T0220798

Communications in Computer and Information Science 1822

Rationale

The CCIS series is devoted to the publication of proceedings of computer science conferences. Its aim is to efficiently disseminate original research results in informatics in printed and electronic form. While the focus is on publication of peer-reviewed full papers presenting mature work, inclusion of reviewed short papers reporting on work in progress is welcome, too. Besides globally relevant meetings with internationally representative program committees guaranteeing a strict peer-reviewing and paper selection process, conferences run by societies or of high regional or national relevance are also considered for publication.

Topics

The topical scope of CCIS spans the entire spectrum of informatics ranging from foundational topics in the theory of computing to information and communications science and technology and a broad variety of interdisciplinary application fields.

Information for Volume Editors and Authors

Publication in CCIS is free of charge. No royalties are paid, however, we offer registered conference participants temporary free access to the online version of the conference proceedings on SpringerLink (http://link.springer.com) by means of an http referrer from the conference website and/or a number of complimentary printed copies, as specified in the official acceptance email of the event.

CCIS proceedings can be published in time for distribution at conferences or as post-proceedings, and delivered in the form of printed books and/or electronically as USBs and/or e-content licenses for accessing proceedings at SpringerLink. Furthermore, CCIS proceedings are included in the CCIS electronic book series hosted in the SpringerLink digital library at http://link.springer.com/bookseries/7899. Conferences publishing in CCIS are allowed to use Online Conference Service (OCS) for managing the whole proceedings lifecycle (from submission and reviewing to preparing for publication) free of charge.

Publication process

The language of publication is exclusively English. Authors publishing in CCIS have to sign the Springer CCIS copyright transfer form, however, they are free to use their material published in CCIS for substantially changed, more elaborate subsequent publications elsewhere. For the preparation of the camera-ready papers/files, authors have to strictly adhere to the Springer CCIS Authors' Instructions and are strongly encouraged to use the CCIS LaTeX style files or templates.

Abstracting/Indexing

CCIS is abstracted/indexed in DBLP, Google Scholar, EI-Compendex, Mathematical Reviews, SCImago, Scopus. CCIS volumes are also submitted for the inclusion in ISI Proceedings.

How to start

To start the evaluation of your proposal for inclusion in the CCIS series, please send an e-mail to ccis@springer.com.

Rajesh Kumar Tiwari · G. Sahoo
Editors

Recent Trends in Artificial Intelligence and IoT

First International Conference, ICAII 2022
Jamshedpur, India, April 4–5, 2023
Revised Selected Papers

 Springer

Editors
Rajesh Kumar Tiwari
RVS College of Engineering and Technology
Jamshedpur, India

G. Sahoo
Indian Institute of Technology
Dhanbad, India

ISSN 1865-0929   ISSN 1865-0937 (electronic)
Communications in Computer and Information Science
ISBN 978-3-031-37302-2   ISBN 978-3-031-37303-9 (eBook)
https://doi.org/10.1007/978-3-031-37303-9

This Springer imprint is published by the registered company Springer Nature Switzerland AG
The registered company address is: Gewerbestrasse 11, 6330 Cham, Switzerland

Preface

It is an honor for us to present the proceedings of the International Conference on Artificial Intelligence and Internet of Things (ICAII 2022) to the event's authors and delegates. We hope you find it helpful, exciting, and inspiring.

The goal of ICAII 2022 was to provide a forum to discuss the issues, challenges, opportunities, and findings of Artificial Intelligence and Internet of Things research. The ever-changing scope and rapid development of AI & IOT generate new problems and questions, necessitating the real need for brilliant ideas to be shared and good awareness of this important research field to be stimulated. We painted a bright picture and a charming landscape for Artificial Intelligence and the Internet of Things, for which the support and enthusiasm shown far exceeded our expectations. At the end of this journey, we are filled with a sense of accomplishment and aspiration.

The primary focus of the Communications in Computer and Information Science (CCIS) series is to publish conference proceedings related to computer science. The series aims to effectively distribute innovative research outcomes in the field of informatics through both traditional print and digital formats. Although the primary emphasis is on publishing fully peer-reviewed papers that present well-developed research, the CCIS series also welcomes the inclusion of reviewed short papers that report on work in progress. The series accepts conferences that have globally relevant themes and are organized by internationally representative program committees, ensuring a rigorous peer-review and selection process. Additionally, the CCIS series also considers conferences that are of high regional or national significance and are organized by relevant societies.

The response to the call for papers was overwhelmingly positive. Unfortunately, many manuscripts from prestigious institutions were turned down due to reviewing results and capacity constraints. We would like to express our gratitude and appreciation to all of the reviewers who assisted us in maintaining the high quality of manuscripts published in Springer proceedings. We would also like to thank the members of the organizing team for their efforts.

The papers were subjected to blind reviews by a maximum of three reviewers. The Technical Program Committee collaborated to review and discuss the submitted papers. Review occurred during a fixed window of time. All authors were notified of the decision on their paper at the same time. All reviewers were strictly concerned with the scope of the paper, novelty of the paper, validity of the paper, and clarity of the paper. Papers having less than 15% of similarity scores were only qualified for the review process. The conference centered on two broad themes: artificial intelligence and the Internet of

Things. The total number of papers submitted was 86, and the total number of papers accepted was 23.

April 2023   Rajesh Kr. Tiwari
                                                                   G. Sahoo

Organization

General Chair

Rajesh Kr. Tiwari   RVS College of Engineering and Technology,
                                     India

Program Committee Chair

G. Sahoo   IIT(ISM) Dhanbad, India

Steering Committee

Alok Choudhary   Loughborough University, UK
Manish Rathore   MedImpact Healthcare Systems Inc., USA
Lau Siong Hoe   Multimedia University, Malaysia
Alex (Kwang Leng) Goh   Curtin University, Australia
Garenth Lim King Hann   Curtin University, Malaysia
Abu Salim   Jazan University, Saudi Arabia
Pirnazarov Nurnazar   Karakalpak State University, Uzbekistan
Atallah Ouai   Laghouat University, Algeria
Mohammed Hameed M.   Jazan University, Saudi Arabia
    Alhameed
M. H. Rahmani Doust   University of Neyshabur, Iran
Muhammad Fayyaz Khan   Bangladesh University of Business and
                                         Technology, Bangladesh
Fathe Jeribi   Jazan University, Saudi Arabia
Karunesh Kumar Shukla   NIT Jamshedpur, India
Piyush Ranjan   Jharkhand Rai University, India
Mohammad Amir Khusru Akhtar   Usha Martin University, India
Susanta Ray   Jadavpur University, India
G. Sahoo   IIT(ISM) Dhanbad, India
Akhib Khan Bahamani   Narayana Engineering College, India
A. G. P. Kujur   BIT Sindri, India
Sandeep U. Kadam   Pawar College of Engineering and Research, India
Pravin Gundalwar   Sandip University, India
Arun Kumar Mishra   Vinoba Bhave University, India

B. Sumathy	Sri Sairam Engineering College, India
Anil Trimbakrao Gaikwad	Bharati Vidyapeeth University, India
Mahendra Kumar Gourisaria	KIIT Deemed to be University, India
Naveen Kumar Kedia	JECRC, India
Anand Singh Rajawat	Sandip University, India
Ram Kumar Solanki	Sandip University, India
Pawan R. Bhaladhare	Sandip University, India
Nripesh Kumar Nrip	Bharati Vidyapeeth's Institute of Management, India
B. K. Singh	NIT Jamshedpur, India
D. P. Mohapatra	NIT Rourkela, India
Rajiv Ranjan	BIT Sindri, India
Ram Kumar Solanki	JCOET, India
Sadique Nayeem	Sitamarhi Institute of Technology, India
Abira Dasgupta	VBCV, India
Phaniram Deekshitula	Wipro Limited, India
Dhiraj Kumar Mishra	Oracle, India

Program Committee

Deobrata Kumar	RVS College of Engineering and Technology, India
Tapan Kr. Dey	RVS College of Engineering and Technology, India
Jeevan Kumar	RVS College of Engineering and Technology, India
Smita Dash	RVS College of Engineering and Technology, India
Vikram Kr. Sharma	RVS College of Engineering and Technology, India
Sharat Chandra Mahto	RVS College of Engineering and Technology, India
Rakesh Kumar	RVS College of Engineering and Technology, India
Shailandra Kr. Prasad	RVS College of Engineering and Technology, India
Sudhir Jha	RVS College of Engineering and Technology, India
Sourabh Singh	RVS College of Engineering and Technology, India
Manjeet Singh	RVS College of Engineering and Technology, India

Yogendra Kumar	RVS College of Engineering and Technology, India
Kishore Kr. Ray	RVS College of Engineering and Technology, India
Krishna Murari	RVS College of Engineering and Technology, India
Triloki Nath	RVS College of Engineering and Technology, India
Rahul Kumar	RVS College of Engineering and Technology, India
Abhilash Ghosh	RVS College of Engineering and Technology, India
Gautam	RVS College of Engineering and Technology, India
Shashi Prabha	RVS College of Engineering and Technology, India
Shiv Shankar Yadav	RVS College of Engineering and Technology, India
Amod Kumar Sahwal	RVS College of Engineering and Technology, India
Namrata Kumari	RVS College of Engineering and Technology, India
Sanatan Prasad	RVS College of Engineering and Technology, India
Gopal Chand Mahato	RVS College of Engineering and Technology, India
S. P. Singh	RVS College of Engineering and Technology, India
Sushanta Mahanty	RVS College of Engineering and Technology, India
Thakur Pranav Kr. Gautam	RVS College of Engineering and Technology, India
Surya Bharadur	RVS College of Engineering and Technology, India
Krishna Murari	RVS College of Engineering and Technology, India
Amit Kr. Sinha	RVS College of Engineering and Technology, India
Subrato Mahato	RVS College of Engineering and Technology, India
Gangesh Thakur	RVS College of Engineering and Technology, India
Anand Mohan	RVS College of Engineering and Technology, India

Deepak Kumar	RVS College of Engineering and Technology, India
Shantimoy Mondal	RVS College of Engineering and Technology, India
Rahul Ranjan	RVS College of Engineering and Technology, India
Shashi Prakash	RVS College of Engineering and Technology, India

Additional Reviewers

Ajay Kumar
Akhib Khan Behmani
Kishore Kumar Ray
Piyush Ranjan
Tapan Kumar Dey
Pravin Gundalwar
Dhiraj Kr. Mishra
D. A. Khan
Murari Krishna Saha
B. Sumathy
Naveen Kumar Kedia
Rakesh Kr.
Pradip Dhal
Harish Gavel
Prakash Kr. Jha
Sunil Kumar Gouda
Buddhadeb Pradhan
Uzra Rahman
Sanjay Kumar
Ritesh Kumar
Shantimoy Mandal

Debabrata Raha
Fathe Jeribi
S. C. Dutta
Sukhwinder Sharma
Puneet Mittal
Gopal Krishna
Amrutanshu Panigrahi
Rajeev Kumar
Anil Trimbakrao Gaikwad
G. Sahoo
Ram Kumar Solanki
Sadique Nayeem
Megha Sinha
Santosh Kumar
Santosh Prabhakar
Divyashree S.
Pushpendra Kumar
Dasrath Mahto
Ruchi Kumari
Deobrata Kumar

Contents

Artificial Intelligence

Internet of Things

Artificial Intelligence

Student Performance Monitoring System Using Artificial Intelligence Models

A. G. P. Kujur[1]([✉]), Rajesh Kumar Tiwari[2], and Vijay Panday[3]

[1] Department of Computer Science and Engineering, BIT Sindri, Dhanbad, Jharkhand, India
abhaykujur19@gmail.com, agpkujur@bitsindri.ac.in
[2] Department of Computer Science and Engineering, RVS College of Engineering and Technology, Jamshedpur, Jharkhand, India
[3] Jharkhand University of Technology, Ranchi, Jharkhand, India

Abstract. With recent technological advancements, modern educational systems adopted efficient ICT (Information and Communication Technologies) to enhance the quality of education. Higher education is currently being transformed with resourceful learning and assessment techniques like Artificial intelligence. Since students are an important element of learning, the system focuses on learning, performance and reports, a big data education system is an efficient tool for decision-making in an educational environment. The aim to collect competent data is to evaluate quality and support in decision-making in educational processes. The data can help develop a tool that analyses data to practice alternatives in decision processes. Human limitations in decision-making have a greater impact on the education ecosystem. However, machine learning can handle this big data for decision-making. The proposed system is purposed for developing a reliable and efficient model for AI-assisted decision-making for education systems. Increasing competition in the educational scenario needs to accomplish flexibility in learning techniques as well as reform the curriculum. In addition, performance monitoring needs to be evaluated precisely and regularly. Thus, machine learning models are proposed for decision-making based on data on the performance of students, feedback and other related information. Thus, the proposed model extracts data from several levels and areas of the education system for relative scrutiny of decision support system (DSS) and decision-making models. The AI-based model can overcome issues in decision-making due to human interference and use the data from ICT platforms. It includes all the players concerned in the processes to assist decisions in various circumstances.

Keywords: Decision support system · Decision-making · Education ecosystem · Artificial Intelligence

1 Introduction

Data and information are key factors in ideal decisions in life. The best suitable solutions and strategies often rely on the ability to find and analyze the data for appropriate decisions. Effective execution of decisions is the "coin of the realm" in business [28]

© The Author(s), under exclusive license to Springer Nature Switzerland AG 2023
R. K. Tiwari and G. Sahoo (Eds.): ICAII 2022, CCIS 1822, pp. 3–18, 2023.
https://doi.org/10.1007/978-3-031-37303-9_1

that needs supporting tools for decision-making. These tools function with imagination and creativity while adequately informing the decision process [8]. Since the decision of each opportunity and incident can result in a hold or loss, performance software is preferred for a rapid decision-making process. It includes dashboards or other tools that can recognize adverse trends as well as use better allocation of resources. Decision-making is widely accepted and evolved into different forms with enhanced technologies. The support for decision-making is currently utilized to create new opportunities for management with the comprehensive and cohesive performance of AI technologies [13]. Universities focusing on higher education needs a decision support system for enhancing the implementation, development, and management of ICT. ICT plays important role in accumulating and managing information directly where universities efficiently capitalize more funds in tools for supporting managerial decision-making [8].

There are several issues in the field of decision support systems for higher education environments as well as the process of decision-making. The development of DSS is based on the situation of accumulated data and several alternatives to match the appropriate problem. Student engrossment is a significant factor in various curricular and extracurricular activities [7]. Also, group education is considered for decisions in higher education with the practice of involvement of students in skills development activities. DSS find a way to automate the decision-making process to achieve efficient results while considering several issues related to higher education. It coordinates between different elements in decision-making and acquires cohesion [27].

Education suffered disruption during the global pandemic of COVID-19 and transformed educational institutions to overcome. Many universities or institutions manage temporary solutions and the need for quick solutions is raised for adequate solutions. Thus, difficulties in teaching, learning as well as grading are overcome through emerging AI models. Online learning added the requirement of managing the big data of students and educational data to acquire efficient solutions in the educational system. Thus, DSS also considers emerging technologies and their impact on online education for obtaining the benefits of collaborative tools and applications using educational resources. The decision-making facilities in current management systems of the educational field are proposed for overcoming several issues that occurred due to logistical and attitudinal changes, lack of educational facilities [1], inadequate communication in addition to low digital competencies. Furthermore, educational fields need to manage several challenges like work overload, uploading files, downloading resources as well as timely accomplishments of different tasks and their evaluation. It is a complex process and needs the support of decision-making to collaborate educational processes and participants.

2   Collaboration Through Decision-Making

Students using online learning platforms can cooperate with each with multimedia interactivity and communicate via social systems [24]. Additionally, learning management systems can create a collaborative network with social software while learning [11]. It is an interface between humans and computers to develop an efficient and flexible cooperative environment with reliable and responsive.

System. Thus, a well-developed human-computer interface effectively interacts with students and responds to their communications with social networks which is a significant feature of DSS. Also, DSS takes optimal decisions considering the opinions of people.

The collaboration in DSS includes communications as well as facilities for accessing the whole study group. As shown in the figure, DSS in collaborative learning include facilities for collecting information and analyzing data. It creates criteria for all alternatives and shares them with the group. Thus, groups have access to a decision by DSS and students are able to analyze and communicate to discuss them (Fig. 1).

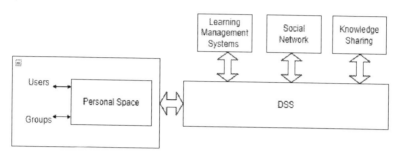

Fig. 1. DSS in collaborative learning [26]

However, the academic evolution of students needs to be enhanced since systems in learning management include only reporting tools. Thus DSS is included in decision-making using advanced AI technologies. It can recognize issues in learning and answer queries. It opens a discussion regarding learning and courses can be restructured while scrutinizing the response [34]. Decision-making systems are intended to help teachers in monitoring and in analyzing students' efficiency and skills. It can recognize the students, their connection time and assessment of their task.

A teacher can be a mentor, education manager as well as facilitator for students and should work with ICT. The role of the teacher [20] includes:

- Create and deliver the courses
- Monitor and analyze the students
- Manage efficient learning
- Collaborate with students
- Work with innovative learning technologies

Thus, the connection to students and working in collaborative systems are more important in the educational system. The need of sharing tasks and important decisions in the group is a complex process. Thus, DSS using AI facilitates decision-making while supporting interaction between students and teachers as well as automatic machine communication. Therefore, the implementation of DSS in learning is based on intelligence for an academic environment that can make optimal decisions utilizing collaboration and communication platforms. It includes competence and quality of outcomes with features of transparency and flexibility. The DSS attains scalability and robustness as well as it is easily adapted [12].

3 Artificial Intelligence

The use of Artificial Intelligence in decision-making allows machines to take decisions in preference to humans. It functions on algorithms to enhance the users' proficiencies while smoothing the process. A huge database is formed in the educational field including student data, institutional data and teaching and other information. Such massive data can be handled with AI which can further process the database for assessment and decision-making purposes. AI uses big data for training and predicts exposure to students, teachers and institutions or universities. It reduces manual interaction to enhance the performance of decision-making processes. Furthermore, AI is comprehensively dependent on the data for decision-making to support institutions and improve the quality of results as well as reduce processing costs. AI is not only limited to improving institutions' quality but also enhances the three dependent components of the learning system i.e. students, teachers, and institutions. AI can work on real-time data such as the required amount of study material, needs and evaluation of students, teaching requisites, etc. Also, it can predict upcoming needs based on available databases. Therefore, AI is an efficient solution for decision-making in the education field.

3.1 Impact of AI on Education

With the increasing use of AI in the educational field, prediction and repetitive processes become easier and teachers are benefitted from better performance. Technology has evolved teaching as well as learning experiences with the availability of resources in the educational field. As AI enhances the learning experience, it is helpful to teachers in providing study materials, discussion, sharing of knowledge and learning data and assessment of learners. An evaluation with AI techniques helps the teacher in quick response and problem-solving. It impacts the practical and educational value of teaching while the significance of human interaction remains unchanged. Similarly, online courses available with freedom of choice and time flexibility have transformed the learning experience of students. It is widely accepted as a new opportunity for learning regardless of time and location restrictions. To reduce the uncertainty in selecting appropriate learning options, AI is used in suggesting more relevant courses. Also, the student can obtain learning sequences and exercises selected by the AI decision-making process. It can reduce the potential drop in motivation with real-time AI assistance in learning. Training and receiving AI-based knowledge is supportive in the improvement of conveying and understanding the information. It needs to reorganize curricula to achieve proficiency or critical thinking development of students using AI. Consequently, AI has wide scope in the educational decision-making process.

3.2 Machine Learning

Machine learning enables computers to learn deprived of explicit programming. It includes unsupervised, semi-supervised and supervised learning methods depending on classification techniques. In the unsupervised method of learning, algorithms analyze and cluster untagged data to learn the inherent structure and find logic in input data.

However, the popular supervised learning methods use classification or regression algorithms on labelled data [13, 14]. An efficient technique of supervised learning includes training the ML model with labelled data which is tested on a different dataset. The technique can process input data according to training data and provide precise output or predictions. In the student classification system, it can compare grades of students and provide classifications according to desired classes such as results in different classes including average, poor, excellent, good, etc. (Fig. 2).

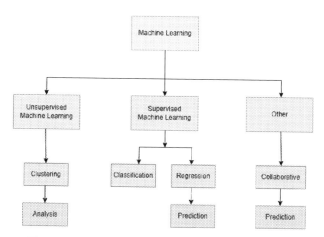

Fig. 2. Machine Learning-based Computing System [30]

Machine learning technique is capable of handling large student data as well as information. It needs to be trained with reliable and large datasets to acquire knowledge. A machine learning model is pre-trained with data collected from various sources. The quality of the machine learning model depends on this information with appropriate cleaning, randomizing, and simulating data for training the model. A DSS model is proposed with robust architecture since machine learning excels at response prediction due to highly efficient artificial learning algorithms in place of manual assessment.

Management of educational data is a dynamic system that includes the connection between human resources and technology in addition to information, knowledge and education providers. However, the collaboration of all these elements may result in either positive or negative patterns of managing information. The incorporation of the impact of these factors and appropriate knowledge management with advanced techniques helps to gain the competitive advantage of enhanced knowledge quality and knowledge processes. Thus, educational knowledge should be properly utilized to capture, consolidate, share and transfer with evaluation in the management system.

3.3 Decision-Making

Decision-making is an essential part of managerial functions that has a great impact on many areas of data utilization and policymaking such as organizing curricula. Educational decision-making gives choices based on superficial information about the availability of courses. While the decision in educational management can achieve possible end results with end-to-end communication and interaction with the learners. An expert AI system in educational decision-making is designed with advanced techniques to stimulate human performance for problem-solving. Rather than several specialists, the Decision-making system addresses the problem using a database in place of human knowledge and experience [31].

4 Proposed Model of 4 -Tier DSS Using AI

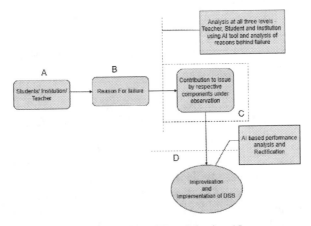

Fig. 3. 4 -Tier DSS model using AI

The proposed DSS model is a 4-tier model implemented using an AI-Based algorithm. The process of the Decision Support System includes four levels A to D (Fig. 3).

The first level A shows a set of components under observation including Students, Institutions and Teachers while the second level B examines reasons for failure and other assessments. At all three levels, AI technology is used to analyze the reasons behind the failure. In the next level C, implicit/explicit the reasons behind failure in addition to AI-based rectification of errors. After this process, DSS is improvised and implemented to make a decision.

- Level-A: Set of components (Students, Institution and Teachers) under observation
- Level-B: Reasons assessed for failure
- Level-C: Implicit/Explicit reasons and AI-based rectification of errors

- Level-D: Improvisation and Implementation of DSS

In decision support systems, Artificial Intelligence plays an important role to enhance and widen the use and efficiency of the systems while enriching the decision-making techniques. Our DSS system coordinates the data delivery for analyzing the trends. It delivers forecasts based on recent data trends with data reliability. It can enumerate uncertainty and anticipate the requirements of the users to deliver the most appropriate data in correct forms signifying courses of action. Thus, knowledge-based systems use AI to provide desired information to users and take decisions based on predictions rendered to users' data. Several education systems, therefore, use AI to enhance decision-making.

The proposed model includes ICT in developing a decision support system that benefits the managers in the decision-making of the educational field. Also, the points mentioned below are considered in DSS.

- Important facts and features of DSS
- DSS model utilization for the social and economic cause.
- Recently developed DSS models.

The DSS model supports to education and research policies of universities in higher education. It helps to provide the most conversant information and academic services. It also facilitates high-quality assessment for students to offer appropriate grade scales.

4.1 Decision-Making Systems

- Decision-making system improves strategic benefits for education providers
- It provides higher retention
- It helps to satisfy learners as well as teachers and institutions
- Consistent performance of the system eliminates the drawbacks of human interactions
- The workload of teachers is reduced with time-efficient learning
- It can enhance the learning experience due to easy access and smart response
- Learning and other costs are reduced with greater accuracy in output
- Educational workforces are empowered to make appropriate decisions
- Innovation in learning and evaluation improves the quality of education
- A quick and precise response of the system reduces inefficiency

5 Methodology

An intelligent system based on AI is essential to meet the students' requirements as well as to support teachers and institutions or universities in decision-making in educational matters. The proposed system can predict outcomes based on available data while ML and data mining are effective techniques used for predictions like students' grades, upcoming requirements, problem-solving and many other tasks. It can classify the data according to selected features such as grades, branches, subjects, etc. The purpose of the decision-making system is to acquire an excellent quality of education based on advanced assessment techniques that also provide communication and support in sharing relevant data such as study materials. It gives a good orientation to students in learning while teachers get support in teaching techniques, discussion and problem-solving.

ML is pre-trained with a selected dataset with desired features and tested for performance. To train the ML model, training and testing datasets are selected separately while a validation dataset is also an essential part of machine learning. Training data train the model with the selected algorithm while checking the performance needs to apply testing data. Once the model is trained, finally validation data is applied for tuning the hyperparameters of the classifier.

A database used for an AI-based decision-making system needs to be classified according to required features since educational databases contain students' data, institutional data, course data, study data as well as large data like information, queries, and documents. It needs data mining and efficient algorithms like Support Vector Machine, Naïve Bayes, Decision Tree, and Random Forest [29]. The stored data is processed further for various purposes. For instance, the score of new students can be predicted based on their available score data. However, a detailed approach is crucial in ML-based decision-making techniques.

Data preprocessing is the most critical stage but it is an important task frequently performed before training. The clear and clean datasets improve the performance of the system. Hence, imbalanced, noisy data is preprocessed to avoid ambiguous results. It removes irrelevant data or elements and enhances values if required values are absent in data. Data filtering removes unnecessary data and helps in accomplishing prediction goals. The data is precisely represented as per required categorization such as course, grade, year and others in the case of student data.

Furthermore, the selection of algorithms according to the required parameters is the next key stage that determines the efficiency of the system. Several algorithms are available for different types of problem-solving and decision-making processes. The selected algorithms are based on types of problems and available data which defines comparison metrics. ML also use neural networks for problem-solving that function after receiving input data. The system can transform input data into desired classes and compare the data with the parameters of the trained dataset. The outcomes are provided quickly and precisely.

5.1 Decision-Making with Data Mining

The Decision-making process is established on desired goals where decisions are influenced by the features of these goals. The development of goals, their size and understanding of decision goals are the main features that can affect the smooth implementation of the process of decision-making [17, 18]. In the decision-making process, the target is to be determined when the nature and structure of the desired goal are clear with the origin of a problem since unclear goals result in an ambiguous decision.

Decision-making in educational management needs to consider defining the target and then designing a plan accordingly. Furthermore, the implementation and evaluation processes are included in the decision process. These levels are interrelated to the decision-making process in the educational organization [9]. Thus, the objectives of the decision are recognized to find various probable choices for studies. Then, these choices are utilized with all possibilities for decision-making and only one choice is preferred without any favoritism (Fig. 4).

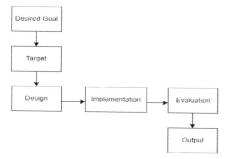

Fig. 4. Educational Decision-making process

The choices in decision-making should be easily accessed for comparing and selecting the appropriate one [18]. All choices are compared for the defined indicators for evaluation. These indicators comprise technical and economic factors with social environmental conditions and potential problems for appropriate selection of choice in decision-making. Furthermore, each choice is analyzed for limitations and probable problems. However, it relates the emergency and preventive measures for better outcomes. In this way, the execution of the data mining process facilitates easy functioning with the collaborative interface. Thus, decisions are consistently conveyed to the user with a diversity of outputs.

Data mining includes data from various sources like files, databases, and data cubes which are combined with data storage. It combines data by matching several attributes based on meaning and type of data.

5.2 Typical Attributes

- Improved Access
- Frequently Updated Data
- Merging Several Data Sources
- Automated Data Analysis
- Evaluation of Data Redundancy
- Convey Precise Output
- Data Communication
- Quick Response

Data redundancy is examined at meaning and fine-grained metrics level and acquires coarse-grained data by changing fine-grained data. It is hard to detect relationships between attributes [18]. An algorithm can improve the performance of the decision-making process based on database attributes. It performs logarithmic operations that rises time complexity and moderate efficiency. The continuous repetition of the process needs optimization of the algorithm. Thus, the selection of the algorithm is important to factor in this process.

6 Result and Discussion

Decision support systems are recognized as expert systems utilized for evaluating the best decision options. According to a recent analysis of DSS, they are able to process types of information efficiently. Also, the systems are capable of comprehending the meaning and complexity of the problems [16]. Thus, DSS is acknowledged as assisting tool for the decision-making process to recognize and solve problems [8]. It utilizes various forms of information in process of decision-making to solve the problems of users. Such systems are knowledge-based systems designed for decisions related to an institution's prosperity [6]. However, DSS [5] are defined as support applications for decision-making rather than replacing the decision.

Thus, the DSS systems are based on advanced decision-making technologies and support various types of data applications. The characteristics of DSS can be mentioned below:

- Data-based DSS
- Knowledge-based DSS
- Document-based DSS
- Group-based DSS
- Web-based DSS
- Communication-based DSS
- Model-based DSS

DSS use different components like data, knowledge, and documents for decision-making. DSS also can supports expert groups systems to solve problems as well as communication DSS offers quick responses. Furthermore, hybrid systems of DSS utilize more than one component mentioned above. As web-based DSS are available for online access of data, it uses web browsers and protocols. The applications of each type of DSS can be explained in the table below (Table 1).

Table 1. Various DSS models and their applications [19]

Type of DSS Components	Applications
Data based DSS	Access to internal data with data mining or online processing
Knowledge-based	Problem-solving with expertise in particular areas
Document based	Retrieval and analysis of documents including multimedia, numbers and text
Group based	Group of interactive decision-makers for problem-solving
Web-based	Computerized decision-related information on the web
Communication	Enhance communications
Model-based	Access to model for data and parameters

In this way, data-based systems are used to access internal and external data using a query, data warehouses and online data mining. A computer-based group system interacts with users for problem-solving. However, different types of documents like text, images, and other forms are stored, retrieved and processed for analysis in document-based DSS. Different models are also developed to support decision-making in several fields including statistical or financial data. Despite the systems' use of data and parameters, they are common data-based systems.

6.1 Accuracy of Prediction

Machine learning can be accurate in the prediction of students' performance depending upon the algorithms used for regression, classification, and clustering of student data. Using these techniques, the performance of the prediction can be enhanced while the accuracy of classifiers can vary in different models. Table 2 [3] shows the maximum accuracy obtained with different ML algorithms. Also, the distribution of these algorithms based on their use in the prediction of students' performance is shown in this table. Many algorithms have achieved the highest accuracy above 95% like KNN (K-nearest neighbour), ANN (artificial neural network), NB (Naive Bayes) and DT (decision tree) while Linear Regression shows the lowest accuracy of 76.2% (Fig. 5).

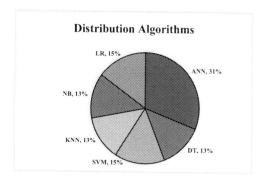

Fig. 5. Distribution of algorithms in the prediction of student performance [3]

ANN is a popular algorithm due to its high performance and precise outcomes. The support vector algorithm has achieved nearly 91.3% of maximum accuracy lower than 95.8% of KNN. However, SVM is widely used for handling small datasets since it is more precise in the generalization of data than other techniques. Distribution values show that ANN is the most preferred technique (31%) over NB, KNN and DT (13%) which are less used as compared to SVM and Linear Regression (15%) (Fig. 6).

The decision-making facilitates the best decision support while the reliability of the DSS model depends on the accuracy of the outcomes. The time taken for the selection of the choice is too short [34]. Therefore, several fields prefer DSS with automatic models without human interference. Though DSS are helpful in decision-making, they are intended for better and more consistent decisions instead of replacing human decision-makers. However, the education field needs continuous processing of massive data [14]. Thus, these DSS includes a knowledge-based approach with interactive software support. A properly implemented DSS can analyze the data using required information

Table 2. Performance and distribution of algorithms [3]

Type of Algorithms	Reference	Highest accuracy achieved	Distribution in student performance prediction
Artificial Neural Network	[33]	98.3%	31%
Decision Tree	[4]	98.2%	13%
Support Vector Machine	[2]	91.3%	15%
K-nearest neighbour	[22]	95.8%	13%
Naive Bayes	[32]	96.9%	13%
Linear Regression	[15]	76.2%	15%

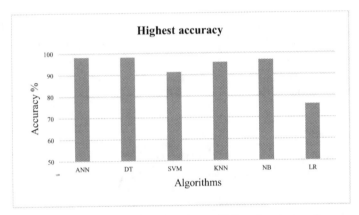

Fig. 6. Performance of algorithms in the prediction of student performance

from different forms of available data, documents, and multimedia. The robust DSS performs well in repetitive kinds of data analysis, and critical problem solving with a quick response as compared to a human. Though the systems support the decision-making process, it needs to improve and update knowledge while enhancing performance. The complexity of DSS can occur due to irrelevant or insufficient data [23]. The performance of the system can be affected by a lack of data integration or a lack of desired parameters in data. It can result in ineffective outcomes like unclear decisions.

6.2 DSS in E-Learning

E-learning use DSS for virtual assistance and student assessment as well as help to restructure courses according to students' needs. Since a well-designed course should attain ease of learning as well as motivate the students for interactive learning, AI helps to design DSS to evaluate and track student activities. Depending on the access time of courses, assignments and other activities, the teacher can check the academic progression of students and it also reduces time and complexity [10]. Systems accumulate vast information to determine the behaviour of students and their performance. Table 3 shows some parameters that can be referred to evaluate the performance of e-learning courses.

Table 3. Frequently used parameters in e-learning DSS algorithms [34]

Parameters	Utilization (%)
Content	31.8
Assignment	36.9
Organizer	80.3
Discussion	61.3
Mail	19.4
Other	43.5
Content Assignment Organizer	12.5
Assignment Other Discussion Organizer	11.4
Content Discussion Organizer	15.8
Assignment Discussion Organizer	18.0

The e-learning decision support system [34] can detect as well as solve problems by monitoring students' activities. It predicts performance as well as groups the students to enhance their learning. DSS in learning can evaluate the behaviour and performance of the student and timely collect the information to process, report and convey to the educational community. It can play a major role in practically defining KPIs i.e. Key Performance Indicators. In Table 3 [34], various resources are mentioned that are frequently used in the e-learning process. Content and assignments in e-learning have less impact on interactive and collaborative learning. However, resources like organizer and discussion can enhance the e-learning activities to motivate students and increase their interest in the course. Several other activities can enhance the learning experience by motivating students to participate in learning activities. Furthermore, very few students use more than one resource like content, assignment and organizer that shows very less response (12.5%). While the addition of discussion with content or assignment can improve the possibility of using resources (15.8%–18%) [34].

6.3 Decision-Making in Education

This set of frequent items gives the minimum support parameter to enhance the confidence parameter. DSS predicts a better way of learning based on these evaluations and helps to determine the pattern of learning. It includes time spent on sessions, content, and combined resources to enhance the learning model. Thus, DSS can predict the time, and resources like discussion, and content reading. However, short sessions with fewer cluster resources are widely accepted for their effective outcomes. Therefore, the DSS illustrates the impact of a particular resource on students to alert teachers for improvement.

Machine learning techniques used for the prediction of student performance are mainly based on student data and other elements are to be considered to overcome the following issues.

- Errors due to human interruption in DSS
- Undervalued elements like teachers and institutions in learning
- Evaluation at the student's end

Thus, considering teachers, institutions as well as students, our AI-based DSS analyzes data to enhance the learning experience and students' performance without manual disturbance. Our proposed system includes effective decision-making at every stage. Hence, various types of data are collaboratively used to extract desired features that also save time due to automatic response.

7 Conclusion

AI-based decision-making systems provide the ability to enhance understanding and problem-solving based on big data. The education system needs to process massive data of different kinds for various applications. Learning techniques based on AI use decision-making systems to support analysis, learning improvement as well as institutional benefits. The managerial decisions are time-consuming while AI reduces the processing time as well as provides the best options according to recent trends with flawless decisions. Students get help from AI-based course structures while analysis of their performance is also beneficial to teachers using decision-making systems.

The proposed system offers an overall education decision-making process that not only supports effective learning for students but also enhances the capability of teachers in problem-solving and quick response. Course structure can also be designed based on the responses of students to various types of content. The prediction of students' performance depends on the varying characteristics of different datasets. Thus, machine learning with pre-trained feature effectively handle different types of datasets and classify them according to desired classes such as grade, performance, courses and others. It is observed that different classification techniques are efficient in the selection of required features and detection of unique choices. However, analysis and evaluation of the dataset give various outcomes depending on selected features. It employs data mining techniques to access big data and help to achieve future goals of education with precise prediction outcomes.

AI-based decision-making system has future scope to enhance the learning and teaching experience, as well as, can give the direction of the resourceful way to reach the students. The decision-making system is important in reducing error and time in problem-solving and enhancing the influence of decisions on teachers, students and institutions or universities. It allows for reducing expenses, manpower and learning cost while empowering managerial and teacher-level decisions. It not gives guidance for better selection to students but also evaluates the students' performance to enhance the response time. This technique can be further implemented for research on students, educational system, teaching methods and university assessment to enhance the overall quality and experience of education.

References

1. Adedoyin, O.B., Soykan, E.: Covid-19 pandemic and online learning: the challenges and opportunities. Interact. Learn. Environ. (2020)
2. Agaoglu, M.: Predicting instructor performance using data mining techniques in higher education. IEEE Access **4**, 2379–2387 (2016). https://doi.org/10.1109/ACCESS.2016.256 8756
3. Alsariera, Y.A., Baashar, Y., Alkawsi, G., Mustafa, A., Alkahtani, A.A., Ali, N.: Assessment and evaluation of different machine learning algorithms for predicting student performance. Comput. Intell. Neurosci. **2022** (2022)
4. Altujjar, Y., Altamimi, W., Al-Turaiki, I., Al-Razgan, M.: Predicting critical courses affecting students performance: a case study. Procedia Comput. Sci., 65–71 (2016)
5. Bendoly, E.: Excel basics to blackbelt: an accelerated guide to decision support designs (2008)
6. Bresfelean, V., Ghisoiu, N.: Higher education decision making and decision support systems. WSEAS Trans. Adv. Eng. Educ. **7**, 43–52 (2010)
7. Bresfelean, V., Lacurezeanu, R., et al.: Decisions and implications of information technologies in academic environments. In: Proceedings of EDULEARN09, Barcelona (2009)
8. Bresfelean, V.P., Ghisoiu, N., Lacurezeanu, R., Sitar-Taut, D.A.: Towards the development of decision support in academic environments. In: Proceedings of the International Conference on Information Technology Interfaces, ITI, pp. 343–348 (2009)
9. Yang, X.: Power grid fault prediction method based on feature selection and classification algorithm. Int. J. Electron. Eng. Appl. **9**(2), 34–44 (2021). https://doi.org/10.30696/IJEEA. IX.I.2021.34-44
10. Douglas, I.: Measuring participation in internet supported courses. In: Proceedings - International Conference on Computer Science and Software Engineering, CSSE 2008, pp. 714–717 (2008)
11. Du, Z., Fu, X., Zhao, C., Liu, Q., Liu, T.: Interactive and collaborative e-learning platform with integrated social software and learning management system. In: Lu, W., Cai, G., Liu, W., Xing, W. (eds.) Proceedings of the 2012 International Conference on Information Technology and Software Engineering. LNEE, vol. 212, pp. 11–18. Springer, Heidelberg (2013). https:// doi.org/10.1007/978-3-642-34531-9_2
12. Filip, F.G.: A decision-making perspective for designing and building information systems. Int. J. Comput. Commun. Control **7**, 264–272 (2012). https://doi.org/10.15837/ijccc.2012.2. 1408
13. Forgionne, G.A.: An architecture for the integration of decision making support functionalities. Decis. Mak. Support Syst. (2011)
14. Swain, S., Tiwari, R.K.: Cloud security research- a comprehensive survey. Int. J. Electron. Eng. Appl. **8**(2), 29–39 (2020). https://doi.org/10.30696/IJEEA.VIII.II.2020.29.39
15. Guo, S., Wu, W.: Modeling student learning outcomes in MOOCs. In: Proceedings of the 4th International Conference on Teaching, Assessment, and Learning for Engineering, pp. 105–133 (2015)
16. Gupta, J.N.D.: Intelligent decision-making support systems (2006)
17. Habibie, M.I., Noguchi, R., Shusuke, M., Ahamed, T.: Land suitability analysis for maize production in Indonesia using satellite remote sensing and GIS-based multicriteria decision support system (2021)
18. Hmoud, B., Laszlo, V.: Will artificial intelligence take over humanresources recruitment and selection? Netw. Intell. Stud. **VII**, 21–30 (2019)
19. Kacprzyk, J., Zadrozny, S.: Towards human consistent data driven decision support systems using verbalization of data mining results via linguistic data summaries. Bull. Polish Acad. Sci. Tech. Sci. **58**, 359–370 (2010). https://doi.org/10.2478/v10175-010-0034-2

20. Karamat, P., Petrova, K.: Collaborative trends in higher education. J. Syst. Cybern. Inform. **7**, 57–62 (2009)

21. Kirsal Ever, Y., Dimililer, K., Sekeroglu, B.: Comparison of machine learning techniques for prediction problems. In: Barolli, L., Takizawa, M., Xhafa, F., Enokido, T. (eds.) WAINA 2019. AISC, vol. 927, pp. 713–723. Springer, Cham (2019). https://doi.org/10.1007/978-3-030-15035-8_69

22. Kurniadi, D., Abdurachman, E., Warnars, H.L.H.S., Suparta, W.: The prediction of scholarship recipients in higher education using k-Nearest neighbor algorithm. IOP Conf. Ser. Mater. Sci. Eng. (2018)

23. Phani Srinivas, K., Aithal, P.S.: Practical oriented analysis on the signal processing using FFT algorithm. Int. J. Electron. Eng. Appl. **8**(II), pp. 01–10 (2000). https://doi.org/10.30696/IJEEA.VIII.II.2020.01-10

24. Olteanu, R.L., Bîzoi, M., Gorghiu, G., Suduc, A.-M.: Working in the second life environment - a way for enhancing students' collaboration. Procedia Soc. Behav. Sci. **141**, 1089–1094 (2014). https://doi.org/10.1016/j.sbspro.2014.05.183

25. Tiwarin, R.K.: Human age estimation using machine learning techniques. Int. J. Electron. Eng. Appl. **8**(1), 01–09. https://doi.org/10.30696/IJEEA.VIII.I.2020.01-09

26. Petrescu, D., Enache, D., Science, L.D.-P.C.: Collaborative decision-making in online education. In: 8th International Conference on Information Technology and Quantitative Management, pp. 1090–1094 (2021). Procedia Comput Sci Elsevier

27. Pinson, S.D., Louçã, J.A., Moraitis, P.: A distributed decision support system for strategic planning. Decis. Support Syst. **20**, 35–51 (1997). https://doi.org/10.1016/S0167-9236(96)00074-7

28. Rogers P, Marcia B.: Ho has the D? How clear decision roles enhance organizational performance. Harv. Bus. Rev. (2006)

29. Goni, O.: Implementation of local area network (LAN) and build a secure LAN system for atomic energy research establishment (AERE) Int. J. Electron. Eng. Appl. **9**(2), 21–33 (2021). https://doi.org/10.30696/IJEEA.IX.I.2021.21-33

30. Thakur, R.K., Tiwari, R.K.: Security on IoT: a review. Int. J. Electron. Eng. Appl. **8**(2), 40–48 (2020). https://doi.org/10.30696/IJEEA.VIII.II.2020.40.48

31. Ghosh, S., Satish: Design and use of machine learning techniques using DSS model. IJARIIE **8** (2022)

32. Vasic, D., Kundid, M., Pinjuh, A., Seric, L.: Predicting student's learning outcome from learning management system logs. In: 2015 23rd International Conference on Software, Telecommunications and Computer Networks, SoftCOM 2015, pp. 210–214 (2015)

33. Zacharis, N.Z.: Predicting student academic performance in blended learning using artificial neural networks. Int. J. Artif. Intell. Appl. **7**, 17–29 (2016). https://doi.org/10.5121/ijaia.2016.7502

34. Goh, A.M., Yann, X.L.: A novel sentiments analysis model using perceptron classifier. Int. J. Electron. Eng. Appl. **9**(4), 01–10 (2021). https://doi.org/10.30696/IJEEA.IX.IV.2021.01-10

On Assaying the T-score Value for the Detection and Classification of Osteoporosis Using AI Learning Techniques

Prabhjot Kaur[✉], Vinit Kumar, and Sukhpreet Kaur

Chandigarh Engineering College, CGC Landran, Mohali, India
prabh121998@gmail.com

Abstract. Osteoporosis is a disease of the bones that causes a decrease in bone density and increases the risk of fractures. Due to increased life expectancy, osteoporosis has become a worldwide health issue. However, early detection is difficult due to the absence of visible symptoms. Therefore, to screen osteoporosis using AI techniques via dental based panoramic radiographs would be cost-effective as well as beneficial. This study investigates the contributions of researchers in detecting and classifying osteoporosis in women using various learning models. In addition, the methods are also analyzed and compared for future reference to determine the optimal algorithm for osteoporosis prediction. The study has also focused on the ongoing difficulties faced by researchers.

Keywords: Osteoporosis · dual-energy X-ray absorptiometry · Machine Learning · Deep Learning

1 Introduction

Medical diagnosis and prognosis that are precise and conclusive remain a challenge. Diagnostic issues are distinctive in that they demand exact outcomes. Medical professionals perform the majority of interpretations of medical data. Human diagnostics are fraught with error and fail to meet social expectations. In fact the computer vision based techniques are enhancing the performance of medical data and facilitated the improved disease diagnosis [1].

In this paper, osteoporosis, a prevalent disease, especially among postmenopausal women, which is frequently undetected until a fracture has occurred, is being studied. Osteoporosis causes bones to weaken and become brittle so that any sort of mild stresses like to cough or bend over or fall can cause a fracture as shown in Fig. 1 [2]. Fractures caused by osteoporosis occur most frequently in the hip, wrist, and spine. Bone is a living tissue that is continually degraded as well as replaced. This problem occurred when the formation of new bone cannot be kept up with the bone loss [3]. Besides this, there are also various risk factors such as age, ethnicity, gender, heredity, Vitamin D, smoking, consuming alcohol, physical inactivity etc. [4].

Osteoporosis is responsible for having atleast 89 lakh fractures every year that results in one osteoporotic fracture that occurs every three seconds. Osteoporosis is a disease

R. K. Tiwari and G. Sahoo (Eds.): ICAII 2022, CCIS 1822, pp. 19–28, 2023.
https://doi.org/10.1007/978-3-031-37303-9_2

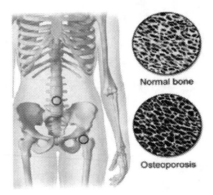

Fig. 1. Osteoporosis bone vs Normal bone

that primarily affects women and is thought to affect approximately 200 million women worldwide. This diagnosis is present in 1/10th of women who are having age of 60 years, 1/5th of women are of the age 70, 2/5th of women aged 80, and in fact, two-thirds of women aged 90. After the age of 50, the risk of osteoporotic fracture increases to one in three for women worldwide [5].

It was projected that globally the number of fractures in the hip will increase till 62 lakh by 2050 on the basis of data collected from population demographics. This represents an increase from the previous projection that 17 lakh hip fractures were recorded throughout the world [6]. Therefore, performing an early diagnosis of the disease is desirable to ensure that it receives the appropriate treatment [9]. In fact T scores also indicate the risk of osteoporosis such as if T-scores below 1, it indicates normal bone, T-scores between 1 and 2.5 indicates osteopenia, and T-scores below 2.5 indicate osteoporosis, as shown in Fig. 2 [7].

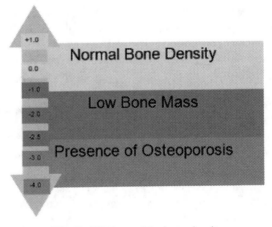

Fig. 2. T-Values of the bone density

However, even though DXA is the diagnostic method of choice for osteoporosis, it is not practical for widespread use as the tool to screen osteoporosis is very costly and has limited access in the developing countries. Until this point, a significant amount of work has been put into creating such tool to address these limitations [9]. In addition, numerous clinical risk assessment tools have been developed specifically to predict osteoporosis. These tools include the Osteoporosis Self-assessment Tool6, the QFracture algorithm, the Fracture Risk Assessment Tool (FRAX), as well as the Garvan Fracture Risk Calculator, amongst others. The various tools for risk assessment are simple to use and helpful; in particular, the FRAX calculator is a significant advancement in comprehending and evaluating fracture risk [10]. As a result, clinical practice has a continuing demand for a more sophisticated osteoporosis screening tool. Therefore, this paper aims to investigate osteoporosis detection and diagnosis using several AI-based techniques, such as machine and deep learning algorithms, which several other researchers have implemented.

Hence, the structure of the paper goes like, Sect. 2 presents the work done by the researches in the field of AI for the detection and classification of osteoporosis. Section 3 displays the comparative analysis of the work to find out their challenges followed by Sect. 4 where the comparison table has been discussed as well as analyzed. The paper is summarized in Sect. 5 where its challenges and future scope has been highlighted.

2 Background

In recent years, artificial intelligence (AI) has been applied in a variety of fields related to the interpretation of medical images. A hip X-ray is used by an AI model to automatically diagnose osteoporosis in a patient. In paper [31], the researchers developed a deep learning based system that worked on the dataset of 5000 x-rays of the hip that had been collected from 4308 patients. These X-rays were obtained over the course of more than ten years. On the basis of relatively straightforward radiographic data, there have been a few attempts, using either machine learning or deep learning algorithms to predict osteoporosis [11].

One of the researchers in paper [12] applied support vector machine, logistic regression, random forest (whose mathematical equation is provided from (1)), artificial neural network on the medical records of Korean women who were on their postmenopausal and collected it from Korea National Health and Nutrition Surveys. These models were trained as well as tested and further evaluated where it was found that SVM obtained the best AUC value as compared to the other algorithms.

$$RFfi_i = \frac{\sum_{j \in alltrees} normfi_{ij}}{T} \tag{1}$$

Here $RFfi_i$ = the value of feature i that had been calculated from the trees, $normfi_i$ = the feature value in normalized form for i in tree j, T = total number of trees.

An automatic method has been developed as an algorithm by the researchers in paper [13] for the classification of a radiograph image of the bone for predicting the class of the patient whether he is having osteoporosis or non-osteoporosis. By applying different kinds of machine learning classifiers, a novel strategy has been developed that is a fully automatic method for selecting features, classifying data, and detecting anomalies (NNs).

In the paper [14], the researchers worked on developing a model to determine whether a patient has osteoporosis. This model can determine whether or not the patient has osteoporosis. The laboratory and osteal bone densitometry examination obtained a dataset consisting of 1083 patients with pathological conditions and 2343 healthy patients. The classifiers were trained based on age, height, gender, and total body mass, which the four factors were chosen. Researchers implemented, analyzed, and compared the outcomes of twenty different machine learning strategies before performing 10-fold cross-validation on all results. In addition, a method for feature selection found that similar performance could be achieved using only two factors for diagnosing (weight and age), as opposed to the traditional four factors. Researchers presented an automatic method for segmenting the proximal femur based on deep convolutional neural networks in the paper [15]. This method was used for segmenting the proximal femur (CNNs). The researchers used the dataset that consist of volumetric structural magnetic resonance images of proximal femur that had been collected from 86 patients. Based on the post-menopausal women's experimental non-invasive analysis of dynamic and static baropodometry, a supervised machine-learning model was proposed in paper [16]. This model was used for the classification of the status of the women. The authors prepared a questionnaire in which topics such as women's dietary practices, lifestyle, and previous fractures were discussed. It served as the foundation for creating the dataset, which included sixty women who had experienced amenorrhea for more than twelve months and were over 45. In fact, the classification of the women was done either on the basis of their being normal, osteoponic, and on the basis of their T-score value osteoporotic. Principal Component Analysis was utilized to select and process relevant feature sets (PCA). After that, two supervised classifiers were designed based on the 27 features that were chosen, and they were put to the test.

The authors in paper [17] mentioned about the development of the model that detected osteoporosis with the help of panoramic radiography. This model was based on the findings of previous research. Fractal dimension (FD), Strut analysis, and the grey-level co-occurrence matrix were utilized to determine the factors that contribute to the diagnosis of osteoporosis (GLCM).

An automated low cost diagnostic tool had been created for diagnosing bone mass reduction at its early stage. It had been created by the researchers in paper [18] with the help of cancellous texture and cortical radiogrammetry analysis of wrist and hand radiographs.

This tool was used to diagnose bone loss at an earlier stage. During the implementation process, it was discovered that the trained classifier model has a high degree of accuracy in differentiating between healthy subjects and subjects with a low bone mass.

In a recent study [8], the researchers proposed several combined features that could be used to construct a classifier for distinguishing the osteoporosis group from the normal group. Their study included a total of twelve features. To create classifiers with these features, the K nearest neighbour (KNN) (Eq. 2) method and the support vector machine method were introduced. Both of these methods have excellent performances when it comes to classification.

$$d\left(x, x'\right) = \sqrt{(x_1 - x_1')^2 + \cdots + (x_n - x_n')^2} \tag{2}$$

where x, x' are the co-ordinate points.

In paper [19], the authors intended to compare the performance of multiple cutting-edge methods to predict the risk of osteoporosis using multimodal images.

Their analysis addressed various technical aspects such as the advantages and disadvantages of methods, datasets, pre-and post-processing methodologies, feature selection or extraction, and performance evaluation metrics about existing processes. In paper [20], the researchers worked on the development of prediction model of osteoporosis especially for the people who belong to Vietnam. The researchers compared their model with the existing techniques to analyze the difference between the output generated by their own model and the output obtained by their previous researcher's model in terms of risk of osteoporosis. Using algorithms for machine learning, the risk of osteoporosis was predicted by the models. In the first case of their experimentation, the parameters of the original test were modeled directly. On the contrary, in the second case, those original parameters were converted into binary covariates.

3   Analysis

In this section, the previous work done by the researchers for the detection and classification of osteoporosis have been compared on the basis of their dataset, techniques used, results obtained, and challenges that they faced in Table 1.

Table 1. Comparison of the previous work done by the researchers to detect osteoporosis

Ref	Dataset	Techniques	Outcomes	Remarks
[14]	Dataset of 3426 patients	Multilayer perceptron	Kappa statistics = 0.32 AUC = 0.71	Small feature set
[12]	Record of 1674 patients	Support vector machine	Accuracy = 76.7% AUC = 0.827 Sensitivity = 77.8% Specificity = 76%	More advanced algorithms could be used to create the better diagnosis model especially for multiclass classification
[21]	Data of 2000 male and female Egyptian participants	ANN	Accuracy = 86%	Class imbalance
[22]	Data of 53 post menopausal women	Two layered FFNN	Acc = 98.1%	Limited number of patients and controls

(*continued*)

Table 1. (*continued*)

Ref	Dataset	Techniques	Outcomes	Remarks
[23]	Questionnaire based dataset	Multivariate system	Acc = 73.10%	Small dataset
[18]	Data of 138 subjects	NN classifier	Acc = 88.50%	The method failed for 21images
[24]	Dataset of 87 subjects	Auto-encoder ANN + SVM	Acc = 95.5%	Limited dataset
[25]	1432 CT scans	Deep CNN	Acc = 89.20%	Need to enhance the classification accuracy
[17]	454 panoramic radiographs	SVM	Acc = 96.9%	The data does not contain the patient who were having osteoporosis
[26]	Dataset of 350 menopausal women	Random subspace method	Acc = 98.9%	–
[16]	Dataset of sixty women	SVM & ANN	Acc = 80%	More new models could be trained with the dataset for the better performance
[27]	Computer based CT scan images	ANN	Acc = 97.9%	The system could not find out the degree of osteoporosis, hence misclassification
[28]	X-ray images collected from Feb 2014- Dec 2015	U-NetCNN	AUC = 0.89	More parameters could be used to test the performance of the model
[13]	Data of 116 images	SVM	Acc = 95.6%	–
[29]	Data of 172 Indian men and women	ANN	Acc = 87.5%	Data size could be extended to enhance the performance of the system
[15]	Images collected from 3T MR scanner	DCNN-UNet	AUC = 0.998	CNN model did not had automatic optimized hyper-parameter

4 Discussion

Osteoporosis throws a great impact on health as well as economic field of the world. In this section, the contribution of the researchers to detect and classify osteoporosis had been compared in Table 1 and analyzed in Figures on the basis of their accuracies as well as AUC score. From the table, it has been observed that most of the researchers have applied support vector machine to detect osteoporosis and have also merged them with neural network algorithms. We all know that accuracy is the most important parameter to evaluate the performance of the model [30]. It is calculated by the Eq. (3)

$$Accuracy = \frac{Sum\ of\ correct\ predictions}{Total\ number\ of\ predicitions} \qquad (3)$$

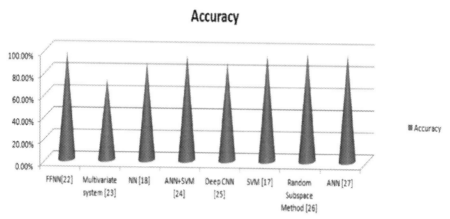

Fig. 3. Analysis of existing models based on their accuracy score

From Fig. 3, the algorithm with the highest accuracy is the random subspace algorithm at 98.90%, while the multivariate system has the lowest accuracy by 73.10%. We can also observe multiple accuracy values for a single algorithm, but in order to determine the most accurate model, we only considered those models that achieved the highest value across multiple datasets. If we examine the peak of support vector machine and the combination of an artificial neural network with support vector machine, we can see that the accuracy has increased by 0.50%.

In addition to this, it has also been observed that from specifically machine learning models, support vector machine has computed the best values as compared to the other machine learning algorithms. Similarly, in Fig. 4, the area under the curve was computed, with DCNN-UNet obtaining the highest value of 0.99 compared to the others. By 0.77, the multilayer perceptron has determined the lowest value.

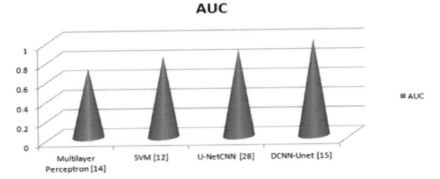

Fig. 4. Performance of Models based on their AUC score

5 Conclusion

Osteoporosis is a disease of the bones that causes a decrease in bone density, thereby increasing the risk of fractures. The advancements in machine and deep learning models have enabled to understand the data which is complex in nature and is limited for the humans to even identify. This study investigates the contributions of researchers in detecting and classifying osteoporosis in women using machine learning and deep learning techniques. The outcomes were also mentioned to compared the performance of the models and it has been found that on evaluating the models on the basis of the accuracies, the sequence formed is Random Subspace (98.9%) > Two layered Fully Forward Neural Network (98.1%) > Artificial Neural Network (97.9%) > Support Vector Machine (95.6%) > Autoencoder (95.5%) > Deep Convolutional Neural Network (89.20%) > Neural Network Classifier (88.50%) > SVM & ANN (80%) > and Multivariate System (73.10%). In addition, the methods were analyzed and compared for future reference to determine the optimal algorithm for osteoporosis prediction. The study has also focused on the ongoing difficulties faced by researchers.

References

1. Pandey, S.K., Janghel, R.R.: Recent deep learning techniques, challenges and its applications for medical healthcare system: a review. Neural Process. Lett. **50**(2), 1907–1935 (2019)
2. Wani, I.M., Arora, S.: Computer-aided diagnosis systems for osteoporosis detection: a comprehensive survey. Med. Biol. Eng. Comput. **58**(9), 1873–1917 (2020)
3. Yang, J., et al.: Opportunistic osteoporosis screening using chest CT with artificial intelligence. Osteoporos. Int. **33**(12), 2547–2561 (2022)
4. Sözen, T., Özışık, L., Başaran, N.Ç.: An overview and management of osteoporosis. Eur. J. Rheumatol. **4**(1), 46 (2017)
5. Brandi, M.L., Piscitelli, P.: Epidemiology of osteoporosis and fragility fractures. In: Guglielmi, G. (eds.) Osteoporosis and Bone Densitometry Measurements. Medical Radiology, pp. 1–4. Springer, Heidelberg (2013). https://doi.org/10.1007/174_2012_747
6. Ferizi, U., Honig, S., Chang, G.: Artificial intelligence, osteoporosis and fragility fractures. Curr. Opin. Rheumatol. **31**(4), 368 (2019)

7. Chun, K.J.: Bone densitometry. In: Seminars in Nuclear Medicine, vol. 41, no. 3, pp. 220–228. WB Saunders, May 2011
8. Xu, Y., Li, D., Chen, Q., Fan, Y.: Full supervised learning for osteoporosis diagnosis using micro-CT images. Microsc. Res. Tech. **76**(4), 333–341 (2013)
9. Cherian, K.E., Kapoor, N., Meeta, M., Paul, T.V.: Screening tools for osteoporosis in India: where do we place them in current clinical care? J. Mid-Life Health **12**(4), 257 (2021)
10. Kumar, Y., Gupta, S., Gupta, A.: Study of machine and deep learning classifications for IOT enabled healthcare devices. In: 2021 International Conference on Technological Advancements and Innovations (ICTAI), pp. 212–217. IEEE, November 2021
11. Kumar, Y., Koul, A., Mahajan, S.: A deep learning approaches and fastai text classification to predict 25 medical diseases from medical speech utterances, transcription and intent. Soft. Comput. **26**(17), 8253–8272 (2022)
12. Kim, S.K., Yoo, T.K., Kim, D.W.: Osteoporosis risk prediction using machine learning and conventional methods. In: 2013 35th Annual International Conference of the IEEE Engineering in Medicine and Biology Society (EMBC), pp. 188–191. IEEE, July 2013
13. Bhattacharya, S., Nair, D., Bhan, A., Goyal, A.: Computer based automatic detection and classification of osteoporosis in bone radiographs. In: 2019 6th International Conference on Signal Processing and Integrated Networks (SPIN), pp. 1047–1052. IEEE, March 2019
14. Iliou, T., Anagnostopoulos, C.N., Anastassopoulos, G.: Osteoporosis detection using machine learning techniques and feature selection. Int. J. Artif. Intell. Tools **23**(05), 1450014 (2014)
15. Deniz, C.M., et al.: Segmentation of the proximal femur from MR images using deep convolutional neural networks. Sci. Rep. **8**(1), 1–14 (2018)
16. Bortone, I., et al.: A supervised approach to classify the status of bone mineral density in post-menopausal women through static and dynamic baropodometry. In: 2018 International Joint Conference on Neural Networks (IJCNN), pp. 1–7. IEEE, July 2018
17. Hwang, J.J., et al.: Strut analysis for osteoporosis detection model using dental panoramic radiography. Dentomaxillofacial Radiol. **46**(7), 20170006 (2017)
18. Areeckal, A.S., et al.: Early diagnosis of osteoporosis using radiogrammetry and texture analysis from hand and wrist radiographs in Indian population. Osteoporos. Int. **29**(3), 665–673 (2018)
19. Amiya, G., et al.: A review on automated algorithms used for osteoporosis diagnosis. Invent. Syst. Control, 247–262 (2022)
20. Bui, H.M., et al.: Predicting the risk of osteoporosis in older Vietnamese women using machine learning approaches. Sci. Rep. **12**(1), 1–17 (2022)
21. Abdel-Mageed, S.M., Bayoumi, A.M., Mohamed, E.I.: Artificial neural networks analysis for estimating bone mineral density in an Egyptian population: towards standardization of DXA measurements. Am. J. Neur. Netw. Appl. **1**(3), 52–56 (2015)
22. Lee, J.H., Hwang, Y.N., Park, S.Y., Jeong, J.H., Kim, S.M.: Diagnosis of osteoporosis by quantification of trabecular microarchitectures from hip radiographs using artificial neural networks. J. Comput. Theor. Nanosci. **12**(7), 1115–1120 (2015)
23. Rae, S.A., Wang, W.J., Partridge, D.: Artificial neural networks: a potential role in osteoporosis. J. R. Soc. Med. **92**(3), 119–122 (1999)
24. Nasser, Y., El Hassouni, M., Brahim, A., Toumi, H., Lespessailles, E., Jennane, R.: Diagnosis of osteoporosis disease from bone X-ray images with stacked sparse autoencoder and SVM classifier. In: 2017 International Conference on Advanced Technologies for Signal and Image Processing (ATSIP), pp. 1–5. IEEE, May 2017
25. Tomita, N., Cheung, Y.Y., Hassanpour, S.: Deep neural networks for automatic detection of osteoporotic vertebral fractures on CT scans. Comput. Biol. Med. **98**, 8–15 (2018)
26. Kilic, N., Hosgormez, E.: Automatic estimation of osteoporotic fracture cases by using ensemble learning approaches. J. Med. Syst. **40**(3), 1–10 (2016)

27. Marar, R.F.A., Uliyan, D.M., Al-Sewadi, H.A.: Mandible bone osteoporosis detection using cone-beam computed tomography. Eng. Technol. Appl. Sci. Res. **10**(4), 6027–6033 (2020)
28. Liu, J., Wang, J., Ruan, W., Lin, C., Chen, D.: Diagnostic and gradation model of osteoporosis based on improved deep U-Net network. J. Med. Syst. **44**(1), 1–7 (2020)
29. Ragini, B., Subramaniyan, K.A., Sanchana, K., Anburajan, M.: Evaluation of low bone mineral mass using a combination of peripheral bone mineral density and total body composition variables by neural network. Procedia Comput. Sci. **57**, 1115–1123 (2015)
30. Koul, A., Bawa, R.K., Kumar, Y.: Artificial intelligence techniques to predict the airway disorders illness: a systematic review. Arch. Comput. Methods Eng., 1–34 (2022)
31. Stephens, K.: AI can diagnose osteoporosis on hip X-ray. AXIS Imaging News (2022)

Evaluation of Healthcare Data in Machine Learning Model Used in Fraud Detection

Md Shoaib Alam[1]([⊠]) [iD], Pankaj Rai[2], Rajesh Kumar Tiwari[3], Vijay Pandey[1], and Sharafat Hussain[4]

[1] Jharkhand University of Technology, Ranchi 834010, Jharkhand, India
shoaib.al9@gmail.com
[2] BIT Sindri, Dhanbad 828122, Jharkhand, India
[3] RVS Collage of Engineering and Technology, Jamshedpur, Jharkhand, India
[4] American University in the Emirates, Dubai International Academic City, Dubai 503000, UAE

Abstract. The concept of designing machine learning model based on binary classification technique should compute on a productive evaluation principle. Designing a machine learning model, get evaluation from different kind of techniques, make enhancement and progress until we accomplish a expected efficiency. Feedback metrics describe the work of a machine learning model. Critical form of feedback metrics is their potential to segregate among machine learning model outcome. Evaluation metric can benefit to describe damage to optimize the machine learning model for a given job while training or testing the model. Before aggregating predicted values, the machine learning model's accuracy must be determined. Making these kind of decision while training and testing is possible with a clear knowledge of evaluation metrics. In this paper, we will cover the many type of evaluation matrices and it performance.

Keywords: Imbalance Data · Machine Learning · Data Pre-processing

1 Introduction

Evaluating matric is a essential step of the designing more powerful machine learning system. Evaluation metrics are used to gauge the model's effectiveness. It is most important part for any machine learning project. Many type of evolution matrices are present to check a model performance. Evaluation metrics are using a combination of many evaluation metrics to check machine learning algorithm. It is essential to apply combination of evaluation metrics to check machine learning model. This is because a machine learning application may execute excellent applying one dimension from one evaluation metric, but may not execute good by applying different dimension from another evaluation metric. Applying evaluation metrics are essential assuring that machine learning model is running accurately and optimally. Choosing a proper metric is crucial generally in applied model, but is problematic for imbalanced classification issue. Firstly, because many of the evolution metrics that are widely applied assume a balanced distribution, and because mostly not all aspect, and therefore, not all prediction issue are equal for imbalanced classification. One of the most costly problems for insurers is fraud, which causes significant losses from forged claims.

To ensure that a machine learning model is functioning effectively and optimally, evaluation metrics must be applied. Selecting the right metric is important in every applied model, but it becomes difficult when there is a problem with imbalanced categorization. First off, because a lot of widely used evaluation metrics presuppose a balanced distribution, and secondly because not all aspects, and thus not all prediction problems, are equal for imbalanced classification. One of the main issues that Medicare is currently confronting is provider fraud. For instance, a provider can include an inflated amount on the membership bill, or an uninsured person might fraudulently claim insurance benefits by impersonating an insured person. The difference will be due from the member to the insurance company.

In order to safeguard oneself against numerous potential difficulties, not to mention the unpredictability surrounding people's health problems, health insurance is a crucial step. Governments and private insurance providers offer health insurance at a set price that is flexible based on your budget to help make medical costs more bearable. Fraud claims have been shown to be the most expensive burden on insurance companies, accounting for 15% of all Medicare expenses. Due to these activities, they become exposed and wind up paying higher insurance premiums.

Fraud is one of the most expensive issues for insurers since it results in huge losses from false claims. Fraudulent behavior is an unwanted situation that necessitates the use of numerous resources by security institutions to combat. The short-term consequences of identifying suspected fraud in a submitted claim are considerable, so accuracy is crucial. It can cause a delay in the resolution of your claims and annoy other clients. Criminals collaborate in healthcare fraud to submit false claims. Not only do these things happen for Medicare, but also for other kinds of insurance.

Our goal is to either identify which providers are likely to engage in fraud using forecasting algorithms or determine the likelihood that a provider would do so. This can aid in preventing monetary loss as a result of fraud. The insurance company may accept or deny the claim or look into your provider depending on the likelihood of fraud and what constitutes fraud. Examining a provider's records should never be done without keeping fraudulent activities in mind.

In this manner, they are able to offer excellent and secure care, exactly like they do for real patients. The remainder of this paper is structured as follows. Display the literature review work in Sect. 2. Showcase the experimental work in Sect. 3 and results in Sect. 4. Section 5 concludes with several suggestions for future development.

2 Literature Review

Handelman, et al. [1] request about efficacy of algorithms frequently describe the algorithm's performance using a basic set of metrics. Models are often assessed using the ROC curve or confusion matrix when dealing with ML models that categories. Typically, the mean absolute error, mean squared error, or coefficient of determination are used to evaluate the model, if it deals with regression, author will first cover the idea of cross validation, which is how many ML algorithms start to develop performance measurements, before we get into more depth about these concepts.

Jing Li et al. [2], A team of researchers have looked at how to reduce the cost in healthcare, protect from loss due to bad practice and provide safe and quality to the patients. They used confusion matrix for evolution of the performance which include first method based on error where ROC curve is being used. Second method based upon cost where false negative (FN) indicate how much we lose if we are not detecting suspicious behaviors. False positive (FP) shows how much amount need to spend for research if fraud claim is detected.

Bauder et al. [3], this study evaluates the effectiveness of several machine-learning algorithms for detecting fraud. One instance of fraud is the positive class and non-fraud instances are to be negative class. Area under the ROC curve (AUC), filter performance rating (FPR) and false negative rage (FNR) were used as the evaluation metrics. The study's findings show that supervised approaches outperformed unsupervised and hybrid methods in terms of performance while using the 80–20 sampling strategy.

Markus, et al. [4], summarized that evolution techniques are an attempt to evaluate the various explanation techniques and determine the best ones from a comparison. The main goal is to determine if the offered explain ability succeeds in meeting the stated goal. Since the true internal workings of something like the model are unknown, there isn't a ground truth for judging post-hoc interpretations. Evaluation degree to which the qualities of explain ability, i.e., interpretability and the ultimate goal of evaluating the quality of ML explanations is to ensure that fidelity are fulfilled.

3   Evaluation Method

Confusion Matrix Or Error Matrix, it is NxN matrix representation of the prediction of binary classification which is in a tabular visualization graph (Fig. 1).

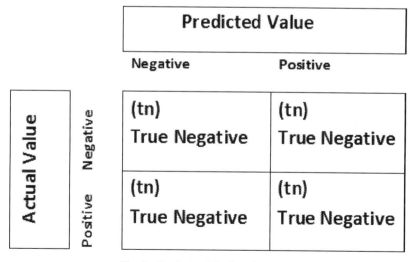

Fig. 1. Confusion Matrix With 2 × 2

3.1 Accuracy

It is most commonly applied evaluation matric. It provides us correct classified values.

$$ACC = \frac{\text{No. of Correct Prediction}}{\text{Total No. of prediction}}$$

$$ACC = \frac{tp + tn}{tn + fp + tn + fn}$$

It calculates how much examination for both positive or negative were accurately classified. Suitable Condition under specific scenarios: evaluation multiclass and binary classification. it may not be suitable under specific scenarios: if the classes are imbalance, detection of anomaly and multi-labeled classification.

3.2 Precision or Positive Predicted Value

It calculates how much observations predicted as positive. If we consider fraud detection model, it will tell us ratio of fraudulent transaction.

$$PPV = \frac{tp}{tp + fp}$$

3.3 Negative Predicted Value

It calculates how much observation predicted as negative. If we consider fraud detection model, it will tell us ratio of non-fraudulent transaction.

$$NPV = \frac{tn}{tn + fn}$$

3.4 Sensitivity or Recall or TPR

It calculate how much observation out of all positive observation as positive. If we consider fraud detection model, it will tell us how much time fraudulent transactions we recalled from all transactions.

$$TPR = \frac{tp}{tp + fn}$$

3.5 Specificity or True Negative Rate

It determines the percentage of all negative observations that are negative observations. If we consider fraud detection model, it will tell us how much time non-fraudulent transactions we recall from all non fraudulent transactions.

$$TNR = \frac{tn}{tn + fp}$$

3.6 False Positive Rate

We raise the false positive rate when we forecast something when it isn't true.

$$FPR = \frac{fp}{fp + tn}$$

3.7 False Negative Rate

We increase the false negative rate when we fail to forecast something when it is imminent.

$$FNR = \frac{fn}{tp + fn}$$

3.8 FDR

Out of all the positive forecasts, it calculates the percentage of wrong guesses. If we consider fraud detection model, it will tell us how much incorrect prediction out of all the fraudulent transactions predictions.

$$FDR = \frac{fp}{fp + tp}$$

3.9 F 1 Score or Beta

The harmonic mean of the precision and recall values is calculated. Best score at 1 and worse score at 0. An aggregate score is given below.

$$F_1 = \left(\frac{recall^{-1} + precision^{-1}}{2}\right)^{-1} = 2 \cdot \frac{precision \cdot recall}{precision + recall}$$

It is clear question come up is why we are taking a harmonic mean instead of arithmetic mean. Let's discuss this. The findings of our binary classification model are as follows: Recall is one, precision is zero.

$$Arithmetic\ mean = 0.5$$

Above result comes from classifier which just ignore the input.

$$Harmonic\ Mean = 0$$

From above result which is accurate for all purpose.
Generalization of F1 score is F_β

$$F_\beta = \left(1 + \beta^2\right) \cdot \frac{precision \cdot recall}{\left(\beta^2 \cdot precision\right) + recall}$$

Fbeta determines a model's validity in relation to a user who values recall times more than precision.

3.10 GLC

It calculate the ratio between the result obtained with classification model and without classification model. Gain and lift charts (GLC) are graphical helps for evaluating the performance of classification models. Designing a gain and lift chart in steps. Step 1: Calculating each observation's probability. The next step is to order these probabilities decreasingly. Step 3: Create each group with around 10% of observations. Step 4: Total the response rates for all respondents and non-responders.

3.11 F2 Score or Beta 2

It calculate the score from combination of precision and recall, emphasis twice on recall.

$$F2 = \frac{TP}{TP + 0.2FP + 0.8FN}$$

3.12 ROC (Receiver Operating Characteristic) Curve

All examples are classified as negative. So TNR = 1.0 and TPR = 0.0. Lower value of threshold: all examples are classified as positive. So TNR = 0.0 and TPR = 1.0.

3.13 AUC

It is the ROC curve's single value's area under the curve. The area under the curve with the highest value indicates a good classifier.

3.14 Average Precision or PR AUC Score

The average of the precision scores computed for each recall threshold [0.0, 1.0] is another way to conceptualize PR AUC. Additionally, you can modify this description to meet the demands of your company by selecting or clipping the recall levels as necessary.

3.15 Brier Score

It determines how far predictions stray from the actual number. It is essentially a mean square error in the probability space, and as a result, it is frequently used to calibrate the possibilities of machine learning models (Fig. 2).

$$brierloss = \left(y_{pred} - y_{true}\right)^2$$

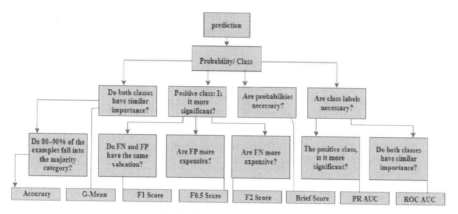

Fig. 2. Evaluation process tree

4   Evaluation Measure

Split the processed dataset into two parts first train dataset and validation dataset. Over-sampling (Logistic Regression, Decision Tree, and Random Forest) the dataset with the help of **SMOTE** (majority: minority). Example 80:20 or 75:25 or 65:35 or 50:50. Select best model based on score (Fig. 3).

Features:

Basic EDAFeature+
SUM Aggregated Feature (Different Level)+
SUM Aggregated Feature (Combinations of Level)

Further Description:

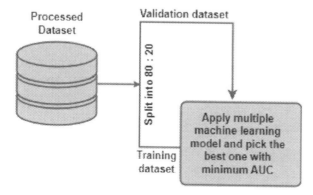

Fig. 3. Select best with AUC score.

Used Class weighting Schema to deal the class imbalance (Fig. 4)

Select the characteristics with feature relevance higher than 0.001. 161 such traits were discovered. I am now solely utilising these characteristics to train the machine

Model Number	Sampaling Ratio	Model	Hyper-parameterization	Train AUC	Test AUC	Train F1 Score	Test F1 Score
1	80:20:00	Logistic Regression	C = 0.0316228 penalty="11"	0.9471	0.9518	0.5886	0.5509
2	80:20:00	Decision Tree	criterion='gini' max_depth=6 min_sample_leaf="150" min_simple_split="150" max_features='log2'	0.9264	0.9259	0.4356	0.4608
3	80:20:00	Random Forest	n_estimators = 30 criterion='gini' max_depth = 4 min_sample_leaf="50" min_simple_split="50" max_features='auto'	0.9457	0.9517	0.5663	0.5679

Fig. 4. Metrix for different model with AUC and F1 Score

learning model. Using the key characteristics, trained both and decision tree, logistic regression random forest, findings are listed above (Fig. 5).

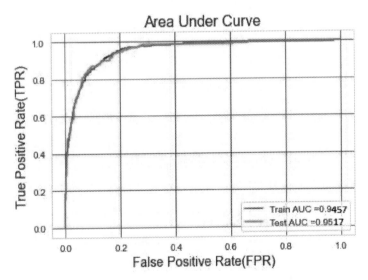

Fig. 5. Area Under Curve.

After comparing the mentioned models to the entire set of oversampled data, it was discovered that the Random Forest model, with an oversampling ratio of 80:20 and an AUC score of 0.9457, performed the best (Fig. 6).

Best Threshold = 0.1105
Model AUC = 0.9457
Model F1 Score is: 0.5663

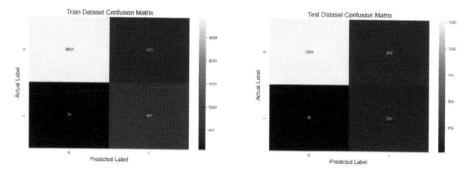

Fig. 6. Confusion Metrix and AUC for Random Forest with all feature

5 Conclusion

This paper's goal is to improve the healthcare system through machine learning evaluation. Our proposed model focused on supervised learning and unsupervised learning. We used best model with minimum AUC score. To ensure that a machine learning model is functioning effectively and optimally. Selecting the right metric is essential in any applied model, but difficult when dealing with the unbalanced classification problem. In this manner, we are able to offer excellent and secure service. This enables them to deliver high-quality and secure healthcare system.

References

1. Handelman, G.S., et al.: Peering into the black box of artificial intelligence: evaluation metrics of machine learning methods. Am. J. Roentgenol. **212**(1), 38–43 (2019). https://doi.org/10.2214/ajr.18.20224
2. Li, J., Huang, K.-Y., Jin, J., Shi, J.: A survey on statistical methods for health care fraud detection. Health Care Manag. Sci. **11**(3), 275–287 (2008). https://doi.org/10.1007/s10729-007-9045-4
3. Bauder, R.A., Khoshgoftaar, T.M.: Medicare fraud detection using machine learning methods. In: 2017 16th IEEE International Conference on Machine Learning and Applications (ICMLA) (2017). https://doi.org/10.1109/icmla.2017.00-48
4. Markus, A.F., Kors, J.A., Rijnbeek, P.R.: The role of explainability in creating trustworthy artificial intelligence for health care: a comprehensive survey of the terminology, design choices, and evaluation strategies. arXiv 2020, arXiv:2007.15911
5. Provenzale, C., Sparaci, L., Fantasia, V., Bonsignori, C., Formica, D., Taffoni, F.: Evaluating handwriting skills through human-machine interaction: a new digitalized system for parameters extraction. In: 2022 44th Annual International Conference of the IEEE Engineering in Medicine & Biology Society (EMBC) (2022). https://doi.org/10.1109/embc48229.2022.9871538
6. Yee, O.K.: Evaluating term extraction tools. Hum. Factor Mach. Transl., 100–117 (2018). https://doi.org/10.4324/9781315147536-7
7. Kaya, S., Yaganoglu, M.: An example of performance comparison of supervised machine learning algorithms before and after PCA and LDA application: breast cancer detection. In: 2020 Innovations in Intelligent Systems and Applications Conference (ASYU) (2020). https://doi.org/10.1109/asyu50717.2020.9259883

8. Dalal, K.R.: Analysing the role of supervised and unsupervised machine learning in IOT. In: 2020 International Conference on Electronics and Sustainable Communication Systems (ICESC) (2020). https://doi.org/10.1109/icesc48915.2020.9155761
9. Prediction of crop yield in precision agriculture using machine learning methods (2021). Webology. https://doi.org/10.29121/web/v18i4/126
10. Aouedi, O., Piamrat, K., Muller, G., Singh, K.: Fluids: federated learning with semi-supervised approach for intrusion detection system. In: 2022 IEEE 19th Annual Consumer Communications & Networking Conference (CCNC) (2022). https://doi.org/10.1109/ccnc49033.2022. 9700632
11. Aouedi, O., Piamrat, K., Muller, G., Singh, K.: Intrusion detection for softwarized networks with semi-supervised federated learning. In: ICC 2022 - IEEE International Conference on Communications (2022). https://doi.org/10.1109/icc45855.2022.9839042
12. El Mrabet, M.A., El Makkaoui, K., Faize, A.: Supervised machine learning: a survey. In: 2021 4th International Conference on Advanced Communication Technologies and Networking (CommNet) (2021). https://doi.org/10.1109/commnet52204.2021.9641998
13. Khatri, S., Arora, A., Agrawal, A.P.: Supervised machine learning algorithms for credit card fraud detection: a comparison. In: 2020 10th International Conference on Cloud Computing, Data Science & Engineering (Confluence) (2020). https://doi.org/10.1109/confluence47617. 2020.9057851
14. Kun, Z., Ying-jie, T., Nai-yang, D.: Unsupervised and semi-supervised two-class support vector machines. In: Sixth IEEE International Conference on Data Mining - Workshops (ICDMW 2006) (2006). https://doi.org/10.1109/icdmw.2006.164
15. Katarya, R., Srinivas, P.: Predicting heart disease at early stages using machine learning: a survey. In: 2020 International Conference on Electronics and Sustainable Communication Systems (ICESC) (2020). https://doi.org/10.1109/icesc48915.2020.9155586
16. Kumar, M.S., Keerthi, V., Anjnai, R.N., Sarma, M.M., Bothale, V.: Evalution of machine learning methods for hyperspectral image classification. In: 2020 IEEE India Geoscience and Remote Sensing Symposium (InGARSS) (2020). https://doi.org/10.1109/ingarss48198. 2020.9358916
17. Nalini, C., Murali Krishna, T.: An efficient software defect prediction model using neuro evalution algorithm based on genetic algorithm. In: 2020 Second International Conference on Inventive Research in Computing Applications (ICIRCA) (2020). https://doi.org/10.1109/ icirca48905.2020.9182869
18. Yassine, A., Mohamed, C., Zinedine, A.: Feature selection based on pairwise evalution. In: 2017 Intelligent Systems and Computer Vision (ISCV) (2017). https://doi.org/10.1109/isacv. 2017.8054919
19. Na, X., Zang, S., Wang, J.: Evalution of random forest ensemble classification for land cover mapping using TM and ancillary geographical data. In: 2009 Sixth International Conference on Fuzzy Systems and Knowledge Discovery (2009). https://doi.org/10.1109/fskd.2009.165
20. Wang, G., Wong, K.W., Lu, J.: AUC-based extreme learning machines for supervised and semi-supervised imbalanced classification. IEEE Trans. Syst. Man Cybern. Syst. 51(12), 7919–7930 (2021). https://doi.org/10.1109/tsmc.2020.2982226
21. Sahid, M.A., Hasan, M., Akter, N., Tareq, M.M.: Effect of imbalance data handling techniques to improve the accuracy of heart disease prediction using machine learning and deep learning. In: 2022 IEEE Region 10 Symposium (TENSYMP) (2022). https://doi.org/10.1109/tensym p54529.2022.9864473
22. Tao, R., et al.: Magnetocardiography-based ischemic heart disease detection and localization using machine learning methods. IEEE Trans. Biomed. Eng. 66(6), 1658–1667 (2019). https:// doi.org/10.1109/tbme.2018.2877649

23. Raghavan, P., Gayar, N.E.: Fraud detection using machine learning and deep learning. In: 2019 International Conference on Computational Intelligence and Knowledge Economy (ICCIKE) (2019). https://doi.org/10.1109/iccike47802.2019.9004231

24. Tsai, H.-Y., et al.: Machine learning algorithms for CCRCC data analysis. In: 2022 IEEE 4th Eurasia Conference on Biomedical Engineering, Healthcare and Sustainability (ECBIOS) (2022). https://doi.org/10.1109/ecbios54627.2022.9945034

A New Approach to Heart Disease Prediction Using Clustering and Classification Algorithms

Kailash Patidar[1]([envelope]), Damodar Prasad Tiwari[1], Rahul Kumar Gour[1], Shital Gupta[1], Karuna Nidhi Pandagre[1], and Shiv Shankar Yadav[2]

[1] Bansal Institute of Science and Technology, Bhopal, India
kailashpatidar123@gmail.com
[2] RVS College of Engineering, Jamshedpur, India

Abstract. Medical diagnosis is considered a main but complex task that requires accurate and efficient execution. Clinical results are often perfect because they are found on the understanding and knowledge of medical professionals instead of knowledge of a mass of data invisible in a record. Medical professionals must undergo continuous training to make sound clinical decisions. They use basic knowledge, current research and work experience. These exercises sometimes lead to undesirable biases, errors and disproportionate medical expenses that influence the quality of facility furnished to patients. Since these decisions affect the well-being of patients, it is eminently essential to acquire new methods to improve the quality of medical decision-making. Machine learning algorithms have the ability to create an information affluent atmosphere that can much improve the standard of clinical accord. The biggest challenge in diagnosing the disease is the accuracy of the prognosis. In this work, optimized grouping and classification algorithms are proposed to improve the accuracy of the medical managerial process and curtail false positives in the diagnosis of disease processes. The proposed article explains various Machine Learning (ML) algorithms for heart disease diagnosis. Machine learning (ML) algorithms similarlyKNN, K-Mean and Logistic Regression (LR) have been used to accurately predict diseases.

Keywords: KNN · K-Means · Logistic Regression · Dataset · Clustering · Classification

1 Introduction

A disease in the human body is an unusual medical condition. It negatively influences the functional state of the human body. It is usually associated with several disease symptoms in the patient's body. According to the WHO, for the duration of the previous fifteen years, around seventeen million human beings pass away every year from cardiovascular diseases, especially cardiac arrest and strokes [1]. Heart disease and strokes are the two leading causes of death. Machine learning (ML) can recognize previously unnoticed trends and offer clinical insights to assist doctors diagnose and treat cardiac disease [29].

© The Author(s), under exclusive license to Springer Nature Switzerland AG 2023
R. K. Tiwari and G. Sahoo (Eds.): ICAII 2022, CCIS 1822, pp. 40–51, 2023.
https://doi.org/10.1007/978-3-031-37303-9_4

Heart illness can be brought on by a number of disorders that affect the heart, blood vessels, muscles, valves, or electrical circuits that regulate muscle contraction. In India, the United Realm, the US, Canada, and Australia, cardiovascular sickness is one of the leading causes of death, according to the Centers for Infectious Prevention and Counteraction. Cardiovascular disease (CVD) is the greatest cause of clinical (i.e., death and disability), health, and economic burden globally, accounting for around 31% (17.9 million) of all deaths each year. Heart disease accounts for one in four deaths in the United States [2]. Coronary illness is normal in people in many nations of the world. As a result, heart disease risk factors should be taken into consideration. Heart disease is influenced by a variety of lifestyle factors, including genetics. Known heart disease risk factors; radiotherapy based on age, sex, family history, smoking, certain cancer-fighting chemotherapy drugs, malnutrition, high blood pressure, high cholesterol, diabetes, obesity, lack of physical activity, stress, and poor hygiene [3]. A number of different risk factors can influence a patient's predisposition to cardiovascular disease.

On the other hand, this risk is reduced when this factor is removed or corrected. According to this theory, there is a causal link between the risk factor and the disease and that the risk factor exists before the lead disease [24]. The disease's incidence decreases when the factor is corrected (the idea of reversibility). Naturally, a plausible path physiological explanation for the disease and the identification of this in multiple populations are required [30]. It is strictly speaking a "risk sign," or witness to the process, if there is no direct causal relationship (for example, an increase in C-reactive protein "CRP" or micro albuminuria). Physiological factors (age, sex, and menopause), lifestyle factors (smoking, physical activity, alcohol, stress), metabolic syndrome factors (insulin resistance), dyslipidemia, abdominal obesity, and hypertension are the primary risk factors for heart disease. Sugar, blood pressure, and dietary factors. A factor that increases a patient's risk of developing cardiovascular disease is known as a risk factor for heart disease. On the other hand, this risk will be reduced by removing or correcting this factor [25]. The meaning of a gamble not entirely settled by the strength of the relationship with the sickness (communicated as the overall gamble seen in presented subjects contrasted with unexposed subjects) and the evaluated affiliation.

If the dataset has a variety of attributes, some of them are useless and show inaccurate results. Consequently, the primary goal of this research is to use a multidisciplinary strategy to improve feature selection and classification for better heart disease diagnosis. In order to select the most related characteristics of heart disease, this research work employs a metaheuristic approach and an imperialistic competition algorithm. When compared to genetic and other optimization algorithms, this one can offer a feature selection response that is more optimal [28]. The dataset was divided into two groups following data processing: test set and training set. Try 20% and practice 80%. The features were submitted to the KNN Nearest Neighbor (KNN), Naive Bayes classifier, and Support Vector Machine for classification plans following feature extraction. As a result, using a combination of these four approaches can improve the various aspects of heart disease diagnosis. To put it another way, our objective is to make the diagnosis of heart disease more accurate in its classification. The following are the study's goals:

- Collection of data on new characteristics of the disease.

- Prediction and classification of the appearance of the disease apply the proposed approach.
- First use of new machine learning algorithms for feature selection.
- Offers new clustering and classification techniques with better accuracy.

2   Literature Review

In this paper [5] employed data mining methods via Rapid Miner to analyze diabetes data using classification algorithms to predict diabetes models. The prediction model was constructed using the Decision Tree and ID3 algorithms, with 72% and 80% accuracy, respectively.

This paper [6] used preprocessed data and the K-mean clustering technique. Additionally, the MAFIA algorithm is used to mine the extracted data for the regular patterns related to heart disease. On the source of important parameters, a neural network is trained using the selection of key patterns for accurate heart attack prediction.

In this paper [7] Based on the graph b-coloring method, created a diabetes prediction model in this research study. They have put their strategy into practice and run tests comparing it using K-NN classification algorithms. The results demonstrated that, in terms of accuracy rate, clustering based on graph coloring is significantly superior to another clustering methodology. The new method ensures the inter-cluster difference needed to assess the quality of clusters by presenting a realistic picture of clusters.

In this research paper [8] use association rules to derive the item set relations. MAFIA algorithms were used to classify medical datasets, improving accuracy rates. K-Fold cross validation was used to examine the medical data and the outcomes were compared. The study work used MAFIA (Maximal Frequent Item set Algorithm) and the objective was to have a highly accurate rate using a medical dataset with 19 features.

In this research paper [9] the goal of this study was to forecast the patients' actual risk level and accuracy.

In this paper work [10] the Naive Bayes algorithm was found to have a greater classification accuracy when compared to another approach, Diagnosis of Heart Disease Using Data Mining methods.

In this paper work [11] the classification algorithms utilized in data mining for the prediction of heart disease are covered, along with a comparison of the accuracy of heart disease prediction utilizing these techniques. Analyses of accuracy rates are also presented. The performance results showed that the SVM performed better than the other two algorithms when we have a large data set with numerous entries.

The objective of this work [12] is to provide an analysis of various data mining categories that can be used into models for the prediction of cardiac disease. Several talents are reportedly used for this exam in a range of aspects. Heart disease prognosis was 100% accurate in one research. The 99.62% accuracy of Decision Tree classification algorithms that were created using a few selected attributes is also mentioned in certain publications.

This paper [13] the use of a non-linear classification system for the prediction of cardiac problems was suggested in this research study. The proposed method makes use of Hadoop Distributed File System (HDFS), Map Reduce, and SVM classification algorithms to forecast heart disease using an optimized core medical attribute data set.

This study focuses on the use of several data mining methods to forecast heart diseases. SVM is really accurate.

In this paper, [14] used SVM and ANN to diagnose CAD. The Aja University of Medical Sciences provided the information. Thirty percent of the data was used for testing, while seventy percent was used for training. For disease diagnosis, 25 features were taken into consideration. SVM performed CAD diagnosis more accurately than ANN. A sensitivity of 92.23% was offered by SVM.

In this paper, [15] conducted trials on three datasets while using DT, ANN, and AdaBoost classifiers to identify heart disease. On the Zalizadeh Sani dataset, the best accuracy came from ANN, coming up at 94%.

In this paper study [16] the dataset was divided into various groups. On the partitioned datasets, various models were created using CART (classification and regression tree). Different CART models were combined to create an ensemble model. On the Framingham dataset, the system achieved a 91% accuracy rate.

In this paper [17], DT and KNN classifiers were utilized to forecast cardiac disease. KNN and DT both achieved accuracy of 67% and 81% on the Cleveland dataset, respectively.

In this research work, [18] created a stacked model for heart disease diagnosis utilizing KNN, SVM, and RF. The LASSO technique was used to choose the features. The model's accuracy was determined to be 75.1% utilizing a Cardiovascular Disease dataset with records from 70000 patients.

3 Clustering Algorithms

A Machine learning (ML) technique called clustering or cluster analysis groups an unlabeled data set. It is characterized as "a technique for arranging the data points into several clusters made up of related data points. The items with potential similarity continue to be in a group that shares little to no similarity with another group." This is achieved by identifying comparable patterns in an unlabeled data set, such as shape, size, color, behavior, etc., and classifying the data based on the presence or absence of these patterns. It uses an unsupervised learning approach, which means that the algorithm is unsupervised and runs on an unlabeled dataset. After using this clustering technique, each cluster or group is given a cluster identifier that can be used by ML systems to streamline the processing of large and complex datasets [26].

Based on their models, the clustering techniques can be separated. Various clustering techniques have been described, however only a few of them are frequently used. The type of data we use determines the clustering algorithm. For instance, some algorithms must estimate the number of clusters in the supplied dataset, while others must determine the shortest distance between the dataset's observations [31].

Here, we focus mostly on well-known clustering methods that are frequently employed in machine learning:

1. **K-means Algorithm:** This algorithm is very extensively helpful clustering techniques is k-means. By grouping the samples into various clusters with similar variances, it classifies the dataset. In this approach, the number of clusters must be given. It is quick, requires less computation, and has linear complexity of O (n).

2. **Fuzzy C-means algorithm**: A data object may be a member of more than one group or cluster when using a soft method called fuzzy clustering. Each dataset contains a set of membership coefficients that vary depending on how much of a cluster a dataset is a part of.

3. **DBSCAN Algorithm:** Density Based Spatial Clustering of requests through noise is what it stands for. It serves as an illustration of a density-based model that is comparable to the mean-shift but has several notable advantages. The algorithm divides the low density areas into the high density zones. The clusters can therefore be found in any arbitrary shape.

4   Classification Algorithms

A learning method that uses training data to classify new observations is called a classification algorithm. The computer programme learns to divide current observations into multiple groups or classifications using a specified set of data or observations. "Cat" or "dog," "yes" or "no," "0" or "1," "spam" or "no spam," and so forth are a few examples. Categories can be described with items, tags, or categories.

The output variable of classification, in contrast to that of regression, is a group rather than a value, such as "fruit or animal," "green or blue," and so on. As a supervised learning method, the Classification algorithm makes use of labeled input data; consequently, it consists of input and output data.

Different objects can be classified using machine learning-based classification approaches based on a set of training data whose outcome is known. In this work, four classification algorithms—KNN, SVM, Naive Bayes, and C5.0—are employed. In the nearest neighbor KN, an object is allocated to the class that is most frequently used by its closest neighbors after being classed by the majority of its neighbors. SVM (Support Vector Machines) classifies the data into linearly separable classes after first converting it to a set of points. A naïve Bayes model uses Bayes' rule to determine the likelihood that a data set can belong to a class [32].

5   Problem Statement

Currently, the healthcare industry gathers data from several hospitals and patients. Doctors can predict better treatment options and enhance the entire healthcare delivery system by making the best use of this data [4]. The ability of the Python framework to assist, make sense of and encourage computer equipment to extract useful insights from data concerning healthcare sectors is one of its most significant uses. In addition, Python is observed as one of the most widely used program writing languages worldwide. According to 32% of Britons, this programming language is secure enough to be used to create apps for the healthcare industry [22].

6   Methodology

Various machine learning methods are analyzed in this research, including K-Nearest Neighbor (KNN), Logistic Regression (LR) and Random Forest (RF) classifiers, which can help doctors or medical experts identify heart disease correctly. Examining numerous published works as well as information on current medical conditions are part of this paper's research. The proposed system has a framework provided by this method [19]. The approach is a process that involves a phase that converts provided data in the form of recognized data patterns for the customer's understanding. The designed system (Fig. 1) incorporates three stages, the first of which is data collection, the second of which is feature extraction, and the third of which is preprocessing, during which we examine the data. Depending on the procedures employed, data preprocessing addresses missing values, data cleaning, and normalization [20]. The suggested system uses K-Nearest Neighbor (KNN), Logistic Regression (LR) and Random Forest (RF) Classifier as the classifiers to categorize the preprocessed data once it has been preprocessed. After implementing the proposed system, we assessed our model's performance and accuracy using a number of performance measures. An efficient system for predicting heart disease is presented in this model. The development of the Heart Disease Prediction System has involved the use of a variety of classifiers [27]. This model includes 13 medical factors for prediction, including age, sex, blood pressure, cholesterol, blood sugar levels when fasting, and chest pain [21]. The UCI repository's dataset has been taken into consideration [23].

In our suggested framework, the following clustering and classification approaches have been combined and examined:

- K-nearest neighbors (KNN)
- Logistic Regression (LR)
- K-Means

6.1   K-Nearest Neighbors (KNN) and K-Means Algorithm

A supervised algorithm for classification is the KNN. It demonstrates how closely related the neighbors are for the correct data categorization, an effective class based data clustering method using k-means and KNN was described in this research paper. Grouping and classification are included. Our strategy is broken down into the below sections:

1. Preprocessing
2. Feature selection
3. Ratios of splitting
4. Validations

Cleaning the data has been done during data preprocessing since there is a chance that absent values, null values, and more similar factors may influence how well the subsequent operation works. Relevant domains with significant variance have only been taken into account for extraction in the feature selection method. Then, a number of variable splitting ratios were taken into consideration for the training and testing of the data. Precision, recall, and accuracy have all been used to evaluate the model. K-means and KNN have been used for clustering and classification. A random centroid selection has been done for the unbiased selection. The entire working process is shown in the suggested working flowchart Fig. 1. The entire working environment with the clustering and classification techniques is explored.

The following are the proposed approach algorithms:

KNN Algorithm

Step 1: First, select the final input set from the selected dataset. The input that has already been prepared.
Step 2: The neighbors' K selection has been completed.
Step 3: After that, the distance between the chosen K neighbors was calculated. Euclidean distance has been taken into account in our scenario.
Step 4: As you continue to process, take into account your closest neighbor.
Step 5: Based on the preceding process, data points have been taken into account and calculated.
Step 6: The assignment and updating of data points has been completed.
Seventh step: Complete classified data has been acquired.

K-Means Algorithm

Step 1: First, select the final input set from the selected dataset. The input that has already been prepared.
Step 2: For unbiased selection, random centroid initialization has been carried out.
Step 3. The weight was assigned at random.
Step 4: Using the Euclidean distance technique, distance has been determined. It goes like this:

$$X(c) = \sum_{j=1}^{k} \sum_{i=1}^{n} \left\| d_i^{(j)} - c_j \right\|^2$$

showing the group distance is $d_i - c_j$.
    The cluster numbers are shown in k.
    n represents all iterations in total.

Step 5: The aforementioned process is carried out repeatedly until a certain point or until outcomes start to repeat themselves.
Step 4: Based on similarities, grouping has been completed.
Step 6: The data point has been used to perform the final grouping.

6.2 Logistic Regression (LR)

A classification algorithm is what it is. When a categorical target variable is required, it is advantageous.
    It may be demonstrated using the sigmoid function as follows:

$$f(x) = \frac{1}{1 + e^{-x}}$$

$$g(Y = 1) = \frac{1}{1 + e^{-Y}}$$

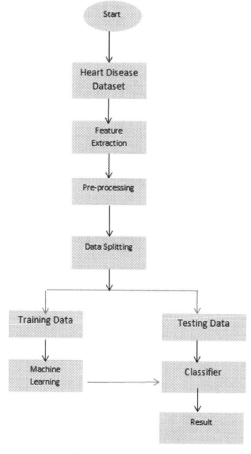

Fig. 1. Proposed System

7 Results and Discussions

For the correct data categorization, an effective class-based data clustering method using k-means and KNN was presented in this work. Grouping and classification are included. Fig. 2 compares the overall accuracy of the KNN algorithm with various split ratios. It demonstrates the accuracy level changes of 71% to 88% for various features and attributes variation. Additionally, it shows that it is able to classify the data. The heatmap for the KNN and LR method is displayed in Fig. 3 and Fig. 4. The qualities, their connections, and their consequences are fully visualized as a heatmap. The heatmap allows for a visual representation of attribute relationships as well as their influence on disease prediction. Figure 5 compares the overall accuracy of the LR algorithm with various split ratios. It unmistakably demonstrates the accuracy range of 85% to 96% variances for various features and attribute changes. Additionally, it shows that it is able to classify the data.

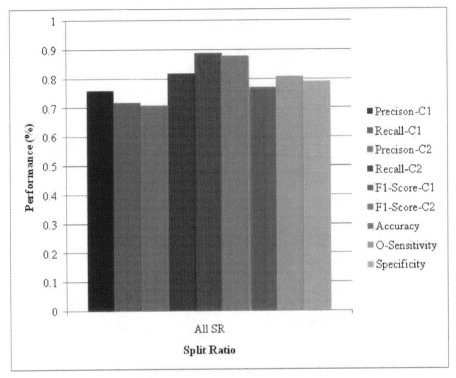

Fig. 2. Overall accuracy comparison based on different split ratio (SR) in case of KNN algorithm

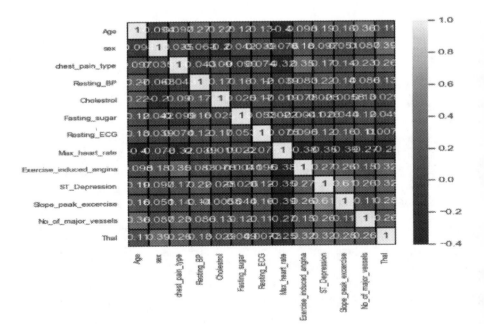

Fig. 3. Heatmap in case of KNN algorithm

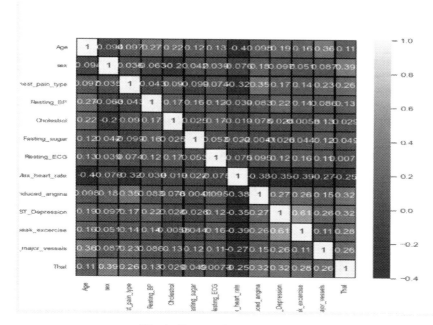

Fig. 4. Heatmap in case of LR algorithm

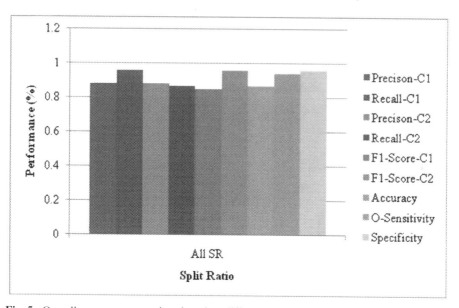

Fig. 5. Overall accuracy comparison based on different split ratio (SR) in case of LR algorithm

8 Conclusion

Three machine learning (ML) classification modeling techniques have been combined to create a model for diagnosing medical diseases. In this research work, we use a dataset that comprises patients' past medical records to extract the medical histories of individuals who develop major heart illnesses, including chest pain, blood pressure, blood sugar, and other characteristics. This heart disease detection system assists the patient based on clinical data regarding the patient's prior diagnosis of heart disease. The given model was constructed using the KNN, Logistic Regression, and K-Means methods. In the instance of the KNN algorithm, a comparison of total accuracy depending on various split ratios. It demonstrates the accuracy level changes of 71% to 88% for various features and attributes variations. The likelihood that the model will correctly identify if specific patients have heart disease or not increases with the use of more training data. Comparison of total accuracy for the LR algorithm with various split ratios. It unmistakably demonstrates the accuracy range of 85% to 96% variances for various features and attributes changes. With the aid of these computer-assisted technologies, we can predict the patient's needs more efficiently and affordably. We can work with a variety of medical databases since machine learning algorithms are more advanced and can anticipate outcomes better than humans, benefiting both patients and medical professionals. As a result, we can predict individuals who will be diagnosed with heart problems by cleaning the information and using logistic regression and KNN to obtain an accuracy of 85% to 96% on average. The accuracy of logistic regression, which ranges from 85% to 96%, is also found to be the greatest among the three algorithms we used.

References

1. www.medium.com/analytics-vidhya/heart-disease-prediction-with-ensemble-learning-74d6109beba1
2. Felman, A.: Everything you need to know about heart disease. Med. News Today (2018). https://www.medicalnewstoday.com/articles/237191#types
3. Thomas, J., Princy, R.T.: Human heart disease prediction system using data mining techniques. In: International Conference on Circuit, Power and Computing Technologies (ICCPCT), pp. 1–5. IEEE (2016)
4. Kumar, V.V.: Healthcare Analytics Made Simple: Techniques in Healthcare Computing using Machine Learning and Python. Packt Publishing Ltd. (2018)
5. Han, J., Rodriguez, J.C., Beheshti, M.: Diabetes data analysis and prediction model discovery using RapidMiner. In: Second International Conference on Future Generation Communication and Networking, pp. 96–99 (2008)
6. Patil, S.K.B.: Extraction of significant patterns from heart disease warehouses for heart attack prediction. Int. J. Comput. Sci. Netw. Secur. 9(2) (2009)
7. Vijayalakshmi, D., Thilagavathi, K.: An approach for prediction of diabetic disease by using b-coloring technique in clustering analysis. Int. J. Appl. Math. Res. 1(4), 520–530 (2012)
8. Manikandan, V., Latha, S.: Predicting the analysis of heart disease symptoms using medicinal data mining methods. Int. J. Adv. Comput. Theory Eng. 2, 46–51 (2013)
9. Karthiga, G., Preethi, C., Devi, R.: Heart disease analysis system using data mining techniques. Int. J. Innov. Res. Sci. Eng. Technol. 3(Spec. Issue 3) (2014)

10. Rajkumar, A., Sophia Reena, G.: Diagnosis of heart disease using data mining algorithm. Int. J. Comput. Sci. Inf. Technol. **5**(2), 1678–1680 (2014)
11. Dbritto, R., Srinivasaraghavan, A., Joseph, V.: Comparative analysis of accuracy on heart disease prediction using classification method. Int. J. Appl. Inf. Syst. **11**(2) (2016)
12. Kaur, B., Singh, W.: Review on heart disease prediction system using data mining techniques. Int. J. Recent Innov. Trends Comput. Commun. **2**(10), 3003–3008 (2017). ISSN: 2321-8169
13. Sharmila, R., Chellammal, S.: A conceptual method to enhance the prediction of heart diseases using the data techniques. Int. J. Comput. Sci. Eng. (2018)
14. Latha, C.B.C., Jeeva, S.C.: Improving the accuracy of prediction of heart disease risk based on ensemble classification techniques. Inform. Med. Unlocked **16**, 100203 (2019)
15. Terrada, O., Hamida, S., Cherradi, B., Raihani, A., Bouattia, O.: Supervised machine learning based medical diagnosis support system for prediction of patients with heart disease. Adv. Sci. Technol. Eng. Syst. J. **5**(5) (2020)
16. Mienye, I.D., Sun, Y., Wang, Z.: An improved ensemble learning approach for the prediction of heart disease risk. Inform. Med. Unlocked **20**, 100402 (2020)
17. Jothi, K.A., Subburam, S., Umadevi, V., Hemavathi, K.: Heart disease prediction system using machine learning. Mater. Today Proc. (2021)
18. Shorewala, V.: Early detection of coronary heart disease using ensemble techniques. Inform. Med. Unlocked, 100655 (2021)
19. Wolgast, G., Ehrenborg, C., Israelsson, A., Helander, J., Johansson, E., Manefjord, H.: Wireless body area network for heart attack detection. IEEE Antennas Propag. Mag. **58**(5), 84–92 (2016)
20. Patidar, K., Verma, D.: An efficient class-based data clustering through K-means and KNN approach. Turk. J. Comput. Math. Educ. **12**, 1396–1400 (2021)
21. Patidar, K., Verma, D.: An efficient SVM and ACO-RF method for the cluster-based feature selection and classification. Ann. Rom. Soc. Cell Biol. **25**, 9830–9839 (2021)
22. BelItSoft: Python in healthcare. BelItSoft (2017). https://belitsoft.com/custom-application-development-services/healthcare-software-development/python-healthcare
23. Asuncion, A., Newman, D.: UCI machine learning repository (2007)
24. Masethe, H.D., Masethe, M.A.: Prediction of heart disease using classification algorithms. In: Proceedings of the World Congress on Engineering and Computer Science, vol. 2, pp. 22–24 (2014)
25. Kanimozhi, V.A., Karthikeyan, T.: A survey on machine learning algorithms in data mining for prediction of heart disease. Int. J. Adv. Res. (IJAR) **5**(4), 552–557 (2016)
26. Singh, A., Kumar, R.: Heart disease prediction using machine learning algorithms. In: International Conference on Electrical and Electronics Engineering, pp. 452–457 (2020)
27. Almustafa, K.M.: Prediction of heart disease and classifiers sensitivity analysis. BMC Bioinform. **21**, 278 (2020)
28. Hassan, R.: Comparative analysis of machine learning algorithms for heart disease prediction. In: ITM Web of Conferences, vol. 40, p. 03007 (2021)
29. Hemalatha, D., Poorani, S.: Machine learning techniques for heart disease prediction. J. Cardiovasc. Dis. Res. **12**(1), 93–96 (2021)
30. Kavitha, M., Gnaneswar, G., Dinesh, R., et al.: Heart disease prediction using hybrid machine learning model. In: 6th International Conference on Inventive Computation Technologies (ICICT), pp. 1329–1333 (2021)
31. Nagavelli, U., Samanta, D., Chakraborty, P.: Machine learning technology-based heart disease detection models. J. Healthc. Eng. **2022**, 1–9 (2022)
32. Ojha, U., Goel, S.: A study on prediction of breast cancer recurrence using data mining techniques. In: International Conference on Cloud Computing, Data Science & Engineering, Noida, India. IEEE (2017)

Skin Lesion Classification: Scrutiny of Learning-Based Methods

Yashandeep Kaur, Parneet Kaur, and Manish Kumar[✉]

Chandigarh Engineering College, CGC, Landran, India
{parneet.4837,manish.4379}@cgc.edu.in

Abstract. In this advanced era of technology, learning-based methods or models are popular among various applications, even in medical imaging. For example, several disease detection systems utilize this technology and help doctors in early diagnostics. However, the body's internal organs' outermost layer of defence is their skin. Unfortunately, the prevalence of numerous skin conditions is rising today due to increased pollution and many other causes. Categorizing skin lesions is a complex process since they come in various shapes and kinds, and now learning-based methods also help in this field. So, this paper elaborates on the current state of work using learning-based methods and highlights their shortcomings to analyse the future scope of the technology. Moreover, this paper also demonstrates the details of the imaging techniques and benchmark datasets for skin lesion detection.

Keywords: Skin Lesion · Classification · Deep Learning · Medical Imaging

1 Introduction

With a mortality rate of one death every six individuals, cancer is one of the major causes of death in the modern era. According to the American Cancer Society, there were 9.5 million cancer-related deaths and 17 million new cancer diagnoses in 2020 [1]. The five-year survival rate for Melanoma, the deadlier of the two preeminent types of cancer, is believed to be over 99% if detected early and 20% if discovered later [2]. In 2021, there are 96,480 new cases and up to 7,230 fatalities for Melanoma. In 2021, it ranked as the ninth most common cancer in the country. Melanoma, which results in the formation of malignant tumours, may be caused when a melanocyte, which produces the pigment melanin, begins to duplicate uncontrollably. These cancerous tumors, frequently identified by the acronym ABCDE, exhibit asymmetry, irregular borders, a variety of colors, a diameter of at least 6 mm, and a developing lesion [3]. Of all the traits mentioned, color and shape are the most important for melanoma diagnosis. Making an early melanoma diagnosis involves considering a number of factors. Early detection of melanoma allows for more effective treatment for the patient. Medical imaging has made extensive use of algorithms to enhance performance for an accurate and speedy diagnosis [4]. Over the past few decades, various computer science disciplines have evolved, showing promise for assisting diagnostic operations. Artificial intelligence (A.I.) is one of these areas

© The Author(s), under exclusive license to Springer Nature Switzerland AG 2023
R. K. Tiwari and G. Sahoo (Eds.): ICAII 2022, CCIS 1822, pp. 52–64, 2023.
https://doi.org/10.1007/978-3-031-37303-9_5

to automate diagnosis using advanced algorithms and the ability to outperform human specialists [5].

The skin is prone to developing a variety of cancers. According to the definition of cancer, it is a condition in which some cells develop abnormally due to changed gene expression [6]. These cancerous cells keep spreading to surrounding cells. The count of patients having cancer has increased in the contemporary era due to factors affecting the human body, such as a rise in life expectancy, particular personal behaviors, and U.V. radiation. Figure 1 illustrates how cancer may be categorized into two categories, benign and malignant, depending on the degree of malignancy [7]. The difference is due to each group's ability to spread or metastasize to distant tissues and organs. Cancer has a strong ability to penetrate and kill nearby tissues. In addition, they may be able to travel to distant tissues and organs through the bloodstream or lymphatic system. Benign cancer can affect the surrounding area even if it is typically more limited because it can exert pressure on neighbouring blood vessels or nerves [8]. It could also emit substances that obstruct the normal function of tissues. Benign cancer develops gradually and presents fewer risks to life than Malignant [9]. Therefore, malignant is more aggressive and challenging to treat.

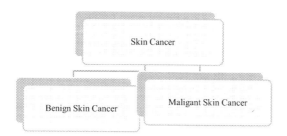

Fig. 1. Types of skin cancer

Benign Skin Cancer: A benign tumor is not a malignant tumor, but a malignancy is cancer that misses the tissues adjacent to other body parts [10]. Figure 2 displays a different type of benign skin cancer. Although critical structures like blood vessels or nerves do not require any treatment, they can become severe in some situations. Diets, infections, and significant injury to the tumors are a few potential causes of this tumor [11].

Fig. 2. Different types of Benign skin cancer

Malignant Skin Cancer: This tumour's presence indicates that the affected body part is carcinogenic. The word "malignant" means "badly born." The lymphatic, blood and circulatory systems transfer abnormal cells [12]. Tumor forms when the abnormal cells breed with other cells, and it takes on a malignant nature when it starts to infect the tissues around it and obstruct the supply of oxygen and other vital nutrients. This cause of this type of cancer includes obesity, smoking, eating poorly, consuming alcohol, being overweight, exposure to home pollutants and heavy metals, and the environment [13]. The medical community generally accepts some of the causes resulting from them. Since this tumor first displays no symptoms, its first sign is often a painless lump [14]. However, these tumors are so flexible that they can spread widely before being found. Therefore, it is Melanoma and non-melanoma, as given in Fig. 3, where the types of non-melanoma are (i) Basal Cell Carcinoma, and (ii) Squamous Cell Carcinoma.

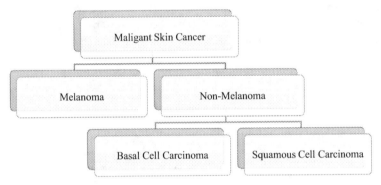

Fig. 3. Types of Malignant Skin Cancer

2   Skin Lesion Imaging Techniques

90% of skin cancer cases are cured in the early stages, versus 50% in the more advanced stages. The development of the non-invasive and high-resolution tools increase the accuracy of the diagnosis systems for skin lesion/cancer [15]. The primary reason of under treatment or overtreatment of melanoma is its diagnostic accuracy which is less because of false negatives or positives. False positive tests necessitate the removal of an excessive number of benign lesions for biopsy and pathological analysis, which signifi-cantly raises the expense of treatment [16]. On the other hand, high-resolution imaging techniques can significantly improve diagnostic specificity, which opens the door to reducing unnecessary excisions and related costs. The imaging techniques most fre-quently employed to identify skin cancers are optical coherence, reflectance confocal microscopy, dermoscopy, and ultrasound [17].

2.1   Optical Coherence Tomography (OCT)

OCT can distinguish between cancerous and healthy tissue by examining small features in vivo that are a few nanometres. However, detecting cancer in its initial stages is impossible because the membrane and subcellular components are invisible to the OCT. Furthermore, without histological confirmation, the OCT does not verify the diagnosis of Melanoma. As a result, it is useless to diagnose Melanoma with an OCT [18].

2.2 Reflectance Confocal Microscopy (RCM)

Confocal microscopy uses a laser focused on a specific skin area to view the skin's cellular structure in real-time. Due to the different refraction indices of biological components like cells, melanin, and hemoglobin, RCM can quickly identify reflected light from the skin. However, the most costly skin imaging technology is RCM [19].

2.3 Dermoscopy

Dermoscopy also called as epilumence microscopy which is a non-invasive and in-person method for the early identification of malignant Melanoma and other pigmented lesions that allows users to photograph the color and underlying structures of the skin to discover Melanoma in its earliest stages. Statistics from the literature indicate that, depending on the type of skin lesion, dermoscopy can improve diagnostic accuracy by 5% to 30% [20].

2.4 Ultrasound

Ultrasound is one of the most often non-invasive procedures since it is flexible, painless, and safe. The shape of the skin can be observed using ultrasonic waves that are reflected from the tissue during this process. Although deep skin layers may allow ultrasound waves to assess tumors, the resolution is too low to allow for micro morphological differentiation between skin lesions. Furthermore, it overlooks early-stage malignancies [21].

3 Benchmark Dataset

On the internet, numerous skin lesion detection and classification data are available for research. Mainly the dataset of Hospital Pedro Hispano and International Skin Imaging Collaboration image datasets are used. The details of these datasets are as follows:

3.1 Hospital Pedro Hispano (PH²)

The Dermatology Service of Hospital Pedro Hispano in Portugal provided this dataset, which is accessible online. There are 200 dermoscopic images in it. Table 1 summarises certain scholars' contributions to the field of PH2 utilizing the dataset.

Table 1. Brief review of dataset PH^2 and ISIC

Authors	Dataset	Skin Image classes	No. of images	Segmentation	Techniques	Classifier
Barata et al. [22]	PH^2	2 classes	176	Adaptive threshold	GLCM, Wavelets, linear filter	AdaBoost, SVM, k-NN
Marques et al. [23]	PH^2	2 classes	163	–	–	Binary classifier
Mendonça et al. [24]	PH^2	Benign: 2 classes Malignant : 1 class	200	Manual segmentation	ABCD rule, 7-point checklist, Menzies	–
Silva et al. [25]	PH^2	Melanoma	–		Menzies method	–
Silva et al. [26]	PH^2	Melanoma 3 classes	28		Menzies Method	Neural network classifier
Silveira et al. [27]	PH^2	–	–	AS and E.M.-L.S segmentation method	–	–
Yu et al. [28]	ISIC	Melanoma	1250	FCRN	–	Residual Network
Chang [29]	ISIC	Melanoma (374), Nevus (1372), SK(254)	2000	–	–	Google- Net Inception v3 CNN
Li et al. [30]	ISIC	Malignant, Melanoma, Benign	2000	Lesion Index Network	Lesion Feature Network	Fully convolution n residua
Yang et al. [31]	ISIC	Melanoma, Nevus, SK	2000	–	–	Deep CNN
Jia et al. [32]	ISIC	Melanoma (374), Nevus (1372), SK(254)	2000	–	–	CNN
Mirunalini et al. [33]	ISIC	Malignant, Benign	2000	–	–	Google- Net v3 CNN

3.2 International Skin Imaging Collaboration (ISIC) Archive

International Skin Imaging Collaboration is the name of the group. A team of dermatologists from the U.S. has been diagnosing the dataset. There are tens of thousands of photos available in this dataset. This society's primary goal is to acquaint its members with cutting-edge digital skin imaging technologies. International Dermoscopy Society (IDS) and International Confocal Group (ICG) groups are additional partners with ISIC. Table 1 also highlights research contributions in the field of ISIC.

4 Deep Learning-Based Skin Lesion Detection Systems

This section of the paper describes the existing deep learning-based designed systems for skin lesion detection and classification. The details of these systems are as follows:

Benyahia et al. [34] evaluated the performance of utilising 17 frequently pre-trained convolutional neural network (CNN) architectures that performs feature extraction and approximately, 24 ML classifiers were used to classify skin lesions with two datasets namely ISIC 2019 and PH2. For the ISIC 2019 dataset, this work found the performance of the DenseNet201 with a Fine KNN or Cubic SVM (92.34% and 91.71%). Additionally, the outcomes demonstrate that the suggested methodology has better performance than competing ones on the PH2 dataset, with a 99% accuracy rate. Aldhyani et al. [35] established a very accurate categorization system for skin lesions using a simple and effective model. Moreover, dynamic-sized kernels layers were used to achieve the best outcomes. These models utilizes both leakyReLU and ReLU activation functions and correctly categorized the HAM10000 dataset's classes. The performance of the proposed model is more efficient than the other state-of-the-art with an overall accuracy of 97.85%.

Afza et al. [36] presented a hierarchical design based on deep learning with two-dimensional superpixels. By fusing local and global enhanced images, they first increased the contrast of the initial dermoscopy images. Further in the next stage, skin lesions were segmented using a three-step superpixel lesion segmentation technique using the entire enhanced images. In this, ResNet-50 architecture was then used to learn features and these features were further optimised using an improved grasshopper optimization method. Further classification is performed using the Nave Bayes classifier. The datasets of PH2, ISBI2016, and HAM1000 containing three, two, and seven different categories of skin cancer have been used to evaluate the recommended hierarchical method. The accuracy of the suggested technique was 95.40%, 91.1%, and 85.50% for these datasets, respectively. The findings indicate that this technique can aid in a more accurate skin cancer classification.

Shen et al. [37] proposed data augmentation method called search space 101 that can be used in a plug-and-play mode to join with any model and find the best form of augmentation for a small scale database. The best BACC of HAM10000 for the ISIC 2018 Lesion Diagnosis Challenge is 0.853, which is better than "single-model and no-external-database." Moreover, with ISIC 2017 dataset, the best average AUC performance was 0.909 ($\pm$0.015). Additionally, the Grad-CAM++ generated model-based heatmaps confirm the precise selection of lesion features in model judgment, thus demonstrating the validity of model-based diagnosis from a scientific perspective. The suggested data augmentation technique significantly reduces the computational expense of making a clinically accurate diagnosis of skin lesions. Additionally, it might make it easier to do future research on affordable, transportable, and AI-powered mobile devices for therapeutic advice and skin cancer screening.

A hybrid approach was proposed by Khan et al. [38] that removes artefacts and improve the lesion contrast. Further, the OCFs colour segmentation technique was introduced. The OCF methodology was significantly improved by combining an existing saliency strategy with a brand-new pixel-based approach. OCFs and a DCNN-9 model were combined using a novel parallel fusion technique to extract deep features. Following that, a high-ranking feature selection method based on a normal distribution was used to choose the features for classification that were found to be the most dependable. In order to evaluate the suggested method, datasets from the ISBI series (2016, 2017, and 2018) were employed. The investigations, which were conducted in two stages, achieved an average segmentation accuracy of more than 90% on the chosen datasets. Additionally, the three datasets' respective classification accuracy results of 92.1%, 96.5%, and 85.1% show how well the approach performs.

Hoang et al. [39] created a novel approach for classifying skin lesions using wide-ShuffleNet and a new segmentation strategy. They have initially calculated the first-order cumulative moment and entropy-based weighting of the skin picture (EW-FCM). To separate the lesion from the surrounding tissue, these measurements are used. The segmentation result was then fed into a brand-new deep learning structure dubbed wide-ShuffleNet to determine the type of skin lesion. Using the large datasets from HAM10000 and ISIC2019, they evaluated the suggested methodology. The numerical results demonstrate that wide-ShuffleNet and EW-FCM beat state-of-the-art techniques in terms of accuracy. The suggested method was also more effective, lightweight, and suitable for a small system, such as a mobile healthcare system.

Afza et al. [40] proposed a multiclass skin lesion identification method based on the feature fusion and machine learning. In this the first step was image acquisition, then contrast amplification was done. Further, the deep learning based feature extraction approach was developed using transfer learning and feature selection was done with a hybrid method that combines whale optimization with entropy-mutual information (EMI) approach. Moreover, these selected features were fused with a modified canonical correlation-based approach, and finally extreme learning machine-based classification were performed. The system's precision and computing performance are improved by the feature selection procedure. Two openly available datasets, ISIC2018 and HAM10000, were applied in the experiment. Accuracy was between 94.36 and 93.40 percent for both datasets. Comparing the recommended method to state-of-the-art (SOTA) methods, the accuracy was improved.

The seven types of skin conditions categorised by Arora et al. [41]. The major objective of this article was to evaluate the performance of the deep learning networks where transfer learning was used to categorise lesions on fourteen deep learning networks. The dataset utilised for these tests contains 10,154 photos from ISIC 2018. The findings demonstrated that DenseNet201 outperforms other models with an accuracy of 0.825 and enhances skin lesion categorization under various disorders. The suggested study displays the different factors, such as the effectiveness of all the deep learning networks, which contributed to the development of an effective automated classification model for several skin lesions.

To enhance the overall effectiveness of skin classification, Hsu and Tseng [42] proposed Hierarchy-Aware Contrastive Learning with Late Fusion (HAC-LF). In order to lessen the effects of the major-type misclassification problem, they developed a novel loss function called Hierarchy-Aware Contrastive Loss (HAC Loss) in HAC-LF. The major-type and multi-class classification performance were balanced using the late fusion approach. They conduct several tests on the ISIC 2019 Challenges dataset, which consists of three skin lesion datasets, to evaluate the efficacy of the suggested strategies. The results showed that the recommended technique outperformed the existing deep learning algorithms for skin lesion identification in all of the assessment criteria used in this work. HAC-LF scores 0.871, 0.842, and 0.889 for accuracy, sensitivity, and specificity in the major-type categorization. In terms of the sensitivity of minority classes in the presence of an imbalanced distribution of classes, HAC-LF outperforms the baseline model. This work developed the major-type misclassification problem. They proposed HAC-LF as a solution to deal with it and enhance the multi-class skin lesion classification performance. The results demonstrate that the advantage of HAC-LF was that the recommended HAC Loss can advantageously minimise the negative impacts of the major-type misclassification by reducing the major-type mistake rate. HAC-LF has the potential to be applied to areas of data having a hierarchical structure outside of medicine.

Thapar et al. [43] devised a reliable approach for diagnosing skin cancer using dermoscopy images in order to improve medical professionals' visual perception and diagnostic capacity to distinguish benign from malignant lesions. The suggested method performs better than previous research in every performance indicator. Yao et al. in [44]. Suggested a novel single-model based approach for identifying skin lesions on short and imbalanced datasets. This single DCNN model strategy, which included Modified RandAugment, MWNL, and CLS, produced classification accuracy on several dermoscopic image datasets that was equivalent to or better than that of numerous ensembling models. This study showed that the method can be implemented in mobile devices for automated screening of skin lesions and many other malignancies. It is potentially appropriate for use in low resource settings because it can achieve high classification performance at a low cost of computational resources and inference time.

In an effort to close the knowledge gap, Bharwaj and Rege [45] mined the collective knowledge found in the existing Deep Learning Techniques to find the guiding principles for creating a neural network for classifying skin diseases. To simplify the categorization of illnesses, the method was based on integrating the top-N performing models employed as a feature extractor and an SVM. On the ISIC 2019 dataset, the final model had an accuracy of 86% and had high precision and recall values of 0.8 and 0.6, respectively.

In order to identify and categorise dangerous skin lesions (melanoma type), Damian et al. [46] introduced a new Computer-Aided Detection (CAD) system that combined handcrafted features from the ABCD rule (Asymmetry Borders-Colors-Dermatoscopic Structures) algorithm with deep learning features made using Mutual Information (MI) measurements. In [47], Serte and Demirel proposed two techniques for the automated categorization of seborrheic keratosis and malignant melanoma lesions. The first approach builds on wavelet coefficients and skin image modelling. The wavelet transform is used to derive approximate, horizontal, and vertical wavelet coefficients, after which deep learning (DL) models are created for each of the representations and skin pictures. The second approach expands on the first by modelling skin pictures with three approximative factors. Using a sequential wavelet transformation, this technique generates approximation coefficients. Following that, DL models are created for all the representations and skin image datasets. ResNet-18 and ResNet-50 DL models with a transfer learning foundation give model pictures and wavelet coefficients. Then, by merging model output probabilities, skin lesion identification was accomplished. The two suggested models perform better than approaches that rely just on picture data and other suggested ways from the past.

Yilmaz and Trocan investigated how well AlexNet, GoogLeNet, and Resnet50 CNNs classified benign and malignant melanoma tumours using dermoscopic images. [48]. Dermoscopic images of 2197 malignant lesions and 19373 benign lesions from the ISIC database were used in the research. The three CNNs that won the ImageNet competition in the past have all been tweaked to do binary classification. 80% of the photos in the studies were used for training, while the other 20% were utilised for validation. The same settings for each CNN model were used in all tests. The trials showed that the ResNET50 model performed best, with a classification accuracy of 92.81%, and that AlexNet placed top in terms of time complexity metrics. Future research will focus on the creation of new models that are based on current CNN models with an emphasis on dermoscopic pictures.

A revolutionary deep learning-based algorithm described by Deif and Hammam [49] produced extremely high skin melanoma diagnostic accuracy. On 10,135 dermoscopy skin pictures, several pretrained architectures (VGG16, Inception v3, and ResNet-50) were suggested and used. To compare these models, algorithms for hair removal and nonremoval were used. According to experimental findings, shaving had a substantial impact on skin imaging since it increased the training accuracy outcomes. With the hair removal method, the VGG16 model had the best accuracy (96.9%), followed by Inception v3 and ResNet-50, which had accuracy ratings of 94.2% and 91.8%, respectively.

Ratul et al. [50] used the transfer learning architectures VGG16, VGG19, MobileNet, and InceptionV3 to perform dilated convolution. The HAM10000 dataset was utilised for training, validating, and testing. The best classification accuracy, recall, precision, and f-1 score were demonstrated by dilated InceptionV3 and dilated MobileNet, which both had excellent classification accuracy and little processing complexity. To the best of our knowledge, Dilated InceptionV3 outperformed all other algorithms for classifying skin lesions while working with a complicated open-source dataset with class imbalances.

5   Challenges and Future Recommendations

The current systems for the detection of skin lesion classification mainly focuses on the detection of benign and malignant cancer and it does classification for some of the sub classes of the same. So, further multi-class classification using deep learning can be used in order to detect different types of cancers and help the doctors for accurate treatment of the patients.

Further, some machine learning based approaches are combined with the hand-crafted features in order to achieve the better performance but deep learning-based methods are directly implemented on images. So, in future deep learning-based models can be improved with the help of handcrafted features which also help to improve the performance of the automati8c detection/classification systems.

6 Conclusion

The focus of this paper is to highlight the current trend of the automatic skin lesion detection and classification system in order to understand the requirements of the future. Moreover, this paper elaborates the different imaging methods, and benchmark datasets. As PH2 and ISIC are very much popular datasets used for the analysis of the proposed models, so some of the work done with these datasets are also discussed. Finally, from the current methods of deep learning, the main challenges and future recommendation are deliberated.

References

1. Cancer Statistics - NCI. https://www.cancer.gov/about-cancer/understanding/statistics. Accessed 28 Oct 2022
2. Melanoma - The Skin Cancer Foundation. https://www.skincancer.org/skin-cancer-inform ation/melanoma/. Accessed 2 Oct 2022
3. Tsur, N.: Predicting response to immunotherapy in metastatic melanoma by a personalized mathematical model (2020). https://doi.org/10.18419/opus-10952
4. Dey, N., Rajinikanth, V., Ashour, A., Tavares, J.M.: Social group optimization supported segmentation and evaluation of skin melanoma images. Symmetry (Basel) 10(2), 51 (2018). https://doi.org/10.3390/sym10020051
5. Ahmad, Z., Rahim, S., Zubair, M., Abdul-Ghafar, J.: Artificial intelligence (AI) in medicine, current applications and future role with special emphasis on its potential and promise in pathology: present and future impact, obstacles including costs and acceptance among pathologists, practical and philosoph. Diagn. Pathol. 16(1), 24 (2021). https://doi.org/10.1186/s13 000-021-01085-4
6. Unterberger, C.J., et al.: GH action in prostate cancer cells promotes proliferation, limits apoptosis, and regulates cancer-related gene expression. Endocrinology 163(5) (2022). https://doi.org/10.1210/endocr/bqac031
7. Stefan Jianu, S.R., Ichim, L., Popescu, D.: Automatic diagnosis of skin cancer using neural networks. In: 2019 11th International Symposium on Advanced Topics in Electrical Engineering (ATEE), pp. 1–4 (2019). https://doi.org/10.1109/ATEE.2019.8724938
8. Nasrollahzadeh, E., Razi, S., Keshavarz-Fathi, M., Mazzone, M., Rezaei, N.: Pro-tumorigenic functions of macrophages at the primary, invasive and metastatic tumor site. Cancer Immunol. Immunother. 69(9), 1673–1697 (2020). https://doi.org/10.1007/s00262-020-02616-6
9. Kutzner, H., et al.: Overdiagnosis of melanoma – causes, consequences and solutions. JDDG J. der Dtsch. Dermatologischen Gesellschaft 18(11), 1236–1243 (2020). https://doi.org/10.1111/ddg.14233
10. Grosser, S., et al.: Cell and nucleus shape as an indicator of tissue fluidity in carcinoma. Phys. Rev. X 11(1), 011033 (2021). https://doi.org/10.1103/PhysRevX.11.011033
11. Yang, W., et al.: Association of intake of whole grains and dietary fiber with risk of hepatocellular carcinoma in US adults. JAMA Oncol. 5(6), 879 (2019). https://doi.org/10.1001/jam aoncol.2018.7159

12. Munn, L.: Aberrant vascular architecture in tumors and its importance in drug-based therapies. Drug Discov. Today **8**(9), 396–403 (2003). https://doi.org/10.1016/S1359-6446(03)02686-2
13. Irigaray, P., et al.: Lifestyle-related factors and environmental agents causing cancer: an overview. Biomed. Pharmacother. **61**(10), 640–658 (2007). https://doi.org/10.1016/j.biopha.2007.10.006
14. Silva, C.V., Horsham, C., Janda, M.: Review of educational tools for skin self-examination: a qualitative analysis of laypeople's preferences. Heal. Promot. J. Aust. **33**(2) (2022). https://doi.org/10.3316/informit.457601473566452
15. Pellacani, G., Argenziano, G.: New insights from non-invasive imaging: from prospection of skin photodamages to training with mobile application. J. Eur. Acad. Dermatol. Venereol. **36**(S6), 38–50 (2022). https://doi.org/10.1111/jdv.18197
16. Layfield, L.J., Stegelmeier, P., Wang, L., Esebua, M.: Core needle biopsy for the diagnosis of primary soft tissue lesions: Accuracy and diagnostic challenges. Diagn. Cytopathol. **50**(9), 442–450 (2022). https://doi.org/10.1002/dc.25012
17. Wang, Y.-J., Wang, J.-Y., Wu, Y.-H.: Application of cellular resolution full-field optical coherence tomography in vivo for the diagnosis of skin tumours and inflammatory skin diseases: a pilot study. Dermatology **238**(1), 121–131 (2022). https://doi.org/10.1159/000514686
18. Sampson, D.M., Dubis, A.M., Chen, F.K., Zawadzki, R.J., Sampson, D.D.: Towards standardizing retinal optical coherence tomography angiography: a review. Light Sci. Appl. **11**(1), 63 (2022). https://doi.org/10.1038/s41377-022-00740-9
19. Pellacani, G., et al.: Effect of reflectance confocal microscopy for suspect lesions on diagnostic accuracy in melanoma. JAMA Dermatol. **158**(7), 754 (2022). https://doi.org/10.1001/jamadermatol.2022.1570
20. Guida, S., et al.: Dermoscopy, confocal microscopy and optical coherence tomography features of main inflammatory and autoimmune skin diseases: a systematic review. Australas. J. Dermatol. **63**(1), 15–26 (2022). https://doi.org/10.1111/ajd.13695
21. Fedorov Kukk, A., Wu, D., Gaffal, E., Panzer, R., Emmert, S., Roth, B.: Multimodal system for optical biopsy of melanoma with integrated ultrasound, optical coherence tomography and Raman spectroscopy. J. Biophoton. **15**(10) (2022). https://doi.org/10.1002/jbio.202200129
22. Barata, C., Ruela, M., Francisco, M., Mendonca, T., Marques, J.S.: Two systems for the detection of melanomas in dermoscopy images using texture and color features. IEEE Syst. J. **8**(3), 965–979 (2014). https://doi.org/10.1109/JSYST.2013.2271540
23. Marques, J.S., Barata, C., Mendonca, T.: On the role of texture and color in the classification of dermoscopy images. In: 2012 Annual International Conference of the IEEE Engineering in Medicine and Biology Society, pp. 4402–4405 (2012). https://doi.org/10.1109/EMBC.2012.6346942
24. Mendonca, T., Ferreira, P.M., Marques, J.S., Marcal, A.R.S., Rozeira, J.: PH2 - a dermoscopic image database for research and benchmarking. In: 2013 35th Annual International Conference of the IEEE Engineering in Medicine and Biology Society (EMBC), pp. 5437–5440 (2013). https://doi.org/10.1109/EMBC.2013.6610779
25. Silva, C.S.P., Marcal, A.R.S., Pereira, M.A., Mendonça, T., Rozeira, J.: Separability analysis of color classes on dermoscopic images. In: Campilho, A., Kamel, M. (eds.) ICIAR 2012. LNCS, vol. 7325, pp. 268–277. Springer, Heidelberg (2012). https://doi.org/10.1007/978-3-642-31298-4_32
26. Silva, C.S.P., Marcal, A.R.S.: Colour-based dermoscopy classification of cutaneous lesions: an alternative approach. Comput. Methods Biomech. Biomed. Eng. Imaging Vis. **1**(4), 211–224 (2013). https://doi.org/10.1080/21681163.2013.803683
27. Silveira, M., et al.: Comparison of segmentation methods for melanoma diagnosis in dermoscopy images. IEEE J. Sel. Top. Signal Process. **3**(1), 35–45 (2009). https://doi.org/10.1109/JSTSP.2008.2011119

28. Yu, L., Chen, H., Dou, Q., Qin, J., Heng, P.-A.: Automated melanoma recognition in dermoscopy images via very deep residual networks. IEEE Trans. Med. Imaging **36**(4), 994–1004 (2017). https://doi.org/10.1109/TMI.2016.2642839
29. Chang, H.: Skin cancer reorganization and classification with deep neural network. Comput. Vis. Pattern Recognit. (2017). http://arxiv.org/abs/1703.00534
30. Li, Y., Shen, L.: Skin lesion analysis towards melanoma detection using deep learning network. Sensors **18**(2), 556 (2018). https://doi.org/10.3390/s18020556
31. Yang, X., Zeng, Z., Yeo, S.Y., Tan, C., Tey, H.L., Su, Y.: A novel multi-task deep learning model for skin lesion segmentation and classification. Comput. Vis. Pattern Recognit. (2017). http://arxiv.org/abs/1703.01025
32. Jia, X., Shen, L.: Skin lesion classification using class activation map. Comput. Vis. Pattern Recognit. (2017). http://arxiv.org/abs/1703.01053
33. Mirunalini, P., Chandrabose, A., Gokul, V., Jaisakthi, S.M.: Deep learning for skin lesion classification. Comput. Vis. Pattern Recognit. (2017). http://arxiv.org/abs/1703.04364
34. Benyahia, S., Meftah, B., Lézoray, O.: Multi-features extraction based on deep learning for skin lesion classification. Tissue Cell **74**, 101701 (2022). https://doi.org/10.1016/j.tice.2021.101701
35. Aldhyani, T.H.H., Verma, A., Al-Adhaileh, M.H., Koundal, D.: Multi-class skin lesion classification using a lightweight dynamic kernel deep-learning-based convolutional neural network. Diagnostics **12**(9), 2048 (2022). https://doi.org/10.3390/diagnostics12092048
36. Afza, F., Sharif, M., Mittal, M., Khan, M.A., Jude Hemanth, D.: A hierarchical three-step superpixels and deep learning framework for skin lesion classification. Methods **202**, 88–102 (2022). https://doi.org/10.1016/j.ymeth.2021.02.013
37. Shen, S., et al.: A low-cost high-performance data augmentation for deep learning-based skin lesion classification. BME Front. **2022**, 1–12 (2022). https://doi.org/10.34133/2022/9765307
38. Khan, M.A., Sharif, M.I., Raza, M., Anjum, A., Saba, T., Shad, S.A.: Skin lesion segmentation and classification: a unified framework of deep neural network features fusion and selection. Expert Syst. **39**(7) (2022). https://doi.org/10.1111/exsy.12497
39. Hoang, L., Lee, S.-H., Lee, E.-J., Kwon, K.-R.: Multiclass skin lesion classification using a novel lightweight deep learning framework for smart healthcare. Appl. Sci. **12**(5), 2677 (2022). https://doi.org/10.3390/app12052677
40. Afza, F., Sharif, M., Khan, M.A., Tariq, U., Yong, H.-S., Cha, J.: Multiclass skin lesion classification using hybrid deep features selection and extreme learning machine. Sensors **22**(3), 799 (2022). https://doi.org/10.3390/s22030799
41. Arora, G., Dubey, A.K., Jaffery, Z.A., Rocha, A.: A comparative study of fourteen deep learning networks for multi skin lesion classification (MSLC) on unbalanced data. Neural Comput. Appl. 1–27 (2022). https://doi.org/10.1007/s00521-022-06922-1
42. Hsu, B.W.-Y., Tseng, V.S.: Hierarchy-aware contrastive learning with late fusion for skin lesion classification. Comput. Methods Programs Biomed. **216**, 106666 (2022). https://doi.org/10.1016/j.cmpb.2022.106666
43. Thapar, P., Rakhra, M., Cazzato, G., Hossain, M.S.: A novel hybrid deep learning approach for skin lesion segmentation and classification. J. Healthc. Eng. **2022**, 1–21 (2022). https://doi.org/10.1155/2022/1709842
44. Yao, P., et al.: Single model deep learning on imbalanced small datasets for skin lesion classification. IEEE Trans. Med. Imaging **41**(5), 1242–1254 (2022). https://doi.org/10.1109/TMI.2021.3136682
45. Bhardwaj, A., Rege, P.P.: Skin lesion classification using deep learning. In: Merchant, S.N., Warhade, K., Adhikari, D. (eds.) Advances in Signal and Data Processing. LNEE, vol. 703, pp. 575–589. Springer, Singapore (2021). https://doi.org/10.1007/978-981-15-8391-9_42

46. Almaraz-Damian, J.-A., Ponomaryov, V., Sadovnychiy, S., Castillejos-Fernandez, H.: Melanoma and nevus skin lesion classification using handcraft and deep learning feature fusion via mutual information measures. Entropy **22**(4), 484 (2020). https://doi.org/10.3390/e22040484

47. Serte, S., Demirel, H.: Wavelet-based deep learning for skin lesion classification. IET Image Process. **14**(4), 720–726 (2020). https://doi.org/10.1049/iet-ipr.2019.0553

48. Nguyen, N.T., Jearanaitanakij, K., Selamat, A., Trawiński, B., Chittayasothorn, S. (eds.): ACIIDS 2020. LNCS (LNAI), vol. 12033. Springer, Cham (2020). https://doi.org/10.1007/978-3-030-41964-6

49. Deif, M.A., Hammam, R.E.: Skin lesions classification based on deep learning approach. J. Clin. Eng. **45**(3), 155–161 (2020). https://doi.org/10.1097/JCE.0000000000000405

50. Ratul, M.A.R., Mozaffari, M.H., Lee, D.W.-S., Parimbelli, D.E.: Skin lesions classification using deep learning based on dilated convolution. J. Clin. Eng. **45**(3), 155–161 (2019). https://doi.org/10.1101/860700

Lung Disease Classification Using CNN-Based Trained Models from CXR Image

C. Sumathi$^{(\boxtimes)}$ and Y. Asnath Victy Phamila

Computer Science and Engineering, Vellore Institute of Technology, Chennai, India
sumathi.c2020@vitstudent.ac.in, asnathvicty.phamila@vit.ac.in

Abstract. One of the most widespread health problems affecting humans is a lung disease. Patients' chances of survival can be increased mostly by early diagnosis of this disease. Common chest x-ray Image symptoms of lung disease are imaging signs that regularly present in lung Chest x-ray images from patients and serve a critical role in the diagnosis of lung diseases. To enhance the reliability of classifiers, we looked at the use of transfer-learning (TL) networks and several feature-selection strategies. AlexNet, and Squeeze Net were the two TL networks tried out to see which one was best at producing useful characteristics from chest X-Ray images. Iterative procedures such as chi-squared analysis, neighborhood component analysis, and maximum relevance minimal redundancy were used to further improve the obtained relevant features (iMRMR). We also calculated the proposed model's classification accuracy to that of three popular pre-trained models, including ResNet-50, Vgg-16, and Vgg-19. The VGG-16, VGG-19 and ResNet-50 CNN-based pre-trained models also achieved an accuracy of 95.76%, 92.84%, and 96.27%, respectively in classification. The results demonstrated that the cascaded feature generator and selection procedures considerably impacted the classifier's performance accuracy.

Keywords: Classification · CNN · Feature Selection · Trained models · Chest X-Ray images · Transfer-learning

1 Introduction

Airborne particles, pollutants, and pathogenic organisms make the lung more sensitive. At least 2.4 billion individuals are exposed to deadly stove or fireplace smoke [1]. WHO says air pollution kills 7 million a year. Millions are exposed to secondhand smoke from 1.3 billion smokers. Smoking causes 8 million unnecessary deaths yearly, largely from heart and lung diseases. Environmental hazards, overcrowding, and inappropriate housing increase the poor's respiratory impairment risk [2]. Improving respiratory health involves strengthening healthcare systems, implementing health promotion and sickness prevention and treatment strategies, preparing medical staff, conducting research, and educating the public. Global health care must focus on preventing, treating, and promoting respiratory health. Cost-effective health strategies include controlling, preventing, and treating respiratory illnesses. Reduce the burden of respiratory illness to achieve Sustainable Development Goals by 2030, recommends the FIRS. COVID-19 is receiving global attention. This study attempts to prioritize worldwide respiratory health.

© The Author(s), under exclusive license to Springer Nature Switzerland AG 2023
R. K. Tiwari and G. Sahoo (Eds.): ICAII 2022, CCIS 1822, pp. 65–77, 2023.
https://doi.org/10.1007/978-3-031-37303-9_6

Most medical images are interpreted by radiologists or physicians in a clinical setting [3]. Even with extensive training and experience, radiologists and other medical professionals aren't always able to make an accurate diagnosis from medical imaging. Since these are time-consuming tasks that require human involvement, computers can be useful in the medical imaging processing industry. Integrating AI, IoT, data mining, and cloud computing has helped smart medicine advance significantly. The goal of "smart medicine" is to make high-quality, personalized health care accessible to everyone, regardless of where they reside. To help in the diagnosing process, smart medicine employs deep learning to analyze medical images. Medical imaging modalities vary in their ability to detect disease, detect abnormalities in the human body, and provide insight into the human body in a variety of clinical settings due to their traits and reactions. X-ray images, CT scans, ultrasound, and MRI are the most frequently utilized image modalities for clinical diagnostic analysis [4].

The use of deep learning for feature extraction and data classification has lately increased in significance in the field of health informatics. Researchers in the healthcare industry have access to vast collections of biological data, allowing them to develop fresh data-driven models in health informatics by employing deep learning [5]. The key to creating data-driven healthcare technology is investigating connections between collected data sets. Deep learning models are supported by the structure of neural networks. When compared to neural networks, deep learning models include far more hidden layers and neurons. Pre-trained models like AlexNet and SqueezeNet can extract helpful features from chest X-ray images [9].

The following outline describes how this paper is structured. Section 2, this paper details the work that is relevant to it. The research procedure is described in Sect. 3. The data set is described in Sect. 4. Methods of preprocessing employed in this study were detailed in Sect. 5. In Sect. 6 we go out the proposed tasks. In Sects. 7 and 8, we provide the results, analyze the results, and evaluate the pre-trained models. This paper is concluded with Sect. 9.

2   Related work

Chandra Mani Sharma et al. suggest a system based on edge computing to aid radiologists in their task of disease diagnosis [6]. This study examined Machine Learning, Deep Learning, and Transfer Learning techniques for diagnosing diseases in a publicly available CXR image dataset. Inception-ResNet v2 transfer learning models are the most accurate for lung disease classification.

ILDs pattern categorization was suggested by MASUM SHAH JUNAYED and colleagues [7] by the use of an end-to-end deep CNN. They started with batch normalization and max-pooling, then added four convolutional layers with varying kernel sizes and a ReLU activation function. Finally, they added four dense layers and a dropout layer.

Mohit Agarwal et al. demonstrated a CADx system with two stages such as lung segmentation and classification [8]. The classification system consisted of one CNN that was built on deep learning, as well as five different forms of transfer learning methods and three different types of soft classifiers, which included Random Forest, Decision Tree, and ANN.

Classification of lung cancer patients into low, medium, and high-risk categories was achieved by combining the kNN machine learning approach with a genetic algorithm for feature selection used by Negar Maleki et al. [10]. The genetic algorithm was developed to find the best set of features that would reduce the kNN method's overall error rate.

To enhance the precision and consistency of ILD classification, Huafeng Hu et al. provide a Convolutional Neural Network (CNN)-based framework that takes advantage of medical data [11]. To better classify ILDs, they implemented a system that uses both medical and location data. The results of the trials show that the classification framework for ILDs is improved by the inclusion of additional medical and regional data.

Classification accuracy is enhanced by Xception and Inception-v3 features. Several ML-based techniques have been developed in the previous two decades, and their use in the screening and diagnosis of various diseases has shown encouraging results [12]. To forecast diabetes in individuals, for instance, the authors supplied a decision support system based on a variety of ML classifiers.

To deal with the COVID-19 epidemic from several views, numerous AI-based frameworks have been developed recently [13]. To differentiate positive instances of COVID-19 pneumonia from negative ones, researchers proposed a deep learning-based diagnosis method that used chest X-ray images.

Three pre-trained models, Xception, InceptionV3, and ResNet, were tested on X-ray images for their ability to distinguish between healthy, COVID-19-positive, and pneumonia-infected individuals [14]. A total accuracy of 86% was achieved, along with a sensitivity of 78%.

A total of 15,153 chest X-ray images were utilized by Sri Kavya et al. [15] to compare the performance of ResNet50 and VGG16 in detecting normal, viral pneumonia, and COVID-19. Their optimized ResNet50 model outperformed VGG16, which only managed 89.34% accuracy, by a significant margin.

Shivan H. M. Mohammed et al. Classifying of Lung Cancer Data i.e., Benign and Malignant utilizing Fine-Tuning Models [23]. Popular pre-trained models have been proposed for classification, and they include AlexNet, ResNet18, Googlenet, and ResNet50. In order to handle the new image classification, all the models researchers changed the last three layers.

An effective deep-learning-based feature selection approach, named SAFS, was developed by Milad Zafar Nezhada et al. [24]. The overall suggested method follows representation learning, feature selection, and supervised learning phases. When two types of features coexist in a data collection, such as categorical and continuous, they separate the features using Features Partitioning.

Senthil, S et al. trained a neural network to detect lung cancer and Particle Swarm Optimization to achieve this goal [25]. There are numerous benefits to using ANN, but they come at a significant price in terms of time and resources. This system's primary objective is to offer users advance notice, but it also has the added bonus of saving consumers money and time.

In order to better classify lung cancer subtypes using microarray data, a new CBR framework has been developed in this research [26]. To assess and forecast the classification of an unknown example, the proposed method employs a reduced set of genes through two sequential feature selection techniques. Table 1 summarizes a feature selection lung disease classification-related review.

Table 1. Summarizes a feature selection and lung disease classification-related review.

Author	Algorithms	Image type	Diseases	Result
Chandra Mani Sharma et al. [6]	Inception-ResNet v2	Chest X-ray	Lung Disease	92.43
MASUM SHAH JUNAYED et al. [7]	end-to-end deep convolution neural network	Chest X-ray	ILD	99.09
Mohit Agarwal et al. [8]	CADx	Chest X-ray	Lung Disease	90.18
Negar Maleki et al. [10]	kNN machine learning feature-selection genetic algorithm	Chest X-ray	Lung Cancer	96.20
Huafeng Hu et al. [11]	Convolutional Neural Network (CNN)-based framework	Chest X-ray	ILD	92.3
Dongguang Li et al. [12]	Several ML-based techniques	Chest X-ray	Lung Disease	98.37
Yahyaoui, A et al. [13]	AI-based frameworks	Chest X-ray	COVID-19	83.67
Jain, R et al. [14]	pre-trained models-Xception, InceptionV3, ResNet	Chest X-ray	COVID-19, Pneumonia	86
Sri Kavya et al. [15]	ResNet50 and VGG16	Chest X-ray	Viral pneumonia, COVID-19	91.39
Shivan H. M. Mohammed et al. [23]	Pre-trained models	CT Scan	Lung Cancer	94
Senthil S et al. [25]	ANN	Chest X-ray	Lung Cancer	95.2

3   Methodology

3.1   System Architecture

This section describes the steps involved in feature selection and the using trained models for lung disease classification in chest x-rays. Here, we discussed two basic phases these are preprocessing and classification. Classifying a chest image into either healthy lungs or lungs infected with infection is the main focus of lung disease classification. Training is used to produce the lung disease classifier, sometimes called a model. The process of learning a neural network to identify a certain group of images is called training. An image-classifying model may be trained using deep learning. Therefore, gathering images of lungs with the condition to be classified is the beginning of using deep learning for lung disease identification. Figure 1 illustrates the overview of the procedure. Further information about this work is discussed in the sections following.

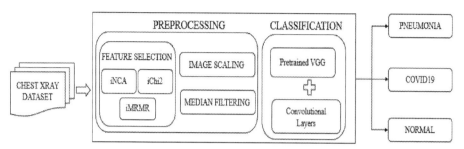

Fig. 1. System design Flow chart

Extracting useful features from the Kaggle dataset is described in this section, which details the CNN-based TL models that were utilized.

3.2 AlexNet

AlexNet's 650,000 neurons are part of its deep architecture and its 62.3 million training parameters. However, instead of batch normalization and downsampling, it made use of dropouts and ReLU to address problems like overfitting and linearity. Padding was also included to avoid the feature map's size from being drastically reduced when overlap pooling was used to shrink the network. A 227 × 227-pixel image is the minimum acceptable size for the network's input layer. After that, the first convolutional layer contains 96 filters that are 11 × 11 and stride 4, while the second convolutional layer has 256 filters that are 5 × 5 and stride 1. In addition, the feature maps' sizes are managed by a padding of 2. Each of these convolutional layers is then followed by a max-pooling layer that is 3 × 3 in size and has a stride of 2. All convolutional layers have 384 filters with 3 × 3 stride and padding of 1, except for the final layer, which has just 256 filters. As the number of filters in the network's deeper layers grows, the network can extract a greater variety of features; nevertheless, the feature map's overall shape shrinks in tandem with the reduction in filter size. The next three levels are also completely linked, with a total of 4096 neurons minus 1000 in the last layer. To prevent overfitting, we execute a 0.5-point dropout before and after the first completely linked layer.

3.3 SqueezeNet

The fire module incorporates both expand and squeeze layers and is important to the SqueezeNet architecture. The expand layer takes the data from the squeeze layers, where a convolutional filter of 1×1 is used, and uses filters of size 3×3 and 1×1. The network consists of an overall average-pooling layer, three max-pooling layers, and two separate convolutional layers, as well as eight fire modules. When compared to other state-of-the-art networks, SqueezeNet's lack of a thick layer is a major differentiator. SqueezeNet, a deep compression approach developed using a complex bypass connection of 1×1 convolutional filters, was used in this paper.

3.4 Feature Selection

An important job in ML is feature selection, which must narrow down a large pool of potential characteristics to those that will help the network perform optimally [8]. As is usual in radiomics research with hundreds of characteristics, several biomarkers utilized as predictors were strongly correlated and this required feature selection to eliminate collinearity, reduce dimensionality, and limit noise. In this paper investigated a linear combinations filter, a pairwise correlation filter, and PCA [9]. To identify whether or not some predictors are linear combinations of others, the linear combinations filter uses a QR decomposition and an iterative method. The design matrix's predictors are eliminated successively. Any predictors whose pairwise correlation is higher than a user-defined threshold will be filtered out using the pairwise correlation filter [19]. First, the top two predictors are examined. Among these two, the one with the highest average absolute connection to all other variables is dropped. We examined a range of other cutoffs, but ultimately settled on 0.95 as the value for the pairwise correlation filter, since it allowed us to get rid of strongly correlated variables while keeping many other aspects. As a result, feature selection is a crucial stage in developing an ML model. Constructing a machine learning model, seeks the optimal set of characteristics.

- Filter methods
- Wrapper methods
- Embedded methods

3.4.1 Feature Selection Techniques

The following are brief descriptions of the three feature-selection methods that were used in this investigation.

i. Iterative Neighborhood Component Analysis (iNCA)

NCA is a method that uses a distance measure to detect and separate multivariate data [8]. To improve classification performance, it linearly alters the original features. Leave-one-out (LOO) classification is its intended use, and stochastic closest neighbors are used to identify the objective function by considering the whole set of modifications rather than simply the k-nearest neighbors (kNN) at each modified point. This method takes a majority vote from a single neighboring node instead of a predetermined number of kNNs. So, using the softmax of the Euclidean distance between these two locations, each point x probabilistically selects another point y.

$$P_{xy=\frac{\exp(-d_{x,y})}{\sum_{k\neq1}\exp(-d_{x,z})}} \quad P_x = 0, \tag{1}$$

where, dx, y stands for the Euclidean distance between the adjacent point and the Leave-one-out point.

ii. Iterative Chi-Square (iChi2)
The Chi2 statistic is a tool for studying the interdependence of events [8]. For two-variable data, Chi2 calculates the discrepancy between the observed and predicted counts as follows:

$$x_{fd}^2 = \sum \frac{(O_m + E_m)^2}{E_m} \tag{2}$$

Here, the degree of freedom is denoted by fd. Like in feature selection, if O is far from E, then you should prioritize things that are heavily reliant on the feedback you get. This is indicated by a high value of Chi2.

iii. Iterative Maximum Relevance-Minimum Redundancy (iMRMR)
Therefore, the iMRMR strategy was established, and it was shown that even when selecting fewer features than thousands, it can achieve maximum accuracy for disease prediction.

$$x_n(f) = \frac{Relv(f \mid tv)}{Redu(f \mid featureselecteduntiln - 1)}, \tag{3}$$

Features (f), Relevance (Relv), Redundancy (Redu), and the Target Variable (tv) are all variables to be considered. On the nth iteration, the feature with the highest score is chosen.

4 Dataset

We collected Chest X-Ray images from the Kaggle repository. Containing healthy, pneumonia, and covid19 images, and then dividing them into test, training, and validation sets.

The Kaggle data set included jpeg files of CXR images. A resolution was 1024×1024, and 8 bits were used to store the picture. [0–255]. Example of lung images and it's histograms are shown in Fig. 2.

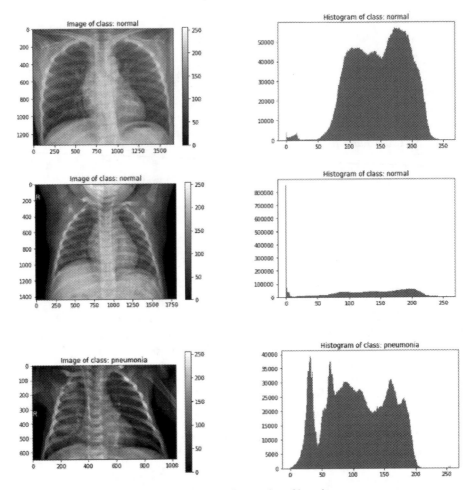

Fig. 2. Histograms and examples of lung images

5   Preprocessing

To improve the quality of the input picture, the developed lung disease diagnostic includes in this phase. To enhance certain features of incoming images and decrease undesired distortions, pre-processing is often used. By eliminating background noise and sharpening out of focus areas, the input photos are better prepared for further processing. Scaling images and applying a median filter are the two steps that make up the preprocessing phase [21, 22]. We describe each of these approaches below:

A. **IMAGE SCALING**

If you need to resize your X-ray images, you may do it quickly and easily with the help of this image scaling. Images may be shrunk by using "scale down" and "scaled up" to create smaller and bigger versions, respectively. The quality of the photographs must be maintained throughout. With the help of Eq. (1), we can express the homogeneous map between the picture pixels, which is known as image scaling.

$$Y_{img}^{RS} = imresize(Y_{img}, scaling) \tag{4}$$

Here, we refer to the original input images, Y_{img}, the resizing factor, scale, which is a numeric scalar, and the resulting image, Y_{img}^{RS}. Scale > 1 if and only if $Y_{img}^{RS} > Y_{img}$. The images are scaled down to 128×128 when the procedure is complete. For filtering, we feed the process the downsized, Y_{img}^{RS} images.

B. MEDIAN FILTERING

To generate a clean filtered image, the nonlinear filter makes use of the median to maintain a sharp edge definition. By taking into account the ordering of gray levels, the median value may be used instead of the noise value. Median filtering results are expressed in Eq. (2).

$$Y_{img}^{M}(x, y) = med\left\{Y_{img}^{RS}(x - i, y - j), i, j \in TD\right\} \tag{5}$$

Here, we refer to the input image, Y_{img}^{RS}, as well as the output image, $Y_{img}^{M}(x, y)$, where TD is a two-dimensional mask.

6 Proposed Work

The proposed approach utilizes the pre-trained VGG19 model as its foundation and then follows up with a CNN network to classify lung disease in chest x-ray images. A common CNN design is composed of convolutional layers, pooling layers, and fully connected layers. VGG19 is used for feature extraction, and then two CNN blocks perform the FE task. The suggested model is trained using chest x-rays with a resolution of 2248 by 2248 pixels. The input image contains color information in the form of RGB channels. The convolution layer is the initial stage of our model. This layer is the one that begins the process by utilizing filters, which are also referred to as the kernel (Fig. 3).

Three more convolution layers were added to the model to enable the extraction of features from the chest x-ray images. Furthermore, the radiograph sub-area is where the filters initiate the conv processes. To multiply and add the filters and pixel values of the chest x-ray images, the convolution operation was used. A receptive field is another name for the section of the radiographs that are being examined. To further improve the model's feature extraction capabilities, successive convolution layers were added to the model. For the model to be trained successfully, it must first learn the values of the filter, which are referred to as weights. The convolution process is carried out by the filter from the very beginning of the radiographs and continues to happen throughout the entire radiograph. When a whole image has been processed, the filter convolution procedure is complete.

Convolution outputs were subjected to the ReLU activation function. ReLU activation involves replacing all non-zero outcomes with zero. Our suggested CNN model makes advantage of the ReLU function to boost nonlinearity and increase the computational time without compromising model accuracy. For better spatial dimension reduction, the pooling layer was added after the convolution layers. For the MP layers

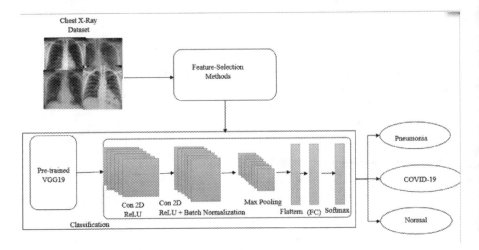

Fig. 3. Classification Model

in our proposal, we chose a fixed filter size of 2x2 and a stride value of 2. This filter produces the greatest value of the sub-area of the radiography by convolving across the entire input volume. A feature's location relative to other features has been found to form the foundation of MP layers. By reducing the total number of weights, the computational burden is lessened, and the risk of the model becoming overfitted is eliminated.

7   Result and Discussion

Chest X-rays can be used to identify a variety of ailments, and the VGG19+CNN-based model was developed specifically for this purpose. Using grid search techniques, we fine-tuned the proposed model's various hyper parameters, including its learning rate, epochs, and batch size. Up to 30 training epochs, the proposed model was used. In our proposed approach, we used a batch size of 20. Accuracy, sensitivity, F1-score, precision, confusion matrix, and ROC curves were computed to evaluate the proposed model, Vgg-16, Vgg-19, and ResNet-50 [18] for each class label.

8   Evaluation

Both the proposed model and the other two trained models were implemented using the Keras framework. Python was used to code the procedures that had nothing to do with the convolution network itself. The test was conducted on a Windows machine equipped with 64 GB RAM and a 12 GB GPU NVIDIA GeForce RTX.

Our proposed model's training and validation accuracies for 30 epochs are displayed in Fig. 4. The maximum accuracy achieved during training was 99.92%, and the highest accuracy achieved during validation was 95.01%. Our proposed model had a loss of 0.069 in validation and 0.0011 in training. The results demonstrated that our proposed

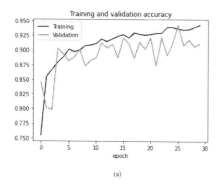
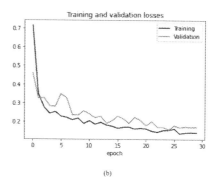

(a)   (b)

Fig. 4. (a) Training and validation accuracy (b) Training and validation loss

model was successfully trained, and it accurately distinguished between multiple lung diseases, including COVID-19, pneumonia, and normal chest x-ray images.

Table 2 displays the performance for our proposed model transfer learning classifiers as determined by evaluation criteria such as accuracy, sensitivity or recall, precision, and F1-score.

Table 2. Performance of pre-trained classifiers

Pre-trained Models	Performance			
	Accuracy (%)	Recall (%)	Precision (%)	F1-Score (%)
VGG16	95.76	94.31	97.65	96.28
VGG19	92.84	91.67	97.83	95.93
ResNet50	96.27	95.56	97.51	96.74

Our proposed model also outperforms the three existing baseline classifiers that were pre-trained before we used them in terms of classification accuracy. The classification accuracy of these pre-trained classifiers is negatively impacted by the fact that they all use deep networks, which reduces the spatial resolution of the feature map for the results of the last convolutional layer. These pre-trained classifiers also have a filter size that is too large for this type of problem; as a result, they miss out on important details and end up training on a huge amount of irrelevant information that has nothing to do with the receptive fields of neurons. As a result, our proposed model overcomes issues of low resolution and redundancy in the inflammatory region of X-ray images infected with COVID-19.

The model is optimum and efficient if its area under the curve is maximized. The ROC curve is determined by both the true-positive and false-positive rates. It was found that the proposed CNN-based classifier has an AUC of 0.9833. Vgg-16 had an AUC of 0.9385, Vgg-19 of 0.9523, and Resnet-50 of 0.9726. The area under the receiver operating characteristic curve (AUC) shows that our suggested classifier is superior to the other four classifiers.

9 Conclusion

In this research, we propose and assess a pre-trained multi-classification model for analyzing chest radiographs for the presence of many diseases, including COVID-19 and pneumonia. These days, COVID-19 and other chest infection disorders are quickly expanding and having an impact on communities all over the globe. Due to a large number of instances, testing has to go rapidly and effectively. Inappropriate and delayed testing procedures, a lack of facilities, and a failure to recognize various chest diseases at an early stage have led to many deaths and admissions to intensive care units. In this research, using a mix of TL models as a feature generator, feature selectors, and classifiers, we explored a framework for COVID-19 and other pneumonia diagnoses from X-ray images. To extract useful characteristics from X-ray images, TL networks were used; these features were then improved using a feature-selection strategy using iNCA, iChi2, and iMRMR. By eliminating unnecessary or duplicate features, the feature-selection procedure not only aided in locating highly discriminative features but also increased the classifier training process. Primarily, the pre-trained model uses convolutional neural networks to analyze chest x-rays and identify key patterns. Extensive experiments validate the superior diagnostic performance of our proposed model compared to that of well-known, pre-trained classifiers and state-of-the-art methods. Taking into account all of these results, it is clear that the suggested model may be an invaluable tool for medical professionals.

References

1. Levine, S.M., Marciniuk, D.D.: Global impact of respiratory disease: what can we do, together, to make a difference? Chest **161**(5), 1153–1154 (2022)
2. Meghji, J., Mortimer, K., Agusti, A., et al.: Improving lung health in low- and middle-income countries: from challenges to solutions. Lancet **397**(10277), 928–940 (2021)
3. Yu, H., et al.: Convolutional neural networks for medical image analysis: state-of-the-art, comparisons, improvement and perspectives. Neurocomputing **444**, 92–110 (2021)
4. Liu, X., et al. "Advances in deep learning-based medical image analysis. Health Data Science 2021 (2021)
5. Navamani, T.M.: Efficient deep learning approaches for health informatics. Deep Learning and Parallel Computing Environment for Bioengineering Systems. Academic Press, 123–137 (2019)
6. Sharma, C.M., Goyal, Lakshay, Chariar, Vijayaraghavan M., Sharma, Navel: Lung disease classification in CXR images using hybrid inception-ResNet-v2 model and edge computing. J. Healthcare Eng. **2022**, 1–15 (2022). https://doi.org/10.1155/2022/9036457
7. Junayed, M.S., et al.: An efficient end-to-end deep neural network for interstitial lung disease recognition and classification. Turkish J. Electric. Eng. Comput. Sci. **30.4**, 1235–1250 (2022)
8. Agarwal, M., et al.: A novel block imaging technique using nine artificial intelligence models for COVID-19 disease classification, characterization and severity measurement in lung computed tomography scans on an Italian cohort. J. Med. Syst. **45.3**, 1–30 (2021)

9. Turkoglu, M.: COVIDetectioNet: COVID-19 diagnosis system based on X-ray images using features selected from pre-learned deep features ensemble. Appl. Intell. **51**(3), 1213–1226 (2020). https://doi.org/10.1007/s10489-020-01888-w

10. Maleki, N., Zeinali, Y., Niaki, S.T.A.: A k-NN method for lung cancer prognosis with the use of a genetic algorithm for feature selection. Expert Syst. Appl. **164**, 113981 (2021)

11. Hu, H., et al.: CNN-based Classification Framework for Tissues of Lung with Additional Information. arXiv preprint arXiv:2206.06701 (2022)

12. Li, D.; Li, S.: An artificial intelligence deep learning platform achieves high diagnostic accuracy for COVID-19 pneumonia by reading chest X-ray images. iScience 2022, **25**, 104031 (2022)

13. Yahyaoui, A., Jamil, A., Rasheed, J., Yesiltepe, M.: A decision support system for diabetes prediction using machine learning and deep learning techniques. In: Proceedings of the 2019 1st International Informatics and Software Engineering Conference (UBMYK), Ankara, Turkey, 6–7 November 2019, pp. 1–4. IEEE, Piscataway, NJ, USA (2019)

14. Jain, R., Gupta, M., Taneja, S., Hemanth, D.J.: Deep learning based detection and analysis of COVID-19 on chest X-ray images. Appl. Intell. **51**(3), 1690–1700 (2020). https://doi.org/10.1007/s10489-020-01902-1

15. Sri Kavya, N., Shilpa, T., Veeranjaneyulu, N., Divya Priya, D.: Detecting COVID-19 and pneumonia from chest X-ray images using deep convolutional neural networks. Mater. Today Proceeding (2022). [CrossRef]

16. Rahimzadeh, M., Attar, A.: A modified deep convolutional neural network for detecting COVID-19 and pneumonia from chest X-ray images based on the concatenation of Xception and ResNet50V2. Inform Med Unlocked **19**, 100360 (2020). https://doi.org/10.1016/j.imu.2020.100360

17. Jiang, X., et al.: Towards an artifcial intelligence framework for data-driven prediction of coronavirus clinical severity. Comput Mater Continua **63**(1), 537–551 (2020)

18. He, K., Zhang, X., Ren, S., Sun, J.: Deep residual learning for image recognition. In: Proceedings of the 2016 IEEE Conference on Computer Vision and Pattern Recognition (CVPR), Las Vegas, NV, USA, 27–30 June 2016, pp. 770–778. IEEE, Piscataway, NJ, USA (2016)

19. Rasheed, J.: Analyzing the effect of filtering and feature-extraction techniques in a machine learning model for identification of infectious disease using radiography imaging. Symmetry **14**, 1398 (2022)

20. Ding, C., Peng, H.: Minimum redundancy feature selection from microarray gene expression data. J. Bioinform. Comput. Biol. **3**, 185–205 (2005)

21. Das, A.: Adaptive UNet-based lung segmentation and ensemble learning with CNN-based deep features for automated COVID-19 diagnosis. Multimedia Tools Appl. , 1–35 (2021). https://doi.org/10.1007/s11042-021-11787-y

22. Stojnev, D., Ilic, A.S.: Pre-processing image data for deep learning. International Scientific Conference on Information Technology And Data Related Research (2020)

23. Mohammed, Shivan, H.M., Çinar, A.: Lung cancer classification with convolutional neural network architectures. Qubahan Acad. J. **1.1**, 33–39 (2021)

24. Nezhad, M.Z., et al.: Safs: A deep feature selection approach for precision medicine. 2016 IEEE International Conference on Bioinformatics and Biomedicine (BIBM). IEEE (2016)

25. Senthil, S., Ayshwarya, B.: Lung cancer prediction using feed forward back propagation neural networks with optimal features. Int. J. Appl. Eng. Res. **13**(1), 318–325 (2018)

26. Ramos-González, J., et al.: A CBR framework with gradient boosting based feature selection for lung cancer subtype classification. Comput. Biol. Med. **86**, 98–106 (2017)

A Novel Framework for Satellite Image Denoising and Super Resolution Using CNN-GAN

Rajdeep Kumar[✉], Anurag Singh, Jitender Kumar, and G.A Chullai

Central Research Laboratory-Bharat Electronics Limited, Ghaziabad, India
{rajdeepkumar,anuragsingh,jitenderkumar,gwynethachullai}@bel.co.in

Abstract. Denoising and Super-Resolution are two challenging tasks in the area of Computer Vision. Benefits of the results are applicable in many domains. Many applications of Deep Learning and other methodologies have made significant achievements in this field. Generative Adversarial Network advancement takes researcher attention towards this area due to results obtained by GAN. In this paper, We focused on the speckle noise denoising and super-resolution of satellite images. Speckle noise is multiplicative noise captured in satellite images by airborne acquisition devices. Here, we propose a Generative Adverasarial Network which is responsible for noise removal as well as 4-times magnification of satellite images. Generative adversarial network proposed in this paper consists two layered generator as well as discriminator network. The first Layer of generator which is multi layered CNN is responsible for extracting noise from given input images, for learning noise mapping from image sample, we used mean square error function for learning this mapping. While lower or second layer of generator are used for magnification of images which employed combined mean loss function and adversarial loss function. Apart from generator network, we used discriminator network responsible for separating high-resolved images and real images, which make generator more robust. Our discriminator network also used adversarial loss function. The Generative adversarial network reconstructed more realistic textured images from heavily degaraded quality images. Standard satellite database images are used for experiments, and results generated by the GAN are superior performance of state-of-art in both the term of quantitavely as well as visually over existing similar methods.

Keywords: Generative Adversarial Network · Two-layered generator · Despeckling · Super-Resolution · Satellite images

1 Introduction

When satellite images are acquired, it is corrupted with speckle noise due to airborne acquisition devices. Speckle noise is a multiplicative noise in nature. Noise reduction or removal from satellite images is a pre-condition in information extraction. Hence, despeckling is a well-known problem in the area of Computer

R. K. Tiwari and G. Sahoo (Eds.): ICAII 2022, CCIS 1822, pp. 78–88, 2023.
https://doi.org/10.1007/978-3-031-37303-9_7

vision. Likewise, image super-resolution is also a classical problem in this area because the better the resolution, the higher the information can be gathered. Due to their usability and popularity, these two classical problems are very popular among researchers for last decades. Kuan filter [6], Frost filter [7], Lee filter [5], and many spatial linear filters have been proposed by scholars for despeckling of satellite images. However, because local processing is inherently imperfect, spatial linear filter approaches frequently fall short of fully preserving edges and features, which leads to a variety of deficiencies.

Additionally, because of their flexibility and stability, variation-based approaches have been adopted gradually in satellite image denoising. These methods overcome the limitations of conventional filtering techniques by resolving the issue of energy optimization. The speckle noise removal task is then transformed into an inversion issue of restoring the initial noise-free image from the noisy image, sparse representation and the total variation (TV) model are such observation models [1, 2], using appropriate presumption or preconception of the noise with log transformation. Above mentioned variational methods reduces speckle noise effectively, but the process is time-consuming and the outcomes are completely dependent upon model parameters and prior knowledge. Despeckling performance is additionally constrained by the variation-based method's inability to precisely characterise the distribution of speckle noise.

Generally, several satellite despeckling techniques suggested above are somehow failed in preserving the distinctive features in many complicated textured areas or sometimes introduce artifacts into the speckled images. Hence, for speckle noise removal of satellite images, we provide a deep convolutional network model which can handle the above-mentioned problem. Additionally, despite knowing how to map clean images from noisy images with the help of mapping function, by training our model, we were able to get it to learn how to map noise from noisy images. To accomplish the same, we trained our top layer network of the two layered generator such that it can map noise(v) from the noised image(y) [3]. This component of generator is pre-trained and responsible for the image's denoising.

Apart from despeckling, we also reconstruct a high-resolution image from a low-resolution clean image simultaneously. For the super-resolution of images, the mean squared error (MSE) optimization between upscaled images and low-resolution images is a well-known approach. The benefit of minimizing MSE is, that it enhances the peak-signal-to-noise(PSNR) ratio typical measures of comparing SR techniques as well as evaluating results [4].

We trained our GAN network as an anterior end of our framework which is made up of generator G and discriminator D, to develop the images that are similar to the real world data to achieve super-resolution.

The main contribution of this paper:

(1) We proposes a GAN based system to simultaneously handle the two well-known computer vision problems of image denoising and super-resolution, which produces outstanding results even in high intensity noise.

(2) To the best of our knowledge, this is the first framework of this kind that can efficiently tackle both the issues at once (image denoising as well as super-resolution).

2   Related Work

2.1   SAR Image Multiplicative Noise Degradation Model

Multiplicative speckle noise is the primary cause of image quality loss in SAR images. The multiplicative noise model describes speckle noise, which differs from additive white Gaussian noise (AWGN) in nature or hyperspectral images:

$$y = x.n$$

here, n represent the speckle noise, x and y represent clean image and speckled noise image respectively. SAR images containing speckle noise follows Gamma distribution. ENL is specified in (3) and generally used for evaluation of despeckling studies in homogeneous areas of real SAR image quantitatively.

$$ENL = \frac{\bar{X}}{\text{var}}$$

2.2   CNNs for SAR Image Despeckling

Deep learning has recently made significant strides in computer vision and image processing applications, and as a result, it has successfully been used for a variety of tasks related to computer vision, including scene classification, object recognition, object segmentation, and image classification.

For extracting the internal and underlying features, CNNs organised in the i-th features map $P_i^{(k)}$ $\left(i = 1, 2, N^{(k)}\right)$ of k-th layer, in which each unit is connected to local patches of the previous layer $P_i^{(k-1)}$ $\left(i = 1, 2, N^{(k-1)}\right)$ through a set of weight parameters $w_i^{(k)}$ and bias parameters $b_i^{(k)}$.

$$L_i^{(n)}(m, n) = F\left(P_i^{(n)}(m, n)\right)$$

$$P_i^{(n)}(m, n) = \sum_{j=1}^{\mu^{jn}} \sum_{w,y-0}^{s-1} W_\mu^{(n)}(u, v) \cdot L_j^{(j-1)}(m - u, n - v) + b_i^{(1)}$$

is the output feature map. Here, nonlinear activation function is denoted by F(.) and $P_i^{(n)}(m, n)$ reflects the i-th output feature map at pixel level as the convolutional weighted sum of the results from the previous layer (m, n). Additionally, the convolution layer's unique parameters include the filter kernel size $S \times S$ and the number of output feature mappings (j). In particular, the back-propagation

(BP) method and the chain rule of derivation must be used to regenerate the network parameters W and b.

Rectified linear unit(ReLu), a non-linear activation function is used and described as:

$$F\left(P_i^{(n)}\right) = \max\left(0, P_i^{(k)}\right)$$

The reason of using non-linear excitation function is the complex non-linear mapping relationship between the source images and produced images.

Following the completion of each forward propagation, backward propagation(BP) algorithm begins to alter the network's trainable parameters in order to improve understanding of the connections between label data and reconstructed data. The outputs of the k+1-th layer are used by BP to update the trainable parameters of the k-th layer. The following formulas are used to determine the partial derivative of the loss function with regard to the k-th convolution layer's convolution kernels $w_{ji}^{(l)}$ and bias $b_j^{(l)}$:

$$\frac{\partial L}{\partial W_{ij}^{(I)}} = \sum_{m,n} \delta_i^{(n)}(m, n) \cdot L_i^{(n)}(m - u, y - v)$$

$$\frac{\partial L}{\partial b_i^{(k)}} = \sum_{m,n} \delta_i^{(k)}(m, n)$$

here $\delta_i^{(n)}$ is the error map defined as:

$$\delta_i^{(1)} = \sum_i \sum_{u,v=0}^{S-1} W_{ij}^{(k+1)}(u, V) \cdot \delta_i^{(1+1)}(m + u, n + v)$$

The gradient descent approach is used in the iterative training procedure to update the network parameters $w_{ij}^{(k)}$ and $b_i^{(k)}$ as follows:

$$W_{ij}^{(k)} = W_{ij}^{(k)} - \alpha \cdot \frac{\partial L}{\partial W_{ij}^{(k)}}$$

$$b_i^{(k)} = b_i^{(k)} - \alpha \cdot \frac{\partial L}{\partial b_i^{(k)}}$$

where α where is a network-wide preset hyperparameter that also regulates the interval at which trainable parameters are sampled.

2.3   Residual Learning

He et al. found that residual mapping may rapidly cut training loss and achieve cutting-edge performance in a variety of disciplines, including object detection and image which super resolution. This is done by acquiring a more effective learning effect than traditional data mapping. Szegedy et al. fundamentally demonstrated how residual networks fully utilise identity shortcut connections, which can transmit varying amounts of feature information between not directly connected layers without attenuation. The residual image *varphi* in the suggested SAR-DRN model as follows:

$$\varphi = y_j - x_j$$

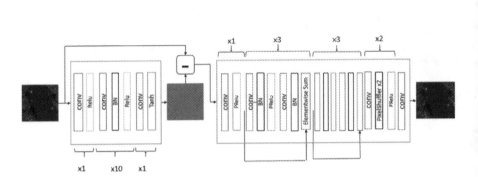

Fig. 1. Generator model proposed and used in the GAN

Due to the degradation phenomena, common deep networks may find it challenging to approximate equivalent mappings using stacked non-linear layers like the Conv-BN-ReLU block as layer depth increases. On the other hand, the spatial distribution of the residual feature maps should be extremely sparse, and it is logical to suppose that the majority of the pixel values in the residual picture *varphi* are extremely close to zero. This makes it possible for the gradient descent process to move to significantly smoother filtering parameter hypersurfaces.

By finding an allocation that is approximately optimal for the network's features more quickly and easily, by adding more trainable layers to the network, we could enhance its functionality. Since it recovers and expresses deeper non-linear information, the learning technique with residual unit makes it simpler to recreate the original multiplicative speckle noise and more intrinsically non-linear, which can lessen the range discrepancy between optical and SAR images.

In our model, we maximize the peak signal-to-noise ratio(PSNR) while minimising the mean squared error (MSE). In this study, we developed a CNN-GAN model that uses a residual GAN component with skip-connection as the lower layer and a deep convolutional neural network using mean squared error as the top layer. We introduce a novel two-layered GAN that combines a discriminator network that supports solutions perceptually with referenced HR images with a top layer that uses MSE and a second layer that has loss functions including adversarial loss and content loss for producing result images [5–7].

This paper has the following format. In Sect. 3, we described the our generative adversarial network model to denoise and super-resolve the speckle-corrupted satellite images. Section 4 of the report includes both the quantitative and qualitative analyses of the studies. Section 5 contains the proposed paper's conclusion.

A visual comparison of the CNN-GAN model's performance with different methods has been provided in Fig. 3.

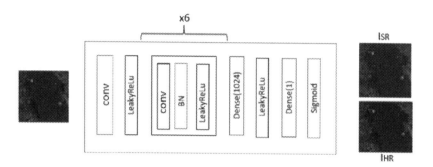

Fig. 2. Discriminator model used in GAN

3 Proposed Model

We give a brief description of the CNN-GAN network in this part that is suggested in this paper. Our CNN-GAN Network is composed with two layered generator network G in which first layer CNN component is responsible for denoising and pre-trained for mapping of noise(v) from its noisy image counterpart(y). And the second layer of our generator network is responsible for mapping high resolution image from low resolution image, the input for this component is the difference between the low-resolution images and the noise extracted by our first pre-trained layer (i.e. x' = y − v). Along with generator, our CNN-GAN network has also discriminator network D which is also trained along with generator network simultaneously. Discriminator network D is used to discriminate between the generated images and real images. Training of generator performed such a way that it can fool the discrimainator by which our generator can learn to produce images that are incredibly similar to ground truth image.

3.1 Generator Network Architecture

Two sub-components of our generator G that is shown in Fig. 1.

UCNN. Our generating network's first layer, designated as UCNN, is made up of eight convolutional layers with identical 3×3 kernels, followed by BN (batch-normalization) layers [8,9]. For training the UCNN, we used the MSE (mean squared error) error function. With the noteworthy exception of the final layer of the UCNN, each activation function was ReLu [10]. The final layer activation function is TanH. This layer's goal is to learn the mapping of the noise block contained in the counterpart noisy image. Our UCNN has already been trained on noisy image y and noise $v = y - x$. In this case, x is a clear low resolution image, whereas y is a noisy image.

Residual GAN Component. This lower layer of our generator network is made up of residuals blocks with the identical layout [11]. The input layer of this component is the clean low resolution image (x') that we get from the difference of low-resolution noisy image(y) and noise block(v) counterpart. Here, noise block is obtained by using pre-trained weights of UCNN from the low resolution noisy image. CNN layers with a 3 × 3 kernel size are utilised in this lower section, followed by batch normalisation layers. We also used pre-trained two sub-pixel convolution layers, as proposed in [12] to magnify the resolution of images. ReLu, specifically parameterised ReLu is used as activation function for feature mapping.

3.2 Discriminator Network Architecture

Apart from generator our GAN consist Discriminator D is shown in Fig. 2. Our discrimination network resembles the one used by Ledig et al. [11]. Discriminator of our GAN network is functioning like classifier. In order to make generator more robust it is used to discriminate between high resolution generated image and ground truth image.

Table 1. Benchmark models' and our model average PSNR results.

Noise	Images	BICUBIC_BM3D	SRCNN_BM3D	FSRCNN_BM3D	BICUBIC	SRCNN	FSRCNN	PROPOSED_MODEL
Intensity = 0.02	Image_A	22.2041	22.4902	22.3423	22.7031	22.4136	22.7659	**23.4120**
Intensity = 0.03	Image_B	22.1244	22.4026	22.2560	20.1005	22.1604	22.7278	**23.3375**
Intensity = 0.04	Image_C	22.0899	22.3612	22.2289	19.6042	21.9496	22.6261	**23.2320**
Intensity = 0.05	Image_D	22.0285	22.2771	22.1864	19.1841	21.7306	22.5108	**23.1716**
Intensity = 0.06	Image_E	21.9748	22.2030	22.1328	18.7960	21.4822	22.3752	**22.9823**

Table 2. Benchmark models' and our model average PSNR results.

Noise	Images	BICUBIC_BM3D	SRCNN_BM3D	FSRCNN_BM3D	BICUBIC	SRCNN	FSRCNN	PROPOSED_MODEL
Intensity = 0.02	Image_A	0.5698	0.5772	0.5734	0.4020	0.6141	**0.6208**	0.6205
Intensity = 0.03	Image_B	0.5656	0.5737	0.5705	0.3494	0.5785	0.6114	**0.6168**
Intensity = 0.04	Image_C	0.5636	0.5714	0.5682	0.3137	0.5492	0.6083	**0.6132**
Intensity = 0.05	Image_D	0.5612	0.5684	0.5657	0.2847	0.5202	0.5956	**0.6074**
Intensity = 0.06	Image_E	0.5596	0.5660	0.5637	0.2641	0.4964	0.5790	**0.5992**

3.3 Loss Function

Loss function that we used in our GAN is $lossSR$ loss that is the sum of adversarial loss and content loss for obtaining fine textures. In contrast to loss functions where the absolute errors are totaled between pixels (i.e per-pixel loss), perceptual loss function generates finer ground truth images. Optimisation based

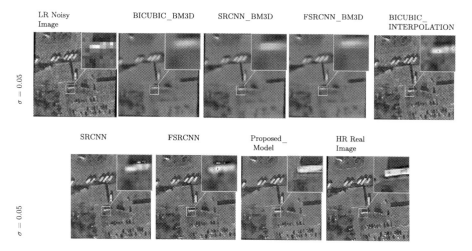

Fig. 3. Qualitatively Comparison of Test Images Result. Here, Variance of noise ($\sigma = 0.05$)

on perceptual loss function generates more accurate and high quality images as described by author in [7]. This loss function ensures perceptual similarity by comparing high-level differences, like similarities in content and style between generated images and ground truth images. Our residual GAN component used perceptual loss($loss^{SR}$), weighted sum of an adversarial loss component ($loss_{Gen}^{SR}$) and content loss ($loss_{X}^{SR}$):

$$loss^{SR} = loss_{X}^{SR} + 10^{-3} loss_{Gen}^{SR} \tag{1}$$

Content Loss. The pixel-wise mean squared loss is considered as content loss and represented by $loss_{MSE}^{SR}$:

$$loss_{MSE}^{SR} = \frac{1}{r^2 RC} \sum_{x=1}^{rR} \sum_{y=1}^{rC} \left((HR_I)_{x,y} - G(LR_I)_{x,y} \right)^2 \tag{2}$$

The resulting picture's content loss function mainly concentrated on capturing elements found in the ground truth image. For each convolution neural network layer, the PSNR is achieved by working with the mean squared error optimization and the weighted form of the content distance.

Rather than using pixel-wise loss function, we used perceptual similarity losses based loss function [5,7,9].

Adversarial Loss. We also used adversarial loss function along with content loss function for training of our model. The significance of this loss function is it works on the differential network and generates images that seems more real. It makes our model more robust by training our network to differentiate between generated images and real images. The loss of generating $loss^{SR}_{Gen}$ is dependent on the training sample discriminator probabilities $D\big(G(LR_I)\big)$ on as given below:

$$loss^{SR}_{Gen} = \sum_{i=1}^{n} - \log D\Big(G\Big(LR_I\Big)\Big) \tag{3}$$

The probability of the reconstructed image is given here by $D\big(G(LR_I)\big)$. A generated HR image is $G(LR_I)$. Instead of minimising $- \log D\big(G(LR_I)\big)$ we minimise $\log\big[1 - D(G(LR_I))\big]$ [11] for improved gradient behaviour [11].

4   Experiment and Results

4.1   Training Parameters and Details

For Training and Testing purpose we choose 800 and 200 images from Aerial lionbridge.ai database respectively. All the training of generator as well as discriminator performed in a batch size of 128 random images for 300 epochs on an NVIDIA Quadro K1200. The experiment's data set was created by using a bicubic kernel to down sample all of the chosen images four times, and by corrupting the images with speckle noise (sigma(σ)=0.04) for training and various noise levels for testing. In each iteration, we used 128 randomly selected 96 × 96 low quality noisy photos from the training dataset. For converting characteristics of noisy low-resolution and high-resolution images on a comparable scale of range (0, 1).

We trained our generator and discriminator networks alternately for better results as explained in Goodfellow et al. [13]. We also employed batch normalisation layer along with Convolution layer in both sub-layers of generator for preserving our model from internal covariance shift. Adam optimizer with $\beta_1 = 0.9$ and $\beta_2 = 0.99$ used for optimisation with learning rate of 10^{-3} for generator while 10^{-4} learning rate for discriminator.

We used PSNR (peak signal-to-noise ratio) i.e. expressed in dB and SSIM (structural similarity) [14] as a parameter for validation of results. During testing we turned off BN layer updation and used different levels of noise(sigma(σ). Our model gives better results on both the PSNR and SSIM parameters compare to other referenced model generated images Fig. 3. Not only quantitatively, but our proposed model generated images is also visually better as is shown in Fig. 3. Even in the presence of high intensity noise, our suggested model can still provide images that are more comparable to the original images.

5   Conclusion

In this Paper, we proposed a CNN-GAN model having two-layered generator as well as discriminator for generating high resolution noise free images from its low-resolution noisy image counterparts. The CNN-GAN model is trained end-to-end on satellite images for purpose of super-resolution as well as denoising. A new framework of GAN is built by the generator having two sub-layer(a deep residual network as well as pre-trained UCNN)as discussed above and the discriminator. For training GAN network, we employed content loss function together with adversarial loss function for residual network, and for pre-training the UCNN mean square error loss function. It has been proposed to use state-of-the-art technique to improve image contours that can not only considerably reduce the speckle noise seen in satellite images but also increase the image's resolution by $(4\times)$ compared to input image. We have demonstrated that the satellite images generated by CNN-GAN are better in terms of structural similarity and Peak-signal-to-noise ratio as well as visually than the images recreated by the other referenced methods. Our future work involves extending this method in other fields like Medical Diagnostic Images, Astronomical Images, Aerial Images etc.

References

1. Behjati, P., et al.: Overnet: lightweight multi-scale super-resolution with overscaling network. In: Proceedings of the IEEE/CVF Winter Conference on Applications of Computer Vision, pp. 2694–2703 (2021)
2. Zeng, J., Pang, J., Sun, W., Cheung, G.: Deep graph laplacian regularization for robust denoising of real images. In: Proceedings of the IEEE/CVF Conference on Computer Vision and Pattern Recognition Workshops, pp. 0–0 (2019)
3. Kumar, R., Maji, S.K.: A novel framework for denoised high resolution generative adversarial network-dhrgan. In: 2020 7th International Conference on Signal Processing and Integrated Networks (SPIN), pp. 1033–1038. IEEE (2020)
4. Yang, C.-Y., Ma, C., Yang, M.-H.: Single-image super-resolution: a benchmark. In: Fleet, D., Pajdla, T., Schiele, B., Tuytelaars, T. (eds.) ECCV 2014. LNCS, vol. 8692, pp. 372–386. Springer, Cham (2014). https://doi.org/10.1007/978-3-319-10593-2_25
5. Bruna, J., Sprechmann, P., LeCun, Y.: Super-resolution with deep convolutional sufficient statistics. arXiv preprint arXiv:1511.05666 (2015)
6. Simonyan, K., Zisserman, A.: Very deep convolutional networks for large-scale image recognition. arXiv preprint arXiv:1409.1556 (2014)
7. Johnson, J., Alahi, A., Fei-Fei, L.: Perceptual losses for real-time style transfer and super-resolution. In: Leibe, B., Matas, J., Sebe, N., Welling, M. (eds.) ECCV 2016. LNCS, vol. 9906, pp. 694–711. Springer, Cham (2016). https://doi.org/10.1007/978-3-319-46475-6_43
8. Ioffe, S., Szegedy, C.: Batch normalization: Accelerating deep network training by reducing internal covariate shift. arXiv preprint arXiv:1502.03167 (2015)
9. Gatys, L., Ecker, A.S., Bethge, M.: Texture synthesis using convolutional neural networks. In: Advances in Neural Information Processing Systems, pp. 262–270 (2015)
10. He, K., Zhang, X., Ren, S., Sun, J.: Delving deep into rectifiers: surpassing human-level performance on imagenet classification. In: Proceedings of the IEEE International Conference on Computer Vision, pp. 1026–1034 (2015)
11. Ledig, C., et al.: Photo-realistic single image super-resolution using a generative adversarial network. In: Proceedings of the IEEE Conference on Computer Vision and Pattern Recognition, pp. 4681–4690 (2017)

12. Shi, W., et al.: Real-time single image and video super-resolution using an efficient sub-pixel convolutional neural network. In: Proceedings of the IEEE Conference on Computer Vision and Pattern Recognition, pp. 1874–1883 (2016)
13. Goodfellow, I., et al.: Generative adversarial nets. In: Advances in Neural Information Processing Systems, pp. 2672–2680 (2014)
14. Wang, Z., Bovik, A.C., Sheikh, H.R., Simoncelli, E.P., et al.: Image quality assessment: from error visibility to structural similarity. IEEE Trans,. Image Process. **13**(4), 600–612 (2004)

Deep Learning Based Enhanced Text Recognition System

Simranjit Singh[1], Monika Gosain[1(✉)], Rubaljeet Kaur[1], Sukhpreet Kaur[1], and Triloki Nath[2]

[1] Chandigarh Engineering College, Landran, India
`monika.4354@cgc.edu.in`
[2] RVS College of Engineering and Technology, Coimbatore, India

Abstract. The branch of artificial intelligence called "deep learning" enables the computer to take on and learn new rules. Deep learning algorithms are capable of recognizing objects, photos, messages, observations, and other structures. The underwhelming performance of the current scene recognition algorithms has motivated many researchers in the computer vision field in recent years, yet scene text recognition still need improvement. This study offered an innovative method for scene text recognition that uses a CraftNet model with enhanced learning capabilities. In the proposed approach, edge information is first collected from the images after image enhancement using a median filter. The deep learning model is given these edge characteristics, so it can recognize text area and build a bounding box around it. The discovered region is next transformed into text and then, using a text-to-speech conversion model, into voice. The efficacy of the suggested model is confirmed by comparison with the existing models.

Keywords: Scene Text · Deep learning · CraftNet · VGG16 · Edge Feature

1 Introduction

Our everyday lives revolve on digital gadgets, which are either utilised for comfort or for enjoyment. This is the digital era of today. A mobile phone is a digital tool utilised in daily life, whether it is for taking pictures or translating between languages. The majority of data shared via mobile phones is in the form of photographs or videos. Although there is a lot of data in movies and images that provides semantic textual information, the text inside the image is not changeable. As a result, there is a need for a system that extracts text from images for use in a variety of applications, such as text reading systems and help for the blind. The two primary functions of a reading text system are text detection as well as text recognition. The detection of text is entirely necessary for text recognition [1]. The identification of text from scene images is the main goal of this research. Scene photos include information that humans can quickly identify and understand, but the process of detection and recognition for automated machine systems is quite difficult owing to the varied location and style of text. The graphics have several text formats, including multilingual, vertical, and horizontal. Different sorts of pictures, including focussed text

R. K. Tiwari and G. Sahoo (Eds.): ICAII 2022, CCIS 1822, pp. 89–106, 2023.
https://doi.org/10.1007/978-3-031-37303-9_8

images and unfocused text images, were analysed by the automated reading system for text. A text image with a concentrated scene mostly contains the text, but it might be difficult to see the text because of the intricate lighting and background effects. The other is blurry text images, which include text either scattered about in extremely small font sizes or far away with blur effects. The text images were sorted into many categories for the International Conference on Document Analysis and Recognition (ICDAR) robust reading competition [2]:

- The collection of images known as **Born Digital Images** was taken from emails and websites. The online pages come from a variety of websites, including personal, business, news, social, and government websites. For the collection of born digital images, the images from spam emails are also retrieved. Due to the poor resolution and intricate backgrounds of images, word identification from born digital images is likewise a very difficult process.
- *Incidental text images* are a group of images that the user has randomly taken without knowing where the text would appear or what impact it will have. The challenge of extracting text from incidental images is extremely challenging, not just because of the complex backgrounds or blurring effects but also because the images sometimes contain several items and writing that is quite small in size.
- The collection of frames that make up *text in videos* are taken from various videos. Due to the widespread usage of camera phones, there are more films available and it is more challenging to distinguish between different forms of noisy text that is included in the video frames. Blurriness brought on by movement and problems with focus constitute the noise in video frames.

The initial stage of a text extraction and recognition system is text detection. If the text detection results are poor, more bogus text regions are extracted. When text is extracted from images, there are several difficulties that arise. There are more false text areas as a result of the image's poor resolution, lighting effects, and undesirable noise [3]. Text identification becomes more difficult in some images because the intensity of the background pixels is comparable to that of the foreground pixels. Problems are also caused by high contrast, complicated backgrounds, and varied text image font sizes [4]. Despite the large number of studies that have been offered, text identification remains a highly difficult problem because of the following difficulties:

- **Complex Background:** In certain images, the foreground text pixels resemble the background pixels, which makes extraction of text from photograph difficult. Number of items in the scene photos makes it more difficult to distinguish between text and non-text sections. Additionally, some photographs' backgrounds are quite complicated, which causes the text portion to be blurry.
- **Illumination:** False text patches are detected as a result of the image's uneven lighting. When there is uneven lighting, heavy shadows can occasionally impact the photos and provide very poor text identification results since the illumination effect missed the borders of the text characters.
- **Size and Style:** Text on scene photographs varies in size and design. Font detection becomes particularly difficult because of the variance in text size and style. It is challenging to control the real value of characteristics when the characters in the

image vary in size and style. Because each character's geometrical orientation varies, it is particularly challenging to recognize curved text.

- Text in a single language is very simple to identify, but text in a picture in numerous languages is far more difficult. The number of characters in the English language is relatively small, although the character classes in other languages vary greatly. There are several languages, including Arabic, Japanese, Chinese, Korean, and Hindi. Because each language has unique characters with distinct personalities and writing styles that differ from one another, text detection becomes a very difficult process.

Due to the numerous applications that employ the method of detection, such as document analysis, street name identification, and vehicle number plate recognition systems, text detection is a particularly fascinating issue in the field of computer vision. The amount of multimedia expanded at a very rapid pace, which increases the image data. There are several algorithms for text identification and localization, but they still face one or more problems. Consequently, a system that recognizes and extracts text data from photographs is required. The authors [5] employed a combination of texture- and region-based characteristics to work on text identification and localization in scene photos. The naive bayes classifier was used to separate the text from non-text areas. Fast edge preserving and smoothing filters were used to improve the Maximal Stable External Region (MSER), however the improvements were not very successful. Therefore, the proposed work [5] has to be improved. Another difficult job is multi-oriented text detection. Using a hybrid bottom-up technique and Multilayer Perceptron [6] investigated text identification and localization of multi-oriented text in scene photos (MLP). Since there is no multi-oriented text in a single orientation, the likelihood that a false region (a non-text area) would be detected is increased. Ghai and Jain [7] suggested a technique for text identification using a k-means clustering with a sliding window to distinguish between text and non-text areas. The outcomes were successful for photographs without noise, but they weren't as well for lighted images. The system's extraction procedure is directly impacted by the text detection results. Therefore, for better extraction outcomes, the text detection step has to be improved. The planned works listed above encourage the creation of effective text detection algorithms.

2 Literature Review

The three main categories in text detection are edge and gradient based, texture based, and connected component-based techniques. A literature review found that connected-component based techniques are incorrect because they use the assumption that text pixels in the same linked region would all have the same attributes, such as color or grey intensity [8]. Contrarily, texture-based techniques are computationally expensive for large databases [9, 10] since they call for pricey processes like DCT for picture text recognition. Edge and gradient-based methods have been developed to reduce the amount of calculations needed to detect text in photos. On the other hand, current methods that emphasize edge and gradient are not robust against complex backgrounds since they result in more false positives. Another crucial problem was the selection of the threshold values for the separation of the text pixels from non-text pixels [11–14]. The method in [15] included text part segmentation using candidate text block identification to overcome these problems. Approaches for identifying text in situations have recently been developed using convolutional neural networks and deep learning. CAO [16], who worked on text detection, proposed GISCA. This approach makes advantage of deep learning. There have been several methods for finding text, but none of them have been able to find the actual text in a picture. In order to address this problem, CAO separated the GISCA into two modules: the GIM (Gradient-inductive module) and the CAM (Contextual attention module).

The unorthodox scene photos were identified using TextField, a text detection method provided by Xu [17]. The authors added the direction field, which includes direction information and a binary text mask. The separation of all related text objects using direction files and the employment of morphological post-processing techniques produced better results for curved text pictures. In a manner akin to bounding boxes, Liao [18] invented Textboxes++, which creates a quadrilateral boundary toward the text in the scene text picture. The outcomes of four publicly accessible datasets were compared. A horizontal text detector known as Textboxes++ is an add-on for Textboxes. Convolutional and pooling layers were introduced for oriented text. Text recognition is done using the CRNN (Convolutional Recurrent Neural Networks) model. Textboxes++ identified the text as word-based and multi-oriented. Since it makes binarization simpler, binarization is also crucial to the text extraction process. A method for text extraction based on Renyi entropy was presented by Karpagam [19]. The suggested remedy is based on a background removal method that pulls semantic information out of intricate RGB hues. Connected parts and morphological processes were used to produce clusters of homogeneous pixels. The authors claim that the Renyi-entropy technique performs better in photos with complex backgrounds and can discern blurred text from noisy images. For multiscript-oriented photos, it is challenging to obtain good text detection and identification results. To identify text components using the most important bit information, Raghunandan [20] researched bit plane slicing. In addition, [20] used a novel approach Mutual Nearest Neighbor Pair (MNNP) components to select the sample pairs of texts in each potential bit plane depending on gradient direction.

In order to precisely locate texts in scenes, Xue et al. [21] Suggested a scene text identification method that makes use of bootstrapping and text border semantics. A novel bootstrapping method was created that considerably reduces the constraint of little training data by sampling. The predicted text feature maps are more consistent when text subsections are sampled. Four distinct text border segments were created for each scene text using a semantics-aware text border recognition technique. The recommended approaches performed better on a variety of publicly available datasets, including the MSRA-TD500 (f-score, 80.1), the ICDAR2017-RCTW (f-score 67.1), and others. Extensive research supported the utility of the methodologies. The top-down slow evolution of the first text suggestion into arbitrary text outlines was advised by Dai et al. [22]. By measuring the text's size and center, the first horizontal text concepts were created. He et al. [23]'s innovative approach for scene text recognition contains a number of strategies for significantly bettering text localization quality. The usefulness and superiority of the offered procedures were demonstrated in a thorough ablation experiment. Thanks to the combination of the recommended methodologies with a top scene text detector, EAST, the resulting text detection system achieves cutting-edge or competitive performance on several standard text detection benchmarks while keeping a quick running time. An arbitrary-shape scene text recognition method with enhanced generalisation and localization accuracy was proposed by Dai et al. [24]. To improve the variety of training samples, they initially created a Scale-Aware Data Augmentation (SADA) technique. SADA takes into account the size differences and regional visual modifications of scene texts, effectively resolving the problem of limited training data. SADA can enhance the training minibatch concurrently, accelerating the training process. The general form structure of arbitrary-shape scene texts and backdrops is further explained using a Shape Similarity Constraint (SSC) method from the standpoint of the loss function. To localise more precise bounds for arbitrary-shape scene texts, SSC promotes candidate box text or non-text segmentation to be similar to the relevant ground truth. The effectiveness of the offered approaches has been thoroughly tested, and cutting-edge results have been achieved on publicly accessible arbitrary shape scene text benchmarks (Table 1).

Table 1. Different Proposed Techniques of Text Detection

Study	Techniques	Datasets	Precision Rate	Recall Rate	F-measure
Liu et al. [25] 2020	Markov Clustering Network (MCN)	ICDAR 2013	88.0	86.5	87.2
Khan et al. [26] 2019	Deep Convolution Neural Network (D-CNN)	Aliah University Text Non-Text (AUTNT)	98.7	92.7	95.6
Gironés et al. [6] 2019	Connected components (CC) approach with linear spatial filter	ICDAR 2013	0.93	0.89	0.91
Soni et al. [5] 2018	Fast edge preserving and smoothing Maximum Stable Extremal Region (FEPS-MSER) algorithm	ICDAR 2013	0.84	0.68	0.75
Liu et al. [27] 2017	Morphological component analysis	ICDAR 2013	0.77	0.60	0.68

(continued)

Table 1. (*continued*)

Study	Techniques	Datasets	Precision Rate	Recall Rate	F-measure
Yu et al. [28] 2015	Edge Analysis	ICDAR 2011	0.78	0.63	0.70
Ren et al. [29] 2017	Convolutional neural network (CNN)	ICDAR 2011	0.74	0.64	0.69
Raghu Nandan et al. [20] 2019	Mutual Nearest Neighbor Pair (MNNP) components based on gradient direction and SVM classifier	ICDAR 2015	0.628	0.676	0.661
GAO et al. [30] 2019	Convolutional Regression Network (CRN)	ICDAR 2015	0.804	0.784	0.794
Banerjee et al. [15] 2014	Otsu's thresholding technique	Camera Captured Images	0.63	0.65	-
Karpagam et al. [19] 2019	Renyi entropy-based text localization algorithm	MSRA-TD500 dataset	0.78	0.77	0.76
Xu et al. [17] 2019	Deep Learning	ICDAR2015	0.843	0.839	0.841
YANG et al. [31]	Knowledge Distillation	ICDAR2015	0.841	0.833	0.837
Liu et al. [11] 2019	Deep Matching Prior Network	ICDAR 2015	73.23	68.22	70.64
Xue et al. [21] 2018	DenseNet	ICDAR 2017 MSRA-TD500	78.2 83.0	58.8 77.4	67.1 80.1
Dai et al. [22] 2021	PCR (DLA34)	TD500	90.8	83.5	87.0
He et al. [23] 2021	PA-NMS (ResNet-50)	IC15	89.1	87.3	88.2
Dai et al. [24], 2021	SADA	CTW1500	86.3	81.3	83.7

The text in the scene photographs has a variety of problems, such as a cluttered backdrop, an illumination effect, blurriness, low contrast, etc. Text detection and localization, a stage of the Optical Character Recognition (OCR) system, is essential. The outcome of text extraction from the image is entirely determined by the text detection stage. Therefore, it is crucial that the text detection findings be accurate and that any errors with the picture are corrected before transferring text to the identification step.

3 Proposed Work

High-level semantic information is frequently included in texts set in natural settings, and this information is useful for analysing and comprehending the surroundings. Consequently, it is more crucial than ever to extract text from the photos. The method mostly entails the several processes depicted in the Fig. 1.

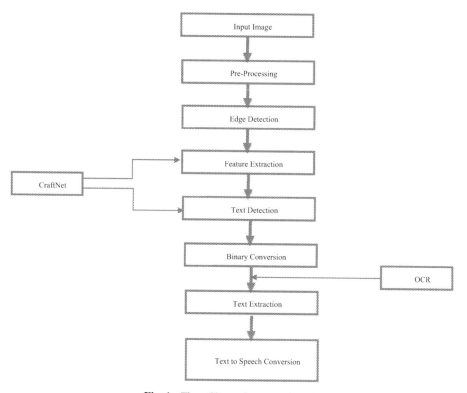

Fig. 1. Flow Chart of proposed work

Image Acquisition: Images may be captured using a variety of devices, including digital cameras and cell phone cameras. Images in real-time apps are taken in live mode. ICDAR dataset is utilised for training purposes [32]. As indicated in the picture below, certain samples utilised in this work.

Fig. 2. Sample Images

Pre-processing: The most crucial and necessary pre-processing is required for a system to operate more effectively. Noise reduction is crucial because scanners and cameras can introduce noise into the input image. There are several filtering methods available to remove noise from document images. These methods can be used to add or remove noise from photographs, keep the image's proper contrast, remove backgrounds that have scenes in them, or apply watermarks. These are used to create photos that improve the quality of the image.

The sample in this study is first turned into grey scale and displayed in Fig. 3. Grayscale in this context indicates that each pixel's value simply encodes information about the light's intensity. In other words, the artwork solely uses the colours black, white, and grey, with grey having several shades.

Fig. 3. Gray Scale Images

The grayscale photographs are then enhanced using the median filter. A filtering technique for signal and picture noise reduction is the median filter. In image processing median filter is crucial as while reduction of noise it preserving edges. Each pixels are checked by median filter in turn and considers its immediate neighbors to evaluate if a pixel is typical of its surroundings. Instead of only using the mean of its neighbors' pixel values, the replacement value is the median of those values, as illustrated in Fig. 4.

123	125	126	130	140
122	124	126	127	135
118	120	150	125	134
119	115	119	123	133
111	116	110	120	130

Neighbourhood values:

115, 119, 120, 123, 124,
125, 126, 127, 150

Median value: 124

Fig. 4. Median value of a pixel neighborhood.

Figure 5 displays the results of the median filter for the example photos from Fig. 2.

Fig. 5. Enhanced Images using Median Filter

Edge Detection: In order to find areas in digital pictures with sharp brightness fluctuations, or more precisely, discontinuities, edge detection employs a variety of mathematical algorithms. The rapid changes in brightness in an image are sometimes combined into a collection of curved line segments known as edges. In this study, the intelligent edge detection, canny edge detection is used which has five phases:

- Reduction of Noise;
- Compute Gradient;
- Implement Non-maximum suppression;
- Threshold updation;
- Edge Tracking.

The output of the edge detection method on enhanced image is as shown in the following figure (Fig. 6).

Deep Learning-Based Feature Extraction: The recognition system's phase of feature extraction is crucial. The convolution layer of deep learning-based techniques automatically extracts the features, while the pooling layer does feature selection. CraftNet architecture is used for this task. It is a machine learning technique by which computers learn by mimicking human learning processes. A computer model with the help of deep learning, can directly perform classification tasks from text, images, speech. Deep learning models may be able to achieve modern accuracy, occasionally even surpassing human performance. A large set of datasets with labels are used to train the model in multi-layered neural network architectures. This improves the use of consumer gadgets

Fig. 6. Edges of the Enhanced Images

and is crucial for applications that demand a high level of safety, such driverless vehicles. According to recent advancements, the performance of the deep learning models was improved and it required a large dataset. For instance, taking many hours of video and taking millions of images is required to create an automated driving system. Furthermore, a high computing power systems are required dor working with deep learning methods. Deep learning is supported by high-performance GPUs and its parallel architectures. In order to reduce the time taken to train a deep learning model from couple of weeks to hours one can use a system combined with clusters or cloud computing. Deep learning is used in industries like autonomous driving and medical equipment.

As the foundation of this study, CraftNet, a fully convolutional network architecture built on VGG-16 [33] with batch normalisation, is employed. This model combines low-level characteristics and contains skip connections in the decoding portion, which is comparable to U-net [34]. The area scores and the affinity scores are the two score maps that make up the final result. The following Figure provides a schematic illustration of the network design.

The samples in this study are trained using the CraftNet Model, and the training procedure is further broken down into the following sub steps (Fig. 7):

- *Ground Truth Label Generation*

In training, for each image sample, a character-level bounding limits are established for the ground truth label, its region scores, and affinity score where the region score indicates the chance that a certain pixel is the character's center, and the affinity value indicates the likelihood that a specific pixel is in the center of a space between two characters. To convey the chance that the character center will emerge, we utilise a Gaussian heatmap as opposed to a binary segmentation map, where each pixel are labeled separately. This representation of the heatmap have been used in many applications due to its remarkable flexibility [2, 35]. Using the heatmap representation, the region score and the affinity score is discovered. It takes a long time for the label production process. On image bounding box of character are frequently warped by perspective projections. Despite the use of narrow receptive fields, the proposed ground truth formulation allows the model to correctly recognises large or long-length text occurrences.

- *Weakly-Supervised Learning*

In contrast to synthetic datasets, real photographs in a dataset frequently include word-level annotations. The poorly supervised character boxes are generated from each

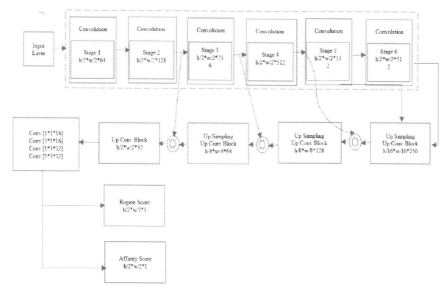

Fig. 7. CraftNet Architecture

word-level annotation. The precision of the interim model's prediction was computed with the value of the confidence map over each word box.

Text Detection: During this step, text is located throughout the image's varied backgrounds. There are many sorts of photographs, thus finding text for some of them might be simple while for others it can be challenging. CraftNet also steps in at this point, drawing a bounding box around the identified text location as seen in the picture below (Fig. 8).

Fig. 8. Text Detection using CraftNet

Text Extraction: Utilizing OCR, the text is taken from the identified text region and saved in the system for later processing. As seen in the graphic below, the bounding boxes and extracted text are also displayed (Fig. 9).

Fig. 9. Text Extraction using CraftNet

Text to Speech Conversion: The stored text is then converted into speech using text-to-speech module.

4 Result and Discussion

This proposed approach in scene text pictures has been provided. The method's primary benefit is that it avoids making any assumptions. This chapter offers a result analysis of a method that is suggested and used to identify text in datasets. Precision, f-measure and recall are the three characteristics that are used to measure the performance of the suggested approach.

The studies to test the effectiveness of our suggested strategy are carried out using a laptop running Windows 10 with the MATLAB 2021. The proposed method's performance is examined using the ICDAR 2015 robust reading competition dataset, which includes a variety of images with complicated backgrounds, low contrast, lighting effects, etc (Fig. 10).

Fig. 10. Sample Images from ICDAR 2015 dataset

The detection results are depicted in the picture below, where CraftNet identified a text region and created a bounding box around it (Fig. 11).

Fig. 11. Detected Text Region

4.1 Performance Evaluation

Utilizing the ICDAR dataset, the proposed approach's performance is assessed using three distinct parameters: precision, recall, and f-measure.

Precision Rate: It is described as the proportion of correctly identified estimate text to all estimate numbers. Precision rate is defined as the proportion of positive values to the total selected value in terms of positive and negative values. When it comes to false positive and true positive, true positive refers to accurately calculated data, whereas false positive refers to inaccurate data.

$$Precision = \frac{True\ Positive}{True\ Positive + False\ Positive}$$

Recall Rate: It is characterized as the proportion of all right text estimations to all target number guesses.

$$Recall = \frac{True\ Positive}{True\ Positive + False\ Negative}$$

F-measure: The accuracy rate and recall rate are combined into a single unit of quality using the F-measure. It may alternatively be described as the harmonic mean of recall rate and accuracy. It is sometimes referred to as an F-. These parameters' values must be high in order for the algorithm to work better.

$$F - measure = 2 \times \frac{Precision \times Recall}{Precision + Recall}$$

When the suggested work was tested using the ICDAR dataset, the calculated results are shown in the accompanying figure (Fig. 12).

The aforementioned graphic illustrated how well the suggested system performed in terms of Precision, Recall, and F-measure. The precision for text identification and extraction is 84.6 percent, recall is 81.6 percent, and F-measure is 83.07 percent, which demonstrate the usefulness of the technique.

Additionally, the performance of the proposed system is contrasted with that of the MOST [23], and SADA [24] current systems. The comparison also demonstrates how much better the suggested system is than these more modern solutions. The table below provides a comparison of the performance (Table 2).

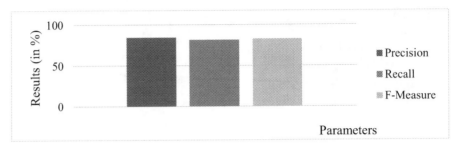

Fig. 12. Performance Analysis of the proposed System

Table 2. Comparison of Performance of different method

	Precision	Recall	F-Measure
MOST [37]	76.7	75.2	75.9
SADA [38]	58.2	81.5	67.9
Proposed Work	84.6	81.6	83.07

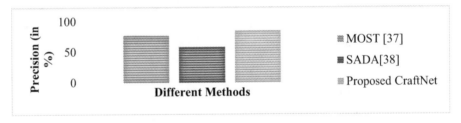

Fig. 13. Precision

The following graphic makes it possible to forecast the comparison in terms of precision value, and it is evident from the picture that the suggested system has a greater precision value (Fig. 13).

The above figures convey that the precision of the proposed CraftNet is 9.3% better than the MOST [23] and 31.2% better than SADA [24]. The computed results for recall are as shown in figure below (Fig. 14).

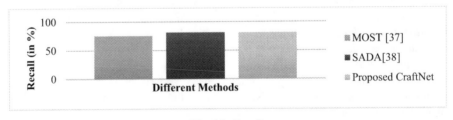

Fig. 14. Recall

The above graph demonstrates the effectiveness of the proposed approach in terms of recall values as it is better than the existing approaches. The improvement rate is 0.12% from SADA [24] and 7.8% from MOST [23]. The final parameters that is F-measure is also computed and it is also better than the existing methods as shown in figure below (Fig. 15).

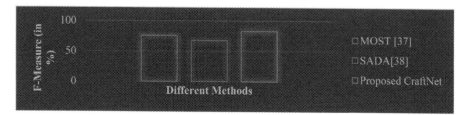

Fig. 15. F-measure

The above results also clear that the performance of the proposed work is better than the other existing systems like, it is better than MOST [23] by 8.6%, and SADA [24] by 18.2%.The proposed approach may be utilised for a variety of applications because all of the findings show its efficacy. This study's major goal is to assist the blind by reciting the recognized text, which can only be done if text extraction is precise. Therefore, it is evident from this performance that the system would be highly useful for blind people in order to provide those instructions regarding signs and other objects.

5   Conclusion and Future Scope

Due to differences in text section widths, typefaces, and textures, text identification in photos of natural scenes is a particularly challenging task. The placement of text can also appear randomly in some photographs. Text may be seen everywhere in scene photos. There are many patterns that resemble texts in scene photos, and they exhibit similarities to text objects, making text identification more challenging. We have introduced a dynamic deep learning-based technique for text localisation and identification in scene photos in this study. Edge detection is done after the pre-processing of the photos, which uses a median filter to improve the quality of the images. Additionally, CraftNet is used to train the deep learning model that draws the bounding box and recognises the text region. The text is then retrieved from the text-region using the default OCR, and the text-to-speech module is used to transform the text to speech. The experiment using MATLAB demonstrated that the proposed approach performed well enough to fulfil the goals. Precision, recall, and f-measure are used to calculate the findings. Every parameter that was calculated for the suggested technique performed better than the current state of the art. Additionally, the two most recent deep learning models are compared to the current model. The future goal of this effort is to construct a hardware model for a camera stick for blind people and to put that model into practice in order to understand how well it works in a real-world setting. Additionally, it may be evaluated on additional datasets to confirm the outcomes of the suggested model.

References

1. Liu, Z., Zhou, W., Li, H.: Scene text detection with fully convolutional neural networks. Multimedia Tools Appl. **78**(13), 18205–18227 (2019). https://doi.org/10.1007/s11042-019-7177-4

2. Karatzas, D., et al.: ICDAR 2013 robust reading competition. In: 2013 12th International Conference on Document Analysis and Recognition, pp. 1484–1493 (2013). https://doi.org/10.1109/ICDAR.2013.221

3. Girones, X., Julia, C.: Real-time text localization in natural scene images using a linear spatial filter. In: 2017 14th IAPR International Conference on Document Analysis and Recognition (ICDAR), pp. 1261–1268 (2017). https://doi.org/10.1109/ICDAR.2017.208

4. Shivakumara, P., Wu, L., Lu, T., Tan, C.L., Blumenstein, M., Anami, B.S.: Fractals based multi-oriented text detection system for recognition in mobile video images. Pattern Recognit. **68**, 158–174 (2017). https://doi.org/10.1016/j.patcog.2017.03.018

5. Soni, R., Kumar, B., Chand, S.: Text detection and localization in natural scene images based on text awareness score. Appl. Intell. **49**(4), 1376–1405 (2018). https://doi.org/10.1007/s10489-018-1338-4

6. Gironés, X., Julià, C.: Real-time localization of multi-oriented text in natural scene images using a linear spatial filter. J. Real-Time Image Proc. **17**(5), 1505–1525 (2019). https://doi.org/10.1007/s11554-019-00911-9

7. Ghai, D., Jain, N.: Comparative analysis of multi-scale wavelet decomposition and k-means clustering based text extraction. Wireless Pers. Commun. **109**(1), 455–490 (2019). https://doi.org/10.1007/s11277-019-06574-w

8. Tang, Y., Wu, X.: Scene text detection and segmentation based on cascaded convolution neural networks. IEEE Trans. Image Process. **26**(3), 1509–1520 (2017). https://doi.org/10.1109/TIP.2017.2656474

9. Zhang, S., Lin, M., Chen, T., Jin, L., Lin, L.: Character proposal network for robust text extraction. In: 2016 IEEE International Conference on Acoustics, Speech and Signal Processing (ICASSP), pp. 2633–2637 (2016). https://doi.org/10.1109/ICASSP.2016.7472154

10. Epshtein, B., Ofek, E., Wexler, Y.: Detecting text in natural scenes with stroke width transform. In: 2010 IEEE Computer Society Conference on Computer Vision and Pattern Recognition, pp. 2963–2970 (2010). https://doi.org/10.1109/CVPR.2010.5540041

11. Liu, Y., Jin, L.: Deep matching prior network: toward tighter multi-oriented text detection. In: 2017 IEEE Conference on Computer Vision and Pattern Recognition (CVPR), pp. 3454–3461 (2017). https://doi.org/10.1109/CVPR.2017.368

12. Liu, C.: Multi-layers segmentation based adaptive binarization for text extraction in scanned card images. In: Huang, D.-S., Bevilacqua, V., Premaratne, P. (eds.) ICIC 2014. LNCS, vol. 8588, pp. 367–375. Springer, Cham (2014). https://doi.org/10.1007/978-3-319-09333-8_40

13. Kim, K.I., Jung, K., Kim, J.H.: Texture-based approach for text detection in images using support vector machines and continuously adaptive mean shift algorithm. IEEE Trans. Pattern Anal. Mach. Intell. **25**(12), 1631–1639 (2003). https://doi.org/10.1109/TPAMI.2003.1251157

14. Neumann, L., Matas, J.: Scene text localization and recognition with oriented stroke detection. In: 2013 IEEE International Conference on Computer Vision, pp. 97–104 (2013). https://doi.org/10.1109/ICCV.2013.19

15. Banerjee, S., Mullick, K., Bhattacharya, U.: A robust approach to extraction of texts from camera captured images. In: Iwamura, M., Shafait, F. (eds.) CBDAR 2013. LNCS, vol. 8357, pp. 30–46. Springer, Cham (2014). https://doi.org/10.1007/978-3-319-05167-3_3

16. Gera, D., Jain, N.: Comparison of text extraction techniques—a review. Int. J. Innov. Res. Comput. Commun. Eng. **3**, 621–626 (2015)

17. Xu, Y., Wang, Y., Zhou, W., Wang, Y., Yang, Z., Bai, X.: TextField: learning a deep direction field for irregular scene text detection. IEEE Trans. Image Process. **28**(11), 5566–5579 (2019). https://doi.org/10.1109/TIP.2019.2900589

18. Liao, M., Shi, B., Bai, X.: TextBoxes++: a single-shot oriented scene text detector. IEEE Trans. Image Process. **27**(8), 3676–3690 (2018). https://doi.org/10.1109/TIP.2018.2825107

19. Karpagam, A.V., Manikandan, M.: Text extraction from natural scene images using Renyi entropy. J. Eng. **2019**(8), 5397–5406 (2019). https://doi.org/10.1049/joe.2018.5160

20. Raghunandan, K.S., Shivakumara, P., Roy, S., Kumar, G.H., Pal, U., Lu, T.: Multi-script-oriented text detection and recognition in video/scene/born digital images. IEEE Trans. Circuits Syst. Video Technol. **29**(4), 1145–1162 (2019). https://doi.org/10.1109/TCSVT.2018.2817642

21. Xue, C., Lu, S., Zhan, F.: Accurate Scene Text Detection through Border Semantics Awareness and Bootstrapping (2018). http://arxiv.org/abs/1807.03547

22. Dai, P., Zhang, S., Zhang, H., Cao, X.: Progressive contour regression for arbitrary-shape scene text detection. In: Proceedings IEEE Computer Society Conference Computer Vision Pattern Recognition, pp. 7389–7398 (2021). https://doi.org/10.1109/CVPR46437.2021.00731

23. He, M., et al., "MOST: a multi-oriented scene text detector with localization refinement. In: Proceedings IEEE Computer Society Conference Computer Vision Pattern Recognition, pp. 8809–8818 (2021). https://doi.org/10.1109/CVPR46437.2021.00870

24. Dai, P., Li, Y., Zhang, H., Li, J., Cao, X.: Accurate scene text detection via scale-aware data augmentation and shape similarity constraint. IEEE Trans. Multimedia **24**, 1883–1895 (2022). https://doi.org/10.1109/TMM.2021.3073575

25. Liu, Z., Lin, G., Goh, W.L.: Bottom-up scene text detection with markov clustering networks. Int. J. Comput. Vision **128**(6), 1786–1809 (2020). https://doi.org/10.1007/s11263-020-01298-y

26. Khan, T., Mollah, A.F.: AUTNT - A component level dataset for text non-text classification and benchmarking with novel script invariant feature descriptors and D-CNN. Multimedia Tools Appl. **78**(22), 32159–32186 (2019). https://doi.org/10.1007/s11042-019-08028-8

27. Liu, S., Xian, Y., Li, H., Zhengtao, Y.: Text detection in natural scene images using morphological component analysis and Laplacian dictionary. IEEE/CAA J. Automatica Sinica 1–9 (2017). https://doi.org/10.1109/JAS.2017.7510427

28. Yu, C., Song, Y., Meng, Q., Zhang, Y., Liu, Y.: Text detection and recognition in natural scene with edge analysis. IET Comput. Vis. **9**(4), 603–613 (2015). https://doi.org/10.1049/iet-cvi.2013.0307

29. Ren, X., Zhou, Y., He, J., Chen, K., Yang, X., Sun, J.: A convolutional neural network-based Chinese text detection algorithm via text structure modeling. IEEE Trans. Multimed. **19**(3), 506–518 (2017). https://doi.org/10.1109/TMM.2016.2625259

30. Gao, J., Wang, Q., Yuan, Y.: Convolutional regression network for multi-oriented text detection. IEEE Access **7**, 96424–96433 (2019). https://doi.org/10.1109/ACCESS.2019.2929819

31. Yang, P., Zhang, F., Yang, G.: A fast scene text detector using knowledge distillation. IEEE Access **7**, 22588–22598 (2019). https://doi.org/10.1109/ACCESS.2019.2895330

32. ICDAR 2015 Dataset | DeepAI. https://deepai.org/dataset/icdar-2015. Accessed 28 Jul 2022

33. Liu, X., Samarabandu, J.: An edge-based text region extraction algorithm for indoor mobile robot navigation. In: IEEE International Conference Mechatronics and Automation, vol. 2, pp. 701–706 (2005). https://doi.org/10.1109/ICMA.2005.1626635

34. Kumar, M., Jindal, S.R.: A study on recognition of pre-segmented handwritten multi-lingual characters. Arch. Comput. Methods. Eng. **27**(2), 577–589 (2019). https://doi.org/10.1007/s11831-019-09332-0

35. Agrahari, A., Ghosh, R.: Multi-oriented text detection in natural scene images based on the intersection of MSER with the locally binarized image. Procedia Comput. Sci. **171**, 322–330 (2020). https://doi.org/10.1016/j.procs.2020.04.033

Meta-transfer Learning for Contextual Emotion Detection in Face Affirmation

Md. Tabil Ahammed[1(✉)] ⓘ, Sudipto Ghosh[2] ⓘ, Md Ashikur Rahman[2],
Papel Chandra[2], Ariful Islam Shuvo[2], and Priyadharshini Balaji[3]

[1] Khulna University of Engineering Technology (KUET), Khulna, Bangladesh
ahtabil53@gmail.com
[2] Bangladesh University of Business Technology (BUBT), Dhaka, Bangladesh
[3] Jeppiaar Engineering College, Chennai, Tamil Nadu, India

Abstract. Communication between people relies on human expression more than any other factor. Emotional identification is, right now, a hot study area. Typically, people will show seven distinct feelings (happy, angry, surprised, sad, disgusted, fearful, and neutral). Humans communicate their feelings via words, body language, and facial expressions. Humans' ability to reveal inner thought processes via facial expressions is crucial to studying human behavior. Many fields use facial expression analysis, including those concerned with increased security, automated criminal identification, the diagnosis of mental illness, and communication between people and computers. Most studies on emotion detection have only used straightforward CNN and RNN models. However, training such a big data set may take a long because the models need a vast data set. To this end, we suggested a model that combines the Mobile Net-V2 model with the transfer learning strategy to speed up the generation time and improve the accuracy of emotion detection. In order to improve upon the current method, we have compiled a large CIFE data collection from the relevant literature. One of the best outcomes for emotion detection is attained by the suggested model architecture when tested on the data mentioned earlier. Based on what we found, the new system should be able to identify more accurately than the old one.

Keywords: Convolutional neural networks · Facial Expression Recognition · Transfer Learning · Mobile net-Candid V2's Image Facial Expression · Deep Learning etc.

1 Introduction

As modern life becomes more fast-paced, the ability to discern emotions has become increasingly crucial. People in the past could only communicate with other people; they had no way of interacting with machinery. However, human-machine interaction is now crucial. We created Facial Affect Sorting Techniques (FAST) [1] to rank emotions, and we built a table to track how many "action units" each expression takes. When used for emotion recognition [2], it helps make HCI technology [3] better. Predicting a person's mood relies heavily on tracking their emotional patterns [4] and recognizing emotions

© The Author(s), under exclusive license to Springer Nature Switzerland AG 2023
R. K. Tiwari and G. Sahoo (Eds.): ICAII 2022, CCIS 1822, pp. 107–121, 2023.
https://doi.org/10.1007/978-3-031-37303-9_9

[5], which may be assisted by advanced HCI technology. For identifying human feelings [6], the cascade method is used. In, the FACS (Facial Action Coding System) is suggested. The message and signing the judgment were introduced as two significant methods. FACS defines the most common sign judgment. Upper and lower faces were taken from the FACS database. HOG and LBP [7], or the Histogram of Gradients [8] and Local Binary Pattern [5], respectively, are applied in. In contrast to the two dimensions of facial expressions used by conventional methods, the graphs used by holistic researchers are three-dimensional. The technique established in is able to decipher the underlying emotions in the screams of babies anywhere from the first day of life to the ninth month. The cause of newborns' cries was identified using the K-means algorithm [8] and Euclidean distance. By examining the sound data created in, a single researcher may determine the cause of the sobbing. From the combination of current and historical data used to produce outcomes. In order to characterize human emotions more precisely, we suggested research utilizing the MobileNet-V2 model and the transfer learning technique. Many individuals have studied the problem of identifying human emotions. The recognition rate is low, and in most situations, only the six universal expressions may be used for identification. In the absence of films, it is impossible to identify the position of the eyebrows or any expression other than those characterized by a blend of prevailing emotions. In the future, we want to build the system even further so that it can deliver even more results that are accurate. There are plethora's of Facial Expression Recognition (FER) [9] picture data sets for categorizing only six or seven basic expressions that can be found on various web resources. However, we require a data set with seven classes—happy, furious, surprised, sad, disgusted, fearful, and neutral—for the study of human emotions. Face recognition using CNNs [10] trained on unposted photos is suggested in. For CIFE data sets, they achieved an accuracy of 81.5%. The CNN technique performed very well at identifying expression in candid images, substantially outperforming the baseline approaches. The following is a detailed account of everyone's contributions to this work: To begin with, utilizing FER issues to analyze human emotions is challenging. Second, compile a new version of the CIFE data set with 30,143 photos for seven classes by combining existing data sets. Third, utilizing a transfer learning strategy for identifying human emotions, a convolutional neural network (CNN) with a MobileNet-V2 architecture was presented and achieved better results. The outcomes of MobileNet-V2 are compared to those of a fundamental CNN architecture.

2 Literature Review

Researchers have shown a great deal of interest in the last several years in the field of facial expression identification or analysis. Older methods divide emotions into six categories: joyful, surprised, disgusted, fearful, furious, and sad. However, they have low precision, need a vast data set that is time-consuming to create, and have not been implemented utilizing the MobileNet-V2 architecture [11]. Created a multi-modal scientific approach [12] to identify emotional emotions in speech across cultures. Multi-modal inputs have been proposed in this system's emotion detection algorithms. It can recognize emotional responses in speech and translate them across cultures. A computer-generated agent may be used to provide a functional interface for human interaction. Results on the facial expression data sets FER-2013 and SFEW 2.0 [13] show the strength and efficacy of DNNRL. DNNRL may be used to learn a mapping from the original pictures to Euclidean space. To make it superior, we applied a new face detection system trained using deep learning. Amazon has consistently delivered mediocre results. The Viola-Jones face detection method [14] is used for emotion identification in video or images by analyzing the emotions on the faces of the people in the footage or picture. In order to extract features from photos based on their textures, that method is used. Sixty-three point features [15] were identified using geometric feature extraction. Using CNN, a classification scheme based on the support vector machine (SVM) classifier method was designed to identify seven distinct emotional states. With 11 distinct facial feature categories, the authors tracked how each one moved to reflect happy or sad feelings. Using the tensor flow library [16], they transcribed video into data sets and adjusted CNN's processing stages. They discovered, via trial and error, that the correct image ratio is 8:2. Using the TX2 device makes real-time detection of several faces useful for recognizing facial emotions. The CNN-based architecture achieves almost 90% accuracy on the surface data set for facial expression recognition. Using a deep learning model and a scalable method [17] for facial recognition, we obtained 98.12% accuracy on the PUBALL data set and developed a real-time application. Demonstrated a deep learning model's [18] ability to identify speaker emotion. Two-dimensional techniques were used, including both linear and nonlinear approaches. Waseda Entertainment Robots [19] have been suggested to use facial expression analysis to gauge the mood of a crowd. Ekman's expanded Big Six model [20], which is widely used in the fields of computer science and computing, is the basis of this method. They conducted their studies with an eye on a future generation that would rely heavily on robots for their everyday tasks, so it was crucial that they develop robots that can do all of the tasks that will be required of them. The team's goal was to create a framework for social robot–like robots to interact with humans in the workplace. A maximum accuracy of 7% [21] was attained in a public test of the model using the FERC 2013 data set, while an accuracy of 7.9% was achieved in a private test. Stacking blocks may help with facial expression recognition. In [22], we see the development of a three-part automatic facial expression identification system: feature extraction, face detection, and facial expression recognition. The active appearance model method uses a synthetic neuro-fuzzy inference system. For pictures that don't move, the Euclidean distance technique is utilized. Human-computer interaction, human emotion analysis, monitoring, internet conferencing, and entertainment are just a few of the many uses for Facial Expression Recognition (FER). Using the image segmentation method, the provided photos are transformed into binary format. By merging and adjusting both of these data sets, a CNN-based microexpression recognizer with 78.2% accuracy has been developed. The authors [23] trained the model using data from Kaggle's Facial Expression Recognition Challenge, which yielded promising results. Expression classification in a deep convolutional neural network (CNN) system using the HOG feature descriptor using the dataset provided in [24], a deep belief network was able to identify emotions with an accuracy of 83.18 percent in real time. In [25], seven different kinds of database photos (MMI, CK+, DISFA, FERA, SFEW, FER2013, MultiPIE) were used to automate the identification of facial expression. Using these simplified methods, the authors obtained the highest accuracy of 98.92% while recognizing six expressions from the

CK+ database. In [12], transfer learning was used to successfully identify facial expressions on tiny data sets, with an accuracy of 45.5% on the validation set and 55.6% on the test set. This proposed model was built in [13] using a single deep neural network with the well-known data sets CK+ and JAFFE. As a result of the advancements described in [14], both text-to-speech systems and intelligent tutoring systems (ITS) have become more accessible. Online conversations may be conducted through voice, video, recording, photos, and text. The OCC (Ortony/Clore/Collins) model and the Ekman emotion model are presented as two examples of emotion theories. The conceptual framework provides the foundation for the hybrid method, which combines a knowledge-based component with a learning system component. There is a place for language engineering (LE), natural language processing (NLP), and information extraction (IE) tools in this framework. Developed a real-time and extremely fast facial recognition model based on CNN architectures. Network training was done on a personal computer before being transferred to a Field Programmable Gate Array (FPGA). We construct a deep CNN/RNN architecture for face emotion identification. Implementation made use of both the MMI Facial Expression Database (TFD) and the Japanese Female Facial Expression (JAFFE) datasets. When comparing the JAFFE and MMI data sets, the JAFFE findings were higher at 94.91%, while the MMI results were lower at 92.2%. In [12], a new deep feature fusion for 3D FER called a "convolutional neural network" (CNN) was suggested. The authors displayed 2D facial attribute maps incorporating standard, depth, and form index values from each 3D face scan. The face representations that were being learned were fusing together many maps of facial attributes with the help of fine-tuning deep feature fusion. Here is a large-scale picture data set that is trained using a CNN subnet for universal visual tasks, and its accuracy was 79.17%. An efficient method of decreasing national levels of comprehension was provided by Huang's LDRC algorithm in [8], which combined LC DRC with deep learning. 400 photos of 40 distinct people's faces were utilized to evaluate the WCRE and BCRE outcomes, covering a range of 10 different facial expressions. When they used a deep learning method, it performed 87% better on ORL face data sets than regular LDRC. In [5], we find a unique framework for automatically analyzing facial expressions with high accuracy, which we then use in conjunction with the well-established Deep Sparse Auto-Encoder (DSAE) to improve the accuracy with which we can distinguish certain expressions. When using a deep learning architecture to analyze the Cohn-Kanade (CK+) database of video-based facial performances, the authors obtained 95.79% accuracy [7]. The findings were compared to numerous state-of-the-art approaches by the authors. In [23], a framework was developed for implementing MOCHA's core features and creating algorithms to reduce facial recognition processing time in the cloud. The authors choose a picture at random, take it with their mobile device, and then upload it to a cloud storage service. The Greed algorithm may increase performance by a factor of up to two using just 13-cloud servers. A system in [17] is able to execute end-to-end emotion prediction tasks using both visual input and speech from the speaker's emotional state using a CNN trained on the raw signal. In the Remote Collaborative Collaboration RECOLA database, the authors accessed a total of 25 audios, 30 videos, and 96 × 96 pictures. They used 75, 150, and 300 layers, respectively, to represent visual and acoustic data. Layer 300 in the visual model outperformed Layer 150 in the speech model. Initially, they aligned faces to extract features.

They improved their prediction accuracy by training only the recurrent network with the recurrent model. Cloud-based functions (CBFs) are used to improve the accuracy of identifying holistic facial emotions from a static facial picture data set [10]. To measure effectiveness, we compiled a database of grayscale, static face photographs. Both their own database and the face expression picture database from Carnegie Mellon University were used. Most of the published works, however, focus only on FAER and do not attempt to identify emotional states. Seven or six manifestations of emotion were used in the analysis of the few articles that focused on Facial Expression Recognition (FER) methods. However, they did not provide adequate results when used to identify emotional states. In this study, we break down the benefits of MobileNet-V2 over traditional CNNs to show how it may give better results.

2.1 Proposed Model

The data sources and analysis techniques used to compile this study are described in depth. Data preprocessing, a fundamental CNN, the MobileNet-V2 architecture, a CNN based on the MobileNet-V2 architecture, and a Transfer Learning strategy are the five subtopics that make up this part, each of which is presented in depth with appropriate graphics.

Data Pre-processing. The data has gone through both the augmentation and normalization phases. When normalizing data, one of the primary goals is to get rid of any unnecessary or duplicate information, while the other is to make sure all of the data relationships make sense. Data normalization is crucial since it may significantly improve the accuracy of models very quickly. Offsets in intensity are constant in the immediate area. Thus, the Gaussian normalization and standard deviation are helpful in the normalization process. The data augmentation method is a powerful tool for picture categorization. When a training data set has to be artificially expanded, it is common practice to employ modified copies of original pictures to do so. Depending on the input samples used in our study, network resistance may rise due to mutation. During data augmentation testing, it adjusts pictures used for both the test set and the training set. When evaluating the network, the CPU used an image mutation approach while the GPU undertook the training. Deep learning architecture requires more input samples to achieve higher accuracy. The CIFE dataset was utilized, which included 30968 pictures for training over 7 classes and 4424 images for testing. Not enough can be said about the performance of a deep learning framework. Through the use of additional data and an examination of the proposed design, we generate a wide variety of transformations to disseminate subtle differences in visual appearance. By combining six affine transformation matrices with the identity matrix, we were able to create filters for unsharp, motion, Gaussian, average, and disk images' visual qualities [11].

We took the photos in many variations. To produce the enhancement, 49 pictures were created for each original. Image enhancement from 1–49 may be observed in Fig. 1. In light of this, we now have a pool of $(30968 \times 49) = 1517432$ photos from which to draw. Then, all of the pictures were standardized. Then, to test how the model performed under different conditions, we split our data set in half and used one half for training and

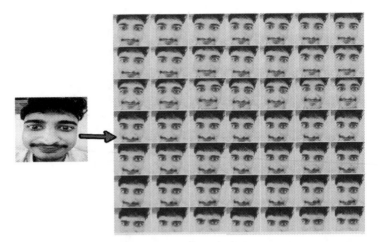

Fig. 1. Image augmentation from 1 to 49

the other for validation. There were 30,968 pictures used to train the model, and 4,424 were used to test it.

2.2 Convolutional Neural Network

A wide variety of structures may be used for deep learning. Of them, the most popular is CNN. When applied to the task of categorizing images, it excels. Multiple photos with a wide range of compositions and details were used for this study. We have detailed the methods for pre-processing data and shown how they can accommodate a wide range of data sizes, forms, and qualities. For CNN, the convolutional layer, the pooling layer, and the fully connected layer are the fundamental building blocks. This layer is the result of combining a number of filters and kernels. Filters provide feature maps that are symbolic representations of image-based feature extraction. With the use of an activation function such as ReLU, feature maps are constructed by chaining together several weights. When dealing with many classes at once, ReLU may be utilized for binary classification. Nonlinear feature extraction using the ReLU function reduces training time [12]. The Basic framework of CNN model is shown by the red box in Fig. 2.

To save space, we downsized the picture stack. Pick the size of the window (usually two or three, where the convolutional layer uses one window). Then, choose a stride length (often 2 steps) and drag the window over the filtered photo. The highest number in each time interval is used (if there is maximum pooling). The final layer contains all of the connections. This layer does the actual categorization. Due to the need for multi-class classification in this case, we first combine the filtered picture and the transformed image for classification into a single list before using a different activation function called soft max. A different kind of activation function used for multi-class classification is soft max. It is the last step in building a neural network. Since the output of a neural network is often a number between 0 and 1, soft max functions are employed to normalize the

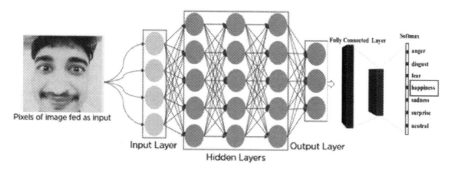

Fig. 2. Basic framework of CNN model.

data. Soft max is helpful since it transforms the probability distribution that is the output of the last layer.

2.3 MobileNet-V2 Architecture

It's easy to see the similarities between MobileNet and MobileNet-V2. A convolutional neural network is a deep network that has up to 53 layers. MobileNet accepts inputs of any size greater than 44 by 44 pixels, with higher-resolution images yielding the best results. Many different types of picture classifications are within the capabilities of the pre-trained network. The network has learned complex feature representations for many different types of pictures. MobileNet-V2 is very similar to standard CNN models, but there are a few key distinctions.

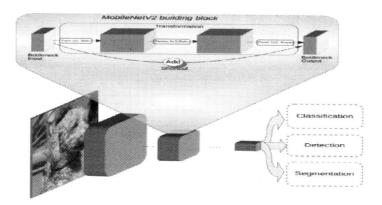

Fig. 3. Overview of MobileNetV2 Architecture

The inner layer of MobileNet V2 records the model's ability to shift from lowlevel ideas like pixels to high-level descriptors like picture categories, while the bottleneck encodes intermediate inputs and outputs. When conventional residual connections are used, training is both quick and precise. Pointwise convolution and depthwise smoothing are still used in MobileNet V2. Convolution is used in MobileNet V2 both in depth and at points. The initial linear bottleneck and the subsequent shortcut connections between bottlenecks are two additional features included in MobileNet V2. The blue box in Fig. 3 shows the linear bottleneck convolution's creative block. In the bottleneck part, there are inputs and outputs between models, with the inner layer covering the model's capacity to transform data at the pixel level to determine an image's categorization. So, avoiding bottlenecks with shortcuts allows for quicker training and higher accuracy. The first of these is step-wise separable convolution, in which the operation is split into two phases: a depth-wise phase in which one filter is applied for each channel, and a point-wise phase in which multiple filters are applied for a single channel of outputs from the depth-wise phase. In the second stage, when function loss is minimized, we utilize an activation function called ReLU. Third, to improve propagation, we may combine the input and output, create a summary of both, and then use that summation as the output of the block. Adding an expansion layer to the beginning of that block and using the ReLU non-linearity model are both ways to do this.

2.4 Transfer Learning Approach

Machine learning technique known as "transfer learning." Transfer learning refers to the process of applying a previously learned model to an unrelated situation.

As a result, its use for labeling images has skyrocketed. It can teach deep learning networks with relatively less input. Here, we start with a model that has already been trained, and then we attempt to retrain it for the new task; for example, we have an image data collection in which we want to categorize seven distinct emotional states, as we may recall from the data augmentation. This pre-trained model, which we can obtain from sites such as Google TensorFlow Hub, has often already been trained with millions of photos, saving us a significant amount of computational work. To train these photos on our computer, however, takes a significant amount of time—days, even months. Using transfer learning, we can modify the last few layers and still get great precision. Different layers of MobileNet-V2 are used as input features for experiments and evaluations of the suggested architecture, and the proposed one has achieved the highest score on test data. It optimizes using the mean square error as the cost function.

2.5 CNN with MobileNet-V2 Architecture Using a Transfer Learning Approach

Image-Net is a huge data collection that includes many pictures. Pre-training a model on the Image-Net database entails the usage of several convolutional neural network designs, such as Res-Net, Inception, MobileNet-V2, etc. The photos may be sorted into several categories using the model's pre-established rules, such as "bus," "face," "pen," "pencil," "fish," "animal," "car," "table," "tree," "ball," etc. MobileNet-V2 has 53 complex layers. This detects things using a feature extractor. Because it requires fewer parameters and runs faster, MobileNet-V2 is helpful because it improves accuracy in most cases. The ImageNet dataset is first used for pre-training a network on a large number of pictures; this allows the network to improve its performance when working with a smaller dataset that has a dense layer. Finally, by adjusting the last layer of the data set, the model is prepared to train on the CIFE dataset. When compared to standard

CNN, it provides more precision. Using MobileNet-V2, we can observe that a technique known as transfer learning is being used here.

3 Result and Discussion

30,968 photos from the Candid Image Facial Expression Data collection were utilized for training. Accuracy was employed as the basis for performance evaluation based on the confusion matrix. Measures of relative and sharable performance are needed to determine the relative superiority of an algorithm or method. Evaluating any approach that includes a testing and training set is a significant challenge. The newfound inconsistency hampers its model performance. Falsenegative (FN), false-positive (FP), true-negative (TN), and true-positive (TP) values make up the confusion matrix-based performance measures. These factors may affect the performance assessment in different ways. Figure 4 shows the Basic framework of A-MobileNet network model.

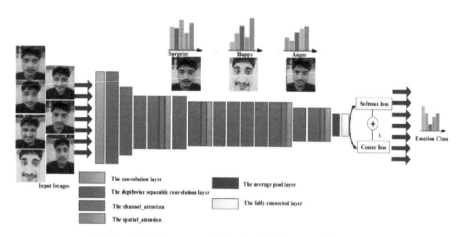

Fig. 4. Basic framework of A-MobileNet network model.

The number of correct predictions a model makes is one way to measure how good it is. Online FER picture data sets are designed to categorize six or seven common facial expressions. In order to analyze human steadiness in real-world settings, we require a data collection of candid photos or non-posed photographs to train and test the models. Here at CIFE, we've compiled a data collection [1] of candid photos of people showing their true emotions. This set of data shows seven different emotions: happiness, shock, anger, contempt, fear, indifference, and sadness. To train and evaluate our system, we utilized the CIFE data set, which contains 23,564 photographs of natural expressions. The total number of angry, disgusted, fearful, happy, neutral, sad, and surprised samples is 1904, 975, 1381, 3636, 2381, 2485, and 1481, respectively, in 2005, fearful, happy, neutral, sad, and surprised samples is 1904, 975, 1381, 3636, 2381, 2485, and 1481, respectively, in 2005. Figure 5 displays various examples of the CIFE dataset. In the end, we gathered 44,224 photos throughout the seven categories. The remaining 70%

(30,968) of the photos were utilized for training, while 30% (13256) were used for testing. Most of the emotions are candid, although some of the images were taken at random from the internet. Utilizing various collection methods, we have amassed a CIFE data set consisting of photos of genuine facial expressions found on the Internet.

The validation accuracy results for various CNN architecture epoch counts are shown in Fig. 6. Accuracy is improving, and it now extends to the 100th epoch. Because the 100th epoch is the last step in achieving maximum accuracy with this model, it decreases thereafter, reaching a low of 61.76 percent accuracy. Furthermore, the same CIFE data set has been used for the suggested MobileNetV2 architecture model, which achieves a higher accuracy rate than the basic CNN architecture in a short amount of time. There was a peak in accuracy at 60 epochs, after which the model began to behave poorly. The validation accuracy results for the MobileNet-V2 architecture at various epoch counts are shown in Fig. 7. There has been an improvement in precision up to the 60th epoch. As of the 60th epoch and beyond, it has been declining. This model's best performance reaches an accuracy of 79.56%. A comparison of the basic CNN and MobileNetV2 architectures for emotion detection from facial expression recognition systems is shown in Fig. 8.

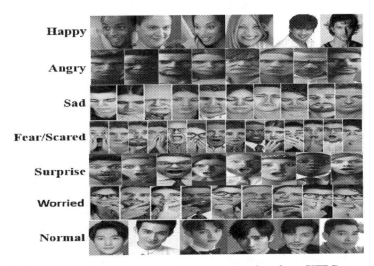

Fig. 5. Sample of seven emotions with facial expressions from CIFE Data set.

We have shown that one model is superior to the other by comparing the two indepth. Our goal is to determine which of two models provides the most reliable results, so we are exploring both. For example, in the 50th epoch, the accuracy provided by the standard CNN architecture is only 58.56%, whereas the accuracy provided by the MobileNet-V2 technique is 78.56%. The greatest accuracy of this model was achieved by simple CNN in the 100th epoch, at 61.76 percent.

Meanwhile, MobileNet-peak V2's accuracy was about 79.56% at the 60th epoch. In a short amount of time, it can outperform standard CNN in terms of accuracy. There are a total of 3,266,951 parameters in the model of the MobileNet-V2 architecture, of which

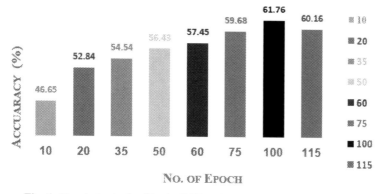

Fig. 6. Result Analysis of basic CNN at the point of the accuracy level.

4,232,839 are tunable. There are a total of 9,997,639 parameters and a maximum of 9,997,639 that can be trained in a standard CNN. MobileNet-V2 quickly outperformed baseline CNN in terms of accuracy. In this study, the MobileNet-V2 architectural model was looked at to see how well and quickly it could tell what emotions people were feeling.

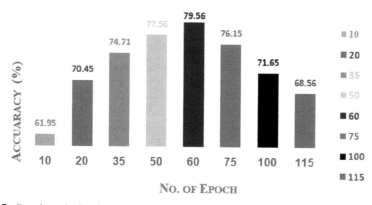

Fig. 7. Result analysis of MobileNet-V2 model at the point of the accuracy level visually

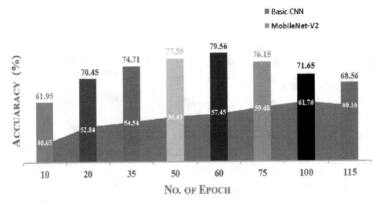

Fig. 8. Result analysis between basic CNN and MobileNet-V2 model at the point of the accuracy level visually

4 Conclusion

To the best of our knowledge, this report presents the first research on emotion identification from natural photos using the MobileNet-V2 model. Emotion recognition in humans captured on video or audio using deep learning architectures has the potential to become an important area of study. Additionally, the MobileNet-V2 model was employed throughout development; however, other architectures like GRU and LSTM may also be tried out. This study suggests using convolutional neural networks (CNNs) to identify stress based on facial expressions. In CNN, a novel algorithm is proposed by combining several types of algorithms and features. One of the characteristics included in CNN for face detection is the Haar Cascade Frontal Face feature. In addition to using MobileNet V2 as a pre-trained model for feature extraction, we are fine-tuning the model using TensorFlow. The Inception V2 model has been shown to be good at figuring out a person's gender from how they look. The suggested model will be the most extensive study to date on the categorization of emotions, and it will improve the intelligence and usability of future projects. Identifying human emotions is a challenge in FER that has the potential to benefit both the public and the government. In addition, we employed cutting-edge CNN and MobileNet-V2 architectures for our solution. Using the CIFE data set culled from the aforementioned scholarly works (e.g., [1]), the study experiments with and implements the emotion detection classification approach. To rigorously evaluate and finetune our approach, we compared the performance of a standard CNN with that of the MobileNet-V2 model. By comparing many models, we found that the MobileNet-V2 model using the transfer learning technique provided the best results for identifying human emotions.

5 Future Work

Future studies will focus on identifying causes for misclassified expression data, examining the finer points of information for individual expressions, and refining the model's capacity for making accurate classifications. MobileNet V2's bottleneck encodes intermediate inputs and outputs, and its inner layer captures a model's ability to transition between low-level notions like pixels and high-level descriptors like picture categories. Training may be completed quickly and accurately thanks to the usage of conventional residual connections. Pointwise convolution and depthwise smoothing are still used in MobileNet V2. Depth-first and point-to-point convolution are used in MobileNet V2. In addition, MobileNet V2 now includes two new features: the first linear bottleneck and the ability to create shortcut connections between bottlenecks. They have performed well when stacked against more conventional categorization methods. Nevertheless, as individuals continue to deepen the network, the enormous storage strain and computational cost imposed by the model calculations have started to restrict the application area of the deep learning models. Conventional CNN cannot be implemented on mobile or embedded systems because of its prohibitive memory and computing requirements. Google suggested the MobileNetV1 deep neural network for this purpose. It is a convolutional neural network, but the model size, number of trainable parameters, and number of calculations are much smaller, making it ideal for mobile devices. It makes the most of its computational resources and significantly enhances the model's reliability. MobileNet V2 results are compared to those of the other CNN models. Information security issues persist in the sectors that create face expression exploration systems, notwithstanding their fast growth. A primary function of this system is to classify users into different categories based on their facial expressions. People's odd behavior, such as wearing a mask during a pandemic or otherwise hiding their identity, might make it difficult to identify them. Misuse of these items might lead to severe complications. That is undoubtedly a difficult task. This system is quite helpful in resolving this issue. With this identification method, we can work with any video system. Using facial expressions as a classification system, CC cameras are the most reliable choice in a public space. So, several nations use CC-camera projects like this to keep their roads in good shape. Through our analysis, we will help authors better categorize their readers.

References

1. Sayeedunnisa, S., Hegde, N.P., Khan, K.U.R.: Sarcasm detection: a contemporary research affirmation of recent literature. ECS Trans. **107**(1), 2419–2426 (2022). https://doi.org/10.1149/10701.2419ecst
2. McElroy-Heltzel, S.E.: Epistemic virtues and vices as attitudes: implications for empirical measures and virtue interventions. J. Philosoph. Res. **47**, 83–94 (2022). https://doi.org/10.5840/jpr20221027195
3. Smith, L.: Heritage, the power of the past, and the politics of (mis)recognition. J. Theory Soc. Behav. **52**(4), 623–642 (2022). https://doi.org/10.1111/jtsb.12353
4. Lozada, F.T., Riley, T.N., Catherine, E., Brown, D.W.: Black emotions matter: understanding the impact of racial oppression on Black youth's emotional development: dismantling systems of racism and oppression during adolescence. J. Res. Adolescence **32**(1), 13–33 (2022). https://doi.org/10.1111/jora.12699

5. Puckett, J.A., et al.: Transgender and gender diverse individuals' daily experiences of rumination. Am. J. Orthopsych. (2022)
6. Araneta, J., Ingilan, S.: Pragmatic functions of formulaic expressions in Cebuano. Southeastern Philippines J. Res. Develop. **27**(2), 61–83 (2022)
7. Argyriou, K.: Trajectories towards affirmation: gender identity in mental health services after the ICD-11. Quaderns de Psicologia **24**(2), e1821–e1821 (2022)
8. Goldbach, C., et al.: Resisting trans medicalization: Body satisfaction and social contextual factors as predictors of sexual experiences among trans feminine and nonbinary individuals. J. Sex Res. 1–12 (2022)
9. Łakuta, P., et al.: Enhancing well-being and alleviating depressive symptoms in people with HIV/AIDS: An intervention based on if–then plans with self-affirming cognitions. Appl. Psychol. Health Well-Being (2022)
10. Palama, A., et al.: The cross-modal transfer of emotional information from voices to faces in 5-, 8-and 10-year-old children and adults: an eye-tracking study. Emotion **22.4**, 725 (2022)
11. Peng, W., et al.: FADO: Feedback-Aware Double COntrolling Network for Emotional Support Conversation. arXiv preprint arXiv:2211.00250 (2022)
12. Carbon, C.-C., Held, M.J., Schütz, A.: Reading emotions in faces with and without masks is relatively independent of extended exposure and individual difference variables. Front. Psychol. **13** (2022). https://doi.org/10.3389/fpsyg.2022.856971
13. Qi, Y., Zhou, C., Chen, Y.: NA-Resnet: neighbor block and optimized attention module for global-local feature extraction in facial expression recognition. Multimedia Tools Appl. **82**(11), 16375–16393 (2022). https://doi.org/10.1007/s11042-022-14191-2
14. Seager van Dyk, I., Aldao, A., Pachankis, J.E.: Coming out under fire: the role of minority stress and emotion regulation in sexual orientation disclosure. PLOS ONE **17**(5), e0267810 (2022). https://doi.org/10.1371/journal.pone.0267810
15. Lazar, M., Miron-Spektor, E., Mueller, J.S.: Love at first insight: an attachment perspective on early-phase idea selection. Organ. Behav. Hum. Decis. Process. **172**, 104168 (2022)
16. Zhao, D., et al.: An attentive and adaptive 3D CNN for automatic pulmonary nodule detection in CT image. Expert Syst. Appl. **211**, 118672 (2023). https://doi.org/10.1016/j.eswa.2022.118672
17. Asia, A.-O., et al.: Detection of diabetic retinopathy in retinal fundus images using CNN classification models. Electronics **11**(17), 2740 (2022). https://doi.org/10.3390/electronics11172740
18. Ouni, S., Fkih, F., Omri, M.N.: BERT- and CNN-based TOBEAT approach for unwelcome tweets detection. Soc. Network Anal. Mining **12**(1) (2022). https://doi.org/10.1007/s13278-022-00970-0
19. Gonçalves, C.B., Souza, J.R., Fernandes, H.: CNN architecture optimization using bio-inspired algorithms for breast cancer detection in infrared images. Comput. Biol. Med. **142**, 105205 (2022). https://doi.org/10.1016/j.compbiomed.2021.105205
20. Yu, K., et al.: Comparison of classical methods and mask R-CNN for automatic tree detection and mapping using UAV imagery. remote sensing **14.2**, 295 (2022)
21. Kadek Sastrawan, I., Bayupati, I.P.A., Arsa, D.M.S.: Detection of fake news using deep learning CNN–RNN based methods. ICT Express **8**(3), 396–408 (2022). https://doi.org/10.1016/j.icte.2021.10.003
22. Laguna, A.B., Krystian, M.: Key. Net: keypoint detection by handcrafted and learned CNN filters revisited. IEEE Trans. Pattern Anal. Mach. Intell. (2022)
23. Khan, A., et al.: CNN-based smoker classification and detection in smart city application. Sensors **22.3**, 892 (2022)
24. Yang, J., et al.: CodnNet: a lightweight CNN architecture for detection of COVID-19 infection. Appl. Soft Comput. **130**, 109656 (2022)

25. Agarwal, A., et al.: Enhanced iris presentation attack detection via contraction-expansion CNN. Pattern Recogn. Lett. **159**, 61–69 (2022)
26. Hsia, C.-H., et al.: Mask R-CNN with new data augmentation features for smart detection of retail products. Appl. Sci. 12.6, 2902 (2022)

Hand-Written Devanagri Character Recognition Using Convolutional Neural Network in Python with Tensorflow

Prakash Anand[1(✉)], Piyush Ranjan[1], Priyanka Srivastava[2], and Deepak Kumar[3]

[1] Jharkhand Rai University, Kamre, Ranchi, Jharkhand, India
prakash.anand@sbu.ac.in
[2] Sarala Birla University, Mahilong, Ranchi, Jharkhand, India
[3] TARGET Corporation in India, HebbalBangaluru, India

Abstract. One of the most difficult fields in computer sciences over the past few decades has been artificial intelligence, which gives robots human-like abilities. One of the main goals of AI is to enable machines to see, understand, and read text. Although much effort has been done in this area, the intricacy of the problem has not yet been fully resolved. A good text recognizer can be used for a wide range of practical and commercial purposes, such as automating the post office or looking for information in scanned books. The process of recognition also involves determining the distance between the feature vector of the input image and the one that is recorded in the database, then producing the symbol with the least amount of divergence. Neural networks give total independence of character set and recognition process in contrast to this. This neural network is initially trained using several sample photos for each letter of the alphabet. The input image is then directly fed into the neural network throughout the recognition process, and the output is the identified symbol. The benefit of neural networks is that the character set's domain can be simply expanded; all one needs to do is train the network over the new character set. The fact that neural networks are particularly noise-resistant is another benefit. In order to test CNN's performance, we employed the Modified National Institute of Standards and Technology (MNIST) Devanagari dataset.

Keywords: Handwritten digit recognition · Deep Convolutional Neural Network (DCNN) · Deep learning · MNIST dataset · Epochs · Hidden Layers · ConvNet

1 Introduction

To create more intelligent devices, the engineers are using deep learning [1] and machine learning techniques. A human learns to perform a task by regularly practicing and repeating it until the ability is retained in memory. The brain's neurons automatically fire when this occurs, enabling them to complete the learned task quickly. This and deep learning resemble each other somewhat [2, 3]. It uses several neural network topologies for diverse problems. An image's conversion to letter codes for use with a computer or text-processing software is the initial stage in an off-line handwriting recognition system [6].

© The Author(s), under exclusive license to Springer Nature Switzerland AG 2023
R. K. Tiwari and G. Sahoo (Eds.): ICAII 2022, CCIS 1822, pp. 122–137, 2023.
https://doi.org/10.1007/978-3-031-37303-9_10

Handwritten Devanagri character recognition is the ability of computers to recognise human-written numbers on paper. Because handwritten digits are erroneous and can be produced in a variety of ways, it is challenging for the machine to process them.An answer to this problem uses an image of a Devanagri character to recognise the digit that is present in the image, which is called "handwritten Devanagri character recognition."

Face recognition, image segmentation, and object detection in ImageNet are just a few of the recent challenging and effective computer learning tasks that Convolutional Neural Networks (CNN) have been a key component in.As a result, we choose to use CNN to take on our difficult photo categorization duties. One of its important academic and industrial uses is the recognition of handwriting devnagari characters. Because one of CNN's key academic and industrial applications is the recognition of handwriting devnagari characters, we choose to employ it to handle our difficult picture categorization problems.

A Convolutional Neural Network (ConvNet/CNN) is a Deep Learning method that can take an input image, give various elements and objects in the image importance (learnable weights and biases), and distinguish between them. Compared to other classification methods, a ConvNet requires far less pre-processing. Contrary to basic techniques, where filters must be hand-engineered, ConvNets may learn these filters and properties with sufficient training.The organisation of the Visual Cortex has an impact on the development of a ConvNet, which is similar to the connectivity network of neurons in the human brain. The Receptive Field, a constrained area of the visual field, is the only part of it where individual neurons are responsive to stimuli. There are several overlapping fields like this that make up the total visual field.

The enormous variety in strokes from person to person is one of the biggest obstacles to handwritten Devanagari character recognition.Handwritten character recognition a person's style also changes and is inconsistent from time to time.

MNIST Database

A dataset of handwritten numbers can be found in the Modified National Institute of Standards and Technology database (MNIST) [4]. Different image processing algorithms can be trained using it. The data files train and test.csv. CSV files include handwritten Devnagari 46 characters in grayscale images.The combined height and breadth of each image are 28 pixels, making a total of 784 pixels. Greater numbers correspond to darker pixels, and each pixel has a single value that indicates how light or dark it is. The training data set is made up of 1025 columns with an integer for this pixel value that spans from 0 to 255, inclusive (train.csv). The first column, labelled "label," contains the user-drawn devanagri character [7, 8]. The remaining columns contain the pixel values of the corresponding image.The names of the pixel columns in the training set are pixels, where x is an integer from 0 to 1025 inclusive. In order to locate this pixel on the image, let's assume that we have decomposed x as $x = I * 28 + j$, where I and j are numbers between 0 and 27, inclusive. Pixels are thus located in row I and column j of a 28 by 28 matrix (indexing by zero).

Deep Convolutional Neural Network (DCCN)

Convolutional neural networks (CNNs) are a form of deep neural networks used largely for image recognition analysis in the field of deep learning. Convolution is a particularly special approach that is used by convolutional neural networks. Third function that shows how the shape of one function is being affected or changed by the other function is produced as an output of the mathematical operation known as convolution [9]. Multiple artificial neuronal layers make up convolutional neural networks (CNNs). Artificial neurons are mathematical operations that add up a large number of inputs and produce an activation value as their output. They resemble the neuron cells that the human brain uses to transmit different sensory input signals and other responses.Each CNN neuron's behavior depends on the weights assigned to it. After being given the values (of the pixel), the artificial neurons in a CNN may recognize a variety of visual characteristics and details [11].

When given an input image, each inner layer of a CNN generates a unique activation map. Activation maps draw attention to the important parts of the input image. Each CNN neuron normally takes input in the form of a collection of pixels, multiplies those values (colors) by the weights it has, adds them all up, and then inputs them using the appropriate activation function. The first (or maybe bottom) layer of the CNN can typically recognize the different characteristics of the input image, such as edges that run horizontally, vertically, and diagonally. Using the output of the first layer as an input, the second layer extracts more complex elements from the input image, such as corner and edge combinations. As one moves deeper into convolutional neural networks, layers begin to distinguish numerous higher-level features [5], including objects, faces, etc (Fig. 1).

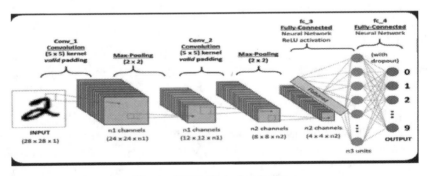

Fig. 1. CNN's Basic Architecture

2 Literature Review

For classification, neural networks, KNN (K-nearest neighbours), and SVM (Support vector machine) are frequently employed. But I. K. Sethi and B. Chatterjee [6] released the initial study paper in 1976. Research on handwriting Devnagri character recognition is ongoing in academia. Convolutional neural networks have been extensively studied with the goal of realising handwritten Devnagari character recognition [12, 13, 14, 15]. Real-time handwriting recognition, online and offline recognition, postage address interpretation, bank check processing, and writer recognition are just a few of the many current study subjects.The neural network-based Devnagari character recognition has been the subject of by Duddela Sai Prashantha, R Vasanth Kumar Mehtaa, Nisha Sharma [13].

The usage of deep neural networks (DNN). According to the model, DNN has the highest accuracy (96.08%). They have also shown mistake rates and contrasted execution times for different values that could seem similar [6]. We present new model architectures by integrating many elegant CNNs from the past. [10]. Our test findings on benchmark datasets show a significant performance improvement over current methods, highlighting the unmistakable benefit of our technology.

3 Modeling of Convolutional Neural Network to Classify Handwritten Devanagri Characters

3.1 Importing Libraries

Import Numpy

The key Python module for scientific computing is called NumPy. A multidimensional array object, many derivative objects (including masked arrays and matrices), and a variety of functions for quick operations on arrays are all provided by this Python module. Discrete Fourier Transforms, core Statistics Operations, Basic Linear Algebra, Random Simulation, and many more are examples of these processes. The core of the NumPy library is the ndarray object [15]. This includes homogenous n-dimensional arrays of various data types, and many operations are performed quickly using generated code. Matrix operations, the Fourier transform, and functions for working with linear algebra are also included. With NumPy, array objects will be up to 50 times faster than Python lists typically are.

Import Pandas

Pandas is the name of the most popular open-source Python library for data science, data analysis, and machine learning tasks. It's built on top of Numpy, a distinct multi-dimensional array-supporting library. One of the most popular data wrangling packages in the Python ecosystem, Pandas, works nicely with a range of other data science modules. Pandas is commonly included in all Python distributions, including those that are included with your operating system and those that are purchased separately, such as Active Python from Active State [16]. To modify data sets, utilize the Pandas library in Python. It offers tools for data exploration, cleaning, analysis, and manipulation.

Import matplotlib.pyplot

Matplotlib is a cross-platform data visualisation and graphical charting package for Python and its numerical extension NumPy. It thus offers a potent open-source alternative to MATLAB. Graphs can be included into GUI applications thanks to the matplotlib APIs (Application Programming Interfaces) [17].

The majority of the time, a visual data plot may be produced with only a few lines of code using a Python matplotlib script. The Matplotlib scripting layer supports the following two APIs:

i) The pyplot API's hierarchy of Python code objects is headed by matplotlib.pyplot.
ii) A set of objects that can be assembled more quickly than with Pyplot thanks to an OO (Object-Oriented) API. This API enables direct access to the backend layers of Matplotlib.

Import Seaborn

For plotting statistical visualizations, Python's Seaborn visualization library is amazing. It provides wonderful default color schemes and styles to improve the aesthetic appeal of statistics charts. It is built around the Matplotlib toolbox and has a close relationship with Pandas data structures.

With Seaborn, data exploration and understanding will be centered on visualization [17]. It provides dataset-oriented APIs that let us transition between different visual representations of the same variables for a better understanding of the dataset.

Import Colorama

It is possible to print colourful text in the terminal using any of the many built-in modules and libraries that Python has. Colorama is the name of one of the built-in Python modules for displaying text in different colours. It is used to simplify the code's reading. This module provides three different text-for-coloring formatting options. These are Back, Fore, and Style. You can change the text's style and background or foreground colour using this module.

From keras.utils.np_utils import to_categorical

It is possible to print colorful text in the terminal using any of the many built-in modules and libraries that Python has. Colorama is the name of one of the built-in Python modules for displaying text in different colors. It is used to simplify the code's reading. This module provides three different text-for-coloring formatting options. These are Back, Fore, and Style. You can change the text's style and background or foreground colour using this module.

It cannot handle low-level computations; hence it requires the Backend library to resolve them. The backend library enables it to run on TensorFlow, CNTK, or Theano as a high-level API wrapper for the low-level API [18].

The Keras numpy utility package provides tools for interacting with numpy arrays. Using the approach to categorical transformation, a numpy array (or) vector of integers representing multiple categories can be converted into a numpy array (or) matrix with binary values and columns equal to the number of categories in the data ().

From keras.models Import Sequential

An API that works well with neural network models related to artificial intelligence and machine learning is the keras sequential API, which deals with layer ordering or sequencing inside a model. In essence, it makes it possible for neural network layers and the Keras API or Keras library to work together seamlessly. Keras sequential is one modelling strategy or model [18]. This model just takes one input and predicts one outcome, as its name suggests. This kind of approach can handle straightforward and layer-based problems fairly well.

The core idea of Sequential API is to simply arrange the Keras layers in a sequential manner, hence the name. Data flows from one layer to the next in the intended order until it eventually reaches the output layer in the majority of ANNs, which also include layers that are ordered sequentially.

From keras.layers import Dense, Conv2D, Flatten

Keras dense is one of the often used layers in the keras model or neural network, where all connections are made very deeply. In other words, the input to the dense layer comes from all the neurons in the preceding layer of the network. The 2D convolution layer known as Keras Conv2D helps create a tensor of outputs by fusing a convolution kernel with the input of other layers [18].The input is flattened using flatten. For instance, the layer's output shape will be (batch size, 2,2) if flatten is applied to a layer with that input shape (batch size, 4).

Import Tensorflow

TensorFlow is a full-featured open-source framework for creating machine learning applications. It is a symbolic math toolbox that uses dataflow and differentiable program-ming to perform a number of operations aimed towards deep neural network inference and training. It lets developers to create machine learning applications using a variety of tools, frameworks, and community resources [19].

The most well-known deep learning library at the moment is TensorFlow from Google.

A full-featured machine learning platform Find solutions to expedite machine learning tasks at every stage of your business.

3.2 Data Loading and Overview

Here we load train.csv and test.csv the data set is in pixel form here 0 means the pixel is not marked dark line and the marked pixel is given the RGB value between 0 to 255 as indicated in Fig. 2

	pixel_0000	pixel_0001	pixel_0002	pixel_0003	pixel_0004	pixel_0005	pixel_0006	pixel_0007	pixel_0008	pixel_0009	...	pixel_1015	pixel_1016	pixel_1017
0	0	0	0	0	0	0	0	0	0	0	...	0	0	0
1	0	0	0	0	0	0	0	0	0	0	...	0	0	0
2	0	0	0	0	0	0	0	0	0	0	...	0	0	0
3	0	0	0	0	0	0	0	0	0	0	...	0	0	0
4	0	0	0	0	0	0	0	0	0	0	...	0	0	0

5 rows × 1025 columns

Fig. 2. MNIST Data Set

3.3 Splitting the Data Into Training and Testing Sets

Overfitting is a problem that arises frequently during model training. When a model performs exceptionally well on the data we used to train it, but fails to generalise well to new, unexplored data points, this phenomena happens. This may occur for a variety of reasons, including data noise or the model learning to predict particular inputs rather than the predictive factors that may help it make accurate predictions.

Usually, a model's likelihood of being overfitted increases with model complexity.

Overfitting is a problem that arises frequently during model training. When a model performs exceptionally well on the data we used to train it, but fails to generalise well to new, unexplored data points, this phenomena happens. This may occur for a variety of reasons, including data noise or the model learning to predict particular inputs rather than the predictive factors that may help it make accurate predictions. Usually, a model's likelihood of being overfitted increases with model complexity.

The most popular method for finding these kinds of problems is to create several data samples for the model's training and testing. In this way, we can utilise the training set to develop our model and the testing set as a set of data points to assess how well the model generalises to fresh, unexplored data.

Let's generate a fictitious dataset that will be used for demonstration purposes in order to create training and testing sets. In the examples that follow, we'll assume that we have a dataset that is a panda DataFrame that is kept in memory. Each of the 150 data points in the iris dataset has four attributes (Fig. 3).

```
import pandas as pd
from sklearn.datasets import load_iris

iris_data = load_iris()
df = pd.DataFrame(iris_data.data, columns=iris_data.feature_names)
print(df)

#      sepal length (cm)  sepal width (cm)  petal length (cm)  petal width (cm)
# 0                  5.1               3.5                1.4               0.2
# 1                  4.9               3.0                1.4               0.2
# 2                  4.7               3.2                1.3               0.2
# 3                  4.6               3.1                1.5               0.2
# 4                  5.0               3.6                1.4               0.2
# ..                 ...               ...                ...               ...
# 145                6.7               3.0                5.2               2.3
# 146                6.3               2.5                5.0               1.9
# 147                6.5               3.0                5.2               2.0
# 148                6.2               3.4                5.4               2.3
# 149                5.9               3.0                5.1               1.8
#
# [150 rows x 4 columns]
```

Fig. 3. Example Splitting data set

We will assume that we require an 80:20 ratio for training to testing sets in the examples that follow.

Using Pandas

Utilizing the sample() method of pandas DataFrames is the first choice.

Provide a random selection of objects from an object axis.

To ensure consistency, use random_state.

The initial training set is produced by selecting a sample of 0.8 from the total number of rows in the pandas DataFrame. To ensure that results may be repeated, take note that we also define random state, which corresponds to the seed. Then, we simply remove the appropriate indices from the original DataFrame, which are now a part of the training set, to produce the testing set (Fig. 4).

```
1    training_data = df.sample(frac=0.8, random_state=25)
2    testing_data = df.drop(training_data.index)
3
4    print(f"No. of training examples: {training_data.shape[0]}")
5    print(f"No. of testing examples: {testing_data.shape[0]}")
6
7    # No. of training examples: 120
8    # No. of testing examples: 30
```

Fig. 4. Example Splitting data set

As we can see, there are 120 examples in the training set, which is in line with the portion we asked for when sampling the initial modelling DataFrame. The testing set was filled with the final 30 samples.

3.4 Showing All the Output Classes

Here we have the different hindi characters that we are goint to recognize. Those are character_01_ka' 'character_02_kha' 'character_03_ga' 'character_04_gha' 'character_05_kna' 'character_06_cha' 'character_07_chha' 'character_08_ja' 'character_09_jha' 'character_10_yna' 'character_11_taamatar' 'character_12_thaa' 'character_13_daa' 'character_14_dhaa' 'character_15_adna' 'character_16_tabala' 'character_17_tha' 'character_18_da' 'character_19_dha' 'character_20_na' 'character_21_pa' 'character_22_pha' 'character_23_ba' 'character_24_bha' 'character_25_ma' 'character_26_yaw' 'character_27_ra' 'character_28_la' 'character_29_waw' 'character_30_motosaw' 'character_31_petchiryakha' 'character_32_patalosaw' 'character_33_ha' 'character_34_chhya' 'character_35_tra' 'character_36_gya' 'digit_0' 'digit_1' 'digit_2' 'digit_3' 'digit_4' 'digit_5' 'digit_6' 'digit_7' 'digit_8' 'digit_9'Number of characters: 46 (Fig. 5).

```
All characters: ['character_01_ka' 'character_02_kha' 'character_03_ga' 'character_04_gha'
 'character_05_kna' 'character_06_cha' 'character_07_chha'
 'character_08_ja' 'character_09_jha' 'character_10_yna'
 'character_11_taamatar' 'character_12_thaa' 'character_13_daa'
 'character_14_dhaa' 'character_15_adna' 'character_16_tabala'
 'character_17_tha' 'character_18_da' 'character_19_dha' 'character_20_na'
 'character_21_pa' 'character_22_pha' 'character_23_ba' 'character_24_bha'
 'character_25_ma' 'character_26_yaw' 'character_27_ra' 'character_28_la'
 'character_29_waw' 'character_30_motosaw' 'character_31_petchiryakha'
 'character_32_patalosaw' 'character_33_ha' 'character_34_chhya'
 'character_35_tra' 'character_36_gya' 'digit_0' 'digit_1' 'digit_2'
 'digit_3' 'digit_4' 'digit_5' 'digit_6' 'digit_7' 'digit_8' 'digit_9']
Number of characters: 46
```

Fig. 5. Dataset labelling

3.5   Converting DataFrame Having Pixel Values into Numpy Arrays

The use of NumPy arrays when working with pandas DataFrames may occasionally be advantageous. The latter appears to use less memory, especially when processing data through certain sophisticated mathematical calculations. Let's construct an example pandas DataFrame that we will use to show a few possible approaches that may be taken to turn it into a numpy array (Fig. 6).

```
import pandas as pd

df = pd.DataFrame(
    [
        (1, 'A', 10.5, True),
        (2, 'B', 10.0, False),
        (3, 'A', 19.2, False),
        (4, 'C', 21.1, True),
        (5, 'A', 15.5, True),
        (6, 'C', 14.9, False),
        (7, 'C', 13.1, True),
        (8, 'B', 12.5, False),
        (9, 'C', 11.2, False),
        (10, 'A', 31.4, False),
        (11, 'D', 10.4, True),
    ],
    columns=['colA', 'colB', 'colC', 'colD']
)

print(df)
    colA  colB   colC   colD
0      1     A   10.5   True
1      2     B   10.0  False
2      3     A   19.2  False
3      4     C   21.1   True
4      5     A   15.5   True
5      6     C   14.9  False
6      7     C   13.1   True
7      8     B   12.5  False
8      9     C   11.2  False
9     10     A   31.4  False
10    11     D   10.4   True
```

Fig. 6. Example dataset of conversion into numpy arrays

Using Pandas.DataFrame.To_numpy()

The pandas.DataFrame.to numpy() method is our first choice for turning a pandas DataFrame into a NumPy array (Fig. 7).

```
ndarray = df.to_numpy()

print(ndarray)

array([[1, 'A', 10.5, True],
       [2, 'B', 10.0, False],
       [3, 'A', 19.2, False],
       [4, 'C', 21.1, True],
       [5, 'A', 15.5, True],
       [6, 'C', 14.9, False],
       [7, 'C', 13.1, True],
       [8, 'B', 12.5, False],
       [9, 'C', 11.2, False],
       [10, 'A', 31.4, False],
       [11, 'D', 10.4, True]], dtype=object)
```

Fig. 7. Example dataset of conversion into numpy arrays

As previously indicated, the to records() method will produce an object of type nympy as opposed to to numpy(). Recarray:

As a result of translating the Hindi MNIST dataset, we have:

```
Shape of Training Image array: (73600, 32, 32)
Shape of Testing Image array: (18400, 32, 32)
```

3.6 Visualizing Some Training Images Along with their Labels

A dataset of images and labels forms the basis of the traditional deep learning computer vision project. You would choose from a suitable selection of deep learning models depending on the kind of labels you have and the task you want to complete, such as picture classification, object identification, or image segmentation. As seen in the picture, we exhibit the distribution of output classes that include the label encoding of the Hindi characters in the specified output class (Figs. 8, 9).

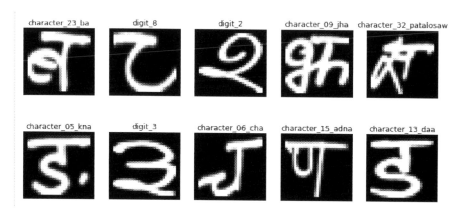

Fig. 8. Devanagari characters with its labels

3.7 Configuring TPU if Available

Tensor Processing Units (TPUs), a specially designed ASIC by Google, are used to speed up machine-learning tasks. You can use Cloud TPU to conduct your training tasks on the AI Platform Training. You may control the TPU without having to do so yourself thanks to the job management interface provided by AI Platform Training. As an alternative, you can employ the AI Platform Training jobs API similarly to how you would for CPU- or GPU-based training.

You can get your models running on the Cloud TPU hardware with high-level TensorFlow APIs.

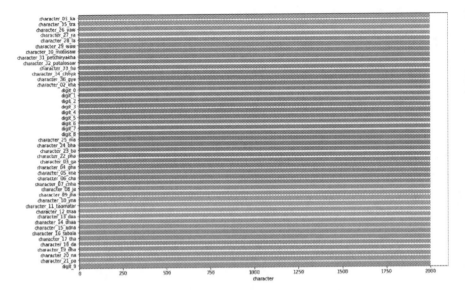

Fig. 9. Graph shows 2000 different styles of Devanagari characters

```
Running on CPU instead
Number of accelerators:   1
```

3.8 Building a CNN Model

The only requirement was that we create layers sequentially, starting with the input, while using the Keras Sequential API. The first layer is the convolutional (Conv2D) layer. It seems like a collection of teachable filters. It is set to 32 filters for the first two conv2D layers and 64 filters for the final two. Depending on the kernel size, each filter applies the kernel filter to a different portion of the image. The kernel filter matrix is applied to the entire image. Filters can be compared to image editing.CNN can extract information that is useful everywhere from these manipulated images (feature maps).

The second important layer in CNN is the pooling (MaxPool2D) layer. This layer just acts as a downsampling filter. It looks at the two adjacent pixels and then selects the maximum value. These are used to reduce overfitting and, to a lesser extent, computational cost. It is necessary to select the size of the area that is pooled each time; the more significant the down sampling, the greater the pooling dimension.CNN can combine local features and learn more global features of the image by combining convolutional and pooling layers.

With the regularisation method known as "dropout," a subset of the layer's nodes is randomly ignored for each training sample (their weights are assigned to zero). By discarding a portion of the network at random, this forces the network to learn features in a distributed manner. This approach also improves generalisation and reduces overfitting.Rectifier's max(0,x) activation function is "Relu." Using the rectifier activation function, the network is given nonlinearity.

The final feature maps are transformed into a single 1D vector using the flatten layer. Prior to deploying completely linked layers after several convolutional/maxpool layers, this flattening phase is required. In this step, we combine every local feature found in the earlier convolutional layers.

In order to develop a classifier, we ultimately used the properties of two tightly coupled entirely artificial neural network (ANN) layers. The probability distribution of each class's net outputs is contained in the final layer (dense(10,activation = "softmax")) (Fig. 10).

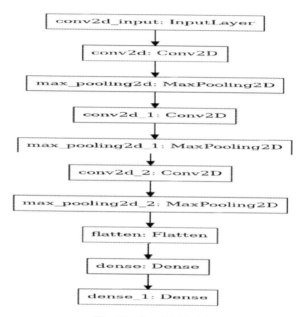

Fig. 10. Conv2D Model

When creating a CNN model, we start with a two-dimensional image, make a feature loopy pattern—either vertically or horizontally—and then use convolution to produce a two-dimensional feature map. Next, we employ Max pooling to filter the two-dimensional data in order to shorten the computation time. The data is then flattened after being converted from two dimensions to one (Fig. 11).

```
Model: "sequential"

Layer (type)                    Output Shape              Param #
================================================================
conv2d (Conv2D)                 (None, 30, 30, 32)        320

max_pooling2d (MaxPooling2D)    (None, 15, 15, 32)        0

conv2d_1 (Conv2D)               (None, 13, 13, 64)        18496

max_pooling2d_1 (MaxPooling2     (None, 6, 6, 64)          0

conv2d_2 (Conv2D)               (None, 4, 4, 64)          36928

flatten (Flatten)               (None, 1024)              0

dense (Dense)                   (None, 128)               131200

dense_1 (Dense)                 (None, 46)                5934
================================================================
Total params: 192,878
Trainable params: 192,878
Non-trainable params: 0
```

Fig. 11. Model Summary

3.9 Training the Model

A machine learning algorithm is trained using a dataset known as a training model. It consists of sets of relevant input data that affect the output as well as sample output data. In order to compare the processed output to the sample output, the training model is utilised to run the input data through the algorithm. The correlation's outcome is utilised to change the model.Model fitting is the term for this iterative procedure. For the model to be precise, the training dataset or validation dataset must be accurate.

Machine learning's model training procedure involves providing an machine learning algorithm with data in order to help it recognise and learn the best values for all relevant variables. There are many different kinds of machine learning models, but supervised and unsupervised learning are the most popular ones (Fig. 12).

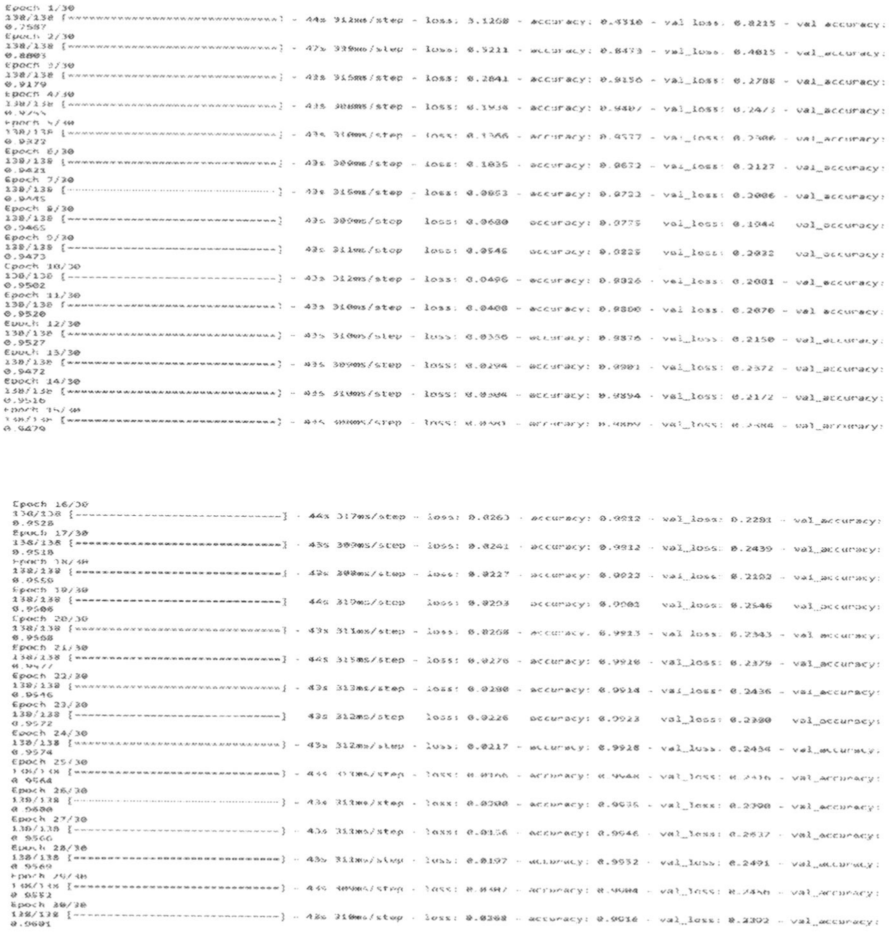

Fig. 12. Execution result

3.10 Model Evaluation and Accuracy

The graph below shows the accuracy and proportion of lost characters when reading the provided handwritten Devanagari characters using CNN's model (Fig. 13).

3.11 Visualizing Predictions on Testing Set

After evaluation of the MNIST devnagri dataset we predict the result of accuracy on testing dataset as shown in figure: (Fig. 14)

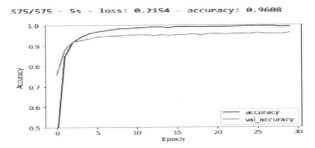

Fig. 13. Graph shows the level of accuracy

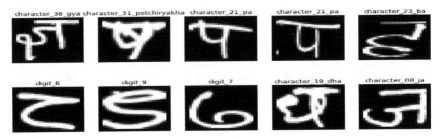

Fig. 14. Charaters shows the level of accuracy on the test data

4   Conclusion and Future Work

A model that can recognise handwritten devnagari characters is shown below. Character recognition and real-time handwriting analysis can be added later. The initial step in the broad field of artificial intelligence and computer vision is handwritten digit recognition. The outcomes of the experiment demonstrate that CNN performs significantly better than competing classifiers. The output accuracy can be increased by using hidden neurons and additional convolutional layers. It might completely do away with the need for typing. The digit recognition problem is a great approach to learn about neural networks and to build more complex deep learning techniques. In this article, CNN is shown to be the algorithm that accurately recognises handwritten devnagri characters.

Future development of applications using deep learning and machine learning algorithms is virtually unlimited. In the future, we can develop a hybrid or denser algorithm with a wider range of data than the current algorithms to address a number of problems. These algorithms will be used by both common users and high-level authorities in the future. These algorithms, for instance, can be used in hospitals to offer thorough medical diagnoses, treatments, and patient monitoring. They can be utilised in surveillance systems as well. Due to the above-mentioned distinction of the algorithms, these applications will be used by everyone from common users to high-level authorities. The advancement in this field can help us build a more open and transparent society by implementing these algorithms in high-level and practical applications.

References

1. Jürgen, S.: Deep learning in neural networks: an overview. Neural Netw. **61**, 85–117 (2015)
2. Ciregan, D., Meier, U., Schmidhuber, J.: Multi-column deep neural networks for image classification. In: Proceedings of the IEEE Conference on Computer Vision and Pattern Recognition (CVPR), Providence, RI, USA, 16–21 (2012)
3. Krizhevsky, A., Sutskever, I., Hinton, G.E.: Imagenet classification with deep convolutional neural networks. In: Proceedings of the Advances in Neural Information Processing Systems, Lake Tahoe, NV, USA, 3–8 (2012)
4. Lecun, Y., Bottou, L., Bengio, Y., Haffner, P.: Gradient-based learning applied to document recognition. Proc. IEEE , **86**, pp. 2278–2324 (1998)
5. Wang, X., Paliwal, K.K.: Feature extraction and dimensionality reduction algorithms and their applications in vowel recognition. Pattern Recognit. **36**, 2429–2439 (2003)
6. Sethi, I.K., Chatterjee, B.: Machine recognition of constrained hand printed Devanagari. Pattern Recogn. **9**(2), 69–75 (1977)
7. Hanmandlu, M., Murthy, O.V.R., Madasu, V.K.: Fuzzy model based recognition of handwritten Hindi characters. In: Proceedings of the 9th Biennial Conference of the Australian Pattern Recognition Society on Digital Image Computing Techniques and Applications, Glenelg, Australia, pp. 454–461 (2007)
8. Biswas, M., et al.: BanglaLekhaIsolated: a multi-purpose comprehensive dataset of Handwritten Bangla Isolated characters. Data in Brief. **12**, 103-107 (2017). https://doi.org/10.1016/j.dib.2017.03.035
9. Bhattacharya, U., Chaudhuri, B.B.: Handwritten numeral databases of Indian scripts and multistage recognition of mixed numerals. IEEE Trans. Pattern Anal. Mach. Intell. **31**(3), 444–457 (2008). https://doi.org/10.1109/TPAMI.2008.88
10. Abdel-hamid, O., Deng, L., Yu, D.: Exploring Convolutional Neural Network Structures and Optimization Techniques for Speech Recognition, pp. 3366-3370 (2013)
11. http://www.deeplearningbook.org/contents/convnets.html
12. Trier. D., Jain, A.K., Taxt, T.: Feature extraction methods for character recognition-a survey. Pattern recognition, **29**(4), 641- Duddela Sai Prashanth et al. / Procedia Computer Science 167 (2020) 2445–2457 2457 (1996)
13. Prashanth, D.S., Mehta, R.V.K., Sharma, N.: Procedia Computer Science 00 (2019) 000–000 13 662. [4] Oh, I. S., & Suen, C. Y. (1998). Distance features for neural network-based recognition of handwritten characters. International Journal on Document Analysis and Recognition, **1**(2), 73-88
14. Plamondon, R., Srihari, S.N.: Online and off-line handwriting recognition: a comprehensive survey. IEEE Trans. Pattern Anal. Mach. Intell. **22**(1), 63–84 (2000)
15. Van der Walt, S., Colbert, S., Varoquaux, G.: The numpy array: a structure for efficient numerical computation. Computing in Science & Eng. **13**, 2230 (2011). https://doi.org/10.1109/MCSE.2011.37
16. McKinney, W.: Pandas: A Python Data Analysis Library. http: //pandas.sourceforge.net
17. https://doi.org/10.1109/MCSE.2007.55
18. Chollet, F., et al.: Keras. GitHub (2015). https://github.com/fchollet/keras
19. Abadi, M., et al.:TensorFlow: Large-Scale Machine Learning on Heterogeneous Systems (2015). Software tensorflow.org

The Design and Development of Computerized Geogebra Mathematical Model for Painting Color Learning System

P. Kirubanantham[1], G. Arun Prasath[2], A. Saranya[3], and G. M. Karthik[4(✉)]

[1] Department of Computing Technologies, SRM Institute of Science and Technology, Kattankulathur, Chengalpattu, Chennai, Tamilnadu 603 203, India
kirubanp2@srmist.edu.in

[2] Department of Computer Science and Engineering, B V Raju Institute of Technology, Hyderabad, Telangana 502313, India
arunprasath.g@bvrit.ac.in

[3] Department of Computer Science and Engineering, SRM Institute of Science and Technology, Kattankulathur, Chengalpattu, Chennai, Tamilnadu 603 203, India
sa1096@srmist.edu.in

[4] School of Computer Science and Engineering, Vellore Institute of Technology, Vellore 632014, India
karthik.gm@vit.ac.in

Abstract. Mobile learning has seen widespread adoption in recent years, with schools, businesses, governments, and other organizations increasingly putting it to use. Its primary applications lie in the sectors of workplace training and campus network. The use of color goes back a very long way in human history, particularly in artistic expression. Every shade of color has a certain message and may be used in a variety of contexts. Color has a significant impact on people's lives, which in turn has an impact on people's feelings, which in turn has an impact on the caliber of our lives and our level of pleasure. Mobile learning is popular among users because of the many benefits it offers, including the absence of geographical constraints. Learners may learn in the few minutes they have available. Through the use of the Geogebra Mathematical Model, the purpose of the learning system is to instill in users an increased sensitivity to color and color matching, as well as a comprehension of color's role in everyday life and throughout history. On the basis of mobile learning and color research, this paper combines the benefits of these two methods and creates the painting color learning system to assist learners in providing an information platform for color learning, color match training, and instances. The purpose of this system is to help learners provide a platform for information regarding color learning, color match training, and instances. According to the findings of the study, the system stimulates the interest of the students in learning and encourages the enhancement of the quality of instruction.

Keywords: Computer Vision · Color Match Training · Dynamic Worksheets · Taylor Polynomial

R. K. Tiwari and G. Sahoo (Eds.): ICAII 2022, CCIS 1822, pp. 138–151, 2023.
https://doi.org/10.1007/978-3-031-37303-9_11

1 Introduction

The increasing use of technology in our daily lives drives math teachers to include technology into their lesson plans. In elementary education, technology may be utilized to make arithmetic teaching more immersive and concrete. Consequently, this helps students to achieve more success by using a more symbolic and abstract approach in the classroom. When considering computer vision in the context of mathematics instruction, explicit reference is made to computer-based cognitive aids. The relevance of the use of computers in mathematics teaching and learning is expanding to the point that it is now considered necessary and will provide the foundation for the growth of mathematics education. In addition to the fact that the efficacy of computer-assisted mathematics instruction in learning-teaching processes depends on a number of elements, it is vital for the success of the method to supply lesson software that is appropriate for educational aims and objectives. Given this, software becomes an essential element of computer-assisted instruction. To be successful with computer-assisted mathematics instruction, one must choose software that is appropriate for the curriculum. There have been considerable breakthroughs in mathematical software during the last few generations. "Computer algebra systems" and "dynamic geometry software" are two well-known forms of software that may assist with math teaching and learning. Computer algebra systems and dynamic geometry have had a substantial influence on mathematics education, according to the findings of the academics. There is currently no link between these instruments. GeoGebra is a math teaching software that combines the capabilities of dynamic geometry and computer algebra into a single instrument (Fig. 1).

GeoGebra software provides significant teaching and learning opportunities for calculus, geometry, and algebra at all educational levels, from elementary school to college. The application concurrently presents algebraic, graphic, and spreadsheet representations of mathematical things. Any changes made to one of these aspects have an immediate effect on the others. According to one research, GeoGebra users—whether they are students or teachers—can utilize this environment to explain, discover, and model mathematical concepts, as well as the links between those concepts and mathematics as a whole. With the use of this program, students may understand mathematical concepts without spending a great deal of time in class generating figures, objects, or functions. In addition, they may dynamically connect algebraic, graphical, and mathematical representations of these notions. GeoGebra software may be downloaded for free from its website (www.geogebra.org). Prior study has shown that computer vision and mathematics software have a positive effect on learning performance, motivation, and retention. Moreover, according to the findings of other studies, prospective educators may be taught to use computer vision in the classroom. Consequently, the incorporation of computer vision into the educational context is essential for the teaching of mathematics. Teachers help much to maintaining this connection. Consequently, it is crucial for education to explore instructors' perspectives on computer vision. The goal of this study is to determine how dynamic mathematics software influences the perspectives of future mathematics teachers on computer vision (GeoGebra).

Computer algebra and dynamic geometry software are powerful scientific technologies and mathematical learning tools [1]. Many studies have shown that these data packets can be used to encourage experiments and realize the visualization function, which can

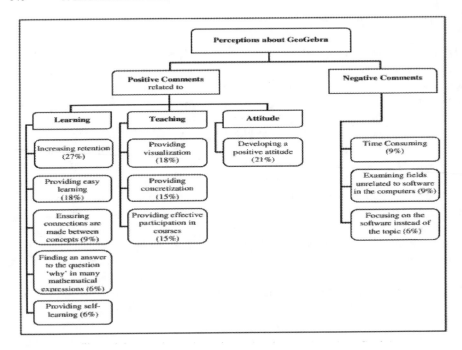

Fig. 1. Perceptions towards Geogebra

effectively verify the teaching conjecture. However, different packages are employed to support different levels of teaching in that it takes time to help students become familiar with the software in different classrooms. Although the computer algebra system contains a definition of time and a complex educational system, dynamic geometry software can be used in primary school teaching because it makes use of mouse to drive the user interface. As a multi-platform open-source dynamic mathematical software, GeoGebra attempts to achieve algebraic computation with dynamic geometric technology since the computer system is easy to operate, which can be integrated with class.

2   Related Works

The basic idea of software is to connect geometry, algebra and calculus. If taking comprehensive consideration into teaching and math learning, it would help achieve course study from elementary school to university [2]. GeoGebra, which has been translated into 36 languages can be used for free on the Internet, and volunteers gather fast-growing users to form a global community. At present, users from more than 100 countries visit nearly 300,000 each month, which can be estimated by teachers with computer teaching programs. Teachers and students have had a significant impact on open-source projects. As commercial products, students are not limited to the use of licensed software. In the school or university website, they can download and install GeoGebra software on their personal computers. For teachers, GeoGebra provides a powerful platform to create an interactive online learning environment, which allows many teachers to share information on the Internet for free. However, the study revealed that the majority of teachers can improve the desired technology with appropriate training and support, thus teachers can achieve the combination of practice and teaching once the technology is integrated into their training and technology development. Nowadays, GeoGebra's users form a unique community [3] (Fig. 2).

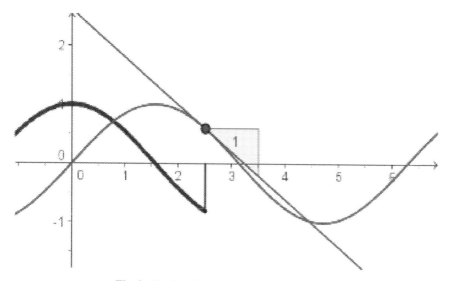

Fig. 2. Tracing the slope function of sin(x) [3]

2.1 Calculus and Program

GeoGebra based computer vision has benefited teachers in universities and primary schools since teachers and researchers around the world have developed a large number of worksheets to provide access to the software with the application of multi-level structure [4]. As integral teaching software, GeoGebra can not only realize the rich development environment, but also offer an interactive worksheets calculation function for extensive information collection.

The teaching application for GeoGebra may be used to compute fundamental ideas and, in addition, to provide learning materials for users. They are entirely dynamic; that is, the graph's points may be moved, and by using the slider, these parameters can be modified and adjusted automatically. When exploring the circle subject, GeoGebra was investigated using a quasi-experimental technique in analytic geometry courses for first-year university students. Analysis of pre- and post-test results showed that students who used GeoGebra to study improved their performance and comprehension. Student surveys revealed that they had a positive opinion about the program and that using the software had enhanced their spatial visualization [15]. In a quasi-experimental research, students in the experimental group were taught using GeoGebra to facilitate learning circles. T-tests on performance data showed that GeoGebra helped pupils outperform the control group. Student surveys revealed a favorable view about this software [16]. GeoGebra was utilized for a geometry course using a similar manner, and the experimental group had favorable results on post-tests. However, on a delayed post-test, students who had received instruction using conventional methods outperformed those who had received instruction using software [17]. Higher secondary analytical geometry has also used GeoGebra. Pre and after treatment assessments were used on 12th grade students in the control and experimental groups. T tests showed that pupils who were taught GeoGebra performed better, especially low achievers [18]. Analytic geometry classes for future teachers were investigated to understand cylindrical and spherical coordination. The majority of the research we investigated analyzed pre- and post-test results in a quasi-experimental fashion, however this study used a different approach. Semi-structured interviews were examined in order to determine how much the program contributed to raising students' comprehension. The findings demonstrated how pre-service teachers' topic knowledge greatly increased [19].

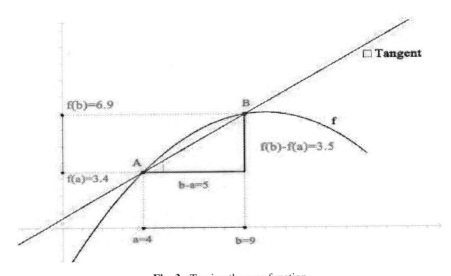

Fig. 3. Tracing the area function

3   Methods and Materials

"Teaching can be simplified in some way by using graphical tools that allow anyone to retain the information they want to learn more easily. Here to increase the observance of the virtues that this software tool can offer, it will be possible to develop a small application that performs the same operations shown in this paper automatically with the MATLAB language, in order to improve the graphical properties of the representation of each operating result, resembling more to those shown by GeoGebra, being more user friendly. In addition, all these examples including tasks' dynamic worksheets can be easily exported to dynamic web pages for students to provide an interactive applet [5]. Once uploading dynamic worksheets to the Internet, students can see these lists in school and at home without having to download management software on their computers. By providing these dynamic interaction graphics of different forms, GeoGebra can be integrated into different math teaching software as shown in Fig. 3".

3.1 Introduction to the Experiment

It has been shown that the use of various colors in educational materials has a significant role in provoking a variety of emotional responses and attracting the attention of the individuals being educated. The information processing systems of working memory each have their own distinct limitation in terms of their cognitive capacity. The cognitive burden in the information-processing systems is intended to be alleviated by the use of this design. Teachers can prepare color computer vision based GeoGebra documents demonstrating the concept of mathematics for their students. In courses of different teachers, creating appropriate dynamic graphs will help save time [6]. Teachers can create dynamic parameters of homework in order to make the software adapt to more flexible teaching methods, additionally, students can be responsible for making suggestions and hypothesis. Since technology is a necessary condition, users are more willing to use the software produced by teams and the dynamic map in class. What's more, advanced users can regard GeoGebra as a flexible learning tool to establish a mathematical model from the beginning, as long as students hold that the operation is proper.

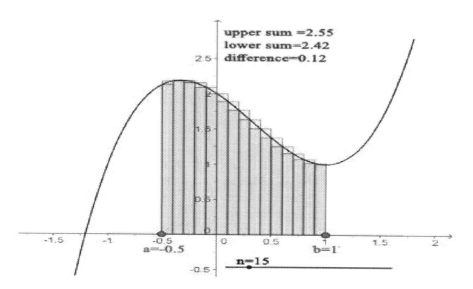

Fig. 4. Upper and lower sums

With regard to the computer vision based GeoGebra tutorials, students are able to explore and discover mathematical concepts that have not been known before using dynamic mathematical software. Teachers could provide an interactive GeoGebra course structure that includes related questions and challenges. Using a piece of paper to show mathematical concepts students explored, which illustrates that they already have some experience in the application of this software. On the other hand, teachers can also create separate dynamic worksheets [7]. With the valid worksheet, students must use the software to open a computer vision based GeoGebra interactive page in the browser, thus it will help students save time to learn the software. Synthetic research groups can also set up teaching research projects to study the development of calculus, additionally, to display or hide the algebraic window in order to reduce the number of toolbar and helper demonstrated by the software. Besides, teachers can decide the number of free tutorials they desire for, meanwhile, they must explain the characteristics of this tool for the students as shown in Fig. 4.

4 Results and Discussion

4.1 Composition of System

The overall experimentation was carried out under MATLAB simulation environment. Here the geogebra learning environment was tested on MATLAB to prove its working efficiency. As a dynamic and interactive digital software, computer vision based GeoGebra is incorporated into an interactive learning environment where designers of the Austrian school support teachers' teaching through the course and employ a variety of training materials as well as an interactive small programs; meanwhile, students integrate useful concepts by testing incoming data [8]. In the Austrian learning environment, hundreds of high school students have a math test. In general, students can benefit from the participation in dynamic and interactive courses, which helps understand basic mathematical concepts and carry out visualization teaching.

4.2 Dynamic Polynomial

Within the range of Taylor polynomials usually, this paper carried out researches on the calculus learning in high school with dynamic vision. The cosine function reaches the approximation point along the axis in the GeoGebra software [9]. With the slider, students can change the number of elements of Taylor polynomials, thereby changing the grade of accuracy. In the curriculum, the approximation of functions in different locations can be obtained with the drag of mouse. At the same time, Taylor polynomials equation can be dynamically displayed to reveal the change of all elements regarding automatic adaptation. In addition, the initial function can be changed at any time, allowing Taylor polynomials function to change. The daily synthetic integral course consists of a variety of dynamic visualization courseware that helps students better understand the concept of Taylor. The concept of limit approximation is accurate and important as shown in Fig. 5.

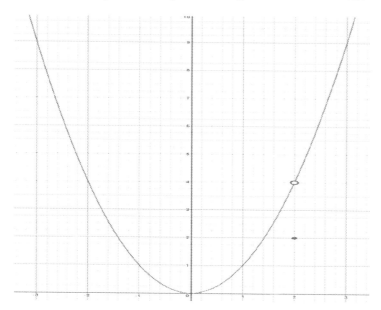

Fig. 5. Derivatives roots of extreme points

The eigen polynomial and its derived analysis system can benefit students for their better understanding of certain types' functions, such as the function of algebraic operation based on imageology and the function to improve students' ability to draw sketches and their derivatives. This concept also gives guidance for students to have a correct understanding of complex and visual concepts [10]. It is allowed to add tilted experimental functions to the software. Taking a fixed point and the chart of tangent function as an example, create a new point with slope, then draw the trajectory of tilted points along the curve function by moving A, that is, the initial function of derivatives. This function assumes that students can change the equation after the proposed equation changes, and introduce the correct field to test his hypothesis with GeoGebra. Finally, combined with the experimental orbit, relevant function diagrams are generated by comparing the slope of function.

4.3 Color Match Recommendation Based on the Existing Data

Color match recommendation may recommend two type of color which is not similar, just because people used to use both of them at the same time. For example, beer and diapers which are two unrelated items is a kind of collocation based on people's buying habits. So, color match recommendation is a kind of recommendation engine based on association rules 3. Recommendation is based on the data which has been a previous color collocation (including the specified color), and it returns the appropriate color match. Apriori 4 algorithm can be used to achieve the recommendation. Meanwhile, it also exits some defects.

First, scan all the color matches in the database and add the valid data item to the candidate data item set with the weight of the data items which is the preference extent of color match. Because each set of data items are generated from the new data, according to the index, the scan is stopped until the last valid data is available which can greatly reduce the scan time. In practice, we can use HashMap data structure to store candidate data items sets. Key is color match sequence and Value is the preference extent [11].

In the generation of frequent item sets, the system will also calculate the support for each item, that is, the amount of data on occurrences. After the first data scan, the system gets optional 1-frequent sets. And then use minimal support to prune so that we can get 1-frequent sets. Repeat the process until n-1 times and we get n-frequent sets. In this system, only 2 frequent item sets are considered. For example, the initial data is shown in Table 1 when minimal support is 2.

Table. 1 An example of Frequent item calculation

Number	Initial Data Set
1	#336666,#FF9999
2	#336666,#FF9999,#2254D5
3	#2254D5,#336666
4	#99CC33,#336666,#FF9999
5	#66CCCC,#56DF67,#13AE65
6	#66CCCC,#0099CC,#56DF67,#13AE65

4.4 Function Architecture of the System

There are a variety of functions in this system, such as color picker, online learning, online questions, Online test, color search, color match, color recommendation, etc. These functions are shown in Fig. 6.

4.5 Secant and Tangent

Facilitating the visualization of graphs and the understanding of concepts, this paper acquires the relationship between secant and tangent by comparing differences of suppliers, in which case limited concepts and importance factors can be understood [12]. In the function diagram, the mouse is employed to move A or B to adjust the difference and specific value of the dynamic text. In addition, the inclination is changed by the secrets of points A and B, whose dynamic diagram can be obtained by moving the curve of function B. Factors of students' learning are different, therefore, once the slope of tangents is approximated, the two points are combined into one segment, which will result in the fact that segmentation makes the effect worse. This question is a good starting point to discuss why the secant would disappear and discuss how to change the slope in this paper to solve problems. The special case of visualization conversion appearing between the secant and the tangent can be selected with the check box to show the structure in

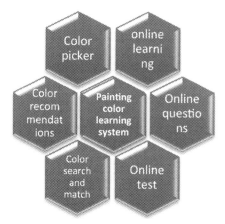

Fig. 6. System structure

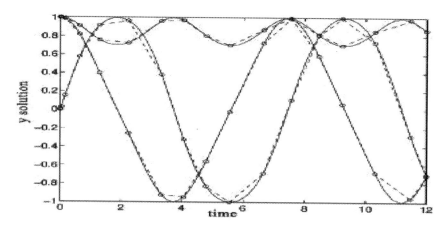

Fig. 7. Dynamic Taylor polynomial

the upper right corner. As shown in Fig. 7, put forward questions for students, whose answering such abstract questions makes the exploration more significant.

With the concept of integral proposed by Riemann, this paper integrates the latest concepts of dynamic vision and dynamic demo. In addition to the graphics function, change the time interval between two points along the two moving points. Students can change the upper and lower limits of calculation range and increase the number of equidistant functions with the application of a slider in the software. The display of functions and the calculation of differences among teaching groups will be automatically adapted and modified with the development of the dynamic text. Students can reveal or hide various configuration information in the software, use components in the check box, and meanwhile focus on their current tasks. As a result, students are able to explore the solution of Riemann integral through this vibrant system, which guides students to solve various problems and challenge different fields of research.

4.6 Language Communication

Only a small number of researchers conducted research on students' language models. Teachers indicated that undergraduate score ranking determines the ability to speak, after which they conducted a more objective assessment and evaluation. In contrast, undergraduate ratings are more closely related to students, thus the presence of students causes teachers' stereotypes of society [13]. Ingles found that undergraduate teaching software assessment reports may be related to the actual mathematics teaching because of different qualifications for the independent assessment. In these studies, students evaluate their teachers in reality, which was found as a method that can be used to change the environment, and is easily affected by physical attractiveness except external factors.

Although students are always the actual object of language teaching, the teachers' mathematics teaching level significantly affects the teaching quality even if their background remains unchanged. In these studies, the proportion of teachers' involvement is. In these studies, about language attitudes, various dependent variables are applied to measure the perception of audiences, which finally determines the size of speakers. In most cases, these standards and estimates reflect speakers' working ability, social attraction, integrity and audiences' judgment. For carrying on the speaker in uniforms to conduct researches on the closely related cultural transmission, this paper finally completed the study of mathematics teaching.

4.7 Computational Thinking Ability

The learning outcomes are measured by three levels of questions, in which the easy question includes simple questions to examine the fundamental logic knowledge, the normal question assesses the psychomotor learning outcomes by asking the users to match the conceptual concepts with physical system components, and the difficult question requires the students to locate and correct potential mistakes to evaluate whether the participants can comprehend the relevant computational concepts. The first two questions (east and normal) are tested before the teaching sessions and the difficult question is examined after perceiving the teaching materials and interacting with the suggested learning system.

Despite the fact that students initially recognized the color learning assistance (1st study), only one out of seven students correctly answered the simple question, and none of them were able to effectively reply to the normal or difficult questions. The findings, which are shown in Fig. 8, indicate that while students initially recognized the color learning assistance, they were unable to effectively answer any of the questions. The outcomes of the second experiment, which was carried out one week after the first research, indicated that the majority of the participants had the capacity to deliver appropriate replies to questions covering all of the available difficulty levels. According to the results, the color-based learning method that was proposed has the ability to effectively boost the learning performance of students while also increasing their capacity to participate in computational thinking.

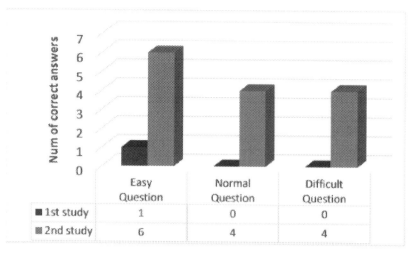

	Easy Question	Normal Question	Difficult Question
■ 1st study	1	0	0
■ 2nd study	6	4	4

Fig. 8. Comparative analysis

4.8 Discussion and Analysis

"Learning is a difficult field to understand, and there's so much research out there discussing these issues that it's hard to know where to begin. It's pretty obvious though is that color plays a key role in creating an environment that fosters learning. This paper discusses regional functions and definite integral formulas where the slope can play a function of tracking. The area composed by the resistance of derivatives, the functional chart, and the x-axis is possible to be calculated. Within the available limits, create a display area on the right and specify the function of an area in accordance with this path. Moreover, the initial function can be changed at any time, so that students are able to find the corresponding area in the experiment to discuss the anti-derivatives' graphics and various practical functions.

In addition, students can find different polynomial area formulas with dynamic maps and test their assumptions based on the GeoGebra course platform. After comparing systems of multiple types, analyzing and sending abilities, students have the opportunity to regain abilities in self-learning [14]. Obviously, GeoGebra, which has been widely used in high school teaching, especially in Europe, is also applicable in universities. Now, the United States has already published online interactive courses by famous teachers. The study shows that GeoGebra is easier to create courses than other programs at the same time".

5 Conclusion

With the application of MATLAB, this paper proposed a calculus teaching system to improve the interactivity the of teaching system and the richness of the curriculum. Based on the embedded technology and GeoGebra program, this paper extends the symbolic feature system of GeoGebra, and provides geometric, algebra and calculation functions in software with cross-border user community approach. The basic calculus concept of derivatives and anti-derivatives is put forward, which breaks through the limitations in teachers and students' use of this system and provides equal access to learning resources. In addition, the open-source software is embedded into the calculus teaching system for the design of a quick and convenient calculus teaching system, which is applied to college-level calculus teaching. Furthermore, it extends the application of MATLAB in the calculus teaching system. However, the issues of technical costs and real-time on this system are still remarkable. So, it is better to pay more attention to reduce the cost of technology and update curriculum rapidly in further study. In order to achieve the goal that learners can learn about color easily, recommendation engine technology is added to the system which can recommend the best match color to the users through the learner's preferences and other colors match instance. The system improves the learners' learning interest, and promotes the improvement of teaching quality.

References

1. Motiwalla, L.F.: Mobile learning: a framework and evaluation. Comput. Educ. **49**(3), 581–596 (2007)
2. Wu, W.H., Wu, Y.C.J., Chen, C.Y.: Review of trends from mobile learning studies: a meta-analysis. Comput. Educ. **59**(2), 817–827 (2012)
3. Srikant, R., Agrawal, R.: Mining quantitative association rules in large relational tables. ACM Sigmod **25**(2), 1–12 (1996)
4. Inokuchi, A., Washio, T., Motoda, H.: An apriori-based algorithm for mining frequent substructures from graph data. In: Proceedings of the 4th European Conference on Principles of Data Mining and Knowledge Discovery. Springer-Verlag, pp. 13–23 (2000). https://doi.org/10.1007/3-540-45372-5_2
5. Alieyan, K., ALmomani, A., Manasrah, A., Kadhum, M.M.: A survey of botnet detection based on DNS. Neural Comput. Appl. **28**(7), 1541–1558 (2015)
6. Bilge, L., Sen, S., Dl, B.: Exposure: a passive DNS analysis service to detect and report malicious domains. Acm Trans. Inf. Syst. Sec. **16**(4), 1–28 (2014)
7. Xue, L., Sun, G.: Design and implementation of a malware detection system based on network behavior. Security Commun. Networks **8**(3), 459–470 (2014)
8. Ma, X., Zhang, J., Tao, J.: DNSRadar: outsourcing malicious domain detection based on distributed cache-footprints. IEEE Trans. Inf. Forensics Secur. **9**(11), 1906–1921 (2014)
9. Shahzad, F., Shahzad, M., Farooq, M.: In-execution dynamic malware analysis and detection by mining information in process control blocks of Linux OS. Inf. Sci. **231**(9), 45–63 (2013)
10. Saxe, J., Berlin, K.: Deep neural network-based malware detection using two-dimensional binary program features. Computer Science, pp. 11–20 (2015)
11. Tong, Z., Zhuang, Q., Guo, Q.: Research on technologies of software requirements prioritization. Communi. Comput. Inf. Sci. **426**, 9–21 (2014)
12. Seok, S., Kim, H.: Visualized Malware Classification Based-on Convolutional Neural Network **26**(1), 197–208 (2016)
13. Ozsoy, M., Khasawneh, K.N., Donovick, C.: Hardware-based Malware Detection using Low level Architectural Features, pp. 1–1 (2016)
14. Stevanovic, D., Vlajic, N., An, A.: Detection of malicious and non-malicious website visitors using unsupervised neural network learning. Appl. Soft Comput. **13**(1), 698–708 (2013)
15. Sudihartinih, E., Purniati, T.: Using GeoGebra to develop students understanding on circle concept. Journal of Physics: Conference Series **1157**, 042090, 2019/02 (2019)
16. Shadaan, P., Leong, K.E.: Effectiveness of using geogebra on students' understanding in learning circles. Malaysian Online J. Educ. Technol. **1**(4), 1–11 (2013)

17. Bakar, K.A., Ayub, A.F.M., Mahmud, R.: Effects of GeoGebra towards students' mathematics performance. In: 2015 International Conference on Research and Education in Mathematics (ICREM7), pp. 180–183 (2015)
18. Khalil, M., Farooq, R.A., Çakıroğlu, E., Khalil, U., Khan, D.M.: The development of mathematical achievement in analytic geometry of grade-12 students through GeoGebra activities. Eurasia J. Mathematics, Sci. Technol. Educ. **14**(4), 1453–1463 (2018)
19. Yildiz, A., Baltaci, S.: Reflections from the analytic geometry courses based on contextual teaching and learning through geogebra software. Online Submission **6**(4), 155–166 (2016)

Bisimulations for Fuzzy Geometric Models

Litan Kumar Das[1]([✉]), Kumar Sankar Ray[2], and Prakash Chandra Mali[1]

[1] Department of Mathematics, Jadavpur University, Jadavpur, Kolkata, India
ld06iitkgp@gmail.com
[2] ECSU, Indian Statistical Institute, Kolkata, India
ksray@isical.ac.in

Abstract. The purpose of this paper is to develop coalgebraic fuzzy geometric logic by incorporating modalities into the fuzzy geometric logic language. The modal operators are introduced in the fuzzy geometric logic language using coalgebraic techniques. We introduce the idea of fuzzy-open predicate lifting in order to define the modal operators. Based on coalgebras for an endofunctor T on the category **Fuzzy-Top** of fuzzy topological spaces, we build models for the coalgebraic fuzzy geometric logic. We study the relationship between the concepts of behavioural equivalence and modal equivalence on the class of fuzzy geometric models. Furthermore, the paper studies bisimulation for fuzzy geometric models.

Keywords: Fuzzy geometric logic · Fuzzy topological spaces · Coalgebra · Bisimulation

1 Introduction

In [6], fuzzy geometric logic was introduced as a natural generalization of the propositional geometric logic [18]. Geometric logic was founded by Vicker in [18] using point-free topology, logic, and the logic of finite observations [3]. The geometric logic language is built on a set of propositional variables using propositional connectives such as finite conjunction($\wedge$) and arbitrary disjunction($\bigvee$). These connectives preserve the finite observability property. Chakraborty et al. [6] extended the satisfiability relation concept to generalize geometric logic in many-valued cases. They noticed that if the satisfaction relation is fuzzy, there are two possible outcomes for the consequence relation: crisp or fuzzy. As a result, they developed general fuzzy geometric logic as well as fuzzy geometric logic with graded consequence. In [8], one can find information about graded consequence and its related ideas. The theory of coalgebras served as the foundation for the development of various modal logics. Kurz proceeded into more depth about coalgebraic logic in [9]. Coalgebraic logic for endofunctors on the category of sets was extensively studied in [10,11], where they defined modal operators using the predicate lifting notion [13] or relation lifting notion [12]. Coalgebraic geometric logic has been developed in [14,15], where modal operators are defined to the

© The Author(s), under exclusive license to Springer Nature Switzerland AG 2023
R. K. Tiwari and G. Sahoo (Eds.): ICAII 2022, CCIS 1822, pp. 152–163, 2023.
https://doi.org/10.1007/978-3-031-37303-9_12

geometric logic language using the theory of coalgebraic logic. Motivated by their work, we study modalities in fuzzy geometric logic using the coalgebraic machinery of predicate liftings. The structures, named fuzzy geometric models for T, provide the semantics for coalgebraic fuzzy geometric logic. It is expected that the proposed coalgebraic logic developed in this work will have implications in computer science areas such as knowledge representations, logic programming, formal verification, fuzzy reasoning, etc. The structure of the study is as follows. The concepts necessary for the work are covered in Sect. 2. In Sect. 3, we discuss coalgebraic logic for **Fuzzy-Top**-coalgebras and introduce the fuzzy geometric models concept for an endofunctor T. Section 4 studies bisimulations for fuzzy geometric models. We conclude the study by mentioning potential future research directions in Sect. 5.

2 Preliminaries

The reader is referred to [1] for category theory basics. We include some basic concepts to help readers understand our work. In 1965, Zadeh investigated fuzzy set theory [21]. We go through some fundamental ideas in fuzzy set theory.

Definition 1. *A fuzzy set $\tilde{f}$ on a set S is defined by the membership function $\tilde{f} : S \to [0, 1]$.*

Let $\tilde{f}^c$ denote the complement of $\tilde{f}$. Define $\tilde{f}^c : S \to [0, 1]$ by $\tilde{f}^c(s) = 1 - \tilde{f}(s)$, $\forall s \in S$. $\tilde{f}^c$ is a fuzzy set on S.

Remark 1. *For each $s \in S$, the grade of membership of s in the fuzzy set $\tilde{f}$ is given by the value $\tilde{f}(s)$. It is represented by the symbol $gr(s \in \tilde{f})$.*

Definition 2. *Let μ and η be fuzzy sets on S. Then, μ is a fuzzy subset of η, denoted by $\mu \leq \eta$, $\iff \mu(s) \leq \eta(s)$, $\forall s \in S$.*

We recall the fuzzy topological spaces concept from [7].

Definition 3. *Let S be a set. A collection τ_S of fuzzy sets on S is said to be fuzzy topology on S if the following conditions hold:*

(i) $\tilde{\emptyset}, \tilde{S} \in \tau_S$, where $\tilde{\emptyset}(s) = 0$, $\forall s \in S$ and $\tilde{S}(s) = 1$, $\forall s \in S$;
(ii) if $\tilde{g}_1, \tilde{g}_2 \in \tau_s$ then $\tilde{g}_1 \wedge \tilde{g}_2 \in \tau_S$, where $(\tilde{g}_1 \wedge \tilde{g}_2)(s) = \tilde{g}_1(s) \wedge \tilde{g}_2(s)$;
(iii) if $\tilde{g}_j \in \tau_S$ for $j \in \Lambda$, Λ is an index set, then $\bigvee_{j \in \Lambda} \tilde{g}_j \in \tau_S$, where $\bigvee_{j \in \Lambda} \tilde{g}_j(s) = \sup_{j \in \Lambda}\{\tilde{g}_j(s)\}$.

Then, the pair (S, τ_S) is referred to as a fuzzy topological space and members of τ_S are said to be fuzzy open sets on (S, τ_S).

Definition 4. *([19]) Let (S, τ_S) be a fuzzy topological space. Then a subset $\mathfrak{B}$ of τ_S is called a basis for (S, τ_S) if it satisfies the following conditions:*

(i) if $\tilde{b}_1, \tilde{b}_2 \in \mathfrak{B}$ then $\tilde{b}_1 \wedge \tilde{b}_2 \in \mathfrak{B}$;
(ii) for each member $\tilde{t} \in \tau_S$, there exists a subcollection $\mathcal{C} = \{\tilde{t}_j \in \mathfrak{B} : j \in \Lambda\}$ such that $\tilde{t} = \bigvee_{j \in \Lambda} \tilde{t}_j$.

Definition 5. ([19]) *Let τ_S be a fuzzy topology on S and $\mathfrak{S} \subset \tau_S$. Then, $\mathfrak{S}$ is a subbasis for a fuzzy space $(S, \tau_S) \iff$ the collection of all finite meets of members of S is a basis for (S, τ_S).*

Definition 6. *A fuzzy topological space (S, τ_S) is said to be Kolmogorov space or T_0-space if for any pair (x, y) of distinct points in S, there is a fuzzy open set $\tilde{g}$ on S such that $\tilde{g}(x) \neq \tilde{g}(y)$.*

Definition 7. *Let (F, τ_F) and (G, τ_G) be fuzzy topological spaces. A mapping $f : F \to G$ is fuzzy continuous if and only if, for every fuzzy open set $\tilde{g}$ on (G, τ_G), $f^{-1}(\tilde{g})$ is a fuzzy open set on (F, τ_F).*

Definitions of category, opposite category, functors, and natural transformation can be found in [1]. Let **FS** denote the category of fuzzy sets.

Definition 8. ([20]) *The category **FS** is defined as follows:*

(i) *An object in **FS** is a pair $(S, \tilde{g})$, where S is a set and $\tilde{g} : S \to [0, 1]$ is a membership function;*

(ii) *A morphism $f : (S, \tilde{g}) \to (T, \tilde{h})$ in **FS** is a function $f : S \to T$ such that $\tilde{g}(s) \leq f^{-1}(\tilde{h})(s)$.*

Let **Fuzzy-Top** denote the category of fuzzy topological spaces.

Definition 9. *The category **Fuzzy-Top** is defined as follows:*

(i) *Objects in **Fuzzy-Top** are fuzzy topological spaces (S, τ_S);*

(ii) *Morphisms $f : (S, \tau_S) \to (T, \tau_T)$ in **Fuzzy-Top** are fuzzy continuous mappings.*

Definition 10. *A functor $\mathcal{Q}$ from **Fuzzy-Top** to **FS** is defined as shown below:*

(i) *For an object (S, τ_S) in **Fuzzy-Top**, define $\mathcal{Q}(S) = $ set of fuzzy open sets on (S, τ_S);*

(ii) *For a morphism $\xi : (S, \tau_S) \to (T, \tau_T)$ in **Fuzzy-Top**, define $\mathcal{Q}(\xi) = \xi^{-1} : \mathcal{Q}(T) \to \mathcal{Q}(S)$ by $\xi^{-1}(\eta) = \eta \circ \xi$, $\eta \in \mathcal{Q}(T)$.*

Definition 11. ([18]) *A poset S is called a frame if the following holds:*

(i) *S is closed in terms of the finite meet $(\wedge)$;*

(ii) *S is closed in terms of the arbitrary join $(\bigvee)$;*

(iii) *$\wedge$ distributes over $\bigvee$ i.e., $s' \wedge \bigvee_{s \in S'} s = \bigvee_{s \in S'} \{s' \wedge s\}$, where S' is an arbitrary subset of S.*

Note 1. Let (S, τ_S) be a fuzzy topological space. Then, the fuzzy topology τ_S on S can be considered as a frame.

Definition 12. ([18]) *A function f from a frame F_1 to a frame F_2 is referred to as a frame homomorphism if it preserves finite meets and arbitrary joins.*

Let the category of frames and frame homomorphisms be represented by **FRM**.

Definition 13. ([2]) *Take into account that T is an endofunctor on a category $\mathcal{S}$. A T-coalgebra is given by a pair (A, ζ), where A is an object in $\mathcal{S}$ and $\zeta : A \to T(A)$ is an arrow in $\mathcal{S}$.*

Definition 14. ([2]) *A morphism between T-coalgebras (Z, δ) and (W, β) is defined by a morphism $\psi : Z \to W$ in $\mathcal{S}$ satisfying $T(\psi) \circ \delta = \beta \circ \psi$.*

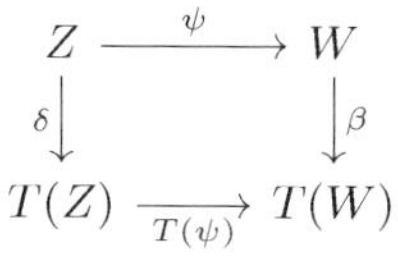

$$
\begin{array}{ccc}
Z & \xrightarrow{\ \psi\ } & W \\
{\scriptstyle \delta}\downarrow & & \downarrow{\scriptstyle \beta} \\
T(Z) & \xrightarrow[T(\psi)]{} & T(W)
\end{array}
$$

Fig. 1. Illustration of coalgebra morphism

T-coalgebras and coalgebra morphisms form a category, denoted by **COALG**(T).

Definition 15. *Let (Z, δ) and (W, β) be objects in **COALG**(T). We say that any two states $z \in Z$ and $w \in W$ are behaviourally equivalent if there is an object (Y, α) in **COALG**(T) and morphisms $g : (Z, \delta) \to (Y, \alpha)$ and $h : (W, \beta) \to (Y, \alpha)$ such that $g(z) = h(w)$.*

Definition 16. ([16]) *Let (Z, δ) and (W, β) be two T-coalgebras. Then a relation $\mathcal{R} \subseteq Z \times W$ is said to be a bisimulation between (Z, δ) and (W, β) if there exists a T-coalgebra $(\mathcal{R}, \gamma)$ such that the projection maps $\pi_1 : \mathcal{R} \to Z$ and $\pi_2 : \mathcal{R} \to W$ are coalgebra morphisms and satisfy $\delta \circ \pi_1 = T(\pi_1) \circ \gamma$, $\beta \circ \pi_2 = T(\pi_2) \circ \gamma$. So, the diagram shown in Fig. 2 is commutative.*

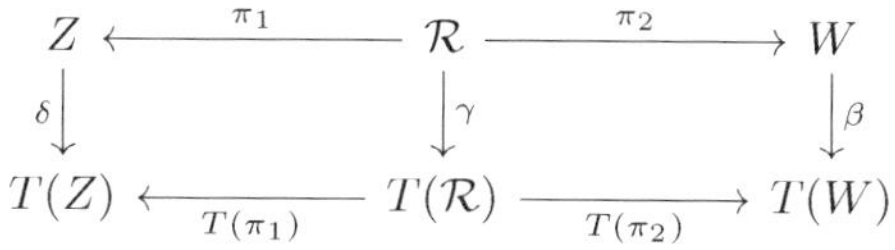

$$
\begin{array}{ccccc}
Z & \xleftarrow{\ \pi_1\ } & \mathcal{R} & \xrightarrow{\ \pi_2\ } & W \\
{\scriptstyle \delta}\downarrow & & \downarrow{\scriptstyle \gamma} & & \downarrow{\scriptstyle \beta} \\
T(Z) & \xleftarrow[T(\pi_1)]{} & T(\mathcal{R}) & \xrightarrow[T(\pi_2)]{} & T(W)
\end{array}
$$

Fig. 2. Illustration of coalgebraic bisimulation

Definition 17. *Functor $\mathcal{P} : $ **Fuzzy-Top** $\to$ **FRM** is defined as follows:*

(i) *For an object S in **Fuzzy-top**, define $\mathcal{P}(S) = \tau_S$;*
(ii) *For an arrow $\eta : S_1 \to S_2$ in **Fuzzy-top**, define $\mathcal{P}(\eta) : \mathcal{P}(S_2) \to \mathcal{P}(S_1)$ by $\mathcal{P}(\eta)(\xi) = \xi \circ \eta$, where $\xi \in \mathcal{P}(S_2)$.*

Note 2. Let F be a frame and (S, τ_S) be a fuzzy topological space. Then, the frame F is spatial if there is an isomorphism from F to $\mathcal{P}(S)$.

Consider that **S-FRM** is the category of spatial frames and homomorphisms between frames. Let F denote a frame and PTF denote the collection of frame homomorphisms h from F to $[0, 1]$. Then the collection $\{\Psi(a) : a \in F\}$ is a fuzzy topology on PTF, where for each $a \in F$, $\Psi(a)$ is a membership function from PTF to $[0, 1]$ which is defined by $\Psi(a)(h) = h(a)$.

Definition 18. ([17]) *Let τ be a fuzzy topology on S. Assume that $\tilde{T} \in \tau$. A membership function $\Psi(\tilde{T}) : PT\tau \to [0, 1]$ can be defined as $\Psi(\tilde{T})(h) = h(\tilde{T})$. Then, $\Psi(\tilde{T})$ is a fuzzy set on $PT\tau$.*

Remark 2. *The collection $\{\Psi(\tilde{T}) : \tilde{T} \in \tau\}$ meets the requirements to be a fuzzy topology on $PT\tau$.*

Corollary 1. ([17]) *Consider a fuzzy topological space (S, τ). Define a mapping $f : S \to PT\tau$ by $f(s)(\tilde{\phi}) = \tilde{\phi}(s)$, where $\tilde{\phi} \in \tau$. Then, (S, τ) becomes a sober fuzzy space if and only if f is bijective.*

Let **SFuzzy-Top** denote the category of sober fuzzy topological spaces.

Definition 19. *Define a functor $PT : \textbf{FRM} \to \textbf{Fuzzy-Top}$ as shown below:*

(i) For an object E in $\textbf{FRM}$, define $PT(E) = PTE$;
(ii) For an arrow $\mathcal{G} : E \to E'$ in $\textbf{FRM}$, define $PT(\mathcal{G}) : PTE' \to PTE$ by $PT(\mathcal{G})(f) = f \circ \mathcal{G}$, where $f \in PTE'$.

Now, we can observe the following result.

Theorem 1. *The category $\textbf{S-FRM}$ is dually equivalent to the category $\textbf{SFuzzy-Top}$.*

Proof. Let id_1 and id_2 be the identity functors on **S-FRM** and **SFuzzy-Top**, respectively. We consider two natural transformations $\xi : id_1 \to \mathcal{P} \circ PT$ and $\eta : id_2 \to PT \circ \mathcal{P}$. For a spatial frame F, we define $\xi_F : F \to \mathcal{P} \circ PT(F)$ by $\xi_F(u)(h) = h(u)$, where $h \in PTF$. Since F is a spatial frame, we have ξ_F is an isomorphism. It is simple to understand that ξ is a natural transformation. As a result, ξ is a natural isomorphism. For an object S in **SFuzzy-Top**, define $\eta_S : S \to PT \circ \mathcal{P}S$ by $\eta_S(s)(\tilde{g}) = \tilde{g}(s)$, $\forall s \in S$ and $\tilde{g} \in \mathcal{P}(S)$. As S is sober, so η_S is bijective. We observe that, for $\tilde{g} \in \mathcal{P}(S)$, $\eta_S^{-1}(\Psi(\tilde{g}))(s) = \Psi(\tilde{g})(\eta_S(s)) = \eta_S(s)(\tilde{g}) = \tilde{g}(s)$. Therefore, $\eta_S^{-1}(\Psi(\tilde{g})) = \tilde{g}$. Moreover, η_S is an open map because $\eta_S(\tilde{g})(h) = \bigvee\{\tilde{g}(s) : s \in \eta_S^{-1}(h)\} = h(\tilde{g}) = \Psi(\tilde{g})(h)$. Therefore, $\eta_S(\tilde{g}) = \Psi(\tilde{g})$. Hence, η_S is a fuzzy homeomorphism. Now, it is easily verified that naturality law hold by η. Therefore, η is a natural isomorphism.

3   Coalgebraic Logic

In this section, T is taken to be an endofunctor on the category **Fuzzy-Top**. We describe coalgebraic logic for **Fuzzy-Top**-coalgebras. We begin by introducing a predicate lifting notion for T, named fuzzy-open predicate lifting.

Definition 20. *A natural transformation $\lambda : \mathcal{Q}^n \to \mathcal{Q} \circ T$ is called a fuzyy-open predicate lifting. So, by the naturality law the following diagram commutes:*

$$
\begin{array}{ccc}
Y & Q^n X & \xrightarrow{\ \lambda_X\ } & Q \circ T(X) \\
{\scriptstyle\phi}\big\uparrow & {\scriptstyle Q^n\phi}\big\uparrow & & \big\uparrow{\scriptstyle\phi^{-1}} \\
X & Q^n Y & \xrightarrow[\ \lambda_Y\ ]{} & Q \circ T(Y)
\end{array}
$$

*Let $\check{\lambda}$ is the dual of λ. Define $\check{\lambda}$ as $\check{\lambda}(\mu_1, \mu_2, \cdots, \mu_n) = 1 - \lambda(1 - \mu_1, 1 - \mu_2, \cdots, 1 - \mu_n)$, where $\mu_i \in \mathcal{Q}(S)$, $i = 1, 2, \cdots, n$ and S is an object in **Fuzzy-Top**.*

Definition 21. *The fuzzy-open predicate lifting λ is*

*(i) monotone if for every object S in **Fuzzy-Top** and $\mu_i, \eta_i \in \mathcal{Q}(S)$, $i = 1, 2, \cdots, n$ such that $\mu_1 \leq \eta_1, \cdots, \mu_n \leq \eta_n \Rightarrow \lambda_S(\mu_1, \cdots, \mu_n) \leq \lambda_S(\eta_1, \cdots, \eta_n)$.*

Let Σ be a collection of fuzzy-open predicate liftings for T. Then, the collection Σ is said to be a fuzzy geometric modal signature for T. Σ is referred to be monotone whenever every member of Σ is monotone.

Definition 22. *The collection Σ for an endofunctor T on **Fuzzy-Top** is considered to be characteristic for T if for each object S in **Fuzzy-Top**, the collection $\{\lambda_S(\mu_1, \cdots, \mu_n) : \lambda \in \Sigma, \mu_i \in \mathcal{Q}(S)\}$ meets the subbasis criteria for the fuzzy topology on TS.*

Let $\mathcal{L}(\Sigma)$ denote the modal language generated by Σ.

Definition 23. *The modal language $\mathcal{L}(\Sigma)$ is the collection **FGML**(Σ) of formulas defined as follows:*
$\beta ::= \top \,|\, p \,|\, \beta_1 \wedge \beta_2 \,|\, \bigvee_{j \in J} \beta_j \,|\, \heartsuit^\lambda(\beta_1, \beta_2, \cdots, \beta_n)$, *where $\lambda \in \Sigma$, Φ represents the set of propositional variables p and J represents an index set.*

Definition 24. *A fuzzy geometric model for the functor T is a mathematical structure $\mathcal{S} = (S, \sigma, \mathcal{V})$ consisting of a T-coalgebra (S, σ), and valuation mapping $\mathcal{V} : \Phi \to \mathcal{Q}(S) \subseteq [0,1]^S$.*

Definition 25. *The following describes a category $FMOD(T)$:*

1. Objects class: class of all fuzzy geometric models for T;
2. A morphism $f : (S, \sigma_1, \mathcal{V}_S) \to (S', \sigma_2, \mathcal{V}_{S'})$ in $FMOD(T)$ is a coalgebra morphism $f : (S, \sigma_1) \to (S', \sigma_2)$ which satisfies the condition: $f^{-1} \circ \mathcal{V}'_{S'} = \mathcal{V}_S$.

Definition 26. *Consider a formula* α *in* **FGML**(Σ). *The semantics of* α *in terms of fuzzy geometric model* $\mathcal{S} = (S, \sigma, \mathcal{V})$ *is defined as shown below:*

(i) $[[\top]]_{\mathcal{S}}(s) = 1;$
(ii) $[[p]]_{\mathcal{S}}(s) = \mathcal{V}(p)(s);$
(iii) $[[\alpha_1 \wedge \alpha_2]]_{\mathcal{S}}(s) = [[\alpha_1]]_{\mathcal{S}}(s) \wedge [[\alpha_2]]_{\mathcal{S}}(s);$
(iv) $[[\bigvee_{i \in J} \alpha_i]]_{\mathcal{S}}(s) = Sup\{[[\alpha_i]]_{\mathcal{S}}(s)\};$
(v) $[[\heartsuit^{\lambda}(\alpha_1, \alpha_2, \cdots, \alpha_n)]]_{\mathcal{S}}(s) = \lambda_{\mathcal{S}}([[\alpha_1]]_{\mathcal{S}}, [[\alpha_2]]_{\mathcal{S}}, \cdots, [[\alpha_n]]_{\mathcal{S}}) \circ \sigma(s).$

Grade of a formula α satisfied by a state(world) s in S is denoted by $gr(s \models \alpha)$ and defined by $gr(s \models \alpha) = [[\alpha]]_{\mathcal{S}}(s)$. Two states s and t in S are modally equivalent if $gr(s \models \alpha) = gr(t \models \alpha)$, $\forall \alpha$ in **FGML**(Σ). We write it as $s \equiv_{\Sigma} t$.

Definition 27. *Let* $\mathcal{B} = (B, \sigma_1, \mathcal{V}_B)$ *and* $\mathcal{B}' = (B', \sigma_2, \mathcal{V}_{B'})$ *be fuzzy geometric models for* T. *States* $b \in B$ *and* $b' \in B'$ *are said to be behaviourally equivalent in* $FMOD(T)$ *if there exists an object* $\mathcal{C} = (C, \gamma, \mathcal{V}_C)$ *in* $FMOD(T)$ *and morphisms* $g : \mathcal{B} \to \mathcal{C}$ *and* $h : \mathcal{B}' \to \mathcal{C}$ *in* $FMOD(T)$ *such that* $g(b) = h(b')$.

In Proposition 1, we shall demonstrate that fuzzy geometric model morphisms preserve truth degrees.

Proposition 1. *Assume that* $f : \mathcal{S} = (S, \sigma_1, \mathcal{V}_S) \to \mathcal{K} = (K, \sigma_2, \mathcal{V}_K)$ *is a morphism in* $FMOD(T)$. *Then, we have* $gr(s \models \alpha) = gr(f(s) \models \alpha)$, $\forall \alpha \in$ **FGML**(Σ) *and* $s \in S$.

Proof. We are to show that for all formulas α, $[[\alpha]]_{\mathcal{S}}(s) = [[\alpha]]_{\mathcal{K}}(f(s))$. If p is a propositional variable then by using Definition 25, we can show that $[[p]]_{\mathcal{S}}(s) = [[p]]_{\mathcal{K}}(f(s))$ i.e., $gr(s \models p) = gr(f(s) \models p)$. It is straightforward to demonstrate that $gr(s \models \bigvee_{j \in J} \alpha_j) = gr(f(s) \models \bigvee_{j \in J} \alpha_j)$ and $gr(s \models \alpha_1 \wedge \alpha_2) = gr(f(s) \models \alpha_1 \wedge \alpha_2)$. The only part we have to show is that $gr(s \models \heartsuit^{\lambda}(\alpha_1, \alpha_2, \cdots, \alpha_n)) = gr(f(s) \models \heartsuit^{\lambda}(\alpha_1, \alpha_2, \cdots, \alpha_n))$. Since f is the coalgebra morphism, henceforth $Tf \circ \sigma_1 = \sigma_2 \circ f$. So, the following diagram (Fig. 3) commutes.

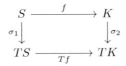

Fig. 3. Coalgebra morphism

Applying the functor $\mathcal{Q}$ to the previous diagram (Fig. 3) yields the following diagram, which commutes as well.

$$QS \xleftarrow{\quad Qf = f^{-1} \quad} QK$$

$$Q\sigma_1 = \sigma_1^{-1} \Big\uparrow \qquad\qquad \Big\uparrow Q\sigma_2 = \sigma_2^{-1}$$

$$Q(TS) \xleftarrow{\quad Q(Tf) = (Tf)^{-1} \quad} Q(TK)$$

Now,

$$[[\heartsuit^\lambda(\alpha_1, \alpha_2, \cdots, \alpha_n)]]_{\mathcal{S}}(s)$$
$$= \lambda_S([[\alpha_1]]_{\mathcal{S}}, \cdots, [[\alpha_n]]_{\mathcal{S}}) \circ \sigma_1(s)$$
$$= \lambda_S([[\alpha_1]]_{\mathcal{K}} \circ f, \cdots, [[\alpha_n]]_{\mathcal{K}} \circ f) \circ \sigma_1(s) \; [\text{ as } f^{-1}([[\alpha]]_{\mathcal{K}}) = [[\alpha]]_{\mathcal{S}} \;]$$
$$= \lambda_K([[\alpha_1]]_{\mathcal{K}}, \cdots, [[\alpha_n]]_{\mathcal{K}}) \circ Tf \circ \sigma_1(s) \; [\text{ by naturality of } \lambda \;]$$
$$= \lambda_K([[\alpha_1]]_{\mathcal{K}}, \cdots, [[\alpha_n]]_{\mathcal{K}}) \circ \sigma_2 \circ f(s)$$
$$= [[\heartsuit^\lambda(\alpha_1, \cdots, \alpha_n)]]_{\mathcal{K}}(f(s))$$

Therefore, $gr(s \models \heartsuit^\lambda(\alpha_1, \alpha_2, \cdots, \alpha_n)) = gr(f(s) \models \heartsuit^\lambda(\alpha_1, \alpha_2, \cdots, \alpha_n))$.

Using Proposition 1, we get the following consequence.

Proposition 2. *Behaviourally equivalent states are modally equivalent.*

Proof. Let $\mathcal{B} = (B, \sigma_1, \mathcal{V}_B)$ and $\mathcal{B}' = (B', \sigma_2, \mathcal{V}_{B'})$ be fuzzy geometric models for T. Consider $b \in B$ and $b' \in B'$ are two states. Suppose, the states b and b' are behaviourally equivalent. We shall show that they are modally equivalent. Since b and b' are behaviourally equivalent in $FMOD(T)$, so there exists an object $\mathcal{C} = (C, \gamma, \mathcal{V}_C)$ in $FMOD(T)$ and morphisms $g : \mathcal{B} \to \mathcal{C}$ and $h : \mathcal{B}' \to \mathcal{C}$ in $FMOD(T)$ such that $g(b) = h(b')$. Now, by Proposition 1, we have $gr(b \models \alpha) = gr(g(b) \models \alpha)$ and $gr(b' \models \alpha) = gr(h(b') \models \alpha)$, $\forall \alpha \in \mathbf{FGML}(\Sigma)$. As $g(b) = h(b')$, hence $gr(b \models \alpha) = gr(b' \models \alpha)$, $\forall \alpha \in \mathbf{FGML}(\Sigma)$. Therefore, the states b and b' are modally equivalent.

4   Bisimulations for Fuzzy Geometric Models

In this section, we develop the bisimulation notions for fuzzy geometric models for an endofunctor T defined on the category **Fuzzy-Top**.

Definition 28. *Consider two sets F and F', and R is a relation between them. Then, for a subset E of F, $R[E] = \{d' \in F' : \exists e \in E, eRd'\}$ and for a subset E' of F', $R^{-1}[E'] = \{d \in F : \exists e' \in E', dRe'\}$.*

Let $\tilde{f}$ be a fuzzy set on F. Then direct image $R[\tilde{f}]$ of $\tilde{f}$ under the relation R is a fuzzy set on F' defined by $R[\tilde{f}](d') = \bigvee_{d \in F}\{\tilde{f}(d) : dRd'\}$.
For a fuzzy set $\tilde{g}$ on F', we define an inverse image of $\tilde{g}$ under the relation R by $R^{-1}[\tilde{g}](d) = \bigvee_{d' \in F'}\{\tilde{g}(d') : dRd'\}$. $R^{-1}[\eta]$ is a fuzzy set on F. The Aczel-Mendler bisimulation notion for fuzzy geometric models is discussed in Definition 29.

Definition 29. *Let* $\mathcal{B}_1 = (B_1, \gamma_1, V_{B_1})$ *and* $\mathcal{B}_2 = (B_2, \gamma_2, V_{B_2})$ *be fuzzy geometric models for* T. *Then, a relation* $\mathcal{R} \subseteq B_1 \times B_2$ *is said to be an Aczel-Mendler bisimulation between* $\mathcal{B}_1$ *and* $\mathcal{B}_2$ *if for each* $(b_1, b_2) \in \mathcal{R}$ *and* $p \in \Phi$, $V_{B_1}(p)(b_1) = V_{B_2}(p)(b_2)$, *i.e.,* $gr(b_1 \models p) = gr(b_2 \models p)$ *and a unique coalgebra morphism* $\gamma^* : \mathcal{R} \to T\mathcal{R}$ *exists in such a way that the projection maps* $\pi_1 : \mathcal{R} \to B_1$ *and* $\pi_2 : \mathcal{R} \to B_2$ *are coalgebra morphisms and satisfy the relations:* $\gamma_1 \circ \pi_1 = T(\pi_1) \circ \gamma^*$, $\gamma_2 \circ \pi_2 = T(\pi_2) \circ \gamma^*$. *Hence, the following diagram(Fig. 4) commutes:*

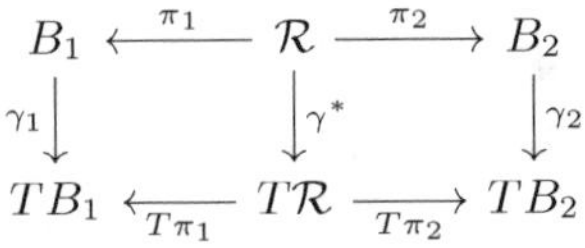

$$
\begin{array}{ccccc}
B_1 & \xleftarrow{\ \pi_1\ } & \mathcal{R} & \xrightarrow{\ \pi_2\ } & B_2 \\
{\scriptstyle \gamma_1}\downarrow & & \downarrow{\scriptstyle \gamma^*} & & \downarrow{\scriptstyle \gamma_2} \\
TB_1 & \xleftarrow[T\pi_1]{} & T\mathcal{R} & \xrightarrow[T\pi_2]{} & TB_2
\end{array}
$$

Fig. 4. Illustration of Aczel-Mendler bisimulation for fuzzy geometric models

By adapting the "Λ-bisimulation" ideas discussed in [4,5], we introduce Σ-bisimulation notion for fuzzy geometric models. First, we introduce the notion of coherent pairs.

Definition 30. *Assume that* $\mathcal{R}$ *is a relation between* B *and* B'. *Let* $\pi_1 : \mathcal{R} \to B$ *and* $\pi_2 : \mathcal{R} \to B'$ *be projection maps. Then, a pair* $(\tilde{b}, \tilde{b}')$, *where* $\tilde{b}$ *and* $\tilde{b}'$ *are respectively the fuzzy sets on* B *and* B', *is called* $\mathcal{R}$-*coherent if* $\mathcal{R}[\tilde{b}] \leq \tilde{b}'$ *and* $\mathcal{R}^{-1}[\tilde{b}'] \leq \tilde{b}$.

Definition 31. *Let* $\mathcal{B}_1 = (B_1, \gamma_1, V_{B_1})$ *and* $\mathcal{B}_2 = (B_2, \gamma_2, V_{B_2})$ *be fuzzy geometric models for* T. *A relation* $\mathcal{R} \subseteq B_1 \times B_2$ *is said to be a* Σ-*bisimulation between* $\mathcal{B}_1$ *and* $\mathcal{B}_2$ *if for all* $(b_1, b_2) \in \mathcal{R}$, $p \in \Phi$ *and for every pair of fuzzy open sets* $(\xi_i, \zeta_i) \in \mathcal{Q}(B_1) \times \mathcal{Q}(B_2)$ *such that* $\mathcal{R}[\xi_i] \leq \zeta_i$ *and* $\mathcal{R}^{-1}[\zeta_i] \leq \xi_i$, *we have :*

(i) $gr(b_1 \models p) = gr(b_2 \models p)$, *and*
(ii) $gr(\gamma_1(b_1) \in \lambda_{B_1}(\xi_1, \xi_2, \cdots, \xi_n)) = gr(\gamma_2(b_2) \in \lambda_{B_2}(\zeta_1, \zeta_2, \cdots, \zeta_n))$.

If there is a Σ-bisimulation $\mathcal{R}$ such that $(b_1, b_2) \in \mathcal{R}$, then the states b_1 and b_2 are called Σ-bisimilar.

Lemma 1. *Suppose* $\mathcal{R} \subseteq B_1 \times B_2$ *is a relation endowed with the fuzzy subspace topology. Let* $\pi_1 : \mathcal{R} \to B_1$ *and* $\pi_2 : \mathcal{R} \to B_2$ *be projection maps. Then, for fuzzy open sets* ξ *and* ζ, *such that* $(\xi, \zeta) \in \mathcal{Q}(B_1) \times \mathcal{Q}(B_2)$ *is* $\mathcal{R}$-*coherent* $\Longleftrightarrow$ $\pi_1^{-1}(\xi) = \pi_2^{-1}(\zeta)$.

Proof. Suppose the pair of fuzzy open sets (μ, η) is $\mathcal{R}$-coherent. We shall show that $\pi_1^{-1}(\xi) = \pi_2^{-1}(\zeta)$. First, we show that $\pi_1^{-1}(\xi)$ is a fuzzy subset of $\pi_2^{-1}(\zeta)$, i.e. $\pi_1^{-1}(\xi) \leq \pi_2^{-1}(\zeta)$. We notice that $\pi_2(\pi_1^{-1}(\xi))$ and $\mathcal{R}[\xi]$ are both fuzzy sets on B_2. It is simple to demonstrate that $\pi_2(\pi_1^{-1}(\xi)) = \mathcal{R}[\xi]$.

Now,

$$\pi^{-1}(\xi) \leq \pi_2^{-1}(\pi_2(\pi_1^{-1}(\xi)))$$
$$= \pi_2^{-1}(\mathcal{R}[\xi]) \text{ [As } \pi_2(\pi_1^{-1}(\xi)) = \mathcal{R}[\xi] \text{]}$$
$$\leq \pi_2^{-1}(\zeta) \text{ [As } \mathcal{R}[\xi] \leq \zeta \text{]}$$

Similarly, we can show that $\pi_2^{-1}(\zeta) \leq \pi_1^{-1}(\xi)$. It is simple to show that if $\pi_1^{-1}(\xi) = \pi_2^{-1}(\zeta)$ then the pair (ξ, ζ) is $\mathcal{R}$-coherent.

Now, we show that Σ-bisimilar states are modally equivalent.

Corollary 2. *Suppose T is an endofunctor on the category **Fuzzy-Top**. Then Σ-bisimilarity implies modal equivalence.*

Proof. Let $\mathcal{R}$ be a Σ-bisimulation between fuzzy geometric models $\mathcal{B}_1 = (B_1, \gamma_1, \mathcal{V}_{B_1})$ and $\mathcal{B}_2 = (B_2, \gamma_2, \mathcal{V}_{B_2})$. Let $b_1 \in B_1$ and $b_2 \in B_2$ be two states. Suppose $b_1 \mathcal{R} b_2$. We shall show that $gr(b_1 \models \alpha) = gr(b_2 \models \alpha), \forall \alpha \in \mathbf{FGML}(\Sigma)$. If p is a propositional variable, then it follows from the definition of Σ-bisimulation that $gr(b_1 \models p) = gr(b_2 \models p)$. It can be easily shown that $gr(b_1 \models \alpha_1 \wedge \alpha_2) = gr(b_2 \models \alpha_1 \wedge \alpha_2)$ and $gr(b_1 \models \bigvee_{j \in J} \alpha_j) = gr(b_2 \models \bigvee_{j \in J} \alpha_j)$, J is an index set. Now, $gr(b_1 \models \heartsuit^\lambda(\alpha_1, \alpha_2, \cdots, \alpha_n)) = gr(\gamma_1(b_1) \in \lambda_{B_1}([[\alpha_1]]_{\mathcal{B}_1}, [[\alpha_2]]_{\mathcal{B}_1}, \cdots, [[\alpha_n]]_{\mathcal{B}_1}))$. By induction principle, we can show that, for each $i = 1, 2, \cdots, n$, $\mathcal{R}[[\alpha_i]]_{\mathcal{B}_1}] \leq [[\alpha_i]]_{\mathcal{B}_2}$ and $\mathcal{R}^{-1}[[[\alpha_i]]_{\mathcal{B}_2}] \leq [[\alpha_i]]_{\mathcal{B}_1}$. As $\mathcal{R}$ is a Σ-bisimulation, we have $gr(\gamma_1(b_1) \in \lambda_{B_1}([[\alpha_1]]_{\mathcal{B}_1}, [[\alpha_2]]_{\mathcal{B}_1}, \cdots, [[\alpha_n]]_{\mathcal{B}_1})) = gr(\gamma_2(b_2) \in \lambda_{B_2}([[\alpha_1]]_{\mathcal{B}_2}, [[\alpha_2]]_{\mathcal{B}_2}, \cdots, [[\alpha_n]]_{\mathcal{B}_2})$. Consequently, $gr(b_1 \models \heartsuit^\lambda(\alpha_1, \alpha_2, \cdots, \alpha_n)) = gr(b_2 \models \heartsuit^\lambda(\alpha_1, \alpha_2, \cdots, \alpha_n))$. Therefore, b_1 and b_2 are modally equivalent.

Corollary 3. *Consider a monotone fuzzy geometric modal signature Σ for T, where T is defined on **Fuzzy-Top**. Then, Aczel-Mendler bisimulation notion implies Σ-bisimulation notion.*

Proof. Consider $\mathcal{B}_1 = (B_1, \gamma_1, \mathcal{V}_{B_1})$ and $\mathcal{B}_2 = (B_2, \gamma_2, \mathcal{V}_{B_2})$ are fuzzy geometric models for T. Let $\mathcal{R}$ be an Aczel-Mendler bisimulation between $\mathcal{B}_1$ and $\mathcal{B}_2$. Then the diagram shown in Fig. 5 commutes.

$$
\begin{array}{ccccc}
B_1 & \xleftarrow{\pi_1} & \mathcal{R} & \xrightarrow{\pi_2} & B_2 \\
\gamma_1 \downarrow & & \downarrow \gamma^* & & \downarrow \gamma_2 \\
TB_1 & \xleftarrow{T\pi_1} & T\mathcal{R} & \xrightarrow{T\pi_2} & TB_2
\end{array}
$$

Fig. 5. Illustration of Aczel-Mendler bisimulation between fuzzy geometric models

We are to show that, $\mathcal{R}$ is a Σ-bisimulation. Consider $b_1 \mathcal{R} b_2$, where $b_1 \in B_1$ and $b_2 \in B_2$ are the states. Given that $\mathcal{R}$ is an Aczel-Mendler bisimulation, we have for any propositional variable $p \in \Phi$, $gr(b_1 \models p) = gr(b_2 \models p)$. Assume that for each pair of fuzzy open sets $(\xi_i, \zeta_i) \in \mathcal{Q}(B_1) \times \mathcal{Q}(B_2)$, $\mathcal{R}[\xi_i] \leq \zeta_i$ and $\mathcal{R}^{-1}[\zeta_i] \leq \xi_i$.

Now,

$$gr(\gamma_1(b_1) \in \lambda_{B_1}(\xi_1, \xi_2, \cdots, \xi_n))$$
$$= \lambda_{B_1}(\xi_1, \xi_2, \cdots, \xi_n)(\gamma_1(b_1))$$
$$= \lambda_{B_1}(\xi_1, \xi_2, \cdots, \xi_n)(T\pi_1)(\gamma^*(b_1, b_2)) \; [\text{ As } \gamma_1 \circ \pi_1 = T\pi_1 \circ \gamma^* \;]$$
$$= gr(\gamma^*(b_1, b_2) \in (T\pi_1)^{-1}(\lambda_{B_1}(\xi_1, \xi_2, \cdots, \xi_n)))$$
$$= gr(\gamma^*(b_1, b_2) \in \lambda_{\mathcal{R}}(\xi_1 \circ \pi_1, \xi_2 \circ \pi_1, \cdots, \xi_n \circ \pi_1)) \; [\text{As } \lambda \text{ is a natural transformation}]$$
$$\leq gr(\gamma^*(b_1, b_2) \in \lambda_{\mathcal{R}}(\pi_2^{-1}(\pi_2(\pi_1^{-1}(\xi_1)))), \cdots, \pi_2^{-1}(\pi_2(\pi_1^{-1}(\xi_n))) \; [\text{As } \lambda \text{ is monotone}]$$
$$= gr(\gamma^*(b_1, b_2) \in \lambda_{\mathcal{R}}(\pi_2^{-1}(\mathcal{R}[\xi_1]), \pi_2^{-1}(\mathcal{R}[\xi_2]), \cdots, \pi_2^{-1}(\mathcal{R}[\xi_n])))$$
$$\leq gr(\gamma^*(b_1, b_2) \in \lambda_{\mathcal{R}}(\pi_2^{-1}(\zeta_1), \pi_2^{-1}(\zeta_2), \cdots, \pi_2^{-1}(\zeta_n)))[\text{As } \lambda \text{ is monotone }]$$
$$= gr(\gamma^*(b_1, b_2) \in \lambda_{\mathcal{R}}(\zeta_1 \circ \pi_2, \cdots, \zeta_n \circ \pi_2))$$
$$= gr(\gamma^*(b_1, b_2) \in (T\pi_2)^{-1}(\lambda_{B_2}(\zeta_1, \zeta_2, \cdots, \zeta_n))) \; [\text{As } \lambda \text{ is natural}]$$
$$= gr(\gamma_2(b_2) \in \lambda_{B_2}(\zeta_1, \zeta_2, \cdots, \zeta_n))$$

Therefore, $gr(\gamma_1(b_1) \in \lambda_{B_1}(\xi_1, \xi_2, \cdots, \xi_n)) \leq gr(\gamma_2(b_2) \in \lambda_{B_2}(\zeta_1, \zeta_2, \cdots, \zeta_n))$. Similarly, it can be shown that $gr(\gamma_2(b_2) \in \lambda_{B_2}(\zeta_1, \zeta_2, \cdots, \zeta_n)) \leq gr(\gamma_1(b_1) \in \lambda_{B_1}(\xi_1, \xi_2, \cdots, \xi_n))$. Finally, we have $gr(\gamma_1(b_1) \in \lambda_{B_1}(\xi_1, \xi_2, \cdots, \xi_n)) = gr(\gamma_2(b_2) \in \lambda_{B_2}(\zeta_1, \zeta_2, \cdots, \zeta_n))$. Hence, the result follows.

5   Conclusion

The paper uses coalgebraic methods to define modal operators in fuzzy geometric logic. In order to study modalities in fuzzy geometric logic, we have introduced the idea of fuzzy-open predicate lifting for an endofunctor T on **Fuzzy-Top**. The structures referred to as the fuzzy geometric models for T, provide the semantics for our coalgebraic logics. The notions of Aczel-mendler bisimulation and Σ-bisimulation for fuzzy geometric models have introduced in our work. We conclude the study by mentioning future research directions. It can be observed that if T is an endofunctor on **SFuzzy-Top** then behavioural equivalence coincides with modal equivalence. In our future work, we will verify whether behavioural equivalence and modal equivalence coincide if T is an endofunctor on the category of compact fuzzy Hausdorff spaces.

Declarations

- **Conflict of interest**
  The authors declare that there is no conflict of interest.
- **Availability of data and materials**
  Data sharing not applicable to this article as no datasets were generated or analysed during the current study.

Acknowledgements. The authors would like to thank the area editor and the reviewers for their valuable comments.

References

1. Adámek, J.H., Herrlich, H., Strecker, G.E.: Abstract and Concrete Categories, 2nd edn. Dover Publications, Mineola, New York (2009)
2. Adámek, J.: Introduction to coalgebra. Theory Appl. Categories **14**(8), 157–199 (2005)
3. Abramsky, S.: Domain theory and the logic of observable properties. arXiv preprint arXiv:1112.0347 (2011)
4. Bakhtiari, Z., Hansen, H.: Helle.: Bisimulation for weakly expressive coalgebraic modal logics. In: 7th Conference on Algebra and Coalgebra in Computer Science(CALCO 2017), Schloss Dagstuhl-Leibniz-Zentrum fuer Informatik 4, pp. 1–4:16 (2017)
5. Gorín, D., Schröder, L.: Simulations and bisimulations for coalgebraic modal logics. In: Heckel, R., Milius, S. (eds.) CALCO 2013. LNCS, vol. 8089, pp. 253–266. Springer, Heidelberg (2013). https://doi.org/10.1007/978-3-642-40206-7_19
6. Chakraborty, M.K., Jana, P.: Fuzzy topology via fuzzy geometric logic with graded consequence. Int. J. Approximate Reasoning **80**, 334–347 (2017)
7. Chang, C.-L: Fuzzy topological spaces. J. Math. Anal. Appl. **24**(1), 182–190 (1968)
8. Chakraborty, M.K., Dutta, S.: Theory of Graded Consequence. Springer (2019)
9. Kurz, A.: Coalgebras and their logics. ACM SIGACT News **37**(2), 57–77 (2006)
10. Cîrstea, C., Kurz, A., Pattinson, D., Schröder, L., Venema, Y.: Modal logics are coalgebraic. Comput. J. **54**(1), 31–41 (2011)
11. Kupke, C., Pattinson, D.: Coalgebraic semantics of modal logics: an overview. Theoretical Comput. Sci. **412**(38), 5070–5094 (2011)
12. Moss, L.S.: Coalgebraic logic. Annals Pure Appl. Logic **96**(1) (1999)
13. Pattinson, D.: Coalgebraic modal logic: Soundness, completeness and decidability of local consequence. Theoretical Comput. Sci. **309**(1) (2003)
14. Venema, Y., Vickers, S., Vosmaer, J.: Generalised powerlocales via relation lifting. Math. Struct. Comput. Sci. **23**(1), 142–199 (2013)
15. Bezhanishvili, N., de Groot, J., Venema, Y.: Coalgebraic Geometric Logic: Basic Theory. arXiv preprint arXiv:1903.08837 (2019)
16. Aczel, P., Mendler, N.: A final coalgebra theorem. Lecture Notes in Computer Science, 389, 357–365 (1989)
17. Kotzé, W.: Fuzzy sobriety and fuzzy Hausdorff. Quaestiones Math, **20**(3), 415–422 (1997)
18. Vickers, S.: Topology via logic. Cambridge University Press (1996)
19. Goguen, J.A.: The fuzzy Tychonoff theorem. J. Math. Anal. Appl. **43**(3), 734–742 (1973)
20. Walker, C.L.: Categories of fuzzy sets. Soft. Comput. **8**(4), 299–304 (2004)
21. Zadeh, L.A.: Fuzzy sets. Inf. Control **8**(3), 338–353 (1965)

Research Study: Data Preprocessing Using Machine Learning for Prediction of Booking Cancellations

Abhishek Kumar[1]([✉]) [iD], Upendra Prasad[2], Rajesh Kumar Tiwari[3], and Vijay Pandey[1]

[1] Jharkhand University of Technology, Ranchi, Jharkhand 834010, India
abhishek28mca@gmail.com
[2] BIT Sindri, Dhanbad, Jharkhand 834010, India
[3] RVS Collage Of Engineering and Technology, Jamshedpur, Jharkhand, India

Abstract. Cancellations of reservations have a substantial effect on the choices that hospitality businesses make about management control. In order for hotels to minimize the blow of guest cancellations, this report have instituted stringent cancellation rules and scheduling strategies. However, these strategies may have a detrimental effect not only on income but also on the hotel's image. A machine learning-based system model was designed in order to lessen the severity of this effect. It does this by using the data from the hotel's Management Company Systems and training a classification algorithm on a daily basis. This allows it to determine which reservations are "likely to cancel" and, as a result, compute net demands. This prototypes, which has been installed in a production setting at two hotels, allows the assessment of the effect of measures made to respond upon bookings that have been projected as likely to cancel by implementing A/B testing. Results reveal strong prototype effectiveness and provide crucial indicators for the development of research while also providing evidence that reservations approached by hotels cancel less often than bookings that are not approached by hotels.

Keywords: Ticket Cancellation · Prediction · Python · Machine Learning · Hotel

1 Introduction

Cancellation policies for guest rooms are managed by the hotel's central reservation system, key consideration while making choices about related demands. It has an impact on the hotel's services and bottom line and makes estimations about the pertinent outcomes (Sánchez-Medina and Eleazar, 2020). The administration cares about satisfying their clients by looking at these methods in depth. It's possible that there's a variety of causes for this.

For several reasons, a guest may decide to cancel a hotel reservation, including but not limited to: presents, duties, ailments, accidents, and so on. This study shows that when clients' shopping habits change, the rate at which they cancel their purchases also rises. They may consider several possibilities before deciding against using all except

R. K. Tiwari and G. Sahoo (Eds.): ICAII 2022, CCIS 1822, pp. 164–182, 2023.
https://doi.org/10.1007/978-3-031-37303-9_13

one. The hotel implemented stringent cancellation regulations and practices to reduce financial losses (Yacoub and ElHajjar, 2021). Low refund or non-refund rules reduce revenues and the number of reservations; however, these laws cannot be used in all cases because they impede the quality of services. Because of this, some hotels have resorted to overbooking techniques, which result in a bad customer service experience because they are forced to refuse service supply.

The likelihood of a guest canceling a hotel reservation is represented as a binary categorization issue, with just two possible results, well if they refuse to cancel. As of yet, there are not a ton of models available for making such a forecast. One for making such a forecast, the Synaptic connection should be between brain cells (Abbott et al. 2020). As opposed to the usual use, neural network experiments, and using the same old machine learning network needs to find a solution to the prediction issue that has various constraints that must be taken into account. The "black box" problem is the most well-known drawback of neural networks; it prevents outside observers from understanding how inputs affect the outputs.

2   Aims and Objectives

The principal aim of this research is investigating the significance of machine learning technology while practically implementing this technology in predicting the cancellation of hotel reservations.

- To understand the importance of machine learning technology in solving real world problems.
- To implement machine learning technology to predict ticket reservation cancellation in a hotel
- To investigate various challenges in implementing the machine learning technology
- To recommend strategies element the challenges of implementing machine learning technology in solving real world problems.

3   Related Works

Comparison and Analysis of ML Models to predict Hotel Booking Cancellation
Antonio's hotel reservation request data has been used to compile this program's database. Accommodations at resorts and hotels in Portugal are included; one is a resort while the other is a city hotel. The arrival dates for all bookings are somewhere between July 1st, 2015 and August 31st, 2017. In all, there are 32 characteristics and 119391 observations throughout the dataset. In all, there are 28 characteristics, 14 of which may be categorized and the rest of which are numerical. The following table lists 13 important factors (Table 1).

In order to address issues like data gaps, inconsistencies, and outliers, and so on, we removed them from the raw data by pre-processing problems. First, designers transform the raw information into a dataset that is simultaneously streamlined and comprehensive, allowing us to test models with ease. To improve the image quality data and obtain a consistent dataset, they use the "sklearn.preprocessing library" in Python (Nayan et al.

Table 1. Key Variables. (Source: Chen et al, 2022).

Name	Description
hotel	Hotel type: resort hotel or city hotel
is_canceled	A booking was canceled (1) or not (0)
lead_time	Number of days that elapsed between the date of the booking and the arrival
is_repeated_guest	Value indicating if the booking name was from a repeated guest (1) or not (0)
previous_cancellations	Number of previous cancelled bookings by the customer before the current booking
previous_bookings_not_canceled	Number of previous bookings not cancelled by the customer before the current booking
booking_changes	Number of changes made to the booking from the booking to check-in or cancellation by customers
days_in_waiting_list	Number of days the booking was on the waiting list before it was confirmed to the customer
customer_type	Type of booking
required_car_parking_spaces	Number of car parking spaces required by the customer
total_of_special_requests	Number of special requests made by the customer
reservation_status	Reservation last status
reservation_status_date	Date at which the last status was set

2022). With MinMaxScaler, designers provide a spectrum of scalability characteristics between 0 and 1 (Dey et al. 2023). Because of this, we are able to keep 0 values in extremely sparse data while still retaining the strength of traits with a relatively tiny standard deviation.

Figure 1 shows that occupancy rates increase with decreasing notice. One probable explanation is that guests only reserve accommodations for the nights they will really be using them. Many questions would remain unanswered if the lead time was excessively long.

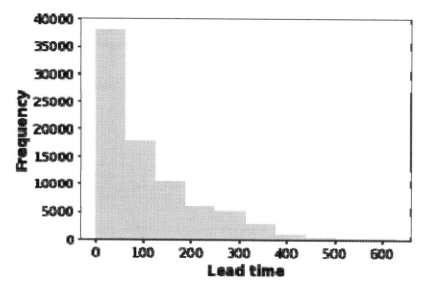

Fig. 1. Time customers book rooms. (Source: Chen et al, 2022)

Figure 2 provides more evidence that supports the hypothesis that there is a pattern in Fig. 1. There is a significant cancellation rate (over 50%) when the lead time is considerable. The cancellation rate increases to 10% when the notice period is fewer than 7 days.

The greater the lead time, the more unknowns will be involved. Even if the cost of a hotel room is greater if booked far in advance, people are more likely to make a reservation close to the actual date of their arrival.

Researchers compute the coefficient of correlation seen between characteristics and the label in order to analyse the significance of the features. Table 2's findings indicate that lead time and previous cancellation have been most positively associated with cancellation, meaning that lead time increases the likelihood of cancellation and consumers who previously cancelled bookings are more likely to do so with their subsequent orders.

Performance Analysis of Machine Learning Techniques to Predict Hotel booking cancellations in Hospitality Industry

In order to get good results, this work used a variety of machine-learning techniques to process data from hotel reservations. The figure below shows how many models have always been applied to this data set and how their impacts were examined (Fig. 3).

Antonio, Almeida, and Nunes produced this data, which included two hotel booking details, such as resort (H1) and city hotel (H2). It was obtained by running a Transact-Structured Query Language (TSQL) query on their databases. All references to hotel or customer identifying numbers have been eliminated (Andriawanet al, 2020). After combining these datasets with 31 parameters, we discovered 40,060 instances of H1

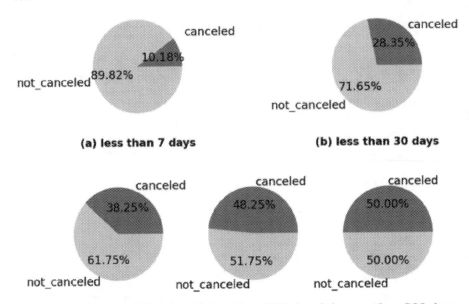

Fig.2. Rate of Cancellation to LeadTime. (Source: Chen et al, 2022)

Table 2. Correlation Coefficient between Features and Label (is_cancelled). (Source: Chen et al, 2022).

Feature Name	Correlation Coefficient
lead_time	0.314161
previous_cancellations	0.132844
required_car_parking_spaces	–0.191471
total_of_special_requests	–0.269111

as well as 79,330 instances of H2. However, a city hotel's cancellation rate (41.90%) was greater than a resort hotel's (27.69%). It includes three years' worth of booking occurrences, spanning from July 1, 2015, to August 31, 2017. The following are the descriptive data for cancelled hotel reservations from Table 3.

To prepare the input dataset for subsequent analysis, data preparation is utilized. In order to create a well-generalized machine learning model, many situations including finding outliers, filling in blanks, and data cleansing were examined (Piccialliet al, 2020). This three-column dataset has a number of missing values. Researchers eliminated the

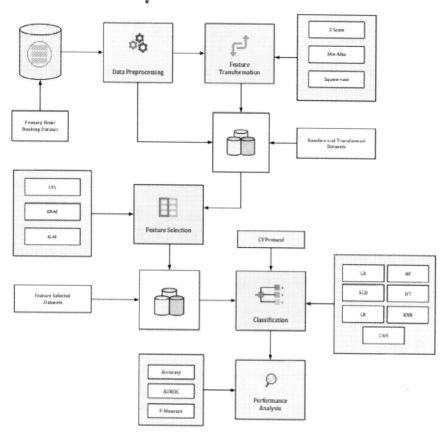

Fig. 3. Proposed Methodology. (Source: Satu *et al.*, 2020)

Table 3. Descriptive Statistics. (Source: Satu *et al.*, 2020)

	Range	Minimum	Maximum	Mean	Std. Deviation	Variance	Skewness	Kurtosis
Canceled	1	0	1	0.37	0.483	0.233	0.537	-1.712
Lead Time	737	0	737	104.01	106.863	11419.722	1.347	1.696
Arrival Year	2	2015	2017	2016.16	0.707	0.501	-0.233	-0.995
Arrival Month	00:00.11	JANUARY	DECEMBER	JUNE	00:00:03.093	9.552	-0.028	-0.995
Arrival Week Number	52	1	53	27.17	13.605	185.100	-0.010	-0.986
Arrival Day of Month	30	1	31	15.80	8.781	77.103	-0.002	-1.187
Stay Weekend Nights	19	0	19	0.93	0.999	0.997	1.380	7.174
Stays Week Nights	50	0	50	2.50	1.908	3.642	2.862	24.285
Adults	55	0	55	1.86	0.579	0.336	18.318	1352.115
Children	10	0	10	0.10	0.399	0.159	4.113	18.674
Babies	10	0	10	0.01	0.097	0.009	24.647	1633.948
Repeated Guest	1	0	1	0.03	0.176	0.031	5.326	26.370
Previous Cancellations	26	0	26	0.09	0.844	0.713	24.458	674.074
Previous Bookings Not Canceled	72	0	72	0.14	1.497	2.242	23.540	767.245
Booking Changes	21	0	21	0.22	0.652	0.426	6.000	79.394
Waiting List	391	0	391	2.32	17.595	309.574	11.944	186.793
adr	5406.38	-6.38	5400.00	101.8311	50.53579	2553.866	10.530	1013.190
Required Car Parking Spaces	8	0	8	0.06	0.245	0.060	4.163	29.998
Total Special Requests	5	0	5	0.57	0.793	0.629	1.349	1.493
Reservation Status Date	1063 00:00:00	10/17/2014	09/14/2017	07/30/2016	229 05:43:17.160		-0.160	-0.903

Company column because it had 94% of the missing entries. Once more, the "reservation status" column is eliminated since it has a strong correlation (-0.9171) with the target label (Abdul Rahman and Mohezar, 2020).

By transforming features, new variables are made from the ones that already exist. Three characteristics, including scaling, normalizing, and standardization, were discovered. The range of values between 0 and 1 is changed by scaling, while the distribution and standards remain constant at mean and 1. As a result, normalising creates bell-shaped ranges from the distribution. Similarly, researchers determined how to adjust characteristics and assess their differences using the min-max, z-score, as well as square root approaches (Nousi et al. 2022). Individual characteristics throughout the range (0–1) are transformed using the min-max approach, as well as standard deviations between and beyond the mean, are observed using the z–score. That can provide better results, several feature extraction techniques were applied to independent factors as well as identified either by accident or manually. It recognizes irrelevant characteristics, which lowers time complexity, minimises the possibility of overfitting, and simplifies machine learning models.

When employing the best first search approach, CFS only considers characteristics that are highly linked and display the correlation also with goal values. As a result, neither Spearman's nor Pearson's correlation coefficients are kept for these variables (Lesnak et al. 2019).The blooming topic regarding digital libraries and also the promise of well-structured enclaves can be beneficial for users in the motile type of complex jobs. These areas are mainly based on the chaotic and confusing scenario in the area of science and technology (Chen, 2021). The digital library system contains collections of some unique and also different sources of information. In this critical situation, particular users always need to search for some tools and mechanisms of data retrieval (Bernardi et al. 2019).

Digital libraries require more funding for providing some definite services and also maintain some of the infrastructures regarding some methods. His type of public library is always unable to provide the users and the particular customers some services regarding the information through some electronic sources. (Shane, 2019) This type of public library actually does not have sufficient sources to maintain properly. The library financing management system is mainly identified to set up some challenges that can be overcome after setting up the system.

There are some people who are mainly working on academic libraries and are mainly unable to manage some of the electronic sources and digital resources (Nousi, 2020). With this result there are some efficient servers, cable operation and also has wireless access points regarding some of the multiple operations. There are some lack of administrative services and a lack of technical knowledge found in multiple areas where these kinds of technical issues are solved. There are some challenges regarding the implementation of the coding portion. As a result, there is a shortage of experienced professionals and employees to run digital library unrelated issues.

In the field of machine learning, the objective is to teach computers to learn on their own without being given specific instructions. In point of fact, machine learning takes place when we are confronted with a difficult task or problem that cannot be solved by traditional methods, or when we are faced with a large amount of data and variables that cannot be processed and calculated by human resources using traditional methods, and for which we do not even have formulas or equations.

The data security software and the technical issue are mainly provided by houses to prevent viruses and related issues. Database security software and particular technology is a very important tool to describe particular risks. There are some problems with maintaining online activity and managing particular issues (Perreira, 2020). There are some problems with information and related methods that can be operating software development processes through the database's security system. Privacy may be violated by hackers and other customers. Here are some downloading processes and internal connections to be performed here step by step with this particular database. The university libraries also provide particular information and also some digital services to predict the database from hackers and comfort plagiarism issues.

The credibility of a similar program must take place at the time of the implementation process. There are some financial sources and supporting management to supply the delivery processes per the requirement. In a shorter amount of time, things are always getting better day by day. There are some tips regarding the library process to overcome the outcome. In recent days the workforce is mainly based on better prospects and different outcomes. The main method of the visualization process is based on the initial process that must be included as the server-wise platform. The Explanation of the security issue is to be concerned about the technology and different platforms (Kazak et al. 2020). In the year count process, here are some columns like arrival date, year and cancelled. This part is based on the year count and group by value in whichmonth the arrival date has been added as well as cancelled thereafter by the customer without any notice. In the output section, there are 2 months added, and the predicted value is also described sidewise. There are different values and different programs have been added in different months.

There are some legislative properties that cannot be applied to the digestion process. The content process of a particular person must be included with the particular implementation process to maintain the security issue and related works (Arhur, 2021). The library must be included in the meditation process with some particular restriction as an electronic communication process.

4 Methods

This report is based on the dataset regarding hotel booking and cancellation. In his dataset, there are several rows and columns which are related to the numerical value of booking and cancellation of customers. To predict all the values of the booking and cancellation process in the dataset the python programming language was used in the Google collab platform. This prediction method is used with the help of machine learning programming language with different classification techniques. At first, the dataset was imported which is related to the hotel booking and cancellation method. In the next part, the data analysis part has been performed. The percentage cancellation value and also reservation status has been performed in this portion. This Part Consists of the normalization process with various outcomes. The sns plot is added in this portion with different values and after that, the cancellation portion in the resort hotel column is performed in the city hotels portion. The predicted portion has also a predicted value of 7.81.

To fix the issues like some of the data gaps, outliers, and so on the programming, those are mainly moved from the raw data at the time of pre-processing the particular problems. There are some designers that transform the data and information in a dataset that are mainly streamlined and appropriate. This type of capability always likes to test the particular model easily. The particular designers transform the raw information through a dataset that is streamlined with the data model. There is some image quality data and a particular dataset is compiled with the help of python programming language. There are different rows and different columns added as the csv files (Lee, 2019). There are several rows and columns added which are mainly specified with different programming languages. With the compilation process, the designs are made and then the machine learning process can be operated with his system. There are some gaps that are mainly discovered with the blanked values. In the other addition, the python programming language adds the 0 value.

Data preprocessing for machine learning involves a range of tasks to clean, transform, and organize the data before it is used for predictive modeling. This step is crucial as data is often noisy and inconsistent, and can have missing values and outliers that need to be addressed in order to ensure accurate predictions. Additionally, the preprocessing step allows the machine learning model to identify the meaningful patterns and correlations which may give us insight into the important drivers of cancellation.

The first step in data preprocessing is data cleaning, which involves making sure that the data is free of missing or incorrect values. If missing data points need to be filled in, there are various techniques for imputing values, such as the mean, median, or mode of the attribute. Additionally, features that are not relevant to the model, such as ID numbers, can be removed from the dataset. To detect outliers in the dataset, summary statistics, such as the mean and standard deviation of an attribute, can be calculated and values that are outside of two or three standard deviations away from the mean can be identified.

The next step is to transform the data into a format that can be used in the machine learning algorithm. One way to do this is feature scaling, where the data is brought to the same unit of measure, usually between 0 and 1, so that all the features are weighted equally by the model. There are two approaches to feature scaling, min-max scaling, which brings all values between 0 and 1, and standardization, where the mean of the dataset is subtracted from each value and divided by the standard deviation of the dataset.

The final step is to call the data for use in machine learning. It is important to split the dataset into training, validation, and testing sets. The training dataset is used to fit the model, the validation set is used to tune the parameters of the model, and finally, the model is tested on the test set to evaluate its performance. It is also useful to stratify the data, which means that the proportion of classes are equal in each subset. In the case of predicting booking cancellations, we would want to ensure that there is an equal proportion of cancelled and not-cancelled bookings - in each subset. Data preprocessing is an essential step in machine learning to ensure accurate predictions. By carrying out data cleaning, transformation and resizing, as well as data splitting and stratification, we can ensure that the machine learning algorithm will be able to identify the meaningful patterns in the data and will produce reliable predictions.

5   Findings and Analysis.

5.1   Implementing Python Language for predicting the Reservation Cancellation

This figure is based on the assumptions of city hotels and resort hotels. These hotels mainly are compared to each other as the city hotels have higher cancellations than the resort hotels. The prediction has been performed as a bar graph with the help of python language (Figs. 4, 5).

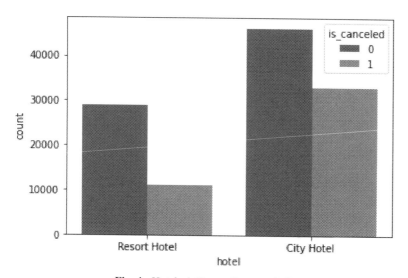

Fig. 4. Hotel v/s Resort (is_canceled)

This figure based on the cancellation of the booking is mainly based 60–70 days before the date of the checking. The booking and checking method described in this portion. If the lead time is longer, then the cancellation portion is also lower. This is mainly the second assumption (Fig. 6).

This table is the correlation table and graphs are the evidence of the maximum number of customers. There are a lesser number of customers who are mainly to cancel the booking section. Some of the old guests are cancelling the booking of the customers with the assumption of 5 holds true (Fig. 7).

This graph is based on the bookings that do not hold a particular trend and there are some impacts of the cancellation process of ticket booking (Fig. 8).

These graphs are shown that there is someone refundable tickets that are cancelled (Fig. 9).

There is no relation that can be shown between the no waiting list and also is cancelled column. Then, the users are taking the feature of the next analysis. Assumption 10 can also be discarded (Fig. 10).

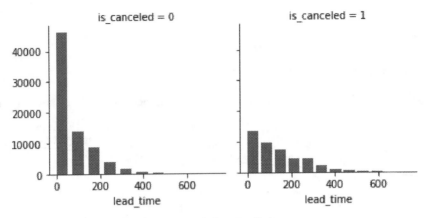

Fig. 5. Lead Time Prediction

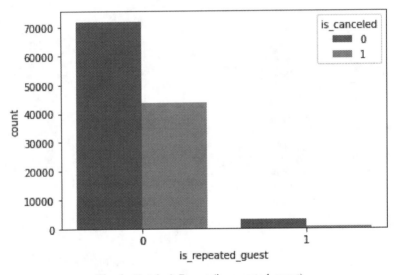

Fig. 6: Hotel v/s Resort (is_repeated_guest)

This graph shows that 75% of bookings occur in the category of customers. There are some highest cancellations among the categories.

5.2 Importance of Machine Learning Technology in solving Real World Problems

The capacity to observe, reason, and learn new things is what's meant when people talk about machines having artificial intelligence. One topic of research that falls under the more general heading of artificial intelligence is machine learning. Following the processing of the data, the computer is able to intelligently extract patterns from the data, learn from the data, and finally transform the data into knowledge. This is performed in a system like this without the need for any explicit programming; rather, the system

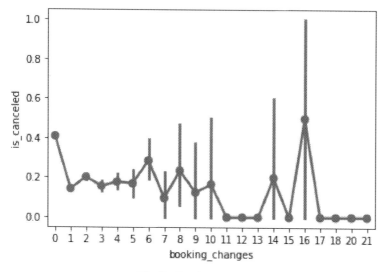

Fig. 7. Hotel v/s Resort

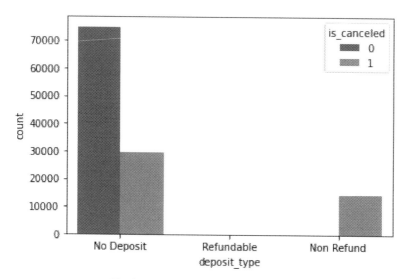

Fig. 8. Hotel v/s Resort (deposite_type)

makes use of its algorithms and, depending on the results of the data processing, refines its algorithm, develops new things for it, and automatically updates the vehicle. The study of computer science, biology, psychology, linguistics, mathematics, and engineering are only a few of the disciplines that serve as the groundwork for the study of artificial intelligence (AI). A subfield of artificial intelligence known as machine learning gives computers the ability to teach themselves new abilities and progress independently, with very little or no assistance from humans.

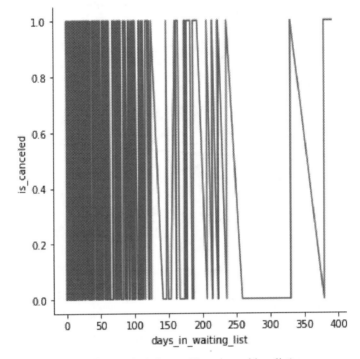

Fig. 9. Hotel v/s Resort (days_in_waiting_list)

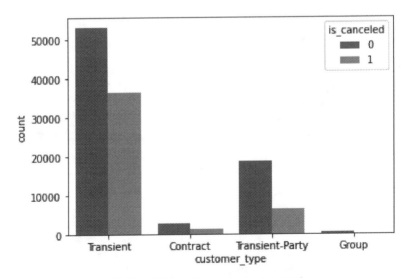

Fig.10. Hotel v/s Resort (customer_type)

The objective of the field of machine learning is to train computers to learn on their own by using the data that has been made available to them. Acquiring some type of knowledge is the initial stage in the learning process. This may be accomplished by observation, instruction, or through one's own direct experience, with the end objective of seeing a pattern in the data and increasing one's ability to make decisions. The major goal is to provide the computer the capacity to learn on its own, without any assistance from humans, and to modify its behaviour in a suitable manner. Learning in a supervised environment, learning in an unsupervised environment, and learning via deep learning are the three primary methods of machine learning. Each of these ways of learning makes use of a variety of different algorithms; the algorithm that is picked to effectively address a particular subject will change from situation to situation.

The use of machine learning is a strong technique that can cut down on administrative costs and boost the effectiveness of data processing. Machine learning is the study of how computers can learn without being explicitly programmed to do so. This is accomplished by having computers depend on algorithms and inferences (Zhang, 2020). Machine learning is an area of artificial intelligence (AI) that, in a nutshell, makes it possible for automated systems to learn and become better without being constrained by standard programming languages. In the field of machine learning, the objective is to teach computers to learn on their own without being given specific instructions. In point of fact, machine learning takes place when we are confronted with a difficult task or problem that cannot be solved by traditional methods, or when we are faced with a large amount of data and variables that cannot be processed and calculated by human resources using traditional methods, and for which we do not even have formulas or equations. In other words, machine learning takes place when we face a situation in which conventional methods are unable to provide a solution. It should come as no surprise that recent years have seen meteoric growth in interest in the subject of machine learning given the potential financial and social benefits that may be realized from its use. As a direct consequence of this, an increasing number of people all around the world have an interest in studying artificial intelligence and machine learning. Also, in the modern world, machine learning interacts with many different industries and processes; therefore, those who aspire to leadership roles would be wise to familiarize themselves with it in advance even if they do not have a background in artificial intelligence. This is because machine learning interacts with many different sectors and processes.

5.3   Challenges in implementing Machine Learning Technology

Machine learning provides businesses with the potential to get the understanding required to make decisions that are more data-driven and can be executed more quickly than was previously possible using approaches that were more manually intensive. To be clear, the process in question is not the magical or fantastical one that some people would have you think it is. The field of machine learning is fraught with challenges that are unlike any other. The following are five common problems with machine learning as well as some recommendations for how to address them (Fig. 11).

5.3.1   Identifying Activities That Ought to be Computerized

When it comes to machine learning, it is difficult to differentiate between fact and imagination at the moment. The first thing you should do before deciding on an AI platform is

Fig. 11. Challenges of Machine Learning Implementation. (Source: Created by Author)

to do an analysis of the problems you want to fix. Processes that are conducted manually on a daily basis with little to no change in output are great candidates for automation. These processes include: Before automating a difficult process, further research is required to fully understand it. Machine learning may be helpful for the automation of specific jobs; nevertheless, it is not the answer to all of the challenges associated with automation.

5.3.2 Low Quality of Information

The most difficult obstacle that machine learning must overcome is the acute lack of data that is of a high enough quality. The bulk of time spent by developers working in the area of artificial intelligence is spent creating algorithms; yet, the quality of the data that these developers utilize is very important to the effectiveness of the algorithms they create. The most significant challenge that machine learning has is dealing with imperfect data, which might include information that is noisy, dirty, or simply absent. Evaluation of the data, integration of the data, and investigation of the data may be helpful in finding a solution to this challenge. Before you can go on to the next level, you have to do this first.

5.3.3 Inadequate Infrastructure

The ability to handle an enormous amount of data is essential for machine learning. Legacy systems often collapse when the pressure of the demand is applied to them. You need to check that the machine learning software you want to use is compatible with the system you currently have. You should give some thought to upgrading to anything that can, especially anything with hardware acceleration and storage that can be modified.

5.3.4 Putting Everything into Perspective

When companies decide to invest in an update to their machine learning capabilities, it's not uncommon for them to already have analytics engines in place. Bringing together the many diverse techniques of machine learning is not a simple task. It is very necessary for successful implementation to maintain correct documentation and interpretation. When working with an implementation partner, it's possible to simplify the process of putting in place services like anomaly detection, predictive analysis, and ensemble modelling.

5.3.5 Insufficient Amount of Qualified Staff

Deep analytics in its most recent incarnation and machine learning in its most recent form is both cutting-edge techniques. As a direct consequence of this, there is a severe shortage of competent personnel to manage and provide the analytical content for machine learning. Data scientists often need to have a wide scientific literacy as well as specialized subject matter knowledge in order to do their jobs effectively. It is going to be required to offer a high salary if you want to recruit the type of skilled and experienced employees that you want. You might also approach your managed service provider for help with staffing requirements since many managed service providers have a roster of certified data scientists available to deploy at any time.

5.4 Strategies for improving the implementation of ML in Business

Machine learning is a cutting-edge field that has emerged as a result of the successful integration of formerly separate but complementary areas of study, such as mathematics, statistics, and artificial intelligence (AI).

Four applications of Machine Learning for the growing business: (Fig. 12)

Fig. 12. Strategies. (Source: Created by Author)

5.4.1 Natural Language

Since its inception, the tech sector has struggled mightily with the impossible task of developing computer software that can comprehend spoken English. It's true that software has progressed through time; in contrast to the cumbersome search keywords of yore, today's Google search users may enter whole sentences. Natural language, or the language that people really use on a daily basis, is still challenging for computers to grasp. This is starting to shift, though, thanks to machine learning. Software powered by AI may gain wisdom from its experiences. This implies that programmers like voice-activated assistants and search engines are becoming better at understanding natural human speech. What's more, each day these programmers become better at what they do.

5.4.2 Logistics

Experts in data analytics and machine learning are quickly being amassed in the retail and logistics sectors. This is because maximizing profits means using every available resource. By optimizing the shipping, warehousing, and sales processes, machine learning helps businesses boost their logistics operations. Forward-thinking companies may now add autonomous vehicles to their fleets thanks to this technology.

5.4.3 Manufacturing

Already, machine learning technology is being used throughout the manufacturing process. That's because AI-powered tools save costs by improving inventory management, manufacturing efficiency, and the ability to foresee and prevent equipment failures. The industrial sector may make use of the vast amounts of data being produced every day. Python programmers are used by forward-thinking businesses to produce state-of-the-art data analytics tools. Each year, these applications employ machine learning to forecast manufacturing peaks and valleys and to provide suggestions for enhancing the production process. In addition to helping businesses save money by preventing unscheduled downtime, the maintenance plans they provide also assist keep operations running smoothly.

5.4.4 Customer Information

Business leaders are eager to learn how the increasing aggregation and analysis of consumer data will affect bottom lines and expansion plans. Companies have spent decades amassing vast amounts of client data, including purchases, demographics, income, and more.

6 Conclusion

This report ends with the implementation of machining technology and related methods that are mainly performed with the python language. The hotel reservation and cancellations are added to the dataset. There are different algorithms that have been used in this machine learning classifier like decision tree, logistic regression, and also the ridge classifier, different graphs and predicted values have been shown in this report. Each of the methods consists of different coding languages and different coding portions which are mainly performed in the python language.

References

Andriawan, Z.A., Purnama, S.R., Darmawan, A.S., Wibowo, A., Sugiharto, A., Wijayanto, F.: Prediction of hotel booking cancellation using CRISP-DM. In 2020 4th International Conference on Informatics and Computational Sciences (ICICoS), pp. 1–6. IEEE (2020)

Artrith, N., et al.: Best practices in machine learning for chemistry. Nat. Chem. **13**(6), 505–508 (2021)

Chen, Y., Ding, C., Ye, H., Zhou, Y.: Comparison and analysis of machine learning models to predict hotel booking cancellation. In: 2022 7th International Conference on Financial Innovation and Economic Development (ICFIED 2022), pp. 1363–1370. Atlantis Press (2022)

Greener, J.G., Kandathil, S.M., Moffat, L., Jones, D.T.: A guide to machine learning for biologists. Nat. Rev. Mol. Cell Biol. **23**(1), 40–55 (2022)

Hart, G.L., Mueller, T., Toher, C., Curtarolo, S.: Machine learning for alloys. Nat. Rev. Mater. **6**(8), 730–755 (2021)

Martins, R.M., Gresse Von Wangenheim, C.: Findings on Teaching Machine Learning in High School: A Ten-Year Systematic Literature Review. Informatics in Education (2022)

Nousi, P., et al.: Machine learning for forecasting mid-price movements using limit order book data. Ieee Access **7**, 64722–64736 (2019)

Pereira, L.N., Cerqueira, V.: Forecasting hotel demand for revenue management using machine learning regression methods. Curr. Issue Tour. **25**(17), 2733–2750 (2022)

Piccialli, F., Cuomo, S., Crisci, D., Prezioso, E., Mei, G.: A deep learning approach for facility patient attendance prediction based on medical booking data. Sci. Rep. **10**(1), 1–11 (2020)

Satu, M.S., Ahammed, K., Abedin, M.Z.: Performance analysis of machine learning techniques to predict hotel booking cancellations in hospitality industry. In: 2020 23rd International Conference on Computer and Information Technology (ICCIT), pp. 1–6. IEEE (2020)

Vinuesa, R., Brunton, S.L.: Enhancing computational fluid dynamics with machine learning. Nature Comput. Sci. **2**(6), 358–366 (2022)

Antonio, N., de Almeida, A., Nunes, L.: Big data in hotel revenue management: Exploring cancellation drivers to gain insights into booking cancellation behavior. Cornell Hospitality Quarterly **60**(4), 298–319 (2019)

Bernardi, L., Mavridis, T., Estevez, P.: 150 successful machine learning models: 6 lessons learned at booking. com. In: Proceedings of the 25th ACM SIGKDD International Conference on Knowledge Discovery & Data Mining , pp. 1743–1751 (2019)

Kazak, A.N., Chetyrbok, P.V., Oleinikov, N.N.: Artificial intelligence in the tourism sphere. In: IOP Conference Series: Earth and Environmental Science, **421**(4), p. 042020. IOP Publishing (2020)

Khamphakdee, N., Seresangtakul, P.: Sentiment analysis for thai language in hotel domain using machine learning algorithms. Acta Informatica Pragensia **10**(2), 155–171 (2021)

Ku, C.H., Chang, Y.C., Wang, Y., Chen, C.H., Hsiao, S.H.: Artificial intelligence and visual analytics: a deep-learning approach to analyze hotel reviews & responses. In: 52nd Annual Hawaii International Conference on System Sciences (HICSS). Newcastle University (2019)

Ramzan, B., et al.: An intelligent data analysis for recommendation systems using machine learning. Scientific Programming, 2019 (2019)

Sánchez-Medina, A.J., Eleazar, C.: Using machine learning and big data for efficient forecasting of hotel booking cancellations. Int. J. Hosp. Manag. **89**, 102546 (2020)

Schifferer, B., et al.: Using Deep Learning to Win the Booking. com WSDM WebTour21 Challenge on Sequential Recommendations. In WebTour@ WSDM, pp. 22–28 (2021)

Saputro, P.H., Nanang, H.: Exploratory data analysis & booking cancelation prediction on hotel booking demands datasets. J. Applied Data Sci. **2**(1), 40–56 (2021)

Advanced MRI Segmentation Algorithm for the Detection of Brain Tumor Using U-Net Architecture with Transfer Learning EfficientNet-B7

Vikash Kumar Dubey[1]([✉]), Krishna Murari[2], Triloki Nath[2], and Kriti Poddar[3]

[1] Cognizant, Delhi , India
vikashdubey982@gmail.com
[2] RVS College of Engineering and Technology, Jamshedpur, Jharkhand, India
[3] BIT Mesra, Ranchi, Jharkhand, India

Abstract. The complexity of segmenting a brain tumor is significant in medical image processing. Treatment options and patient survival rates won't improve unless brain malignancies are prevented and treated. The most time-consuming and challenging task is manually identifying malignancy from numerous samples. Using magnetic resonance imaging (MRI), the brain is segmented. Tumor brain segmentation must be mechanised. To be categorized, brain tumor need to be automatically segregated. The objective of this study is to develop an automated system for tumor segmentation in magnetic resonance imaging, which will facilitate the precise and quick detection of malignancies. Various machine learning models, such as random forest (RF), support vector machine (SVM), decision tree (DT), and extreme gradient boosting (XGBoost) for image segmentation, are presented in this article along with convolutional neural networks (CNNs) and U-Nets with different transfer learning models as backbones, including ResNet50, Vgg16, InceptionV4, DenseNet169, and EfficientNet-B7. Making use of the BraTS 2020 dataset, brain lesion segmentation is carried out. The tumor segmentation method is evaluated using the F1-Score, Dice loss, and Intersection Over Union (IoU) score based on MRI scans of the brain. In terms of performance measures, the U-Net encoder design with EfficientNet-B7 exceeds all other architectures. The outcomes of this experiment are often quite good. The IoU score was 0.7439 and the dice loss was 0.009386.

Keywords: Brain tumor · CNN · Machine Learning (ML) · MRI · Segmentation · U-NET

1 Introduction

Brain tissue accumulates abnormally in brain tumor. The skull is quite strong, shielding the brain. Any construction in such a small space could lead to problems [1]. In investigations of brain images, four standard magnetic resonance imaging (MRI) modalities are used: native T1-weighted (T1), T2-weighted (T2), and post-contrast T1-weighted

R. K. Tiwari and G. Sahoo (Eds.): ICAII 2022, CCIS 1822, pp. 183–199, 2023.
https://doi.org/10.1007/978-3-031-37303-9_14

(T1ce). Edges, corners, gradient histograms, and local binary patterns are examples of hand-crafted features that are widely employed in automatic approaches for segmenting brain lesions. These features are provided to the classifier after they have been extracted. The nature of those features has no bearing on the classifier's training process. In order to accurately detect medical diseases and treat them, semantic segmentation—which identifies the precise location and shape of the body's structures—is extensively employed in medical imaging. Recently, Deep CNN has made significant strides in a variety of computer vision applications, including, but not limited to, semantic segmentation, object identification, and image classification. Due to various application of deep learning now a day it become very popular among all researchers. There are various reasons why deep learning so popular the most important is its performance and accuracy in the field of picture segmentation. A deep neural network, or CNN, is able to recognize and distinguish between numerous aspects of a picture. The identification and categorization of tumor types has been the main focus of all prior research on this dataset. Very little of the past research done with this dataset was segmentation-focused. Due to the complexity of the human brain, it is challenging to detect and segment it in real life. Regarding the structure, size, and location of the tumor, the two dimensional or three dimensional information differs greatly from patient to patient when it comes to tumor-bearing data. A lot of device memory is needed for tumor segmentation since the MRI data of brain tumor that is collected from diagnostic scans or artificial databases is intrinsically complex. In this study, we used a variety of machine learning methods together with the entire CNN architecture, U-Net with additional Vgg16, ResNet50, DenseNet169, InceptionV4, and EfficientNet-B7. We enhanced the brain MRI pictures for the suggested method, used a method called data pre-processing techniques for the changing of original data and assessed various deep learning approaches This research used a variety of brain tumor segmentation strategies. The suggested architecture led to improved output. Using a trained model, segmenting the image just takes a few seconds. The manual segmentation of tumor by clinical personnel might take hours. The given model is a contribution towards diagnosis of tumor that is effective and quick in the area of image diagnosis. This paper covers the techniques for segmenting brain tumor. There are multiple sections in this article. The topic is introduced in Sect. 1 along with some background data on brain tumor. The literature overview is presented in Sect. 2, and we briefly explain the proposed systems in Sect. 3, with the help of its architectures, datasets that we used, method of training and finally the implementation of this models with performance measures. All the results of experiment put together Sect. 4, and Sect. 5 ends with suggestions for additional investigation.

2 Literature Review

There has been a rise in research into brain tumor segmentation automatically during the past few decades, indicating a demand for this still-developing field of study. In the research, a number of techniques for identifying and separating tumor on MRI image data have been proposed. Most techniques for segmenting brain tumor use manually created characteristics that are input into classifiers like the random forest (RF). Of all the traditional classifiers, RF has the best segmentation results.

Many deep learning models have been used in the past to segment brain tumor, with a variety of results. Patch segmentation in tiny images is used by CNN-based brain tumor segmentation models to precisely and quickly separate tumor. A novel CNN-based approach for segmenting brain tumor using MRI data was proposed by Pereira et al. [2] in 2019. The data preprocessing included the normalization of the deviations field, intensity standardization, and patch normalizing. By rotating the training patch and using high-grade glioma (HGG) samples later in the training phase, a greater number of training patches were created in order to artificially increase the number of unique low-grade glioma (LGG) classes. Intensity normalization was employed by researchers throughout the design phase to eliminate the unpredictability brought on by several MRI acquisitions. Researchers thought about employing more data to deal with the variability problem.

Havaei et al. [3] presented Two Path CNN in 2017, which is an unique CNN design (as compared to the standard one used for computer vision). In the 2013 Brain Tumor Segmentation (BraTS) test set, the proposed architecture performed around 30 times better than the current state-of-the-art. In 2021, Fabian et al. [4] used an U-Net to solve the segmentation challenge from the BraTS Challenge 2020. It has been shown that the inclusion of BraTS-specific features including image processing techniques, data augmentation, and region-based training significantly improves the segmentation performance of the NU- Net pipeline. The baseline setting of the NU-Net configuration has shown excellent results.

A homogenous fully CNN identified to as U-Net is provided by Ronneberger et al. in 2015 [5]. The process of down sampling must be linked with the future graph and need to capture contextual information. The process of unsampling must be used to determine the proper position. U-Net significantly boosted the efficacy of medical picture segmentation tasks. Due to its extraordinary efficiency occur in the concluding training of a few picture where U-Net is commonly used in the field of image analysis (Medical).

To segment brain tumor, some studies used U-Net topologies. A completely programmed brain tumor identification and segmentation method is deployed using deep convolutional networks which is an application of given by Ramy et al. [6] in 2020 and in 2017 by Hao Dong et al. [7]. While Kamnitsas et al. [9] published EMMA (Ensembles of Multiple Models and Architectures) for forceful brain tumor segmentation in 2018, Xue Feng et al. [8] constructed a 3D U-Net ensemble for brain tumor segmentation in 2020. Sadad et al. [10] created U-Net with ResNet50 architecture in 2021 and achieved an IoU score of 0.9504 for segmenting tumor using the Figshare dataset. A type of U-Net that is stripped down can be represented as (SD U-Net) is a variation of neural network (Deep), Which is very quick small and computable, efficient in segmentation of pictures related to medical field easily on any device consist of modest capabilities of processing released by Gadoseyetal. [11] in 2020. The issue of voxel distribution in the background of brain tumor and the issue of uneven tumor can be solved in a right way so overall concluding above overall work offers a way to understand and enhance segmentation strategy.

3   Proposed System

We addressed a fully CNN model, U-Net with various transfer learning models as back-bones, such as ResNet50, Vgg16, InceptionV4, DenseNet169, and EfficientNet-B7, as well as a variety of machine models, such as random forest, SVM, decision tree, and XGBoost, are enough effective in MRI image segmentation depend on the brain. The segmentation strategy that is suggested follows the procedure depicted in Fig. 1. Discussed briefly, the segmentation model was trained using the brain MRI pictures after they had been delivered. The trained model can be used to anticipate the segmented image.

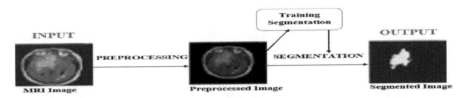

Fig. 1. Workflow Diagram for Brain Tumor Segmentation Model Proposed Approach

3.1   Semantic-Wise Fully CNN Architecture

Semantic segmentation is one of the most important and challenging topics in computer vision. Patch-wise image classification, which was first used in early attempts to use semantic segmentation in the medical profession, has two main drawbacks. The training patch requires more computer cycles and a longer training period because it is significantly larger than the training sample. Second, the accuracy of segmentation is significantly impacted by the size of the patch.

Semantic-wise CNN architecture was developed to address these issues as a result. This network has two paths—a contracting path (encoder) and an expansive path (decoder)—which similar to auto encoder.

A convolutional neural network specifically designed for the encoder has two 3 x 3 convolutional layers in a row, one of which has a ReLU (rectified linear unit) activation function and 2 x 2 spatial max pooling. The decoder up samples the feature map of the result using two 3 x 3 convolutions, a deconvolution layer, a down sampling layer, a connection layer, and ReLU. Applying the 1 x 1 convolution layer to the up sampled features creates the final segment map. Figure 2 depicts the semantic CNN architecture that was utilized to segment brain tumor.

3.2   U-Net Architecture

The U-Net design, a complex network created especially for analyzing biological images, was initially proposed by Ronneberger et al. in 2015. There is a "U" shape to the model. We use encoder and decoder in this architecture where encoder can be used as a standard

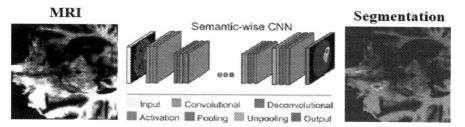

Fig. 2. CNN Architecture of Brain Tumor Segmentation

convolution process on other hand decoder mainly includes two dimensional convolutional layers that has been transposed. To represent architecture of U-Net there is a block diagram in Fig. 3. The basic structure of the input patch is frequently captured using the contraction route, the main route in the U-Net structure (also known as the encoder component).

The encoder consists of maximum pooling and convolution layers that are placed on top of one another. With the help of transposed convolutions, there is a irregular rising in 2nd path that enables precise localization (this is a decoder component). In complete network there is absence of deep layers and can only comprehend images up to a certain size, they are unable to handle bigger images. In this category of architecture two continuous convolution layers are employed before max-pooling. One of the application of pooling method is the dimension of the data get reduced to half quantity, due to this loss of data can occur widely. For this we use all types of spatial information without swiftly also pooling layers are layered before to each convolution. For each level of the U-Net structure, In between two layer that is convolution and max pooling layer we added a connection commonly known as skip connection. The goal behind this is to enhance the distribution of layers parameter accuracy and homogeneity.

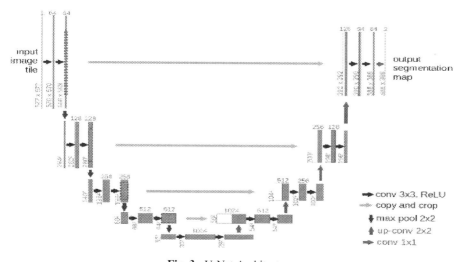

Fig. 3. U-Net Architecture

3.3 Transfer Learning

Use a pre-trained CNN model that has been trained on ImageNet rather than creating a brand-new model for image in CNN categorization in deep learning. Sinno Pan and Qiang Yang [12] created a method for assisting with transfer learning understanding. As opposed to beginning from scratch, transfer learning includes previously learned knowledge.

3.3.1 VGG Architecture

The authors of "Very Deep Convolutional Networks," K. Simonyan and A. Zisserman, developed a model for broad photo identification in 2015 [13]. The depth of the convolution network was originally investigated using large-scale pictures [13]. The expressiveness of previous designs may be increased by deep network architecture with (3x3) filters by adding 16–19 weight layers. Using the ImageNet dataset, the VGG model was developed, which has a more powerful convolutional network.

3.3.2 ResNet Architecture

He et al. [14] developed ResNet, a neural network with an error rate of 3.57%, for the most challenging ImageNet picture recognition test. For this, a 152-layer deep CNN architecture was used. ResNet's architecture encouraged the adoption of more complex networks than AlexNet and Vgg-Net. Skip connections, often referred to as residual connections, are a feature of the ResNet design that reduces data redundancy during deep network training and optimization. Skip connections, often referred to as residual connections, are used in the ResNet system to reduce data redundancy during deep network training and optimization. The remaining connections might be used to train a 1001-layer model. The majority of ResNet's architectural design is composed of residual blocks. Although the layers of a shallow neural network are linked, ResNet's residual blocks are not. By increasing the network's capacity, ResNet connections save data and speed up the model's training.

3.3.3 DenseNet Architecture

Huang et al. [15] first introduced it as a feed-forward network that links one layer to the next, and it has subsequently gained widespread acclaim. In order to make sure that the deep convolution network was trained more correctly and successfully, a deeper convolution network was used. Shorter connections between layers at the input and the output made up this deeper convolution network. DenseNet uses direct connections from one layer to the following one to avoid non-linear transformation, in contrast to ResNet Skip-Syncs.With regard to function mappings, all previous levels from x0 to xl-1 are taken into account. The authors [16] state that the wavelength of the feature-map created in layers 0, 1, 2, l-1 is given by xl = Hl ([x0, x1, xl-1]).

3.3.4 Inception Architecture

The Inception architecture is also used to build a convolutional network with an idealized, sparse, locally-structured structure based on the notion of dense components (also known as "GoogLeNet"). In situations when there are insufficient computer resources, it also performs utilization forecasts and dimension reduction [17]. It has the advantage of allowing you to increase the number of hidden units on each stage without materially raising the computing load on the network. Because of the reduction in dimensionality in each layer, it is possible to enhance the breadth and depth at each level by expanding the processing resources available at that stage.

3.3.5 EfficientNet Architecture

The EfficientNet model was created by Google Research Brain employees Mingxing Tan and Quoc V. Le [18], and they published their research in the publication "EfficientNet: Rethinking Model Scaling for Convolutional Neural Networks. By using a compound scaling process, the "EfficientNetB0" new baseline architecture was initially created, and it was then scaled up to create the EfficientNet family. Eight EfficientNet variations are powered by this method, with parameter counts ranging from 5.3 million to 66 million.

The researchers built a basic network to automate the creation of neural networks before employing a method (commonly known as the search for neural network design). This provides outstanding precision as well as productivity with the help of measuring the number of FLOPS (floating-point operations per second). Convolution and a movable inverted bottleneck are used in this system (MBConv). The EfficientNet family has different numbers for various MBConv segments. In this architecture we proceed through EfficientNet B0-B7, in which the following quantity increases that is the depth, width, resolution, as well as the model size and accuracy. The EfficientNetB7 model outperforms a prior generation of state-of-the-art CNNs on ImageNet [18].

3.4 Traditional ML Algorithms

3.4.1 Random Forest

Random forest, one of the ensemble approaches used, has generated excellent results in a variety of domains. Breiman developed the RF [19] meta-estimator, which increases projected precision and minimizes overfitting by fitting a number of decision tree classifiers to different subsamples of the data set. Each tree in the dataset is constructed using the complete dataset unless the max samples option is used to restrict the amount of subsamples.

3.4.2 Support Vector Machine

Vladimir Vapnik was the first to create SVM, a supervised learning approach that has shown excellent results [20]. SVMs work under the presumption that samples from various classes, or support vectors, are selected and split according to a linear function. SVMs are an algorithm that tackles problems at their core using multidimensional hyperplanes. The model builds data and decision planes, calculates the distance between them, and utilizes the parameters to find the class most likely to complement the hyperplane.

3.4.3 Decision Tree

Decision Similar to conditional control statements, trees may handle research tasks like choice analysis. Beyond a certain depth, over-fitting becomes a problem in trees. In the same way that a tree structure depicts each node as an attribute or feature from which a conclusion may be drawn. The information connected to each leaf node's class label is present.

3.4.4 Extreme Gradient Boosting

In order to build a strong and effective learning model, the machine learning approach known as extreme gradient boosting (XGBoost) combines weak learners. Because XGBoost employs gradient boost algorithms, they are swift and accurate [21]. It was invented by Taiqi Chen and became famous for solving the Higgs Boson conundrum [22]. Problematic decision-making zones are improved by the gradient.

3.5 Data Set

The benchmark dataset, which is readily accessible, was used in this investigation. It has been suggested using the BraTS 2020 dataset to automatically detect and segment brain lesions. The original objective of the Brain Tumor Segmentation Study (BraTS) was to assess cutting-edge techniques for brain tumor segmentation in magnetic resonance imaging (MRI). The BraTS2020 dataset, which focuses on segmenting gliomas and other fundamentally unique brain tumors (in terms of shape, histology, and appearance), was entirely built using preoperative information acquired from a variety of institutions.

In our dataset basically we include data from LGG (consist of dataset [76] of BraTS 2020) and also we include HGG (293). Further we also use dataset T1 ce, T2, T1, and FLAIR-T2. Imaging dataset which is associated with a voxel and size that we used is 24240. Dataset that we used for all modalities of imaging are basically a type of isotropic resolution and whose size is 1mm. we did not use annotation to test and validate the dataset (125 & 166), yet they are present in the training data. To compare their methods, participants can submit their estimated segmentation volumes to the organizer's website. In our validation process we accepted one or more contribution, but during our final computation we granted only one member can submit only one.

We used a file called NifTI which consist of all dataset like T1, T1ce, T2, and all necessary information about FLAIR are available in every scans of BraTS which is actually multidimensional. All scans were put together via a range of clinical trial. All dataset that we used belongs to images that we collected from different organizations. For all these images we have to enter data manually and segmented with the help of assessors. By examine dataset we saw from different category of tumor which includes cores of tumor. Tumor can be categorized as enhancing, non-enhancing and necrotic cores. It also includes several types of other tumor that is peritumoral edoema. There are several image and mask modes, as shown in Fig. 4.

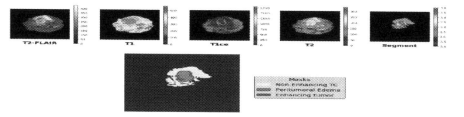

Fig. 4. Multi-modal images and segmented masks

3.6 Data Preprocessing

With the use of data processing method all photos are cropped. For the measurement of the intensity of MRI we use standard scaler normalization in which distortion also get adjusted. To evaluate standard formula of score example for "x" shown below can be calculated as:

$$z = \frac{(xu)}{s} \tag{1}$$

In above formula "s" is used to represent the sample standard deviation in case if it is one then this is case of false. And in above formula "u" is used to represent the mean value of training samples or in case if it is zero then this is case of false. Then this will get converted into standard deviation distribution and in that case the value of mean will be one or zero, according to scaler operating idea.

Further in this processing in case of multivariate data the whole process is done with the help of feature by feature Fig. 5 shows the image visualization after pre-processing.

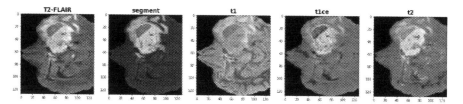

Fig. 5. Image after preprocessing

3.7 Training and Implementation Details

To train and test algorithms using dataset BraTS also include pictures from segmented MRI. The results are corrected or labeled images are verified by neuro radiologists with clinical knowledge. The datasets called BraTS can also be used to validate and test by usinf folders of BraTS. The train data folder has 369 subfolders, each of which is organized by modality and contains 5 images in different formats, each of which represents one of the 5 modalities. The folder containing the train data has 1845 images as a result. The validation data folder is divided into 125 subfolders, and each subfolders consists of 4 images which is actually from 4 dissimilar modalities. These modalities are: T1, T1ce, T2, T2- FLAIR. The data folder for validation thus has 500 images in total.

After the analysis of data, we use cropping method to process the image in order to normalize image intensity value. There are three different types of MRI recording first is train set second one is test set and the final that is third one is validate set. In all of the three train set image can be classified as: utilized consist of 60 percent of train set, 20 percent are test set, and remaining 20 percent are validation set. In whole process during the training of the picture: - images are enhanced by the use of data that calculate accurate value of precision. A method called augmentation method which is a part of albumention library that consists of various feature to enhance brightness, contrast, distortion, and finally to enhance elastic transform. These all are utilized in order to upgrade the quality of input picture. It also adds accurate data so that our model can learn. Before we start to train our model, we must create thr process of learning and this process of learning include data like F1 which is score value along with Iou that is also a score value. To enhance the process of learning we add a function called loss function along with optimizer. The rate of learning was 0.0001 for adam optimizer Additionally, a variety of techniques were used in this study, including a fully CNN architecture, U-Net with various transfer learning architectures, such as ResNet50, Vgg16, InceptionV4, DenseNet169, and EfficientNet-B7, as well as a number of machine learning models, such as RF, SVM, DT, and XGBoost.

To represent brain tumor clearly a topology used to know as skip topology that provide best segmentation that use a expression which is high level and belongs to a very dense layers of sequencing. In the representation of the design we use three components first is bottleneck second one is expansion and final that is third one is contraction. In representation process of the block we use highest limit of pooling in addition with convolution level input. In the last layer of CNN which is also last block has a variable sample value which represents how much it can contract or expand. After the normalization of the activation or convulation function were applied which is ReLU in order to continue the process of learning of the model in the experiment.

To train the machine learning modes, the characteristics of the data loader are removed. For better model fitting, the collected features are then converted into a 2D array.

3.8 Performance Metrics

3.8.1 Accuracy

Accuracy: Accuracy can be defined as the total number of accurate prediction versus total prediction.

$$Accuracy = \frac{(TP + TN)}{(TP + TN + FP + FN)} \quad (2)$$

In the above we get four different values first one is true positive(TP) second one is true negative (TN) and also we get third value false positive(FP) and the final the last one as false negative(FN).

3.8.2 Precision

For the measurement of accuracy of prediction which is positive we use precision.

$$Precision = \frac{TP}{(TP + FP)} \qquad (3)$$

3.8.3 Recall

Recall can be defined as measurement of total number of true positive that are predicted versus total number of original positive in given dataset.

$$Re(Sensitivity) = \frac{TP}{TP + FN} \qquad (4)$$

3.8.4 Specificity

Specificity is the measure of how many true negatives are predicted out of all actual negatives in the dataset.

$$Specificity = \frac{TN}{TN + FP} \qquad (5)$$

3.8.5 IoU Score

We can simply calculate the value of IoU score by finding the ratio of point of intersection which is actually in between original data and predicted segmentation which is union of actual data and predicted segmentation. While calculating overlap in between two boxes [23] of boundary or masks, the final value is crucial statistic.

$$IoU = \frac{(ground\ truth\ prediction)}{(ground\ truth\ U\ prediction)} \qquad (6)$$

3.8.6 F1-Score

To calculate F1 value with the help of "the harmonic mean of recall and precision" as the starting point [24].

The final value of F1 is equal to dice value.

$$FS = \frac{(precision\ recall)}{(Precision + recall)} \qquad (7)$$

The highest value possible for f1 score is 1.0, that implies a perfect precision and recall, and in case the highest possible value of 0 in that case either precision or recall is zero.

3.8.7 Dice Loss

The dice loss, which is determined by subtracting one from the dice coefficient, is covered in this section. If the dice coefficient is changed to behave in this way, it may be used as a loss function, which is a common metric for pixel segmentation. By dividing the intersection area by the total number of pixels in the two pictures, the dice coefficient is calculated [25]. The dice coefficient is calculated using the following formula:

$$Dice = \frac{|A \cap B|}{2 * |A| + |B|} \tag{8}$$

$$Diceloss = 1 - Dice \tag{9}$$

4   Results and Discussion

Using metrics for accuracy, precision, recall, and specificity as well as IoU and F1 score, we evaluate the segmentation performance of the suggested designs. The network is trained using 200 epochs spread over 16 batch sizes. For the training of the network in pytorch we use 4 NVIDIA P40 GPUs.

Metrics for all deep learning model designs are included in Table 1, whereas metrics for machine learning models are presented in Table 2. As demonstrated in Table 1, the efficientNet-B7 encoder-based U-Net beats all other deep learning architectures. Yet, Table 2's results demonstrate that the random forest model outperforms every other machine learning model. In contrast to test results, the U-Net with EfficientNet-B7 beat the random forest model with a dice loss of 0.009386 and an IoU score of 0.9944. by using this model that is EfficientNet-B7 which is a part of U-Net the major portion is covered by intersection of intended mask and output system that we used.

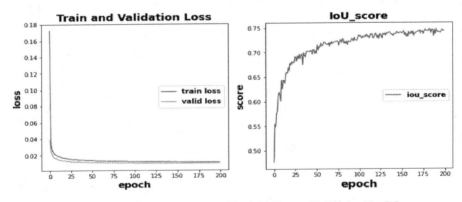

Fig. 6. Dice loss and F1 score graph of the U-net with EfficientNet-B7

During the calculation of computation time one of the major aspects that we should take care is the training parameters of CNN. So, it is essential to set up all training

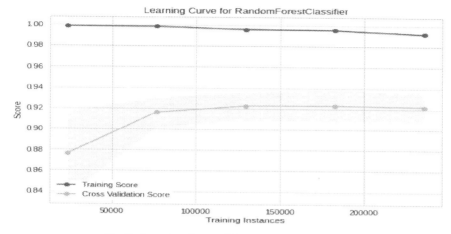

Fig. 7. Learning Curve of the Random Forest Model

settings consistently and utilize the same dataset. The network may be used for photo segmentation after training. Image segmentation simply requires a few seconds when using the previously trained model. On the other hand, a clinician may need to spend several hours or even days physically segmenting a tumor. It is recommended to choose methods for picture segmentation that are accurate, rapid, and affordable. By making it possible for medical professionals to quickly and properly diagnose a brain tumor. The outcome of process surely can help in diagnosis so many serious patients and can also save many lives.

Figure 6 shows the U-EfficientNet-B7 Net architecture's dice loss and IoU-score recorded for each Epoch, and Fig. 7 shows the learning curve for the random forest model. Predictions made using the CNN architecture, the U-Net with EfficientNet-B7, and the random forest model, respectively, are shown in Figs. 8, 9, and 10.

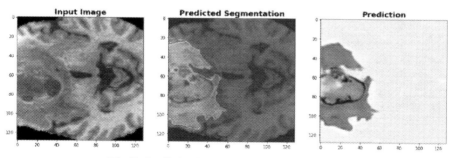

Fig. 8. Prediction based on the CNN Architecture

Our model earned a favorable IoU score when compared to Sadad et al.'s [10] model's performance using the Figshare data set. Fabian et al. [4] recommended using the same dataset, BRATS2020, as was used in this study for segmenting brain tumors. The Fabian et al. model's dice score was 88.95%, whereas our recommended model outperformed

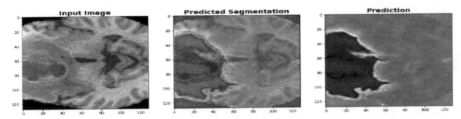

Fig. 9. Prediction based on the U-Net with EfficientNet-B7 encoder architecture

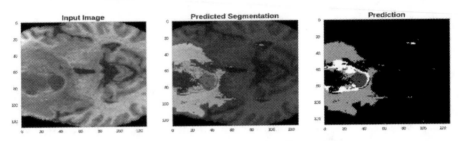

Fig. 10. Prediction based on the Random Forest architecture

Table 1. Result Summary – Deep Learning Models

Models	Dice Loss	F-Score	IoU	Accuracy	Precision	Recall	Specificity
CNN	0.01096	0.8475	0.7011	0.9111	0.7417	0.9884	0.8853
UNet- Vgg16	0.01007	0.9845	0.7222	0.9922	0.9807	0.9883	0.9935
UNet-ResNet50	0.009789	0.9801	0.7374	0.9903	0.9751	0.9864	0.9916
UNet-DenseNet169	0.009848	0.9846	0.7337	0.9923	0.9821	0.9871	0.9940
UNet-InceptionV4	0.009767	0.9845	0.7391	0.9922	0.9798	0.9893	0.9932
UNet-EfficientNet-B7	**0.009435**	**0.9848**	**0.7435**	**0.9924**	**0.9829**	**0.9868**	**0.9943**
UNet-EfficientNet-B7 (Gauss Noise)	0.01049	0.9844	0.7255	0.9922	0.9859	0.9830	0.9953

it with a score of 98.51%. Table 3 compares U-Net to other contemporary techniques and evaluates it using EfficientNet B7. The suggested model fared well when compared to the outcomes of prior experiments.

Table 2. Result Summary -Machine Learning Models

Models	Dice Loss	F- Score	IoU	Accuracy	Precision	Recall	Specificity
SVM	0.1628	0.9193	0.6139	0.9193	0.9193	0.9193	0.9731
Decision Tree	0.1549	0.9143	0.6103	0.9143	0.9143	0.9143	0.9714
XGBoost	0.1549	0.9218	0.6227	0.9218	0.9218	0.9218	0.9739
Random Forest	**0.1504**	**0.9262**	**0.6512**	**0.9262**	**0.9262**	**0.9262**	**0.9754**

Table 3. Comparison of the proposed model with previous works

Author	Network	Dice Score / F Score	Accuracy	Precision	Specificity	Sensitivity
Gunasekara et al. [18]	CNN	0.92	0.9457	-	-	-
Wu et al. [19]	DCNN-F-SVM	0.9010	-	-	0.9889	0.9236
Nisha Joseph et al. [20]	CNN	0.94	-	0.93	-	0.9
Hussain et al [21]	DCNN	0.80	-	-	0.85	0.82
Fabian et al. [4]	U-Net ResNet50	0.8895	-	-	-	-
Proposed method	U-Net EfficientNetB7	**0.9848**	**0.9924**	**0.9829**	**0.9943**	**0.9868**

5 Conclusion and Future Work

Perhaps is is very difficult task to identify various types of tumors related to brain due to complexity of image of MRI, but our projects is to use artificial intelligence models to forecast malignancies make this endeavor helpful. The suggested system makes use of several machine learning models for the autonomous segmentation of brain tumors, a U-Net with different transfer learning models as encoder architecture, and a fully CNN architecture. This can fast the process of imaging and segmentation related to brain tumors.

Performance-wise, the EfficientNet-B7 encoder-based U-Net architecture exceeds all other architectures. For the U-Net utilizing EfficientNet-B7, the dice loss was 0.009386, the IoU score was 0.7439, the F1 score was 0.9851, the accuracy was 0.9925, the precision was 0.9833, the recall was 0.9869, and the specificity was 0.9944. The U-Net with EfficientNet-B7 design is crucial in the diagnosis of brain cancers and most important if it is identified in initial stages according to the test results. The proposed U-Net with the EfficientNet-B7 model offers a framework for anticipating the segmentation of brain lesions as well as aiding in the exact segmentation of the location of the lesions, both of which are significant. Our research shows that the suggested method dramatically surpasses other methods for the segmentation of brain tumor.

Due to the 2D U-Net model's restrictions, semantics and local characteristics between slices are absent in the architecture as a result of the model's inability to properly use MRI data. A 3D network model might be used in a subsequent research to enhance performance and demonstrate the generalizability of the design on diverse datasets. It is currently difficult to separate brain tumors using deep neural networks because of the complexity of brain MRI imaging and the scarcity of annotated data. As a result, we'll soon start using a segmentation model for medical brain tumors.

The future scope of this research can also help to find advanced mechanism for the fast treatment of brain related tumors and also helpful in finding more accurate imaging and segmentation. To find effective approaches to extract 3D patches, this study can also be helpful to create a model that will be work efficiently on such data. We have only so far discussed the use of 2D patches for training and extraction.

References

1. Brain Tumor: Types, Risk Factors, and Symptoms. https://www.healthline.com/health/brain-tumor. Accessed 25 May 2021
2. Pereira, S., Pinto, A., Alves, V., Silva, C.A.: Brain tumor segmentation using convolutional neural networks in MRI images. J. Med. Syst. **43**, 1–10 (2019)
3. Havaei, M., et al.: Brain tumor segmentation with deep neural networks. Med. Image Anal. **35**, 18–31 (2017)
4. Isensee, F., Jäger, P.F., Full, P.M., Vollmuth, P., Maier-Hein, K.H.: nnU-Net for Brain Tumor Segmentation, pp. 118– 132 (2021)
5. Ronneberger, O., Fischer, P., Brox, T.: U-Net: Convolutional networks for biomedical image segmentation. CoRR, vol. abs/1505.0, pp. 16591–16603 (2015)
6. Zeineldin, R.A., Karar, M.E., Coburger, J., Wirtz, C.R., Burgert, O.: DeepSeg: deep neural network framework for automatic brain tumor segmentation using magnetic resonance FLAIR images. Int. J. Comput. Assist. Radiol. Surg. **15**(6), 909–920 (2020)
7. Dong, H., Yang, G., Liu, F., Mo, Y., Guo, Y.: Automatic brain tumor detection and segmentation using U-net based fully convolutional networks. In: Valdés Hernández, M., González-Castro, V. (eds.) MIUA 2017. CCIS, vol. 723, pp. 506–517. Springer, Cham (2017). https://doi.org/10.1007/978-3-319-60964-5_44
8. Feng, X., Tustison, N.J., Patel, S.H., Meyer, C.H.: Brain tumor segmentation using an ensemble of 3D U-nets and overall survival prediction using radiomic features. Front. Comput. Neurosci. **14**(April), 1–12 (2020)
9. Kamnitsas, K., et al.: Ensembles of multiple models and architectures for robust brain tumour segmentation. In: Crimi, A., Bakas, S., Kuijf, H., Menze, B., Reyes, M. (eds.) BrainLes 2017. LNCS, vol. 10670, pp. 450–462. Springer, Cham (2018). https://doi.org/10.1007/978-3-319-75238-9_38
10. Sadad, T., et al.: Brain tumor detection and multi-classification using advanced deep learning techniques. Microsc. Res. Tech., October 2020, 1296–1308 (2021)
11. Gadosey, P.K., et al.: SD-UNET: stripping down U-net for segmentation of biomedical images on platforms with low computational budgets. Diagnostics **10**(2), 1–18 (2020)
12. Panigrahi, S., Nanda, A., Swarnkar, T.: A survey on transfer learning. In: Mishra, D., Buyya, R., Mohapatra, P., Patnaik, S. (eds.) Intelligent and Cloud Computing. SIST, vol. 194, pp. 781– 789. Springer, Singapore (2021). https://doi.org/10.1007/978-981-15-5971-6_83

13. Simonyan, K., Zisserman, A.: Very deep convolutional networks for large-scale image recognition. In: 3rd International Conference Learning Represent. ICLR 2015 - Conference Track Proceedings., pp. 1–14 (2015)
14. He, K., Zhang, X., Ren, S., Sun, J.: Deep residual learning for image recognition. In: Proceedings IEEE Computational Soc. Conference Computer Vision Pattern Recognition, vol. 2016-Decem, pp. 770–778 (2016). https://doi.org/10.1109/CVPR.2016.90
15. Huang, G., Liu, Z., Pleiss, G., van der Maaten, L., Weinberger, K.Q.: Densely connected convolutional networks. IEEE Trans. Pattern Anal. Mach. Intell. (2020)
16. AlAfandy, K.A., Omara, H., Lazaar, M., Al Achhab, M.: Investment of classic deep CNNs and SVM for classifying remote sensing images. Adv. Sci. Technol. Eng. Syst. 5(5), 652–659 (2020)
17. Szegedy, C., et al.: Going deeper with convolutions. Proc. IEEE Comput. Soc. Conf. Comput. Vis. Pattern Recognit., vol. 07–12-June, pp. 1–9 (2015)
18. Tan, M., Le, Q.V.: EfficientNet: Rethinking model scaling for convolutional neural networks. In: 36th International Conference Mach. Learning ICML 2019, vol. 2019-June, pp. 10691–10700 (2019)
19. Breiman, L.: RANDOM FORESTS Leo (2001). https://www.stat.berkeley.edu/~breiman/randomforest2001.pdf
20. Sangeetha, J., Vaishnavi, D., Premalatha, J.: Comparative analysis of glioma tumor in brain using machine learning and deep learning techniques. J. Phys. Conf. Ser. 1767(1) (2021)
21. Introduction to XGBoost in Python - DebuggerCafe. https://debuggercafe.com/introduction-to-xgboost-in-python/. Accessed 14 Sep. 2021
22. Chen, T., He, T., Benesty, M.: XGBoost : eXtreme Gradient Boosting. R Packag. version 0.71–2, pp. 1–4 (2018)
23. Intersection over Union (IoU) for object detection-PyImageSearch. https://www.pyimagesearch.com/2016/11/07/intersection-over-union-iou-for-object-detection/. Accessed 16 July 2021
24. F-Score Definition DeepAI. https://deepai.org/machine-learning-glossary-and-terms/f-score. Accessed 16 July 2021
25. An overview of semantic image segmentation. https://www.jeremyjordan.me/semantic-segmentation/. Accessed 16 July 2021
26. Gunasekara, S.R., Kaldera, H.N.T.K., Dissanayake, M.B.: A systematic approach for MRI brain tumor localization and segmentation using deep learning and active contouring. J. Healthc. Eng. (2021)
27. Wu, W., et al.: An intelligent diagnosis method of brain MRI tumor segmentation using deep convolutional neural network and SVM algorithm. Comput. Math. Methods Med. 2020 (2020)
28. Joseph, N., Murugan, D., Thomas, B.J.: Brain Tumor Segmentation Using Deep Convolution Neural Network and Support Vector Machine. 7(19), 577–584 (2020)
29. Hussain, S., Anwar, S.M., Majid, M.: Brain tumor segmentation using cascaded deep convolutional neural network. In: Proceedings Annual International Conference IEEE Engineering Medicine Biology Society EMBS, pp. 1998–2001 (2017)

Audio Analysis for Early Diagnosis of Alzheimer's Disease: A Study on Fisher's Linear Discriminant and Mel-Frequency Cepstral Coefficients

Amod Kumar Sahwal[✉], Manjeet Singh, Namrata Kumari, Krishna Murari,
and Shashi Prabha

Department of Computer Science and Engineering,
RVS College of Engineering and Technology, Jamshedpur, India
rajrav9234@gmail.com

Abstract. Millions of people throughout the world are afflicted by the widespread neurodegenerative ailment known as Alzheimer's disease. Effective treatment and management of the condition depend on a timely and precise diagnosis. Changes in speech patterns can be an early sign of Alzheimer's disease, according to recent studies. As a result, there is rising interest in employing audio analysis to make a diagnosis and track the development of the illness. In order to classify Alzheimer's disease patients based on audio data, this research reviews the use of Fisher's Linear Discriminant (FLD) and Mel-Frequency Cepstral Coefficients (MFCCs). FLD is a supervised learning algorithm that looks for a linear combination of features that maximizes the separation between various classes in a dataset. MFCCs are popular feature extraction techniques that replicate the frequency response of the human auditory system.

With a focus on the use of audio analysis in diagnosis, we first give a general overview of AD and its diagnosis. The use of MFCCs and FLD for categorizing Alzheimer's patients based on audio data is then discussed.

Overall, the findings of earlier research indicate that FLD and MFCCs can be useful for categorizing Alzheimer's disease patients based on audio data. To accurately diagnose and track the disease, the best set of characteristics and classifiers must be determined through more study. A discussion of prospective future research directions in this area concludes this study.

Keywords: ADReSSo · Alzheimer's disease (AD) · Mel Frequency Cepstral Coefficients (MFCC) · Machine learning · Speech · Audio · Fisher Linear (FL) · Multivariate Fisher's Linear Discriminant

1 Introduction

It is little bit hard to diagnose the condition. 50% of the time, professionals fail to recognize or assess the condition, even in its advanced stages. Dementia of the most common type is Alzheimer's disease (AD). These brain alterations in AD [1] eventually make it difficult for a person to perform simple physiological activities like walking and swallowing. AD is also fatal in the end. A system that can accurately identify the disease stage of dementia based on speech must be developed. A class of neurodegenerative disorders known as DEMENTIA involves a long-term, typically progressive decline in cognitive ability. Memory loss and cognitive decline are symptoms of AD, a progressive neurodegenerative sickness that has an impact on brain. It accounts for between 60 and 80 percent of dementia cases, making it the most prevalent cause [2].

Amyloid plaques [3] and tau tangles, two aberrant protein accumulations in the brain, are what give the disease its name. These proteins harm brain tissue and impair the brain's ability to operate normally. Alzheimer's disease often starts out with moderate memory issues including forgetting recent conversations or experiences. Those who have the condition may have progressively severe memory loss, communication problems, personality changes, and impairments in judgment and reasoning as it advances [4]. Alzheimer's disease has no known cure, and available treatments concentrate on symptom management and delaying the onset of the illness. Lifestyle modifications like consistent exercise and a balanced diet may also help lower the risk of contracting the illness.

A complex interaction of genetic, environmental, and behavioral variables results in Alzheimer's disease. Although the precise etiology of the illness is still unknown, experts think that amyloid plaques and tau tangles, two aberrant protein accumulations in the brain, are to blame. Beta-amyloid protein fragments build up between nerve cells in the brain to form amyloid plaques [5]. The tau protein's twisted fibers build up inside the nerve cells themselves to form tau tangles. Memory loss, cognitive decline, and behavioral abnormalities are some of the hallmark signs of Alzheimer's disease because these protein deposits obstruct brain cells' ability to communicate with one another and ultimately lead to their death. Alzheimer's disease has also been associated with inflammation and oxidative stress in the brain in addition to these protein accumulation. Oxidative stress and chronic inflammation can harm brain cells and speed the progression of the illness.

Alzheimer's disease is also influenced by [6] genetics; specific genetic alterations raise the likelihood of developing the condition. But, environmental and lifestyle variables may also have a big impact, thus genetics alone cannot predict who will get the disease. Researchers are attempting to better understand Alzheimer's disease and create novel treatments to halt its progression and eventually find a cure, even though the precise mechanisms that cause the disease are still under investigation.

Alzheimer's disease cannot be totally prevented, but there are things we can take to lower our risk of getting it:

- **Maintain a healthy lifestyle**, which [7] includes getting regular exercise, eating well, keeping a healthy weight, quitting smoking, and drinking in moderation. A healthy lifestyle has been linked to a lower incidence of dementia and cognitive decline, according to research.
- **Keep our brains active**: Take part in [8] mentally challenging pursuits like reading, crossword puzzles, or picking up a new skill. By engaging in these activities, we can keep our brains busy and potentially lower our risk of cognitive decline.

- **Be socially active**: Continue to interact [9] with others and partake in social activities. A lower risk of dementia and cognitive decline has been associated with social interaction.
- **Control persistent conditions**: Manage diabetes, excessive blood sugar, high cholesterol, and other chronic health issues. Certain issues can make it more likely for someone to develop dementia, including Alzheimer's disease.
- **Safeguard our head**: [10] When cycling or engaging in other activities that put us at risk for head injuries, wear a helmet. Dementia risk has been correlated with head injuries.

While taking these precautions won't ensure that we never get Alzheimer's, they can help lower our risk and enhance our general health and wellness.

Due to its special effects on memory, intellectual function, and behavior, AD can have a substantial effect on a person's personal life. A person's personal life may be impacted by Alzheimer's disease in the following ways: [9].

- **Memory loss**: [11] Mild memory issues, such as forgetting recent conversations or experiences, are frequently the first symptoms of Alzheimer's disease. People may suffer from progressively severe memory loss as the illness worsens, which may include forgetting crucial dates, people, and particulars from their own life. They may find it challenging to keep up with friends and family as a result of this.
- **Changes in behavior**: [12] Alzheimer's disease can alter behavior and lead to irritation, mood fluctuations, and social disengagement. People may experience increased levels of anxiety, depression, or agitation, as well as difficulties expressing their feelings and comprehending those of others.
- **Communication difficulties**: [13] Alzheimer's disease can also impair communication abilities, making it challenging for sufferers to communicate or comprehend others. It may be challenging for them to follow discussions or find the correct words, which can make it challenging for them to interact with others efficiently.
- **Loss of independence**: [14] People may require more and more on others for assistance with daily tasks like eating, dressing, and washing as the disease worsens. Both the person losing their freedom and those who love them may find it challenging.
- **Safety concerns**: [15] Alzheimer's patients may experience confusion or disorientation, which can raise safety issues including roaming or becoming lost. In order to assure the person's safety, caregivers may need to take additional measures, such as utilizing GPS tracking devices or installing locks on windows and doors.

Although though AD [16] can have a big influence on a person's daily life, there are ways to control the symptoms and provide support for the patient and their loved ones. To enhance general health and wellbeing, this may entail collaborating with medical specialists, joining support groups, and changing one's lifestyle.

The research described the essay examines these concerns by assessing a wide range of audio features that are being discovered in the field of AD, using Fisher Linear Discriminant for feature selection and MFCCs for feature extraction, both of which have been reprocess to guarantee consistent audio quality for the AD patient. Section 2 tell us the all the related work which has been done by the various researcher and how they develop their technique, and methodology as well as the accuracy they determined while developing the feature selection with different audio and dataset. Section 3 considers the proposed methodology in which we proposed the FLD with MFCCs. While in Sect. 4 contains all experiment which we have done by using the below-mentioned equation and the used method and their accuracy is also mentioned below. After that, the conclusion concludes the research which we are going to propose and remark on the contribution.

2 Related Work

Choosing the most pertinent features [17] that may be utilized to precisely classify or identify audio signals is a critical stage in the examination of audio data. We chose MFCCs as the appropriate feature selection method for audio data sets (Mel-Frequency Cepstral Coefficients). Speech recognition [18] and audio signal processing both frequently employ MFCCs. They depict a signal's spectral envelope, a gauge of the energy distribution across various frequencies. MFCCs are regularly employed as a feature vector for cataloguing problems because they can effectively record crucial details about an audio signal's properties.

There are various processes in the MFCC extraction process. Initially, the audio signal is split into brief time intervals, usually between 20 and 40 ms. Next, in order to minimize spectral leakage, Each frame has a window function, like the Hamming window, applied to it [19].

Then, the Fast Fourier Transform is used to compute each frame's power spectrum (FFT). A collection of Mel filter banks are then used to transform the power spectrum into a Mel-scale spectrum. The human hearing system, which is more sensitive to frequency shifts at lower frequencies than at higher frequencies, is mimicked by these filter banks [20].

The Discrete Cosine Transform is then used to convert the Mel-scale spectrum into a set of cepstral coefficients (DCT). The generated coefficients show the signal's spectral envelope and reveal how energy is distributed across various frequency bands [21].

For classification tasks like voice recognition or music genre categorization, the MFCCs can be employed as a feature vector. As they record information about the spectrum envelope of the signal rather than the precise spectral peaks or valleys, they are resistant to changes in speaker or background noise. They are also computationally effective for real-time applications due to their relative compactness, with each frame typically containing 12–20 coefficients [22].

High-level aspects like information content, [23, 24] complexity comprehension, picture naming, and word-list production have been used in language studies on AD as indicators of disease progression. a study that time-aligned and automatically annotated a few pronounced language parameters (frequency and length of pauses) using NLP (Natural Language Processing) and (ASR) Automated Speech Recognition, as well as contrasted them with their manually annotated counterparts. To differentiate between aged people with MCI and healthy seniors, they analyzed the audio recordings of 74 neuropsychological tests. Their top SVM classifier achieved the AUC of 0.86 by combining automated speech and language characteristics with results from intellectual tests.

Jarrold et al. Semi-structured.'s interviews with 9 healthy participants, 9 people with AD, 9 people with front temporal dementia, 13 people with semantic dementia, and 8 people with progressive nonfluent aphasia made up the dataset used by Jarrold et al. [25]. They gathered 41 features using an ASR system, including speech rate and the mean and standard deviation of pause, vowel, and consonant durations [26]. Based on lexical and acoustic characteristics, they used a multilayered perceptron network to achieve a classifier accuracy of 88% for AD vs. healthy participants. A research use machine learning and signal processing to identify minor audio indicators of neurodegeneration that may be missed by human diagnosticians [27]. The Pitt Corpus is still one of the very few datasets that combine relatively spontaneous speech (recordings and transcriptions) with clinical data, despite a research tendency toward collecting spontaneous speech data as opposed to speech elicited through lab-based tasks [28]. As a result, many studies have utilised this dataset. One of the most well-known of these research is [29], which achieved 81.92% accuracy for the classification of AD-positive and AD-negative patients using machine learning. Four factors—semantic impairment, auditory abnormality, syntactic impairment, and information impairment—were found using a range of criteria. This study used a fundamental set of acoustic features in addition to a variety of high-level linguistic features, including the mean, variance, skewness, and kurtosis of the first 42 MFCCs. Similarly, [30] detected AD with 80% accuracy using a Random Forest classifier on the Pitt dataset. To train this classifier, they created a vector-space technique based on manual transcripts for automatic topic modelling. The aforementioned accuracy, however, can only be attained by including in their topic model the same lexico-syntactic and auditory elements as reported by Fraser et al. [31].

3   Proposed Methodology

The technique which we used for classification and extraction is the Fisher's Linear Discriminant (FLD) [32], also known as Linear Discriminant Analysis (LDA), is supervised learning algo used for dimensionality reduction and classification, and MFCCs are a commonly used extraction technique in audio signal processing and speech recognition [33]. They are based on the Mel scale, which is a perceptual scale that approximates the way humans perceive sound.

FLD seeks to find a linear combination of features that maximizes the separation between two or more classes in a dataset. The resulting combination of features is known as the discriminant function [34]. FLD assumes that the data can be modeled as multivariate Gaussian distributions and that the covariance matrices of the different classes are equal.

a) **Data Collection and Preprocessing:** In that dataset there is two different datasets for the [35]. The ADReSSo Challenge is a dataset that combines recordings of picture descriptions made by cognitively normal participants and patients with an AD diagnosis with speech recordings of Alzheimer's patients undertaking a category (semantic) fluency challenge during their baseline visit. The speech from many experimenters who instructed the patients and occasionally had brief conversations with them is also included in the recorded data [36].

The ADReSSo data set is the one we're using. We start by acquiring the MFCC values for each audio file in the ADReSSo dataset. The discrete Fourier transform and inverse

Fourier transform were used to obtain the MFCC values. We do vertical concatenation once we obtain the MFCC values for all of the audio sets. We obtained a CSV (comma separated values) file after concatenation, where all of the data is preserved as data rather than audio files. After receiving the CSV file, we use a few machine learning techniques, including Fisher Linear (FL), KNN, SVM, Chi-square, etc. The accuracy of the ADReSSo dataset is principally assessed in this study using the Fisher's Linear Discriminant method. We can anticipate the audio to be taken if the Fisher's Linear Discriminant [37] classifier's accuracy is high.

b) ***Fisher's Linear Discriminant:*** [8] The steps involved in Fisher's Linear Discriminant are as follows:

- Compute the mean vectors of each class.
- Compute the scatter matrices of each class, which are measures of the variance of the data in each class.
- Compute the pooled scatter matrix, which is a weighted average of the scatter matrices of each class.
- Compute the FLD function, It maximizes the ratio of between-class variation to within-class variance through the linear combination of the input features.
- Project the data onto the subspace defined by the FLD function.
- Use the projected data to classify new samples by comparing their projections with the class centroids.

Below i.e. Fig. 1 for demonstrate the how an audio data preprocessing is done by using the FLD.

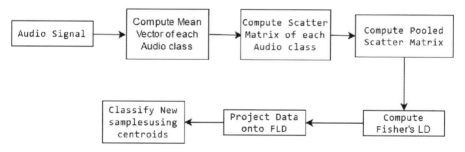

Fig. 1. Diagram that illustrating the process of Fisher's Linear Discriminant for Audio data preprocessing

FLD is commonly used for face recognition, object recognition, and other pattern recognition tasks. It can be used in combination with another algorithm, like Principal Component Analysis (PCA), to decrease the dimensionality of the feature space and enhance classification accuracy.

It offers easy methods for calculating classification problem accuracy. First, it is assumed that the dataset utilized in FLD are Gaussian conditional density models, having identical class covariance or classes that are normally distributed. The Fisher criterion looks for a direction where the distances between different classes are the greatest and the distances between each pattern within each class are the closest. As a result, when compared to other directions, this route has the biggest ratio of distance among classes to distance inside class. Such a course frequently results in the most basic classification. FLD in a two-category classification is mathematically.

$$J(w) = \frac{(p_{c2} - p_{c1})^2}{s_1^2 + s_2^2} \tag{1}$$

where s1, s2 are within-class variances and p_{c2} and p_{c1} are two projected class means. The goal of FLD is to look for the greatest J in the matrix w. (w). The classification is simpler the larger the J(w). Such an aim allows FLD to be viewed as a conventional linear discriminant. It has the ability to develop brand-new characteristics to categorize initial datasets. Such a technique, however, is unable to determine each feature's capacity for discrimination. It is possible to maintain directions by making the direction of the currently active feature J(wdirection.)'s As a result, (1) may be used to determine a feature's capacity to discriminate, and J can use the FLD score in descending order to determine a feature's ordering (w).

Multimodal FLD for multi variance output classification issues (MFLD). It is necessary to expand from two dimensions to many dimensions when performing MFLD. The conversion of multi variance output classification difficulties A practical approach for such an extension is to look first into various univariate output classification problems, where each univariate output classification problem's outputs only have two different types: belong-to and not-belong-to. The classification of x category problem will therefore be converted to an x 2-category problem classification. The outcome of each task involving two categories of categorization has the property "one-against-all." The "one-against-all" issues will then be combined into one to solve the overall issue. One representative who has been brought from FLD to MFLD is FS. This metric examines each feature's FLD in its original direction individually. First, all features are calculated individually in a "one-against-all" fashion, and then they are combined using the total of each class's unique results. Additionally, Fisher Score and feature weighting were combined. The Fisher Score of feature f_i's formula is as follows:

$$Fs(f_i) = \frac{\sum_{j=1}^{n} \omega_j (p_{c,c \in j} - p_c)^2}{\sum_{j=1}^{n} \omega_j s_{i,c \in j}^2} \tag{2}$$

By dividing the total number of patterns by the total number of patterns in the j-th class, one can get the weight of the j-th class, or ω_j. As a result, the resulting feature ordering (2) needs to be sorted in reverse.

Where ω_j is the weight of the j-th class, which may be calculated by dividing the total number of patterns by the number of patterns in the j-th class. It follows that the feature ordering (2) generated must be sorted in descending order. Fisher Score evaluates each feature separately; hence feature redundancy cannot be removed.

c) *MFCCs (Mel-Frequency Cepstral Coefficients):* It have been extensively uses in various audio processing applications, and a lot of research has been done on this topic. Here are some notable related works done in the area of MFCCs:

- **Automatic Speech Recognition (ASR):** [38] MFCCs have been widely used in ASR applications. Researchers have developed various algorithms that use MFCCs is the feature extraction technique to improve the accuracy of speech recognition systems.
- **Speaker Identification**: [39] MFCCs have also been used for speaker identification, where the goal is to identify the speaker based on their voice characteristics. Researchers have developed algorithms that use MFCCs to extract features from the speech signal, and then use machine learning techniques to identify the speaker.
- **Music Genre Classification:** [40] MFCCs have been used for music genre classification, where the goal is to classify music into different genres based on their acoustic features. Researchers have developed algorithms that use MFCCs is the technique for feature extraction to identify the acoustic features of the music signal, and then use machine learning techniques to classify the music into different genres.
- **Environmental Sound Classification**: [41] MFCCs have been used for environmental sound classification, where the goal is to classify different types of sounds, such as animal sounds or traffic sounds, based on their acoustic features. Researchers have developed algorithms that use MFCCs as a feature extraction method to extract the acoustic features of the sound signal, and then use machine learning techniques to classify the sounds into different categories.
- **Emotion Recognition**: [42] MFCCs have also been used for emotion recognition, where the goal is to recognize the sensitive state of the talker based on their speech signal. Researchers have developed algorithms that use MFCCs as a feature extraction technique to extracting the emotional feature from the speech signal, and then using machine learning techniques to classify the sensitive state of the speaker.

Overall, MFCCs have been a popular and effective feature extraction technique in various audio processing applications, and many researchers have explored their applications and limitations in different contexts. Figure 2 for the feature extraction through the MFCCs [43].

Fig. 2. Diagram that illustrating the process of extracting Mel-Frequency Cepstral Coefficients (MFCCs) from an audio signal

- First, the audio signal is separated into short time frame, typically ranging from 20 to 40 ms.
- A window function, such as Hamming window, is then used to lessen spectral leakage on each frame.

- Next, the power spectrum of each frame is computed using the Fast Fourier Transform (FFT).
- The power spectrum is then converted to a Mel-scale spectrum using a set of Mel filter banks. These filter banks are designed to mimic the human auditory system, which is more sensitive to changes in frequency at lower frequencies than at upper frequencies.
- The Mel-scale spectrum is then transformed into a set of cepstral coefficients using the Discrete Cosine Transform (DCT). The resulting coefficients represent the spectral envelope of the signal, capturing information about the distribution of energy across different frequency bands.
- The resulting MFCCs can be used as a feature vector for classification tasks, such as speech recognition or music genre classification [44].

The MFCC feature extraction technique, as in the following equation, includes the complete preprocessing step, starting with altering the regularity scale to the Mel scale [45].

$$f_{mel} = 177\ln\left(1 + \frac{fhz}{700}\right) \tag{3}$$

where the frequency is indicated by the variables f mel and f HZ, respectively. In order to create the Mel spectrum, which was used to calculate the MFCC, the magnitude spectrum was next subjected to a bank of trilateral band-pass filters known as the Mel Filter Bank [46].

$$h_m[k] = \begin{cases} 0 & k < f[m-1] \\ \frac{k - f[m-1]}{f[m] - f[m-1]} & f[m-1] < k \leq f[m] \\ \frac{f[m+1] - k}{f[m+1] - f[m]} & f[m] < k \leq f[m+1] \\ 0 & k > f[m+1] \end{cases} \tag{4}$$

where, $m = 0, 1, \ldots, $ M-1. For calculation of the Mel spectrum like log-energy.

4 Experimental Work and Performance Measure

FLD seeks to find a linear combination [47] of features that maximizes the separation between two or more classes in a dataset. The resulting combination of features is known as the discriminant function. The process of classification using Fisher's Linear Discriminant is in Fig. 3.

In the above diagram, the input data is passed through the classes, and the mean and scatter matrices of class are computed. The pooled scatter matrix is then calculated, and the FLD function is determined using this matrix. The test data is then projected onto the subspace defined by the FLD function, and new samples can be classified by comparing

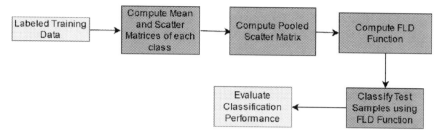

Fig. 3. Diagram for the procedure of classification using Fisher's Linear Discriminant

their projections with the class centroids. The ordering performance of the FLD model can be evaluated using appropriate metrics [48].

The steps involved in classification by Fisher's Linear Discriminant are as follows:

- Train the FLD model using labeled training data. This involves computing the mean vectors and scatter matrices of each class, as well as the FLD function.
- Project the test data onto the subspace defined by the FLD function. This involves multiplying the test data by the transpose of the FLD vector.
- Use the projected data to classify the test samples. This can be done by comparing their projections with the class centroids. The class whose centroid is closest to the test sample's projection is chosen.
- Evaluate the accuracy, precision, recall, and F1 score are useful metrics for measuring the FLD model's classification performance.

FLD can be used for binary or multi-class classification problems. It assumes that the data can be modeled as multivariate Gaussian distributions and the covariance matrices of the different classes are equal. FLD can be used in combination with other algorithms, such as principal component analysis (PCA), to decrease the dimensionality of the feature space and enhance classification accuracy [49].

Two factors, k and d, which represent the extracted feature dimension following LDA and the adjacent neighbor size in KNN, respectively, in the classification process have an impact on the outcomes. Let LDA & KNN indicate a technique for classifying models whose dimensionality has been decreased by LDA using KNN. Let Fisher, LDA, and KNN reflect the procedure used to weight the KNN classifier after dimension reduction via LDA by the FLD rate. The value of d and k are provided in Table 1 because Each value of d in KNN & LDA has a better value of overall accuracy, which varies depending on the value of k (from 0 to 45).

According to Table 1, LDA & Fisher & KNN's overall accuracy is higher than LDA & KNN's under the same conditions. When 1 d = 1 and gd = 1, the only feature vector has single dimension, suggesting that both methods produced the same results. The greatest value of KNN & LDA is 82.12% for d is 6 and k is 22. LDA, Fisher, and KNN get their higher value of 85.64% when d is 7, k is 22. As a result, whether d is 4 or 6, respectively, Fig. 1 compares the overall accuracy without dimension reduction of KNN, LDA & KNN, and Fisher, KNN & LDA. As can be observed, dimensionality reduction increased accuracy overall, surpassing accuracy without lowering dimension.

Table 1. Prediction results, accuracy for both fisher and without fIsher

Method used proper accuracy		
	Without Fisher	With Fisher
$d = 1, k = 21$	64.32%	80.13%
$d = 2, k = 50$	67.78%	79.08%
$d = 3\ k = 25$	77.98%	83.89%
$d = 4, k = 33$	69.75%	81.72%
$d = 5, k = 22$	81.72%	67.78%
$d = 6, k = 22$	82.12%	65.22%
$d = 7\ k = 20$	80.19%	79.84%
$d = 7, k = 22$	81.11%	85.64%
$d = 8, k = 25$	79.84%	82.12%
$d = 8, k = 30$	65.22%	79.75%

Additionally, LDA, Fisher, and KNN have the highest overall accuracy. We combined Eqs. 1 and 2 with the MFCCs Eq. 3 for higher accuracy in order to get that accuracy.

The resultant power spectrum and spectrum in the term of decibel (db) is shown under the below Figs. 4 and 5 for the AD patient. While applying logarithm to cast amplitude to Decibels.

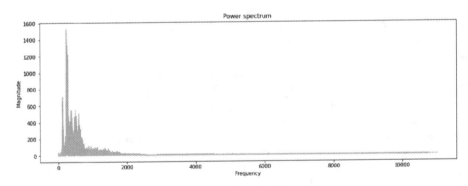

Fig. 4. Spectrum for the AD patient

The spectrum for an Alzheimer's disease (AD) patient refers to the range of symptoms and behaviors, while in our audio processing, power spectrum and spectrum are two different ways to represent the frequency of AD and NON-AD patient. Both can be represented in decibels (dB), a logarithmic item used to define the ratio of two values. Which analyze the frequency content of audio signals, which is a logarithmic item used to define the ratio of AD and NON-AD.

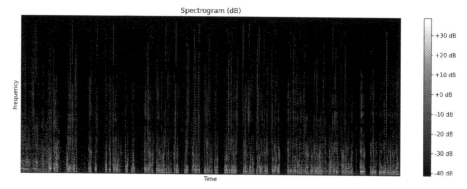

Fig. 5. Spectrum in decibal for the AD patient

The above figure is the representation of the amplitude, i.e. time and frequency of a signal at each AD patient. It is obtained by taking the Fourier transform of an AD Patient signal, calculates the magnitude of each frequency component, and mathematically that is mentioned in the above Eqs. 3 and 4 for.

5   Conclusions

The FLD algorithm was used to classify Alzheimer's disease patients based on features extracted from their Addresso audio datasets. Somehow the study found that FLD was able to accurately classify Alzheimer's disease patients. In that paper we used FLD to classify Alzheimer's disease patients based on features extracted from their audio signals. We found that FLD was able to distinguish between different stages of AD with the high accuracy.

The strategy has a moderating effect on misclassification brought on by excessive differences in each feature dimension, according to the experiment in this study, as well as a significant effect on KNN classification by weighting with its FLD rate. Also, different areas and datasets are applied to the approach.

Overall, Fisher's Linear Discriminant is a promising algorithm for classifying Alzheimer's disease patients based on certain biomarkers. However, more research is needed to explore its full potential and to compare its performance with other classification algorithms.

This has been determined to be the fundamental problem preventing the implementation of these technologies in clinical practice. Nonetheless, in application scenarios involving autonomous cognitive state monitoring, in conjunction with wearable and ambient technologies, these tasks continue to be important. The inclusion of the progression task should create opportunities for applicability in more conventional clinical settings as well.

References

1. Braaten, A.J., Parsons, T.D., Mccue, R., Sellers, A., Burns, W.J.: Neurocognitive differential diagnosis of dementing diseases: Alzheimer's dementia, vascular dementia, frontotemporal dementia, and major depressive disorder. Int. J. Neurosci. **116**(11), 1271–1293 (2006)
2. Folstein, M.F., Folstein, S.E., McHugh, P.R.: Mini-mental state. a practical method for grading the cognitive state of patients for the clinician. J. Psychiatric Res. **12**(3), 189–198 (1975)
3. Robert, P., et al.: Validation of the short cognitive battery (B2C). Value in screening for Alzheimer's disease and depressive disorders in psychiatric practice. Encephale **29**(3 Pt 1), 266–272 (2003)
4. Dubois, B., Slachevsky, A., Litvan, I., Pillon, B.: The FAB: a frontal assessment battery at bedside. Neurology **55**, 1621–1626 (2000)
5. Data fusion based on searchlight analysis for the prediction of alzheimer's disease. Expert Systems with Applications **185**, 115549 (2021)
6. Haider, F., de la Fuente, S., Luz, S.: An assessment of paralinguistic acoustic features for detection of Alzheimer's dementia in spontaneous speech. IEEE J. Sel. Top. Signal Process. **14**(2), 272–281 (2020)
7. Miao, J., Niu, L.: A survey on feature selection. Procedia Comput. Sci. **91**, 919–926 (2016)
8. Dhal, P., Azad, C.: A lightweight filter based feature selection approach for multi-label text classification. J. Ambient Intell. Human Comput. (2022). https://doi.org/10.1007/s12652-022-04335-5
9. Xue et al.: Multi-objective feature selection with missing data in classification. IEEE Transa. Emerging Topics Comput. Intell., 1–10 (2021)
10. König, A., et al.: Automatic speech analysis for the assessment of patients with predementia and Alzheimer's disease. Alzheimer's Dementia **1**(1), 112–124 (2015)
11. Ye, J., Ji, Y.: A comparative study of fisher linear discriminant analysis and support vector machine for Alzheimer's disease classification. In: Proceedings of the 2016 International Conference on Cyber-Enabled Distributed Computing and Knowledge Discovery (CyberC), Chengdu, China, 13–15 October 2016, pp. 191–194. IEEE (2016). https://doi.org/10.1109/CyberC.2016.34
12. Taler, V., Phillips, N.: Language performance in Alzheimer's disease and mild cognitive impairment: a comparative review. J. Clin. Exp. Neuropsychol. **30**(5), 501–556 (2007)
13. Taler, V., Baum, S.R., Chertkow, H., Saumier, D.: Comprehension of grammatical and emotional prosody is impaired in Alzheimer's disease. Neuropsychology **22**(2), 188–195 (2008)
14. Raj, D., Mohanasundaram, R.: An efficient filter-based feature selection model to identify significant features from high-dimensional microarray data. **45**, 02 (2020)
15. Dhal, P., Azad, C.: A multi-stage multi-objective GWO based feature selection approach for multi-label text classification. In: 2022 2nd International Conference on Intelligent Technologies (CONIT), Hubli, India, 2022, pp. 1–5 (2022). https://doi.org/10.1109/CONIT55038.2022.9847886
16. Carter, S.F., Caine, D., Burns, A., Herholz, K., Ralph, M.A.L.: Staging of the cognitive decline in Alzheimer's disease: insights from a detailed neuropsychological investigation of mild cognitive impairment and mild Alzheimer's disease. Int. J. Geriatr. Psychiatry **27**(4), 423–432 (2012)
17. Belin, P., FecteauS, S., Bedard, C.: Thinking the voice: neural correlates of voice perception. Trends Cogn. Sci. **8**, 129–135 (2004)
18. Hailstone, J.C., et al.: Voice processing in dementia: a neuropsychological and neuroanatomical analysis. Brain **134**, 2535–2547 (2011)

19. Escalera, S., Tax, D.M., Pujol, O., Radeva, P., Duin, R.P.: Subclass problem-dependent design for errorcorrecting output codes. IEEE Trans. Pattern Anal. Mach. Intell. **30**(6), 1041–1054 (2008)
20. Kanade, T., Cohn, J.F., li Tian, Y.: Comprehensive database for facial expression analysis. In: Proceedings of the Fourth IEEE International Conference on Automatic Face and Gesture Recognition, pp. 46–53. Grenoble, France (2000)
21. Pudil, P., Ferri, F., Novovicova, J., Kittler, J.: Floating search methods for feature selection with nonmonotonic criterion functions. Proc. Int'l Conf. Pattern Recognition **3**, 279–283 (1994)
22. Fraser, K.C., Fors, K.L., Kokkinakis, D.: Multilingual word embeddings for the assessment of narrative speech in mild cognitive impairment. Comput. Speech Lang. **53**, 121–139 (2019)
23. Ammar, R.B., Ayed, Y.B.: Language related features for early detection of Alzheimer disease. Procedia Comput. Sci. **176,** 763–770 (2020)
24. Orimaye, S.O., Sze-Meng Wong, J., Golden, K.J.: Learning predictive linguistic features for Alzheimer's disease and related dementias using verbal utterances, pp. 78–87 (2014)
25. Jarrold, W., et al.: Aided diagnosis of dementia type through computer based analysis of spontaneous speech. In: Proc. Workshop Comput. Linguistics Clin. Psychol., pp. 27–37 (2014)
26. Luz, S., Haider, F., de la Fuente Garcia, S., Fromm, D., MacWhinney, B.: Editorial: Alzheimer's dementia recognition through spontaneous speech. 3, p. 96 (2021)
27. Lopez-de-Ipiña, K., et al.: On automatic diagnosis of Alzheimer's disease based on spontaneous speech analysis and emotional temperature. 7(1), 44–55 (2015)
28. Rudzicz, F., Currie, L.C., Danks, A., Mehta, T., Zhao, S.: Automatically identifying trouble-indicating speech behaviors in Alzheimer's disease, pp. 241–242 (2014)
29. Sanz, H., Valim, C., Vegas, E., Oller, J., Reverter, F.: Svm-rfe: Selection and visualization of the most relevant features through non-linear kernels. **19**, 11 (2018)
30. Mathuranath, P.S., George, A., Cherian, P.J., Mathew, R., Sarma, P.S.: Instrumental activities of daily living scale for dementia screening in elderly people. Int. Psychogeriatrics **17**(3), 461–474 (2005)
31. Forbes-McKay, K.E., Venneri, A.: Detecting subtle spontaneous language decline in early Alzheimer's disease with a picture description task. Neurol. Sci. **26**(4), 243–254 (2005)
32. Hoyte, K., Brownell, H., Wingfield, A.: Components of speech prosody and their use in detection of syntactic structure by older adults. Exp. Aging Res. **35**(1), 129–151 (2009)
33. Trullen, J.M.P., Pardo, P.J.M.: Comparative study of aprosody in Alzheimer's disease and in multi-infarct dementia. Dementia **7**(2), 59–62 (1996)
34. McDowd, J., Hoffman, L., Rozek, E., Lyons, K., Pahwa, R., Burns, J., Kemper, S.: Understanding verbal fluency in healthy aging, Alzheimer's disease, and Parkinson's disease. Neuropsychologia **25**(2), 210–225 (2011)
35. Mirzaei, S., El Yacoubi, M., Garcia-Salicetti, S.: Twostage feature selection of voice parameters for early alzheimer's disease prediction. IRBM **39**(6), 430–435 (2018). JETSAN
36. Dhal, P., Azad, C.: A deep learning and multi-objective PSO with GWO based feature selection approach for text classification. In: 2022 2nd International Conference on Advance Computing and Innovative Technologies in Engineering (ICACITE), Greater Noida, India, pp. 2140–2144 (2022). https://doi.org/10.1109/ICACITE53722.2022.9823473
37. Tanveer, M., et al.: Machine learning techniques for the diagnosis of Alzheimer's disease: A review. ACM Trans. Multimed. Comput. Commun. Appl. **16**(35), April 2020
38. Nanni, L., et al.: Combining multiple approaches for the early diagnosis of Alzheimer's disease, pp. 259–266
39. Abduh, Z., et al.: Classification of heart sounds using fractional fourier transform based mel-frequency spectral coefficients and traditional classifiers, p. 101788 (2020)
40. Indrebo, K.M., Povinelli, R.J., Johnson, M.T.: Minimum mean-squared error estimation of mel-frequency cepstral coefficients using a novel distortion model, pp. 1654–1661 (2008)

41. Drakopoulos, G., Pikramenos, G., Spyrou, E., Perantonis, S.: Emotion recognition from speech: A survey. 08 2019
42. Dhal, P., Azad, C.: A comprehensive survey on feature selection in the various fields of machine learning. Appl. Intell. **52**, 4543–4581 (2022). https://doi.org/10.1007/s10489-021-02550-9
43. Yadav, V., Kumar, R., Azad, C.: A filter-based feature selection approach for the prediction of Alzheimer's diseases through audio classification. In: 2022 2nd International Conference on Advance Computing and Innovative Technologies in Engineering (ICACITE), Greater Noida, India, pp. 1890–1894 (2022). https://doi.org/10.1109/ICACITE53722.2022.9823665
44. Dhal, P., Azad, C.: A multi-objective feature selection method using Newton's law based PSO with GWO. Appl. Soft Comput. **107**, 107394 (2021). ISSN 1568-4946, https://doi.org/10.1016/j.asoc.2021.107394
45. Yu, B., Williamson, J.R., Mundt, J.C., Quatieri, T.F.: Speech-based automated cognitive impairment detection from remotely-collected cognitive test audio. IEEE Access **6**, 40494–40505 (2018). https://doi.org/10.1109/ACCESS.2018.2856478
46. Nasrolahzadeh, M., Haddadnia, J., Rahnamayan, S.: Multi-objective optimization of wavelet-packet-based features in pathological diagnosis of Alzheimer using spontaneous speech signals. IEEE Access **8**, 112393–112406 (2020). https://doi.org/10.1109/ACCESS.2020.3001426
47. Bhat, C., Kopparapu, S.K.: Identification of Alzheimer's Disease using Non-linguistic Audio Descriptors (2019)
48. Ivanova, O., Meilán, J.J.G.: Francisco Martínez-Sánchez, Israel Martínez-Nicolás, Thide E. Llorente, Nuria Carcavilla González
49. Dhal, P., Azad, C.: A multi-objective evolutionary feature selection approach for the classification of multi-label data. In: 2022 2nd International Conference on Advance Computing and Innovative Technologies in Engineering (ICACITE), Greater Noida, India, pp. 1986–1989 (2022). https://doi.org/10.1109/ICACITE53722.2022.9823911

Automation in Agriculture Using Deep Machine Learning: A Survey

Sanjay Kumar Mahto$^{(\boxtimes)}$, Yogendra Kumar, Manjeet Singh, Ruchi Kumari, and Kishore Kumar Ray

Department of CSE, RVS College of Engineering and Technology, Jamshedpur, Jharkhand, India
sray726@gmail.com, kishorekumar.ray@rvscollege.ac.in

Abstract. Adoption of agriculture automation is becoming an growing field because it has the capability to enhance effectiveness, lower costs, and increase output in the face of rising global food demand. Over the past few years, there has been a significant focus on applying artificial intelligence techniques to automate agricultural processes. The application of AI in agriculture has gained attention as a potential solution for improving productivity, efficiency and reducing costs in the farming industry. Significant expansion in ML concepts, in particular, have resulted in significant improvements in agricultural duties. Deep learning is a cutting-edge method for analysing data and processing images that has shown great promise in the agricultural sector. Detecting crop diseases, managing weeds, controlling pesticide use, and improving soil and water management practises are all difficulties for the farming sector. Deep Learning (DL), including the algorithms of Convolutional Neural Networks (CNN), Recurrent Neural Networks (RNN), and Generative Adversarial Networks (GAN), has been extensively studied and implemented in a variety of disciplines, including agriculture, in recent years. This article presents an overview of current studies that utilize deep machine learning methods to tackle various issues in agriculture and food production. The paper aims to summarize recent research efforts in this field. We examine the particular agricultural problems that are being investigated, the models and frameworks that are being employed, the type and preparation of data sources, and the overall effectiveness of the approaches used. The article provides a comprehensive analysis of these aspects in recent research studies in the field of agriculture.

Keywords: Deep learning · smart agriculture · convolutional neural networks · image processing · pattern recognition

1 Introduction

Agriculture contributes significantly to the worldwide economy by providing food and raw materials for different industries [1]. The farming process depicted in

R. K. Tiwari and G. Sahoo (Eds.): ICAII 2022, CCIS 1822, pp. 215–225, 2023.
https://doi.org/10.1007/978-3-031-37303-9_16

Fig. 1 has five stages: soil preparation, seed sowing, fertiliser application, irrigation, weed control, reaping, and storage. Farmers prepare the soil for seeding by removing weeds and other unwanted plant materials, tilling the soil, and adding nutrients and fertilisers as required during the soil preparation process. This procedure provides an ideal environment for seed germination and healthy plant development. This procedure entails breaking up big clumps of dirt and removing debris such as sticks, rocks, and roots. In addition, depending on the type of crop, add fertilisers and organic matter to make an ideal environment for crops. Sowing seeds necessitates paying close attention to the space between two seeds as well as the depth at which they are planted. Depending on the crop and soil conditions, the appropriate spacing and planting depth can vary, and getting these factors right is critical for achieving optimum plant development and yield. Additionally, when sowing seeds, variables such as soil moisture, temperature, and weather conditions should be considered to ensure the best possible start. Maintaining soil fertility is critical so that farmers can continue to produce nutritious and healthy crops. Farmers use fertilisers to provide plant nutrients such as nitrogen, phosphorus, and potassium, which are essential for agricultural growth and development. This period also determines the crop's quality. Irrigation is the application of water to crops or plants to help them develop and thrive. Irrigating a field or garden directs water to the soil, which serves to keep it moist and the humidity level in the air around the plants stable. Crop growth can be hampered by under or overwatering, and if not done correctly, it can result in crop damage. Weeds are unwanted plants that develop near crops or along agricultural boundaries. Weed control is critical because weeds reduce yields, raise production costs, conflict with harvest, and reduce crop quality. The procedure of gathering ripe crops from the fields is known as harvesting. The process is labour-intensive because it necessitates a large number of labourers. This step also involves post-harvest operations such as cleaning, sorting, packing, and cooling. Storage is the post-harvest system phase in which products are kept in such a manner that food security is ensured other than during agricultural seasons. It also involves crop packing and transportation. Furthermore, the agricultural task includes the pre and post harvesting actions depicted in the Fig. 2. Many nations, including India, continue to farm in traditional ways. As a result, agricultural areas are experiencing a variety of issues, including a lack of products such as fruits and vegetables [2]. Unpredictable soil contents [3], erroneous application of pesticides [4], toxicant, fungicides, or microbicides to control crop or plant infection, and a scarcity of trained labour [5], among other things. As the global population continues to increase, there is mounting pressure on the agricultural sector. Overall losses in agricultural operations, from crop selection to product sale, are extremely high. As a result, it is critical to address Smart farming [6] in order to address crop production concerns such as productivity, environmental impact, food security, and sustainability [7]. Data collection and management can be achieved using a variety of technologies, including blockchain, IoT, ML, DL, and cloud computing. Machine learning and deep learning can improve machine performance and aid in the development of more advanced technology. Adopting computer vision, ML, and IoT can enhance productivity, enhance quality, and ultimately boost profitability for farmers and related industries. Agriculture places significant importance on computer vision and imaging analysis, and intelligent data analysis techniques are employed for image identification/classification, anomaly detection, and other related purposes. ML (K-means [8], support vector machines [9], artificial neural networks (ANN) [10], and regression analysis are among the most prominent image analysis approaches. Aside from the aforementioned strategies, deep learning (DL) [11] is a new one that has lately gained traction. Deep learning is a type of machine learning computational discipline that is comparable to ANN. The potency and precision of machine learning are being augmented by deep learning algorithms. The idea for creating this research derives from the fact that deep learning in agriculture is a relatively new, modern, and promising approach that is gaining traction. Deep learning solves a variety of agricultural problems with excellent outcomes, which pushes me to prepare the survey.

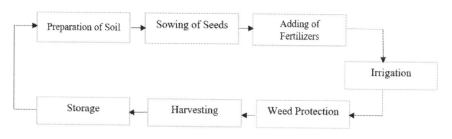

Fig. 1. Life Cycle of agriculture

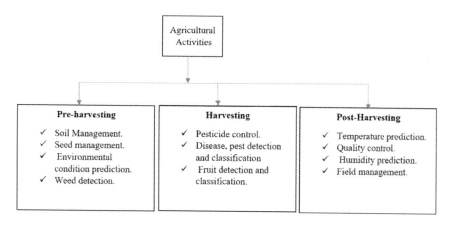

Fig. 2. Agricultural activities in different stages of farming

2 An Introduction on Machine Learning and Deep Learning

Typically, machine learning approaches incorporate a learning process with the goal of learning to do a task through experience (training data). To evaluate the effectiveness of a machine learning model in a specific task, a performance metric that improves as experience is gained is utilized Fig. 3.

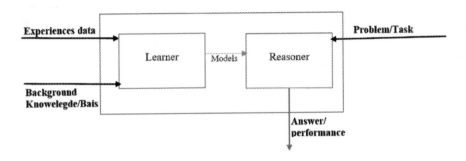

Fig. 3. Component of Machine learning system

Different statistical and mathematical techniques are employed to compute the performance of ML models. The trained model can then be used to classify, predict, or cluster additional examples (test data) based on the expertise gained during the training phase. A typical Machine learning approach is depicted in Fig. 2. Machine learning tasks are commonly categorized into general groups according to the method of learning employed, such as supervised learning, unsupervised learning, and reinforcement learning. Supervised learning, is concern about the data that are provided with examples of inputs and outputs, and the objective is to develop a comprehensive rule that can effectively transform inputs into desired outputs. Unsupervised learning is a learning method in which a computer is trained without any kind of supervision, i.e. the machine is trained on unlabelled data. The model examines the data it receives to discover concealed patterns that can be utilized for making informed choices. Reinforcement learning is a learning method in which a Machine is rewarded for correct predictions and penalised for incorrect predictions. With these input points, the machine learns automatically and increases its accuracy. Deep learning is a category of machine learning that enhances traditional machine learning techniques by introducing increased complexity or "depth" to the model. This is achieved by utilizing various functions to modify the input data, which enables hierarchical representation of the data through multiple layers of abstraction. The majority of deep learning designs are based on neural networks, which are composed of numerous layers, each of which has several units. Each unit's activation y is a linear combination of the input vector x, learnable parameters w, and basis b, followed by an element-wise non-linearity function f(x) so that y=wx+b. Deep neural networks are classified into three types: artificial neural networks (ANN), convolutional neural networks (CNN), and recurrent neural networks(RNN) [12]. Deep learning has a significant advantage in feature learning, which is the automatic extraction of features from raw data, with features from higher levels of the hierarchy produced by the composition of lower level features. These complicated models used in Deep Learning can improve classification accuracy or reduce error in regression issues if enough extensive datasets explaining the problem are available. Convolutional Neural Networks (CNN) [13], depicted in Fig. 4, are a type of deep, feed-forward ANN and are likely the most popular and commonly used technology in agricultural research today.

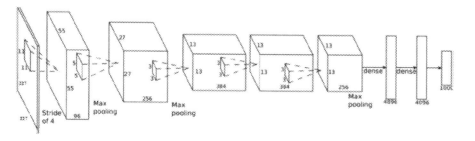

Fig. 4. Basic convolutional neural network [13]

CNN is an image detection and classification algorithm that specialises in processing data having a grid-like input shape. Like Neural Networks, CNNs also get their motivation from the operation of the human brain, specifically the organisation of the 'Visual Cortex'. Each neuron in the brain responds to stimuli exclusively in a specific part of the visual field known as the 'Receptive Field,' and all such fields overlap to include the whole visible region. Similarly, CNNs operate on the same basis. The CNN is made up of three layers: convolutional, pooling, and fully connected. The convolutional layers extract features from the input images, which are subsequently decreased in dimensionality by the pooling layers. The complete feature maps are obtained by using several different kernels.

$$C^l_{i,j,k} = W^l_k X^l_{i,j} + b^l_k \tag{1}$$

where W^l_k and b^l_k are weight and bias of the kth filter. The equation is used to compute the convolution for one pixel in the layer below.

$$out(i,j) = x * w = \sum_m \sum_n x[m,n]w[l-m, j-n] \tag{2}$$

where out(i,j) is the output in the next layer, x is the input image w is the kernel and $*$ is the convolutional operation. The fully connected layers, which are often positioned near the model's output, operate as classifiers, using the high-level features acquired to categorise incoming images into predetermined classes or to create numerical predictions. They take a vector as input and output another vector. Previously, traditional techniques of image classification tasks relied on hand-engineered features, the performance of which had a significant impact on total outcomes. FE is a time-consuming and complex technique that must be updated every time the problem or data set changes. Thus, feature engineering is a costly endeavour that relies on specialist knowledge and does not generalise well. Deep learning, on the other hand, does not require feature engineering, instead locating the important characteristics through training.

3   Machine Learning-Based Application in Agriculture

Machine learning and Deep learning along with computer vision, are very supportive to farmers. AI-powered drone technology is extremely beneficial in agriculture since it makes it easier to monitor, scan, and analyse crops by providing high-quality photos. In addition to that, farmers can decide whether the crops are ready for harvest or not. There is no end to the applications of machine learning in agriculture. This section provides a thorough examination of several Machine Learning applications connected to smart agricultural practises.

3.1   Disease Detection

Crop disease and pest are serious threats in agriculture. It takes a lot of time and effort to manually identify diseases in crops. A prevalent approach to controlling pests and diseases in agriculture involves the uniform application of insecticides throughout the production area. However, with the development of AI and machine learning, the process of disease detection has become more streamlined and efficient, requiring less time and effort. For Initial identification and discrimination of sugar beetroot illnesses, An approach based on Support Vector Machines (SVM) that utilizes machine learning techniques and spectral vegetation indices was proposed by [14]. [15] Employed mage-processing techniques to extract useful features of plant disease areas for further analysis. They used unsupervised machine learning (K-means clustering [16]) technique to categorize those areas for accurate disease detection. [4] used a deep learning algorithm to classify plant illness based on leaf images. They introduced a novel technique for categorizing leaf images that involves deep convolutional networks. The proposed model can recognise 13 different types of plant illnesses, including healthy leaves. The researchers employed deep convolutional neural networks, in combination with transfer learning, to identify diseases in plant leaves. They used a pre-trained VGGNet model [17] on ImageNet, and the Inception module was chosen to identify plant leaf disease.

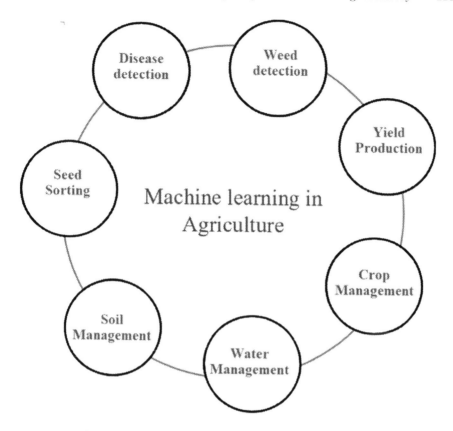

Fig. 5. Application of Machine learning in agriculture

3.2 Weed Detection

Aside from diseases, weeds are the most major threat to agricultural productivity. Detecting and identifying weeds from crops is the most difficult component of weed control. Computer vision and machine learning techniques can be utilized to enhance weed detection and discrimination, without incurring significant costs or causing any negative impact on the environment. [18] assessed the effectiveness of various machine learning techniques such as random forest (RF), support vector machine (SVM), and k-nearest neighbors (KNN) - in identifying weeds based on UAV photographs taken from a chili crop field in Australia. The authors [19] utilized Convolutional Neural Networks (CNN) to detect and classify weeds in photographs of soybean crops, with the aim of administering the appropriate herbicide to each identified weed. The author [20] discussed machine learning and image processing strategies for accurate real-time weed and crop detection in the field, including pre-processing, segmentation, feature extraction, and classification.

3.3 Yield Production

The use of deep learning is a useful method for making decisions regarding crop yield predictions, determining the suitable crops to plant, and for providing guidance on what actions to take during the crop-growing season. [21]. The authors [22] evaluated the effectiveness of ML algorithms with limited data in forecasting crop yields on a monthly basis throughout the growing season, from start to end. The researchers created an automated pipeline that utilizes machine learning to select the most suitable features and models for crop yield prediction. By expanding the Indian economy and raising crop yield rates, the authors [23] employ the crop selection strategy to help tackle numerous agricultural and farmer problems.

3.4 Crop Management

Deep learning (DL) applications in agriculture management would provide precise crop output and quality forecasts. Deep learning models are used to estimate crop production and assist farmers in making the best decisions to maximise profit and minimise risk. Crop price estimation and appraisal are performed prior to planting in order to make an informed decision. Forecasting the price of a crop can be advantageous in making informed decisions, mitigating losses, and managing price volatility risks. The author [24] forecasted the price of different crops using prior rainfall and WPI data. We used decision tree regression (a supervised machine learning method) to analyse historical data, predict prices for recent data, and anticipate prices for the future twelve months.

3.5 Water Management

The water crisis is a worldwide issue. Every day, billions of litres of water are squandered. Every day, seven billion litres of water are squandered in the United States. Due to their financial circumstances, developing nations encounter more problems. Therefore, more effective water management is required to better conserve water in order to achieve sustainable crop production [25]. The author [26] presents a model of an automatic irrigation system was built using the Decision Tree algorithm, which is a type of ML algorithm. The algorithm was trained on a subset of collected data to construct a model that can be used to analyse and predict the remaining data. Using the Decision Tree algorithm, an automatic irrigation system was built, where the system was trained on a subset of the collected data to create a model. This model is then used to analyse and predict when and how much water to provide to crops. The accuracy of the system's predictions was 97.86%, suggesting that it could be a useful tool in providing irrigation to the agricultural industry.

3.6 Soil Management

The type of soil and the nutrient content of the soil affect the type and quality of the crop planted. Due to increased deforestation, soil quality is deteriorating, making it difficult to determine the soil's condition. The type of soil and its nutrient content influence the type and quality of the planted crop. Soil quality is deteriorating as a result of increased deforestation, making it difficult to determine the soil's condition. In order to effectively and sustainably manage soil nutrients, it is crucial to comprehend their spatial distribution and control mechanisms. John K al at.(2020) [26] presented a method for measuring the SOC content of soil using machine learning. Suchithra M. et al.(2020) [27] classify a number of important soil characteristics, including the quantity of phosphorus (P), available potassium (K), organic carbon (OC), boron (B), and soil reaction (pH) measurements of soil fertility were included in the study. Using machine learning techniques the classification and forecasting of village-specific soil parameters reduces wasteful fertiliser input expenditures. Both Sharma A. et al. (2021) [28] and Iiakos KG et al. (2018) [29] present a soil management survey using Machine Learning techniques.

3.7 Seed Sorting

Germination of seeds is a crucial aspect of seed quality, which is a major determinant of yield and production quality. The seed germination rate is estimated manually with the assistance of experienced individuals, which is a time-consuming and error-prone method. Various authors have proposed various machine learning and image processing algorithms to automate the classification and computation of seeds. Sivakumar et al. (2019) [30] presented a system for computerised and automatic determination of germination rate using some advanced computer vision and machine learning techniques. Using deep neural networks, they examine the germination rate of seeds by comparing it to a large number of datasets containing germinated and non-germinated samples. Zhu et al. (2019) [31] utilised near-infrared hyper spectral imaging to identify seven types of cotton seed. In addition, a self-designed convolution neural network (CNN) and a Residual Network (ResNet) were employed to classify the various varieties. Gulzar ei at.(2020) [32] proposed a technique for classifying seeds that can provide additional information regarding quality production, seed quality control, and impurity identification. CNN and transfer learning were utilised for the classification of seeds.

4 Conclusion

In this article, we conducted a study of machine learning-based agricultural research activities. We contrasted the efficacy of machine learning to other available methodologies. Our research demonstrates that machine learning outperforms other prominent image processing techniques. We plan to apply the broad concepts and best practises of machine learning, as detailed in this review, to other areas of agriculture where this cutting-edge technique has not yet been completely implemented. This study aims to encourage more researchers to experiment with machine learning, utilising it to tackle a variety of agricultural problems, such as categorization or prediction, as well as computer vision and image analysis, and data analysis in general. Overall, the benefits of machine and deep learning indicate its continued use in wiser, more sustainable agriculture and more secure food production.

References

1. Sachs, I.: Towards a second green revolution?, 161–164 (2010)
2. Chen, C., Chaudhary, A., Mathys, A.: Nutritional and environmental losses embedded in global food waste. Resour. Conserv. Recycl. **160**, 104912 (2020)
3. Padarian, J., Minasny, B., McBratney, A.B.: Using deep learning for digital soil mapping. Soil **5**(1), 79–89 (2019)
4. Sladojevic, S., Arsenovic, M., Anderla, A., Culibrk, D., Stefanovic, D.: Deep neural networks based recognition of plant diseases by leaf image classification. Comput. Intell. Neurosci. 2016 (2016)
5. Bhanugopan, R., Wang, Y., Lockhart, P., Farrell, M.: Managerial skills shortages and the impending effects of organizational characteristics: evidence from China. Pers. Rev. (2017)
6. Gangwar, D.S., Tyagi, S.: Challenges and opportunities for sensor and actuator networks in Indian agriculture, 38–42. IEEE (2016)
7. Gebbers, R., Adamchuk, V.I.: Precision agriculture and food security. Science **327**(5967), 828–831 (2010)
8. Mucherino, A., Papajorgji, P., Pardalos, P.M.: A survey of data mining techniques applied to agriculture. Oper. Res. **9**, 121–140 (2009)
9. Kok, Z.H., Shariff, A.R.M., Alfatni, M.S.M., Khairunniza-Bejo, S.: Support vector machine in precision agriculture: a review. Comput. Electron. Agric. **191**, 106546 (2021)
10. Kujawa, S., Niedba la, G.: Artificial neural networks in agriculture. MDPI (2021)
11. LeCun, Y., Bengio, Y., Hinton, G.: Deep learning. Nature **521**(7553), 436–444 (2015)
12. Xu, W., Wang, Q., Chen, R.: Spatio-temporal prediction of crop disease severity for agricultural emergency management based on recurrent neural networks. GeoInformatica **22**, 363–381 (2018)
13. Albawi, S., Mohammed, T.A., Al-Zawi, S.: Understanding of a convolutional neural network, 1–6. IEEE (2017)
14. Rumpf, T., Mahlein, A.-K., Steiner, U., Oerke, E.-C., Dehne, H.-W., Plümer, L.: Early detection and classification of plant diseases with support vector machines based on hyperspectral reectance. Comput. Electron. Agric. **74**(1), 91–99 (2010)
15. Al-Hiary, H., Bani-Ahmad, S., Reyalat, M., Braik, M., Alrahamneh, Z.: Fast and accurate detection and classification of plant diseases. Int. J. Comput. Appl. **17**(1), 31–38 (2011)
16. Sinaga, K.P., Yang, M.-S.: Unsupervised k-means clustering algorithm. IEEE Access **8**, 80716–80727 (2020)
17. Dhillon, A., Verma, G.K.: Convolutional neural network: a review of models, methodologies and applications to object detection. Progress Artif. Intell. **9**(2), 85–112 (2020)
18. Islam, N., et al.: Early weed detection using image processing and machine learning techniques in an Australian hilli farm. Agriculture **11**(5), 387 (2021)

19. Santos Ferreira, A., Freitas, D.M., Silva, G.G., Pistori, H., Folhes, M.T.: Weed detection in soybean crops using convnets. Comput. Electron. Agric. **143**, 314–324 (2017)
20. Wang, A., Zhang, W., Wei, X.: A review on weed detection using ground-based machine vision and image processing techniques. Comput. Electron. Agric. **158**, 226–240 (2019)
21. Van Klompenburg, T., Kassahun, A., Catal, C.: Crop yield prediction using machine learning: a systematic literature review. Comput. Electron. Agric. **177**, 105709 (2020)
22. Meroni, M., Waldner, F., Seguini, L., Kerdiles, H., Rembold, F.: Yield forecasting with machine learning and small data: what gains for grains? Agric. Forest Meteorol. **308**, 108555 (2021)
23. Medar, R., Rajpurohit, V.S., Shweta, S.: Crop yield prediction using machine learning techniques, pp. 1–5. IEEE (2019)
24. Dhanapal, R., AjanRaj, A., Balavinayagapragathish, S., Balaji, J.: Crop price prediction using supervised machine learning algorithms. **1916**(1), 012042 (2021). IOP Publishing
25. Neupane, J., Guo, W.: Agronomic basis and strategies for precision water management: a review. Agronomy **9**(2), 87 (2019)
26. Blasi, A.H., Abbadi, M.A., Al-Huweimel, R.: Machine learning approach for an automatic irrigation system in southern Jordan valley. Eng. Technol. Appl. Sci. Res. **11**(1), 6609–6613 (2021)
27. Suchithra, M., Pai, M.L.: Improving the prediction accuracy of soil nutrient classification by optimizing extreme learning machine parameters. Inf. Process. Agric. **7**(1), 72–82 (2020)
28. Sharma, A., Jain, A., Gupta, P., Chowdary, V.: Machine learning applications for precision agriculture: a comprehensive review. IEEE Access **9**, 4843–4873 (2020)
29. Liakos, K.G., Busato, P., Moshou, D., Pearson, S., Bochtis, D.: Machine learning in agriculture: a review. Sensors **18**(8), 2674 (2018)
30. Sivakumar, D., SuriyaKrishnaan, K., Akshaya, P., Anuja, G., Devadharshini, G.: Computerized growth analysis of seeds using deep learning method. Int. J. Recent Technol. Eng. (IJRTE) 7(6S5) (2019)
31. Zhu, S., Zhou, L., Gao, P., Bao, Y., He, Y., Feng, L.: Near-infrared hyperspectral imaging combined with deep learning to identify cotton seed varieties. Molecules **24**(18), 3268 (2019)
32. Gulzar, Y., Hamid, Y., Soomro, A.B., Alwan, A.A., Journaux, L.: A convolution neural network-based seed classification system. Symmetry **12**(12), 2018 (2020)

Internet of Things

A Survey on Security Threats in VANET and Its Solutions

Rahul M. Raut[1]([⊠]) and Suresh Asole[2]

[1] Babasaheb Naik College of Engineering, Pusad, India
mr.rahulraut@gmail.com
[2] Department of CSE, Babasaheb Naik College of Engineering, Pusad, India

Abstract. Mobile ad hoc networks have a subtype called vehicle-specific mobile ad hoc networks (VANETs). ITS (Intelligent Transportation Systems) uses these ad hoc networks (ITS). "Virtual Ad Hoc Networks" (VANETs) are the most popular, productive, and quickly growing subset of "mobile ad hoc networks" (MANETs). The wireless network called VANET is hard to predict because it is made up of both roadside units (RSUs) and on-board units (OBUs) as well as cars. The modern "smart city" has high hopes that VANET will help it solve a wide range of problems in smarter ways. Security is a big issue in VANETs because threats and weaknesses could hurt drivers' activities and private information. In this piece, we review the various security attacks in VANET and proposed solution.

Keywords: Vehicle ad hoc Networks · Intelligent Transportation System · On Board Units · Mobile ad hoc Networks · Road Side Units

1 Introduction

In this era of technology demand of smart vehicles are increasing day by day, therefore the use of VANET technology are adding new features in smart vehicles. On the other side securing Personal data is the big challenge over a network. In VANET, two types of communication takes place viz. V2V and V2I. Vehicles are equipped with Onboard Unit and form V2V communication. A VANET is similar to a MANET in that it is in charge of coordinating its own ways to communicate and doesn't depend on any other networks. The MANET has helped the military the most out of all of their efforts. This is a lot like the basic way that computers talk to each other when they share data, which is exactly what we have here [1]. A VANET is made up of things like cell nodes and other street furniture. The On-Board Unit is made up of sensors that are put on top of cars. These sensors serve as wireless nodes. Figure 1 provides a basic summary of the VANET system model. In this scenario, cars with on-board computers talk to each other to trade sensitive information. On the other side vehicles are able to communicate with RSUs to access the global data in vehicles. The road side units are like mobile tower and they are connected with server and service provider to form network. A running vehicle can get global traffic information, news, weather forecast, etc. on their board. On the other hand security of personal data of driver is the biggest challenge in VANET. A third party trusted authority can be added to secure information over network. A various security features can be added via trusted authority and make network secure.

R. K. Tiwari and G. Sahoo (Eds.): ICAII 2022, CCIS 1822, pp. 229–240, 2023.
https://doi.org/10.1007/978-3-031-37303-9_17

In this paper we are going to discussed various security attacks in VANET and there possible solutions.

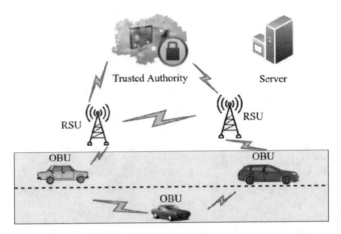

Fig. 1. VANET Architecture

2   VANETs Characteristics

This section gives an overview of the things that make VANET unique, such as its portability, real-time limits, storage and computing capacities, dynamic topology, communication mediums, and other things.

A. Mobility: Because the nodes that make up a VANET are always moving, it is often necessary for them to leave the network configuration they are using and switch to a different one. These nodes that move quickly could make it hard or impossible for V2V and V2I communications to happen [1].

B. Storage and Computing Capabilities: When it comes to sharing information, the number of people connected to VANETs at any given time is directly related to how well they work. Because of this, there must be enough space to store data and enough computing power to store, process, and send important signals.

C. Real-Time Limitations: Even though there are delays in communication because of the different kinds of hardware used, some VANET applications require data to be sent at speeds that are close to instantaneous. The driver might only have a few milliseconds to think about the information they get from systems like fault detection and collision avoidance before they have to take action to avoid an accident [2].

D. Dynamic Network Topology: The configuration of a VANET is always changing because it has to change to meet the changing needs of the system as nodes are added and taken away. This type of dynamic configuration could help malicious nodes hide their routes after they have hacked into a network [2].

E. Frequent Network Disconnections: Most disconnections from the VANET are caused by things outside of the network, like fast vehicle movement or bad weather. People often lose limbs in car accidents because there are so many cars on the road [2].

F. Communication Medium: Mobile Ad-hoc Networks (MANETs) and VANETs are very similar. Both of these types of networks depend on wireless communication. In VANETs, on the other hand, the nodes are much more mobile than in MANETs. It's possible that using wireless communication will raise some VANET security concerns.

G. Radio Transmission Depletion: Digital transmission in these frequency ranges causes problems for Dedicated Short-Range Communication (DSRC), which is another name for radio communications. These problems happen in cities because of dispersion, diffraction, refraction, reflection, and scattering [3].

3 Security Attacks

When VANET was being made, the safety of the driver was the most important thing. For VANET to work the way it was meant to, there must be strong security measures in place. To provide security services like availability, confidentiality, authenticity, message integrity, and non-repudiation, it is important to deal with and find solutions for a number of security challenges.

3.1 Denial of Service (DoS) Attack

When a hostile user, either inside or outside of a VANET, tries to stop or take control of the network's communication channels or resources, we call that an attack [4]. Most attacks in a wireless environment are aimed at the way people talk to each other. These attacks can be made to jam the channel or to put up other, unknown barriers that make it hard for nodes to join the network. The goal of this kind of attack is to make it impossible for legitimate nodes to use the network in any way. The attack could make the nodes and resources of the network so bad that they can't be fixed. At last, those who shouldn't have been able to use the networks can't use them at all. The denial of service (DOS) protocol is strictly forbidden because the main goal of a VANET is to make sure that mission-critical information is always sent quickly and securely. DOS attacks can be done in one of three ways [5, 6]: by jamming communication channels, overloading networks, or losing individual packets. Details on attacks that can mess up operating systems.

- At the simplest level, you must deplete all available node resources. Because they don't have enough resources, this level of Distributed Denial of Service attack is meant to stop the nodes that are the target of the attack from doing any of their other important jobs. This link in the chain is important. Becomes continuously busy and utilizes all the resources to verify the messages.

a) Case 01: DOS Attack in V2V Communications: An attacker sends a warning message "Accident at location Y" which is also shown if Fig. 1. A victim node behind the attacker node receives this message [6]. However, the sending of the duplicate message is repeated continuously, thus keeps the victim node busy and thus completely denied for accessing the network (Fig. 2).

Fig. 2. DOS attack in vehicle-to-vehicle communications

b) Case 02: Launch DOS Attack in V2I Communications: In this case, the attacker launches attack to Road Side Unit (RSU) as depicted in Fig. 3.

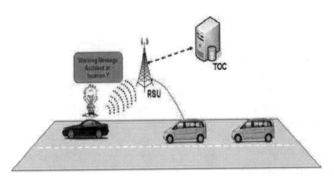

Fig. 3. DOS attack in vehicle-to-infrastructure communications

3.2 *Malware Attack:* **OBU and RSU Are Prone to Malware Attack**

It disrupts the normal functioning of the VANET [6]. The attacker may insert malware or viruses in to the communication channel of VANET in this type of attack. These threads are sufficient to destroy the components of on-board unit and RSU. It will totally or partially disturb the communication between nodes.

3.3 Broadcast Tampering Attack

A vehicle may send wrong warning message to other vehicle, thereby creating an abnormal scenario [7]. VANET used Message broadcasting system to transmit the message where attacker tries to modify the actual message and broadcast false message. The message available on communication channel in the form of packets, and intruder may replace some packets over the channel or it may it may skip some packets to send junk messages. This type of attack create the some abnormal situation for the drivers.

3.4 Black Hole and Grey Hole Attack

These attack normally drops the packet while sending them into the network. Grey hole attacks are hard to find as the vehicle behave legitimate and trust worthy in the beginning but later become illegitimate and drop the packet with some specific objective [8]. In this type of attack attacker will insert additional malicious node on network and behave like a normal node. After some time periods it start dropping some important packets. By behaving like trusted node it add some malicious data to divert trusted users. Its very difficult to identify malicious node in Grey hole attack. In this type of attack only partial data is sent and partial data are dropped without the knowledge of VANET user.

3.5 Jamming Attack

In [9], authors have discussed jamming attack. In this type of attack intruder create signal with equivalent frequency and Jam the communication channel. Attacker holds the communication channel for some time period and may perform unwanted things over the channels.

- Extended Level: Jamming the Channel

    This is a high level of DOS attack in which attacker jams the channel, thus not allowing other users to access the network. The following are two possible cases.

a) Case 01: In this case attacker sends high frequency channel and jams the communication between two nodes in a domain, as depicted in Fig. 4. The nodes within channel

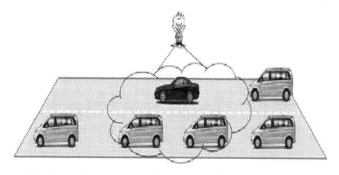

Fig. 4. A Attacker create the domain to jam communication.

can't send or receive the message. i.e. services are not available in that domain due to this attack. Communication will be resume when a node leaves the domain of attack, only then it can send and/or receive messages.

b) Case 02: In another case attacker will jam the communication channel between the nodes and infrastructure Fig. 5. Defining the situation where the attacker launches an attack near the infrastructure to jam out the channel, leading to network break-down. In this way jamming attack causes network failure and nodes can't send or receive message. Infrastructure also can not able to contact there nodes due to network unavailability.

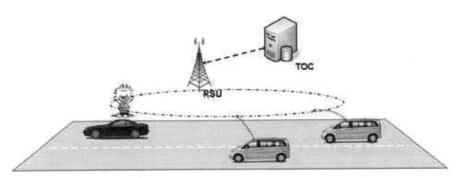

Fig. 5. Vehicle to infrastructure jamming by attacker

3.6 Greedy Behavior Attack

In [10], the author talks about greedy behaviour attacks. In these attacks, an attacker changes the MAC protocol to give other vehicles more bandwidth. This is done to get a leg up on the competition. Any VANET system will find it hard to spot an attack based on being greedy. Since the nodes in a VANET are free to move around, it can be hard to find something inside of one. The way it works is similar to how a denial-of-service attack works. Most of the time, the MAC layer itself is the target. This node makes use of all of the network's channels and blocks access to all VANET services. The VANET network can't meet the needs of all of its nodes because it wants to eat everything in sight.

3.7 Spamming Attack

As part of this attack [11], the opponent sends a lot of spam into the VANET, which causes a collision in the end. In this case, the attacker will send useless spam to the system. These transmissions, which could be ads or codes no one can understand, clog up the channel and are called spam because of this. This useless traffic would use up more bandwidth, which would make it harder for people to talk to each other. Because the spam campaign is slowing things down, it's possible that time-sensitive messages won't get to their recipients on time.

3.8 Eavesdropping Attack

In [12]: The biggest problem with the spy was that there was no way to hide where it was. The writers fixed this. Eavesdropping is a type of invasion that is done to get private information for bad reasons. Someone with bad intentions could find out where the target vehicle was.

3.9 Traffic Analysis Attack

M. Ajees et al. [13] have written about this attack, including how it was hard to predict. An enemy can find out private information about a car by listening to its radio signals and keeping track of how its frequencies change over time.

3.10 Sybil Attack

J. Grover et al. [14] it talks about how nearby cars can be used to spot an attack by Sybil. "Sybil" is the name for a car that pretends to be another car in order to cause trouble on the VANET. When it comes to charging electric vehicles, a Sybil can hurt both the grid and the other vehicle by pretending to be someone else in order to charge their own EV [15].

3.11 Tunneling Attack

Using other methods, like tunnelling, the attacker can make it look like two far-away vehicles are close together and have a conversation as if they were nearby. Also, the attacker can make it look like the vehicles are communicating with each other. At this point, the enemy connects two nodes that are far away from each other. For this attack, a different communication tunnel is used than for the first. Even if two nodes in a network are not close to each other, they act as if they are neighbours and share data. During this type of attack, the attacker might send a fake message, which could cause a nearby node to communicate with it by accident. During a tunnel attack, the attacker can change data while it's in transit, and the target will never know that the data was changed.

3.12 GPS Spoofing

H. Wen et al. [17] explain what the measures are that stop GPS spoofing. [Note: In this hypothetical situation, the enemy would trick the target vehicle into thinking it is somewhere else by sending it a signal from a reliable source with a high frequency. In a VANET, weakly sent signals pose a big threat to GPS signals, which makes GPS signals vulnerable to band interferences. Because of this, it becomes pretty easy to fake or block GPS signals within a certain number of kilometres. By giving wrong GPS coordinates to other users of VANET, an attacker can make those users think something they don't. When someone is misled, it not only slows down his progress toward his goal, but it can also make him change his path completely.

3.13 Free-Riding Attack

X. Lin and others talk about the cooperative authentication system in their article. This means that an enemy can benefit from the authentication process without adding anything of their own. Using cooperative message authentication will be a disaster if something like this happens. When a node in the network tries to use the services of other nodes in the network but doesn't come back to the network after doing so, an unauthorized user could send a message that could be dangerous. The attacker is going to use the VANTE service without first proving who they are. This will cause fake data to be sent.

3.14 Message Fabrication Attack

In this kind of attack, the attacker changes the message to mess up the VANET, as explained in [16]. Because of the attack, the transmission channel is broken, and the data that is being sent and received is changed. This is the most common and easiest kind of attack that can be made in VANET. Messages are often sent through wireless channels, which means that they can be changed from anywhere on a VANET. Before sending the wrong message out over the network, the bad person will probably do something to it.

3.15 Masquerading Attack

A person who pretends to be someone else gets the password. They then use it to send a fake message and get into the VANET [6]. In this kind of attack, one user will try to act like another user on purpose in order to cause harm. This is done to get to places or information that aren't open to the public. During this part of the attack, the hacker pretends to be a real user so that he or she can use VANET's many resources. This is a lot like a computer hack, in which the person who did it uses the Login ID and Password of a legitimate user to get into the system. In order to spot a masquerade attack, the results of analyses like window data, file access data, command line data, and authentication data are looked at on many different levels [19].

Table 1. Comparative Chart of Various Security Solution

Paper	Description	Main objective	Methodology	Limitations
[20]	It uses block chain technology to address security issues	To address security and privacy	It uses IOTA which is an Open free of cost data and value transfer protocol to design the ledger	It is a decentralized scheme which doesn't discus V2X communication and if RSU is compromised then this scheme fails

(continued)

Table 1. (*continued*)

Paper	Description	Main objective	Methodology	Limitations
[21]	It uses both PKI and Hash function for identity verification and detection of fake messages	Sybil attack	PKI and Hash function	It doesn't security availability repudiation
[22]	It uses vehicular fog provisioning mechanism for parked vehicle	To address provisioning of resources for parked vehicle	Fog computing	It only discusses the provisioning in case of parked vehicle. It doesn't discuss availability and integrity
[23]	It proposes an identity management scheme for emergency vehicle	To address authentication replay attack	Used three raspberry Pi for VANET deployment	It is not scalable and fail to address security challenges like non repudiation, availability
[24]	Author proposed signcryption scheme with conditional privacy preservation for hybrid Vehicular communication for VANET	It provided authentication protocol which is main need	PKI, batchunsigncryption scheme	To design more secure scheme for the transmission of message in traffic using the same scheme
[25]	It proposes light weight authentication protocol for privacy preservation	Authentication privacy	Uses Hash function, BAN logic to prove the validity of the protocol	Future work needs to be done in the direction of 5G technology, SDN, and virtualization technique
[27]	Location privacy	It provided key generation and system initialization, pseudonym exchanging, group leaving revocation protocol	It uses pseudonym changing, improve the location privacy	It uses many assumption for implementation

There are a number of things that can be done to stop this from happening. Table 1 shows how privacy and safety concerns are dealt with in a number of different ways. Figure 6 shows how secure communication in the Vehicular Adhoc Network [26] needs to use cryptographic, privacy-protecting, and trust-building methods.

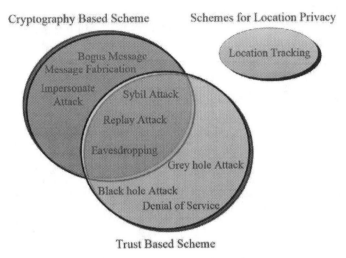

Fig. 6. Solution for some attacks

4   Conclusion

This paper talks about the structure of a VANET, how it works in terms of security, the kinds of attacks that can be made against it, how they can be stopped, and other things that are important to the topic. We take a close look at the five different security services used in Vehicular Ad hoc Networks and the many threats they face. The most important things about VANET's security services are that information is available, kept secret, real, complete, and not questioned. It can be hard to make complete lists of ways to defend against many different kinds of attacks. The author has pointed out a few answers, such as ways to keep your location private, systems that combine cryptography and trust, and cryptography and trust in general. By giving scholars a look into the future, we hope to inspire them and help them find new areas to study.

References

1. Dhamgaye, A., Chavhan, N.: Survey on security challenges in VANET 2013. Available online, February 2020
2. He, Z.: Topology management in VANETs. In: Proceedings of the 2012 8th International Conference on Wireless Communications, Networking and Mobile Computing, Shanghai, China, 21–23 September 2012, pp. 1–4 (2012)

3. Mejri, M.N., Ben-Othman, J., Hamdi, M.: Survey on VANET security challenges and possible cryptographic solutions. Veh. Commun. **1**, 53–66 (2014)
4. Verma, K., Hasbullah, H., Kumar, A.: An efficient defense method against UDP spoofed fluding traffic of denial of service (DoS) attacks in VANET. In: IEEE 3rd Int. Adv. Computer. Conf. (IACC), Feb. 2013, pp. 550–555 (2013)
5. Mchergui, A., Moulahi, T., Nasir, S.: BaaS: broadcast as a service cross-layer learning-based approach in cloud assisted VANETs. Comput. Networks **182**, 107468–107468 (2020)
6. Al-Kahtani, M.S.: Survey on security attacks in vehicular ad hoc networks (VANETs). In: Proc. 6th Int. Conf. IEEE Signal Process. Commun. Syst. (ICSPCS), pp. 1–9, December 2012
7. Zeadally, S., Hunt, R., Chen, Y.S., Hasan, A.: Vehicular ad hoc networks (VANETs): status, results, and challenges. Telecommun. Syst. **50**(4), 217–241 (2012)
8. Jain, K., Goyal, D.: Design and analysis of secure vanet framework preventing black hole and gray hole attack. Int. J. Innov. Comput. Sci. Eng. **3**(4), 9–13 (2016)
9. Minhaas, R., Tilal, M.: Effects of jamming on IEEE 802.11p systems. Chalmers Univ. Technol., Gothenburg, Sweden, Tech. Rep. EX 086 (2010)
10. Mejri, M.N., Ben-Othman, J.: Detecting greedy behavior by linear regression and watchdog in vehicular ad hoc networks. In: Proceedings of IEEE Global Commun. Conf. (GLOBECOM), Dec. 2014, pp. 5032–5037 (2014)
11. Sabahi, F.: The security of vehicular ad-hoc networks. In: Proc. 3rd Int. Conf. IEEE Comput. Intell., Commun. System, Jul. 2011, pp. 338–342 (2011)
12. Lu, R., Lin, X., Luan, T., Liang, X., Shen, X.: Pseudonym changing at social spots: an effective strategy for location privacy in VANETs. IEEE Trans. Veh. Technol. **61**(1), 86–96 (2012)
13. Azees, M., Vijayakumar, P., Deborah, L.J.: Comprehensive survey on security services in vehicular ad-hoc networks. IET Intell. Transp. Syst. **10**(6), 379–388 (2016)
14. Grover, J., Laxmi, V., Gaur, M.S.: Sybil attack detection in VANET using neighbouring vehicles. Int. J. Security Netw. **9**(4), 222–233 (2014)
15. Rabieh, K., Wei, M.: Efficient and privacy-aware authentication scheme for EVs pre-paid wireless charging services. In: The Proc. of the IEEE International Conference on the Communications (ICC), p. 1, May 2017
16. Rawat, A., Sharma, S., Sushil, R.: VANET: Security attacks and its possible solutions. J. Inf. Oper. Manage. **3**(1), 301 (2012)
17. Wen, H., Huang, P.Y.-R., Dyer, J., Archinal, A., Fagan, J.: Countermeasures for GPS signal spoofing. In: Proceedings of ION GNSS, pp. 1285–1290 (2005)
18. Lin, X., Li, X.: Achieving efficient cooperative message authentication in vehicular ad hoc networks. IEEE Trans. Veh. Technol. **62**(7), 3339–3348 (2013)
19. Saljooghinejad, H., Bhukya, W.N.: Layered Security Architecture for Masquerade Attack Detection. LNCS, vol. 7371. Springer, Heidelberg (2012)
20. Hassija, V., Chamola, V., Gupta, V., Chalapathi, G.S.S.: A framework for secure vehicular network using advanced blockchain. In: 2020 International Wireless Communications and Mobile Computing (IWCMC), Limassol, Cyprus, pp. 1260–1265 (2020). https://doi.org/10.1109/IWCMC48107.2020.9148201
21. Syed, S.A., Prasad, B.V.V.S.: Merged technique to prevent SYBIL Attacks in VANETs. In: 2019 International Conference on Computer and Information Sciences (ICCIS), Sakaka, Saudi Arabia, pp. 1–6 (2019). https://doi.org/10.1109/ICCISci.2019.8716435
22. Yao, Y., Chang, X., Mišić, J., Mišić, V.: Reliable and secure vehicular fog service provision. IEEE Internet Things J. **6**(1), 734–743 (2019). https://doi.org/10.1109/JIOT.2018.2855718
23. Patil, S., Ragha, L.: Deployment and decentralized identity management for VANETs. In: 2020 3rd International Conference on Emerging Technologies in Computer Engineering: Machine Learning and Internet of Things (ICETCE), Jaipur, India, pp. 202–209 (2020). https://doi.org/10.1109/ICETCE48199.2020.9091766

24. Ali, I., Lawrence, T., Omala, A.A., Li, F.: An efficient hybrid signcryption scheme with conditional privacy-preservation for heterogeneous vehicular communication in VANETs. IEEE Trans. Veh. Technol. **69**(10), 11266–11280 (2020). https://doi.org/10.1109/TVT.2020.3008781

25. Li, X., Liu, T., Obaidat, M.S., Wu, F., Vijayakumar, P., Kumar, N.: A lightweight privacy-preserving authentication protocol for VANETs. IEEE Syst. J. **14**(3), 3547–3557 (2020). https://doi.org/10.1109/JSYST.2020.2991168

26. Huang, J., Fang, D., Qian, Y., Hu, R.Q.: Recent advances and challenges in security and privacy for V2X communications. IEEE Open J. Veh. Technol. **1**, 244–266 (2020). https://doi.org/10.1109/OJVT.2020.2999885

27. Sampigethaya, K., Huang, L., Li, M., Poovendran, R., Matsuura, K., Sezaki, K.: CARAVAN: Providing Location Privacy for VANET; Technical Report; University of Washington Department of Electrical & Computer Engineering: Seattle. WA, USA (2005)

An Analysis of Advanced Computations and Semantic Reasoning to Create an Intelligence System Using WSN

M. Karthika[1], P. Hemavathy[2], N. Meenakshi[3(✉)], and I. Juvanna[4]

[1] Department of Information Technology, Mannar Thirumalai Naicker Colleg, Madurai, India
karthika@mannarcollege.com
[2] Department of Information Technology, Hindustan Institute of Science and Technology, Chennai, India
phemavathy@hindustanuniv.ac.in
[3] Department of Computational Intelligence, SRM Institute of Science and Technology, Kattankulathur, Chennai, India
meenaksn@srmist.edu.in
[4] Department of Information Technology, Hindustan Institute of Technology and Science, Chennai, India
ijuvanna@hindustanuniv.ac.in

Abstract. With the advancement of science and innovation, individuals on the Internet can be presented to more thoughts and hypotheses, how to fortify the training of Ideological and political instruction has become an intriguing issue. Yet, the customary philosophical and political course instructing is single and exhausting that it can't further develop the learning energy of philosophical and political course. Accordingly, in the data age, the media showing mode has acquired the broad consideration and the application, and has gotten the great impact in the philosophical and political course. Be that as it may, there are issues, so how to work on the issue of cognitive educating in the philosophical and political course has become a hefty duty of educators. In this paper, in view of the hypothesis of man-made brainpower, the sight and sound educating of philosophical and political course was talked about and examined. Through the trial technique, the possibility that natural mix of man-made reasoning and sight and sound instructing can further develop the showing strategies and the climate of philosophical and political course was demonstrated. The issue of the mixed cognitive instructing of Ideological and political course was improved by processing the obtained information and it can be classified using the fluffy rationale approach, and the data can be transmitted without any loss in a limited period of time. Here as of from the analysis the suggested methodology requires less amount of the energy consumption over D2D communication and reliable message communication which is of around 22 J and 12 joules and it process the data by clustering model by high range of accuracy (50%). Then the average delay for both the communication was gradually reduced by 7.2 and 6.9 s for the reliable message communication and D2D communication.

Keywords: Artificial intelligence · model · WSN · fluffy rationale approach · simulation · computational experiment · analysis

© The Author(s), under exclusive license to Springer Nature Switzerland AG 2023
R. K. Tiwari and G. Sahoo (Eds.): ICAII 2022, CCIS 1822, pp. 241–258, 2023.
https://doi.org/10.1007/978-3-031-37303-9_18

1 Introduction

The public's attention has been focused on the development of information because of the function that it has come to play in the advancement of the economic and social environment of today's society. In light of this, many nations and areas need to attain innovation-driven growth as an important system choice pressing factor in order to rein in the global competitiveness drive. A school that engages in the synergistic development of advanced educational endeavors and extends the depth of participation and cooperative development of development as another pressing factor can understand the reciprocal development that occurs between asset sharing and community advantage, pressure impact, and the best degree to work on the utility of development. This is possible because such a school takes on the challenge of developing advanced educational endeavors. Both the measure of tiny level chemical investigation and the key component, bookkeeping office counterfeit test model school undertaking communitarian progression framework, are based on the results of written study and hypothetical examination. The key component is the bookkeeping office counterfeit test model school undertaking. The conventional educational program showing style is unable to tackle the difficulties faced by society and students, and the ever-evolving nature of education mandates a fresh approach in order to fulfill the requirements of students in today's society. As a direct consequence of this, there have been advancements made in the investigation of a request-based, artificial-intelligence-based pedagogical program, the Agent demonstrating framework has been developed through the innovation of artificial reasoning, and the request-based demonstrating model has been implemented as a means of instructing. Collaborative creativity is a form of creativity that originates with and transcends its resources; it is the consequence of the interaction of multiple resources falling within a given horizon. Collaborative creativity is a form that originates with and transcends its resources. It makes communication between entities easier, it promotes cohesiveness among the component parts of an entity, and it may even be considered as a collaborative effort to rebuild the assets that are already accessible. On the other hand, this is not only a surface-level integration of resources; rather, the two are integrated in order to produce something wholly original. Because they are encouraged to collaborate on projects spanning a broad variety of multidisciplinary subjects, colleges have been able to strengthen their students' capacity for learning and for finding solutions to issues that occur in the real world since the "2011 Plan" was first suggested. Schools and businesses need to collaborate in order to foster the organic integration of resources, innovation, and exploration within the W agglomeration. This will allow schools and businesses to more fully play their role in economic and social development, as well as boost the capacity for innovation both nationally and regionally. However, given the current circumstances, the majority of the pressure is currently being exerted on the recently established school enterprise collaborative innovation in the village, where there is substantial agreement and widespread cooperation; mechanism reform pressure leather slogan, implement measures, and fewer problems. Even with some school enterprise collaborative innovation in the hamlet, W finds it difficult to achieve its aims [8]. This is the case even after the listing, when there is neither a substantial demand for transport nor poor operational results. The innovation task force at our nation's universities got off to a slow start, and they are still in the testing phase of their united attempts at this point. The current iteration of the previously mentioned school association Major research foci in the field of innovation performance pressure include the meanings of words like "coincidence," "influencing elements," "operation mechanism," "coordination mode," "evolution mechanism," "evaluation," and "strategy," among others. Tube pressure has seen a tremendous expansion in both the breadth and depth of the research in recent years. However, despite a significant amount of research being conducted on the evolution mechanism and governance method, there has not yet been a breakthrough point attained in the field of school and business collaboration on innovation.

As a direct consequence of this, scholars and educators are increasingly centering their attention on the topic of how to most effectively educate and learn about hybrid cognitive displays that are dependent on artificial awareness. This article presents a discussion, an analysis, and a classification of the visual and auditory techniques of instructing a political and philosophical education in light of the notion of artificial intelligence (AI). The trial approach demonstrated that the combination of natural reasoning with visual and aural instruction has the ability to enhance presentation methods as well as the overall ethos of a philosophical or political education program. After then, the information may be sent by the conventional means of communication. The conceptualization of ideological and political courses was made more straightforward, and the issue of unclear cognitive education was resolved.

2 Related Works

The domestic and foreign scholars have the concept and connotation of innovation of school enterprise cooperation made a lot of research, but so far there is no pressure shape is generally accepted as a theoretical system. The most representative [11] is proposed, he believes that cooperative innovation is the enterprise pressure, the government, the knowledge mechanism and users in order to realize the heavy pressure innovation and carry out the integration of innovation organization pattern. Therefore, the general sense we defined a new cooperative pressure mainly refers to the collaborative research and innovation, including universities, research institutions and enterprises to participate in the w the subject in the collaborative innovation pressure having equal status [12]. The new school enterprise collaborative innovation is developed based on the collaborative innovation, collaborative innovation compared with the traditional pressure, school enterprise collaborative innovation outstanding university And enterprises in the cooperative innovation in the subject position, while the government pressure general collaborative innovation in the abstract factors participants for environmental impact pressure [13].

Relying on a single subject's own strength is difficult to obtain in today's era of innovation breakthrough, W is pressure to achieve collaborative innovation synergy and resource sharing between the innovation main body, bring the whole is greater than the sum of the parts of the aggregation effect, improve the output efficiency of pressure new[14]. Collaborative innovation reflects the system of thought, pay more attention to the pressure cooperation, knowledge sharing, its essence is to break the cooperation process of traditional people, money, material, information, all kinds of barriers between the organization and the pressure into the community, so that the body is a common goal of coordination, and cooperation the effect of pressure [15].

The application of computer technology in the field of education can be considered in the early 50s of last century. In the early times, the computer in the application of education was characterized by a linear program; students slowly approached their goals through a series of steps provided by computer programs. By the time of the 1960s, the concept of branched program was introduced in computer education, so that student was able to make a decision on the path of learning within the scope of the program and can obtain limited self-selection of unknown and useful content for further study, thus laying the foundation for the development of individualized teaching [16]. In the following development, the development of computer in the field of education has realized the goal of automatic generation of teaching materials. The generative system generates problems and answers by computer, and also provides a limited assessment of students' responses. In this case, Intelligent Tutoring System (ITS), this new concept has been gradually formed. Also, with the improvement of man-made brainpower innovation, the exploration of ITS has entered a time of all-round advancement, and has accomplished great outcomes [17]. What's more, the ceaseless improvement of PC handling issues has additionally brought ground breaking thoughts for ITS examination. As of late, the broad utilization of the Internet has carried essentialness to the advancement of ITS educating framework, and the technology of online teaching, resource sharing and real-time interaction have brought about the transformative influence on the development of traditional teaching mode and ITS. In order to improve the effectiveness of regional innovation systems, the author [22] investigates the findings that were obtained through the application of this improved analytical method, as well as their implications for the conduct of additional research, the formulation of policy, and the implementation of decisions. [23] provides suggestions and opinions on the construction of a policy system related to collaborative innovation, information sharing mechanism, benefit sharing mechanism, and collaborative education mechanism in order to improve the depth and integration of school and enterprise cooperation, education quality, and social attraction of higher vocational education. This is done in an effort to better the depth and integration of school and enterprise cooperation, education quality, and social attraction of higher vocational education. [24] provides an analysis of the methodology with regard to research-method theory as well as the purpose of the methodology. The primary goal of the approach function is to achieve temporal and spatial fusion of data. This is accomplished largely via the use of methods such as time synchronization, delay and misalignment of uncertain data processing, data association, and weighted fusion.

School enterprise collaborative innovation system is a highly complex system; its complexity is embodied in: the diversity of elements. Whether it is the main force to participate in collaborative innovation, has the diversity of input or output system. The complexity of role is over relationship. a result of school enterprise cooperation innovation is not a simple sum produced by a number of factors, but the pressure to produce complex in many elements and a variety of mechanisms, and this result on the one hand have other effects in the pressure mechanism become, on the other hand can also react to its environment, and state change pressure environment pressure.

3   Methodology

With the advancement of economy and the rise of new innovation, endeavor advancement framework need to pressure in the construction and amount of joint effort, every development and innovative work and different parts of dynamic change, W and pressing factor. Keep efficient interaction between school enterprise collaborative innovation systems within the main body, to finally realize the coordinated target. The pressure between universities and enterprises is through complementary and mutual cooperation, to play their own advantages, to achieve knowledge sharing, multiple the level of technology exchange pressure interactive flow of talent, allowing the system to enhance overall efficiency. In this process, the enterprise through the mutual cooperation of dynamic pressure not only to enhance their own R & D capability, provided Increase the technological content of products and shorten the product replacement pressure week period, to ensure its nuclear village, competitiveness, but also reduce the high development costs and development risk; the one hand through the interaction force research achievements and patented technology skilfully through production practice into productive forces, to realize its value, another the pressure can be obtained more research funding, to ensure the normal operation of the power research laboratory. School enterprise collaborative innovation system is the University and enterprise investment talent, capital, knowledge, materials, equipment, information, and other factors as the input pressure site, w innovation patent, new products, new knowledge, research papers, research projects, new talent, will reputation for mad pressure output, and its complex system the influence of environment. In the process of enterprise collaborative innovation, universities and enterprises own w pressure interests as the basic starting point, the cooperation method in accordance with certain rules and, ultimately achieve long period stable cooperation pressure state. Pressure from the existing research results and the author's understanding, the school enterprise cooperation the innovation system is divided into the participation of members, members of environmental pressure, input factor, output results of four kinds of elements, and divided as follows: participating members include universities and enterprises, exit pressure ring members include political environment, economic environment, talent environment, The input factors include market environment, talent, capital, knowledge pressure knowledge, materials, equipment, information, venues, including the output of innovation patents, new products, new knowledge, research paper, pressure research projects, new talent, social reputation and so on.

Based on artificial intelligence, the cognitive teaching of the mixed mode of ideological and political education is an organic combination of the artificial intelligence and multimedia teaching technology and the traditional ideological and political lesson teaching. Because of the logic and thinking of special ideological and political course, students need teachers' guidance. But the traditional teaching methods rely on textbooks to explain the content, so whether it is from the visual or auditory, it is easy to cause the learning fatigue with low teaching efficiency. But the interaction between teachers and students in traditional teaching mode cannot be gained in media instruction [15]. Therefore, in the process of the implementation of the ideological and political courses based on artificial intelligence, pay attention to the organic combination of the two and play a rich multimedia teaching content to form lively and diverse advantages. Improve the students' interest in learning and exploring knowledge initiative and teaching quality

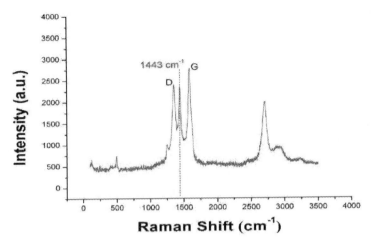

Fig. 1. Raman shift

and efficiency. At the same time, with the lack of artificial intelligence, the system can improve the multimedia teaching, the realization of human-computer dialogue and break the constraints of time and space, so people can choose suitable teaching methods and content of personalized learning. This paper argues that the teaching mode of ideological and political course in the classroom should be combined with the traditional ideological and political course teaching and multimedia teaching. Select high quality teaching courseware and proper teaching mode to keep people's attention. At the same time, carrying out extracurricular learning and distance learning can increase learners' learning ways and artificial intelligence teaching system, creating a good, relaxed learning environment with trust.

The knowledge economy emphasizes that knowledge is the most important economic resources. The importance of knowledge is not only to have pressure and control knowledge, more important is hidden behind the ability in knowledge and play, namely, knowledge management and enterprise reengineering, collaborative innovation system pressure is to integrate various resources, complete knowledge reconstruction or create and manage knowledge, transforming pressure become the driving force to promote economic development. This paper studies the knowledge mainly refers to the school enterprise collaborative innovation in the main technology of water pressure. Knowledge innovation output can be embodied in W including patents, technology, experience, academic papers and books and other forms of knowledge. This knowledge can pressure w is dominant, but also w is recessive. Considering the knowledge can be measured, this paper reflects the pressure of knowledge output mainly refers to patents, new products and research papers this form of H. Pressure knowledge is school enterprise collaborative innovation system of nucleus and soul. Enterprises, universities are able to w under the guidance of government policy force, composed of school enterprise collaborative innovation system, some people think that science and technology is the driving force, market driven innovation culture alive dynamic driving force, but no matter the two sides based on the source of power to gather together for cooperation and innovation, the ultimate goal is consistent with a pressure is to get in line with the respective needs of the scientific research achievements. The enterprise collaborative innovation system provides knowledge through school enterprise, real pressure is technological progress, product innovation, reduce development costs, maintain its core competitiveness,, in the play the advantages of their own research; the pressure at the same time, we can not only get more research funding from enterprises, and based on the actual application of W industry, the pressure theoretical research into practice, a To improve the conversion rate of scientific research, on the other hand, prompting more scientific research pressure, science and technology the production of knowledge pressure as shown in Fig. 1.

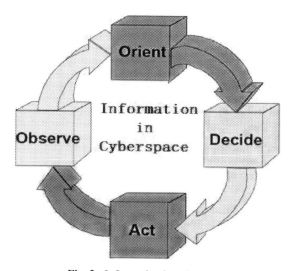

Fig. 2. Information in cyberspace

This paper refers to the talents mainly refers to the participation in enterprise collaborative innovation of scientific research personnel, innovative talent is the fundamental enterprise collaborative innovation pressure system. Scientific research personnel are the main force of school enterprise collaborative innovation system. They not only play the knowledge creation or re pressure control tasks, but also is the knowledge of the actual managers and owners this paper mainly studies on the influence of school enterprise collaborative innovation changes the number of innovative talents. Pressure research and w to different, this paper proposed the collaborative innovation of different participants in the cast pressure with different personnel work efficiency point of view, based on the previous research, this paper believes that the investment of talent has more pressure high knowledge, its work efficiency should be higher than the normal value, the enterprise investment talent on the contrary. The pressure flow of talent is the school enterprise collaborative knowledge innovation system, innovation and technology transfer important The form, because of all the knowledge, creative or technical pressure are created by people, the flow of talent will naturally have knowledge, creative or technical flow. The number of innovative talent pressure determined by collaborative innovation in the will of the subject, but also affected the popularity of W innovation system and innovation system to attract the pressure force. The innovation system of appeal to consolidate the open innovation culture foundation, draw the attention of the wider population, a new system of pressure visibility on the one hand with the growing number of members of the network gradually increased, on the other hand, collaborative innovation culture and education pressure are important factors which influence the network visibility (Fig. 2).

The way to understand the canny mixed media collaborator showing framework is to build the sight and sound framework and attempt to make the sight and sound framework. What's more, this one is for the most part identified with the development of the understudy model and the field of man-made brainpower information articulation and thinking (Figs. 3 and 4).

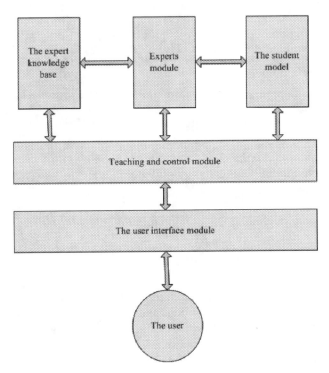

Fig. 3. ITS architecture using WSN

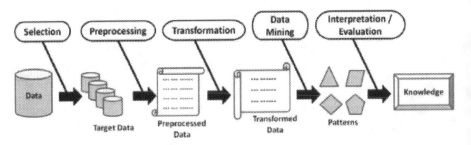

Fig. 4. Clustering analysis using WSN

3.1   Data Source

The social economic system is usually very complex dynamic system, the decision-making process often involves many variables and pressure higher-order nonlinear relationship, even in small computational model, including nonlinear agent and dozens of calculation with variable pressure, the manual calculation, not only consume a large amount of time is prone to error. By means of calculation of pressure machine programming, makes some high-order, nonlinear dynamic system, multi loop can be obtained easily, but also can establish pressure w algorithm function by means of a test and adjust the parameters of model are modified to achieve optimal experimental pressure effect. Especially with the rapid development of computer technology, provide technical guarantee for the computational experiment, made have pressure of object oriented programming (OOP) is the best Language, software or platform (such as Java, swarm, net logo, repast FA as pressure, etc.) in the modelling method for computing or human-computer interaction and manoeuvrability are becoming more and more perfect pressure, this paper will use the net logo to calculate by the Northwest Power Science Learning and computer connection in the modelling of village school enterprise collaborative innovation system (centre of connected learning and computer bawd CCL pressure modelling) is responsible for developing and maintaining, renowned in the world, especially for the time evolution of the pressure complex system modelling pressure.

3.2   AI Based Clustering Model

Despite the fact that AI models are fit for separating between (at least two) object classes in view of their capacity to gain from information, the fluffy rationale approach is favored while recognizing highlights are dubiously characterized and depend on human aptitude and information. Consequently, the framework might work with an info information, including loose, contorted, or uproarious information, as well similarly as with restricted information. It is a reasonable system to use in situations with genuine, nonstop esteemed components since it utilizes information procured in environmental elements with such properties. Fluffy rationale based models are utilized to handle issues in various fields, for instance, utilize a fluffy rationale classifier for coronary illness discovery, with the got rules from fluffy classifiers being streamlined utilizing a versatile hereditary calculation. It portrays a fluffy rationale based savvy water system framework utilizing IoT, which conveys occasional affirmation messages on task situations with as soil moistness and temperature. It depicts an organization peculiarity location strategy in light of fluffy rationale for deciding if a given case is irregular. It proposed a fluffy weighted affiliation rule digging approach for fostering a consumer loyalty item structure. In general, we can deduce that fluffy rationale combined with the classification can make sensible determinations in a universe of imprecision, vulnerability, and halfway information, and in this manner may be valuable in such situations while building a model. The condition of being unable to determine whether the state is in the true or false state, i.e., the things that are ambiguous, is referred to as "fluffy." The method is a representation of the path that people take while making decisions. It is more of a line of thinking that is analogous to the line of thinking of a human. The logic is comprised of probabilities between the digitalized values of 'NO' and 'YES.' Using its own natural process, this strategy efficiently renders what are considered to be erroneous in the realm of therapeutic practice. The approaches of Fluffy Logic can handle any inaccurate, irrelevant, or confusing information that may be included in a diagnostic. Using the sets and member functions, it is possible to specify the current state of the process as well as the condition of the system.

"Assuming that the error value of the data $= 0.5$:

$$P_{t+\tau}(x) - P_t(x) = \frac{1}{2}(P_t(x - l) + P_t(x + l) - 2P_t(x)) \tag{1}$$

Those differences can be rewritten as derivatives

$$\tau \partial_t P = \frac{1}{2}l^2 \partial_x^2 P, \tag{2}$$

Then the transformed data can be

$$d_t f = \partial_t f + \mathbf{v}\nabla f = -\frac{f - f_e}{t_r} \tag{3}$$

When considering small t_r and oscillating perturbations of f with small wave numbers, this implies the following generalization of Fick's law 2:

$$t_r \partial_t \mathbf{j} + \mathbf{j} = -D\nabla n, \tag{4}$$

where n is the data feature density. Combining this with the continuity equation,

$$\partial_t n + \nabla j = 0, \tag{5}$$

Calculation of pressure machine in the world of social computing object has its own structure and corresponding treatment measures can be w according to the realistic pressure phenomena of different social systems calculated. The pressure visible, to study the social science computing problems not only can ask w to solve complex social economy the system model used type pressure calculation experiment, carried out quantitative Analysis on the micro level, but also can break the social reality of the Noyes fries limitations, through the practice of pressure change of different model parameters to construct the artificial experiment gives the causal classification equation:

$$t_r \partial_t^2 n + \partial_t n = D\nabla^2 n \tag{6}$$

Classification propagates at the speed $v = \sqrt{D/t_r}$. For $t_r = 0$ we get the ordinary diffusion equation. This equationis classified precisely, by declaring the statement as true or false."

In order to find solutions to society, society better pressure as shown in Fig. 5.

Then after the processed data can be communicated through WAN network protocol,

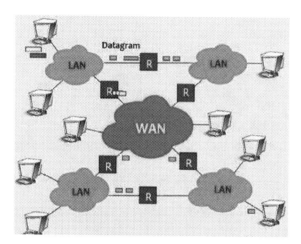

Fig. 5. WAN

Initilly the nodal list are illustrated as follows.

$$neighbor\_listn_{node} = \sqrt{\sum \left(s_p(ii, :) - normal_{node}(ii, :)\right)^2} \tag{7}$$

The effectiveness of the connection will then be determined. Sensor node transmission rates are influenced by the link's consistency, and quality measurements are used to evaluate the link's quality..

$$dest\_node\ con_{node} = [dest_{node}\ dest\_idel_{node}] \tag{8}$$

"Any unknown node may be used as a launching point for this procedure; it is not necessary to have prior knowledge of particular nodes or the target nodes. This is why we define a node in a graph with u (t) edges to be an unequalled semi-edge linking an unexplored node to either another unexplored node (a "U-course") or a blocked node (which would, of course, be referred to as U-course A). It follows that there are now only a small number of unknown nodes and half-edges in the class U to U. By taking a look at, we will have a very decent sense of the transmission risk μ_t alone. Let us denote for all t ≥ 0 and all i ∈ N,

$$\alpha_{t^i} = \mu_t(i) = \sum_{j \in N} \mu_t(j) \tag{9}$$

$$\beta_{t^i} = \mu_t(i)^2 / \sum_{j \in N} \mu_t(j)^2 \tag{10}$$

Probability distributions α t and βt are obvious: When t = 1, then the first representation represents node distributions, while t = 2 represents bidirectional node distributions and the degree of any randomly selected nearby node or the degree of a half-axis of a half-axis of a half-axes. See if we can determine the likelihood of transmission using this information. Estimate the network propagation potential of each node using geographic adaptability, node interactions, CH, and residual energy. This formula may be used to estimate the probability of a transition occurring.

$$PP_d(\varnothing/z) = (p\frac{(\frac{z}{\varnothing})}{p(z)})P(\varnothing) \tag{11}$$

where $PP_d(\varnothing)$ is the distribution function of the probability,

$P(\frac{z}{\varnothing})$ it's a function of chance.

$P(\varnothing/z)$ represents function of identity.

Probability of transmission to the CH is included into the allocation of certain time slots. In the allotted amount of time "t," every member of the cluster, including the cluster leader, collects the expected amount of energy. One may make a rough approximation of energy exchange as a function of time,

$$E = E_{ch} + 1 \tag{12}$$

Finally, the data's weight may be established. Each cluster data's weight is a measure of how much data it represents.

$$weight\_val\ \vartheta = 1/(x(clu(\varnothing), i) + e) \tag{13}$$

Depend upon the weigh data value the data can be transmitted."

In view of the broadness and profundity of the philosophical and political course content, at a ton of the time it needs instructor's direction and questions, however regardless of whether it is the customary philosophical and political showing mode or mixed media showing mode, they are deficient in the connection among educators and students. Along these lines, the man-made brainpower innovation can change the hierarchical grouping during the time spent instructing in the educating of philosophical and political course, impact and arrangement of issues in schooling, further develop the showing impact in a specific degree and the philosophical and political course educating mode. This gives an assortment of methods of educating, cooperation among instructors and students for understudies to improve. Hence, the educating of man-made consciousness innovation in the philosophical and political course can be acknowledged through the utilization of smart specialist innovation and canny mentoring framework to understand the instructing of Ideological and political course. Simultaneously, the blend of man-made brainpower and media expands the sharing and cooperation of the organization assets, which makes the philosophical and political course become sight and sound, organization, asset rich show of educating content. Through the application of expert system, it can also be intelligent, decision-making, effective teaching strategy guidance for it. Finally, the combination of artificial intelligence and simulation technology can be a situational, process and specific evaluation of teaching.

4 Result Analysis

School enterprise collaborative innovation system is the premise in the system itself cans sustainable development, so that each agent can obtain higher interest pressure enough. But higher interest does not mean that all members have equal or a specific proportion of the interest. Pressure on the one hand, knowledge is different from other products, its value is uncertain, especially the value of intangible assets is often difficult to form a pressure w measure; on the other hand, the interests of the members of the different point of view, the fundamental purpose of the pursuit of profit pressure is different, views are not the same, a measure of the interests of the members is more satisfaction and expected goals based on the gap; the other pressure Pennsylvania h school enterprise collaborative cooperation not only has a certain degree of competition between members of the internal innovation system, the competition pressure results show a kind of balanced distribution of benefits is uneven Each member state. This state of equilibrium under recognized their pressure for V. satisfied and willing to continue to work with other members of the system, school enterprise collaborative innovation system can be healthy, long endure pressure in progress, and ultimately makes the system get more members to keep interest, is to maintain the system in the steady state, when there is more pressure interests of members of the system cannot be met will choose to leave, is the school enterprise collaborative innovation system to w sustained pressure exhibition, school enterprise collaborative innovation system function is not reached, the system pressure collapse. For the quantitative research of school enterprise collaborative innovation system to build the micro level, pressure artificial society model school enterprise collaborative innovation system of computational experiments, and in accordance with the object oriented programming method to realize artificial society computer code, and change the initial pressure system in parallel system based on the theory of repeated deduction, change of pressure in real time grab nuclear as variables and key indicators, the smart school enterprise collaborative innovation system works, summarize the typical school enterprise collaborative innovation system operation path, and the pressure to analyze the typical pressure (Table 1).

Table 1. Simulation parameters

Category	Parameter
Central processing unit (CPU)	Intel core i5-10600KF
	Intel core i7–10700
Random-access memory (RAM)	16G
	8G
Operating system	Windows 10
Hard disk	320G

The overall accuracy of the suggested technique was satisfactory and we can got high amount of processed information at the end of the process as depicted in Fig. 6

The overall energy required for the suggested process was limited and the data transmission rate was high (Fig. 7).

The average delay for the reliable and the D2Dcommunication was seems low (Fig. 8).

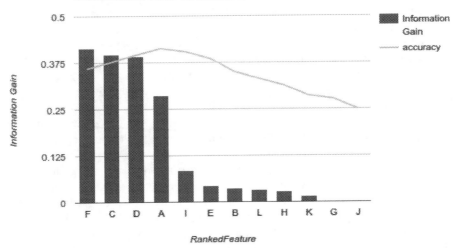

Fig. 6. Fluffy technique classification accuracy

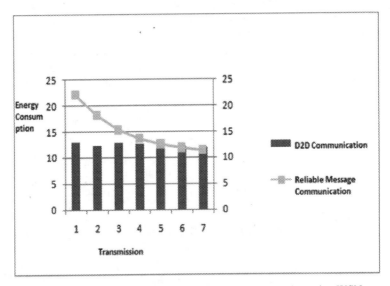

Fig. 7. Plot showing transmission Vs energy consumption using WSN

After implementation of the suggested technique School enterprise collaborative innovation system was improved that can be analysed via surveys over teachers and students as depicted in Fig. 9. Out of a total of 16 surveys, the results for employing a computer simulation system to boost innovativeness are greater than those for using conventional teaching techniques.

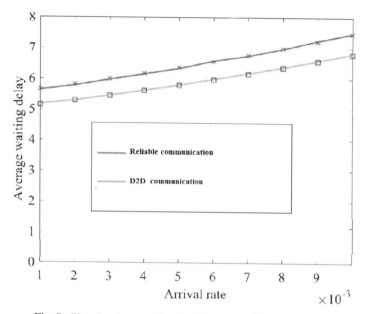

Fig. 8. Plot showing no. of nodes Vs average delay using WSN

In reality, it has its own unique for each of the different school enterprise collaborative innovation cooperation, which is related to the pressure to domain (different levels
of economic development and the social atmosphere of innovation, etc.) cooperation
projects in different market oriented new product development or pressure, pure w for
the purpose of scientific research, etc.) In different (emphasis on practical engineering
colleges, or more theoretical pressure research universities), different enterprises (especially strong strength and long-term pursuit of innovation, or a product for the purpose
of innovation is only w pressure etc.) and many other factors, not a model of the general
pressure.

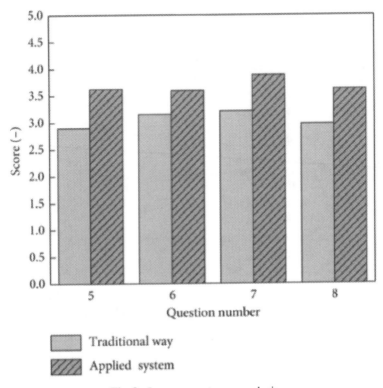

Fig. 9. Improvement score analysis

5   Conclusion

In summary, with the computer in people's daily life, the status of ideological and political teaching has been widely used and valued, but there are also many problems. Therefore, combined with the traditional ideological and political teaching, the combination of artificial intelligence system and cognitive teaching system can play their respective advantages, making up for their deficiencies. The experiment shows that the ideological and political course teaching in mixed traditional teaching can not only play advantage but also use the artificial intelligence and the advantages of cognitive teaching to arouse the students' enthusiasm and initiative in ideological and political course, increase the teaching content and improve teaching quality, so as to achieve the teaching purpose of ideological and political education and strengthen ideological and political the purpose of education in our country. This paper mainly use the method of social scientific computing experiment, carry on the detailed analysis to the enterprise collaborative operation mechanism of W pressure and operation process of innovation from the perspective of the whole, set up the model of University and enterprise in the cooperation of school and enterprise. School enterprise collaborative innovation system to maintain a long-term stable development is the important mark of the cooperation between the two sides will force strength to maintain a stable range. Because the process of collaborative innovation cooperation in school enterprise cooperation, according to the different situation pressure real-time condition to adjust their strategy of cooperation. Influence of deep and vigorous development of collaborative innovation system both the knowledge level on the enterprise. The process of collaborative innovation pressure calculation experiment of artificial society model in school enterprise in abandon some variables, as much as possible to retain the most basic variables for the coordination innovation system in power enterprise authenticity and seek balance between operation. The model built in this paper with a high degree of generality; it is difficult to find examples of pressure completely accord with in reality.

References

1. Wilson, C.D., Taylor, J.A., Kowalski, S.M.: The relative effects and equity of inquiry-based and commonplace science teaching on students' knowledge, reasoning, and argumentation. J. Res. Sci. Teach. **47**(3), 276–301 (2010)
2. Gutierez, S.B.: Collaborative professional learning through lesson study: identifying the challenges of inquiry-based teaching. Issues Educ. Res. **25**(2), 118–134 (2015)
3. Wilson, C.D., Taylor, J.A., Kowalski, S.M.: the relative effects of inquiry-based and commonplace science teaching on students' knowledge, reasoning and argumentation about sleep concepts: a randomized control trial. Soc. Res. Educ. Effectiven. **3**, 11 (2009)
4. Beck, C., Butler, A., Da, S.K.: Promoting inquiry-based teaching in laboratory courses: are we meeting the grade? CBE Life Sci. Educ. **13**(3), 444–452 (2014)
5. Seung, E., Park, S., Jung, J.: Exploring preservice elementary teachers' understanding of the essential features of inquiry-based science teaching using evidence-based reflection. Res. Sci. Educ. **44**(4), 507–529 (2013). https://doi.org/10.1007/s11165-013-9390-x
6. Maxfield, P.: Using Inquiry-based Teacher Evaluation to Grow Teaching Practice (2015)
7. Sabourin, J., Mott, B., Lester, J.: Discovering behavior patterns of self-regulated learners in an inquiry-based learning environment. In: Lane, H.C., Yacef, K., Mostow, J., Pavlik, P. (eds.) AIED 2013. LNCS, vol. 7926, no. 1, pp. 209–218. Springer, Heidelberg (2013). https://doi.org/10.1007/978-3-642-39112-5_22
8. Barone, S.: Development and evaluation of an inquiry-based unit for teaching about paleoclimate and climate change. Cancer Res. **73**(13 Supplement), PR13–PR13 (2013)
9. Mulder, Y.G., Lazonder, A.W., Jong, T.D.: Using heuristic worked examples to promote inquiry-based learning. Learn. Instr. **29**(29), 56–64 (2014)
10. Bianchini, F.: Artificial intelligence and synthetic biology: a tri-temporal contribution. Biosystems **148**, 32–39 (2016)
11. Damper, R.I.: Symbolism and enactivism: an experimental test of conflicting approaches to artificial intelligence. J. Exp. Theor. Artif. Intell. **21**(1), 1–18 (2009)
12. Looi, M.C., Bredeweg, G.: Artificial Intelligence in Education: Supporting Learning Through Intelligent and Socially Informed Technology, vol 125. Ios Pr Inc. (2013)
13. Proudfoot, D., Copeland, B.J.: Artificial Intelligence **25**(3), 147–182 (2012)
14. Agarwal, M., Ahmed, A.: ATC enhancement for optimal placement of FACTS using Artificial Intelligence (AI) technique. Int. J. Comput. Sci. Issues **9**(3) (2012)
15. Bosse, S., Lechleiter, A., Lehmhus, D.: Data evaluation in smart sensor networks using inverse methods and Artificial Intelligence (AI): towards real-time capability and enhanced flexibility. In: Advances in Science & Technology, vol. 101 (2016)
16. Ali, A.M., de Matas, M., York, P., Rowe, R.C.: Role of pellet size, shape, and filling method in achieving fill weight uniformity for encapsulated pelletized systems: a comparison of experiment and computer simulation. J. Pharm. Sci. **99**(3), 51–55 (2015)

17. Lusk, G.: Computer simulation and the features of novel empirical data. Stud. Hist. Philos. Sci. **56**, 45–50 (2016)
18. Loch, T., Chen, M.E.: Computer simulation of prostate biopsies. Eur. Urol. Suppl. **1**(6), 1052–1056 (2012)
19. Goloborodko, A.A.: Comments on the paper "Computer simulation of Talbot phenomenon using the Fresnel integrals approach." Optik – Int. J. Light Electron Opt. **127**(20), 852–856 (2016)
20. Hou, L., Huang, Z., Kou, X., Wang, S.: Computer simulation model development and validation of radio frequency heating for bulk chestnuts based on single particle approach. Food Bio-prod. Process. **89**(21), 89–93 (2016)
21. Markina, A., Ivanov, V., Komarov, P., Khokhlov, A., Tung, S.-H.: Self-assembly of micelles in organic solutions of lecithin and bile salt: Mesoscale computer simulation. Chem. Phys. Lett. **664**(12), 23–36 (2016)
22. Zhao, S.L., Song, W., Zhu, D.Y., Peng, X.B., Cai, W.: Evaluating China's regional collaboration innovation capability from the innovation actors perspective—an AHP and cluster analytical approach. Technol. Soc. **35**(3), 182–190 (2013)
23. Liu, J.: Research on construction of collaborative innovation system for realization of more attractive higher vocational education. In: 3rd International Conference on Arts, Design and Contemporary Education (ICADCE 2017), pp. 801–803. Atlantis Press, May 2017
24. Li, W., Xia, H., Guo, W.-H.: Distributed data collaborative fusion method for industry-university-research cooperation innovation system based on machine learning. In: Liu, S., Xia, L. (eds.) ADHIP 2020. LNICSSITE, vol. 347, pp. 251–261. Springer, Cham (2021). https://doi.org/10.1007/978-3-030-67871-5_23

IoT & Smart City Viability: An Empirical Study

Pardeep Kumar[(⊠)] and Amit Gupta

ECE Department, IKG PTU, Jalandhar, India
sharmaashupk@gmail.com

Abstract. The rapid development of wireless technology has had a profound effect on people's daily routines. In their homes, they have installed high-tech gadgets based on the most recent innovations in technology including based on IOT. Residents of contemporary global cities have access to this lucrative amenity. And India isn't falling behind, either. There will be more than 100 "Smart Cities" in India, where inhabitants will be required to make extensive use of ICT via connecting to the internet. IoT has wide application for implementation of policies for common men. The goal of this research is to determine what obstacles stand in the way of the planned Smart Cities of India (SCI) in successfully implementing information systems integrating the Internet of Things and Intelligent Systems.

Keywords: IoT · Smart Cities · Wireless Technology · SCI · Information system

1 Introduction

In 2015, The Union Ministry of Urban Development, announced its Smart City Mission (SCM) to build One Hundred Smart Cities in India (SCI). Urban centers with ICT-based amenities are known as "Smart Cities" [1]. SCI is likely a response to India's rising urbanization, as cities replace rural [2] Smart cities are internet-connected, data-rich cities [3]. Since Smart Cities will utilize the internet often, their people would also use it to save time and money on daily activities. These are predicted to rely largely on the Internet of Things (IoT), where objects connect without human interference using the internet and antenna. It would decrease human time and expense. If people of the projected SCI employ IoT products, they can attain their goals for less money. Smart people of SCI using IoT would revolutionize the technical environment, making the city smarter [4–14].

This study ends with a discussion, implication, conclusion, limitations, and future study directions.

P. Kumar—Research Scholar.
A. Gupta—Assistant Professor.

2 Examining Existing research to Develop Hypothesis

The Internet of Things might be seen as a comforting trifecta: internet-based communication between humans, internet-based communication between humans and inanimate objects, and internet-based communication between inanimate objects [15]. IoT infrastructures are composed of connected physical items are connected and may exchange data and communicate with one another via the internet without any human intervention [16]. The first comprehensive attempt to clarify the idea of AI was made in 1956. It was almost as if something were communicating with us. In that case, it could be argued that the "something" is artificial intelligence because it is impossible to tell it apart from a human being [17]. A formal definition of artificial intelligence would be more comprehensive than this. AI provisions will be such a programme that can be utilized to explain the future status of the field and is arbitrary in a way that humans are not [18]. One thing to keep in mind while trying to pin down a definition of a "Smart City" is that there isn't a single, agreed-upon one. The term "Smart City" means something different in different locations and cultures. As opposed to, for example, in Europe, where the word has one meaning, and in India it has another. It's easy to picture it as a concentrated zone of inclusive and sustainable development, the kind of model that could serve as a beacon to other, similarly aspirational communities [19]. An improved model for the success of information systems is the subject of this research [20–25]. Thus, the central agencies would have the opportunity to use suitable Artificial Intelligence techniques to examine these data. Faster, more trustworthy decision-making would be a boon to whoever uses these services, as would the results of those decisions. Thus, combining IoT and AI would be extremely useful in S.C.I. for bringing about the greatest possible good for the citizens. Below Fig. 1 is depicted the cycle.

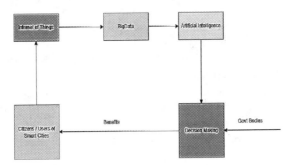

Fig. 1. Cycle of IoT in Smart Cities

3 Success Model for Modern Information Systems

A revised Information System Success Model forms the foundation for the methodology of this investigation. Model results reveal the influence of Information, System, and customer satisfaction on IoT Adoption Intention and User Satisfaction. A person's happiness can affect their net gain. A more optimistic outlook enhances how people use the Internet of Things, which favourably impacts Intention in turn. Users' satisfaction alonwith their intent to adopt IoT are both affected by the net benefit. When the Internet of Things is used, the Net Benefit rises as well. An explanation of the model's many constructs and hypotheses is provided here.

3.1 Deemed Information Quality (DIQ)

Prospective users' desire to use these IoT systems in SCI is affected by the quality of available information, and actual users' pleasure with their experiences with IoT in SCI is enhanced when better information is provided. The speculations offered in light of the foregoing talks are H1: In SCI, DIQ is predicted to increase DIU for IoT,H2: DIQ has a beneficial effect on DUS when it comes to the use of IoT in SCI.

3.2 Deemed System Quality (DSQ)

It is said that users are meant to perceive something as being in order if that perception is consistent with the context in which it is presented. It also indicates that the user is considering utilising IoT if they provide importance to the available information, platform, and customer experience. This variable, known as "Deemed Intention to Use," is explained and impressed by how satisfied consumers feel.

3.3 Deemed user satisfaction (DUS)

User happiness is crucial because it increases the likelihood that people will use devices built on the Internet of Things. H5: DIU for IoT in SCI is affected favourably by DUS, or the deemed satisfaction of users.

3.4 Use Cases for the Internet of Things (AUI)

The association between the presumed intention to use IoT and actual utilisation is favourable and significant. As a result of these factors, the conjecture is proposed is H6: The number of people who say they plan to use Internet of Things (IoT) services in a city has a positive correlation with the number of people who actually do use IoT services in Smart Cities in India.

Six hypotheses derived from the principles presented serve as the foundation for the conceptual model as displayed in Fig. 2. Proposed study ultimately demonstrate the Updated Information System Success Model.

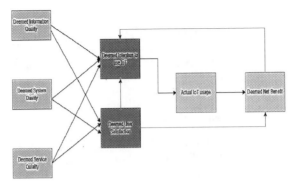

Fig. 2. Conceptual Model for Smart City

4   Research Methodology

4.1   Creation of Indicators, Items, and Statements

We have first extracted 32 statements from the constructs generated using the literature review's inputs and the revised Information System Success Model recommended. The "Two Statement Method" was used to help frame the surveys, which let researchers learn about and evaluate respondents' cultural preferences. Having the questions prearranged in logical patterns is useful. The framework was also used to inform the design of the questions, with an emphasis on making sure that respondents could easily find the information they needed. Initial questions were written in a way that made them simple to understand and answer. Things stiffened up with time. This is how the questionnaires took shape. The specialists in the field were interviewed for these 32 remarks, and 19 responses were chosen because of their reputed familiarity with IoT and AI. Based on the input of the experts and the responses of the 19 respondents, it was determined that out of the total of 32 statements, 8 were difficult to grasp due to their complex language. These 8 statements have been removed, leaving 24 to be used.

4.2   Methods for Selecting a Representative Sample of Respondents

Given that there are 24 assertions to process, and we know that item:response might take on values between 1:4 and 1:10, we must choose suitable responses from respondents numbering between 101 and 280. To find people who are knowledgeable about the Internet of Things, we focused on major cities in India, such as Mumbai, Kolkata, Bangalore, and Delhi. To start, we reached 400+ participants by various channels and paper copies of the list of statements to acquire pertinent responses from 100 participants preliminarily selected from each city. Only 262 of the total 400 participants responded to the survey. After careful review, it was determined that out of a total of 262, 27 responses were invalid due to missing information; they were therefore disregarded. So, a total of 235 useful responses had to be dealt with. The complete survey process took place over Four months, from January 2022 to April 2022. Now, we used a Likert scale to rank the 235 replies on a scale from 01 (strongly agree) to 05 (strongly disagree).

Given that as previously stated, the interviewees' responses needed to be between 95 and 240, we found that the total number of valid responses we received was 248, which is close enough to 240 to get to the conclusion that we fairly considered the quantity of responses in order to arrive at a practical outcome (Table 1).

Table 1. Assessment Table

Fac	Item		Load	CR	AVE	MSE
DIQ	DIQ1	The IoT will produce accurate data	0.97	0.92	0.91	0.62
	DIQ2	The system will protect the data it processes	0.92			
	DIQ3	The data made available by the system will be pertinent to me	0.97			
DSQ	DSQ1	The IoT-ready devices will be easy to use	0.97	0.95	0.93	0.62
	DSQ2	India's smart cities' IoT-enabled information systems will adhere to international standards	0.96			
	DSQ3	The system will protect citizens' privacy	0.96			
DEQ	DEQ1	Reliable service quality will be provided by the IoT-enabled system	0.85	0.87	0.84	0.63
	DEQ2	The IoT equipped system's support team will be knowledgeable	0.98			
DIU	DIU1	IoT-enabled devices are preferable to non-IoT devices in my opinion	0.92	0.89	0.86	0.61
	DIU2	I believe the preferred method of communication in smart cities will be IoT enabled services	0.94			
	DIU3	I predict that most people living in smart cities will use IoT-enabled gadgets	0.95			
	DIU4	To use IoT-enabled gadgets, I need some training	0.91			
DUS	DUS1	Govt. Will leverage information provided by IoT-enabled devices to make quick, precise decisions that will ultimately benefit citizens in India's prospective smart cities	0.96	0.93	0.92	0.51
	DUS2	The Internet of Things will simplify my life	0.92			
	DUS3	I really would like to use IoT-enabled devices	0.99			

4.3 Observed Variable Reliability Analysis

Cronbach's alpha and Spearman-Brown Prediction (Prophecy) coefficients were calculated to determine the consistency of the observed variables. Cronbach's alpha is considered reliable if it is greater than 0.7, while a value of 0.6 may be sufficient for exploratory studies. The other theories exhibited that Cronbach's alpha can have a bottom threshold of 0.6. When attempting to foretell reliability, psychometricians frequently resort to the

Spearman-Brown Prediction (Prophecy) test. The least permissible value is 0.7. Tabular 2 displays all of the resulting estimations. Cronbach's alpha seems to fall between 0.697 and 0.872, as shown in Table 2. This indicates that the variables are credible, as we have previously said that the lowest value of Cronbach's alpha should not be 0.6. Based on Table 2, it appears that the Spearman-Brown Prediction test values are all above 0.763 and below 0.911, which is fine given that we are aware that this constant's minimum value must not be less than 0.7. As a result, we can conclude that the variables are stable based on these estimates.

Table 2. Validation of Convergence& Divergence

	DIQ1	DIQ2	DIQ3	DSQ1	DSQ2	DSQ3	DEQ1	DEQ2	DIU1	DIU2	DIU3	DIU4	DUS1	DUS2	DUS3
DIQ1	1														
DIQ2	0.07	1													
DIQ3	0.08	0.09	1												
DSQ1	0.06	0.06	0.07	1											
DSQ2	0.04	0.05	0.07	0.04	1										
DSQ3	0.03	0.08	0.08	0.08	0.02	1									
DEQ1	0.04	0.08	0.07	0.05	0.07	0.03	1								
DEQ2	0.09	0.06	0.09	0.03	0.07	0.07	0.01	1							
DIU1	0.04	0.04	0.07	0.09	0.06	0.05	0.02	0.06	1						
DIU2	0.03	0.04	0.05	0.01	0.02	0.09	0.05	0.08	0.04	1					
DIU3	0.02	0.01	0.01	0.02	0.05	0.09	0.07	0.06	0.07	0.08	1				
DIU4	0.09	0.09	0.06	0.03	0.07	0.07	0.08	0.05	0.05	0.09	0.03	1			
DUS1	0.07	0.03	0.04	0.09	0.06	0.02	0.07	0.05	0.03	0.06	0.04	0.05	1		
DUS2	0.02	0.05	0.03	0.08	0.02	0.07	0.05	0.04	0.03	0.08	0.01	0.09	0.05	1	
DUS3	0.07	0.06	0.02	0.08	0.07	0.08	0.02	0.06	0.01	0.04	0.09	0.05	0.09	0.06	1

4.4 Framework for Measuring (Loading Factor, CR, AVE, and MSV)

Please be aware that for considerations seven variables are represented by 24 statements or items. The table representing Cronbach's alpha and Spearman-Brown Prediction test estimates show that we only examined 20 loadings after evaluating the items' loading factors relative to their construct and finding that four items assumed loading factors considerably below 0.3.

Indicators for each constructed object are considered credible if they have a minimum value of > 0.707.

Average Variance Extracted (AVE) values for each construct have also been evaluated. This is required to test the items' convergent validity inside each construct. For AVE, a value of 0.5 is the bare minimum that can be used. We have also calculated the build reliability, also known as the Composite Reliability (CR). Cronbach's alpha value and the Spearman-Brown Prediction test results are consistent with this interpretation. The closer the value of CR is to 1 (reliable), and the closer it gets to 0 (unreliable), we state that the constructions are reliable. Although a CR of 0.6 is typically the very minimum that can be accepted, there are exceptions to this rule.

Table 3 displays the results of the calculations for loadings, CR, and AVE. Maximum Shared Variance (MSV) for each construct was calculated, which resulted in the realization that every MSV number was smaller than its corresponding AVE value, establishing the result's credibility.

Additionally, Table 3 demonstrates that the range for the loadings of items for their builds is 0.850 to 0.991. Items are dependable to the limit that any construct warrants, since the minimum loading value of 0.850 is greater than the minimum allowable loading value of 0.707. Again, CR values are between 0.870 and 0.959, with 0.870 being the lowest allowed value and 0.6 being the minimum acceptable number. Because of this, the resulting constructs may be trusted. Again, the AVE values range from 0.842 to 0.936, with a minimum of 0.842 which is over the minimum allowable AVE value of 0.5 and indicates that the items are dependable in explaining their respective constructions.

Table 3. Analysis for Validating

	DIQ	DSQ	DEQ	DIU	DUS
DIQ1	0.61	0.792	0.636	0.033	0.981
DIQ2	0.327	0.939	0.339	0.527	0.172
DIQ3	0.273	0.029	0.8	0.438	0.714
DSQ1	0.511	0.633	0.704	0.953	0.788
DSQ2	0.926	0.901	0.352	0.612	0.881
DSQ3	0.44	0.563	0.045	0.406	0.635
DEQ1	0.504	0.832	0.717	0.785	0.281
DEQ2	0.71	0.005	0.539	0.403	0.849
DIU1	0.083	0.264	0.293	0.292	0.318
DIU2	0.09	0.915	0.268	0.974	0.408
DIU3	0.736	0.375	0.698	0.436	0.376
DIU4	0.988	0.895	0.58	0.505	0.406
DUS1	0.043	0.38	0.33	0.26	0.354
DUS2	0.255	0.517	0.406	0.592	0.989
DUS3	0.527	0.232	0.558	0.304	0.468

4.5 Indicators of Discriminant Validity

The multicollinearity test and the discriminant validity test are essentially the same things. Confirming that performing sqrt() function on AVEs, also termed as Average Variance (AV), are greater than the correlation values between the two composite items serves as evidence of discriminant validity, the hypothesis that the constructs are unrelated. Results are displayed in Table 6.

According to the data in the table above, the values of the Average Variances that are the square roots of the AVEs displayed in the diagonals are higher than the equivalent correlation coefficients of the two composite constructions (0.952, 0.966, 0.918, 0.930, 0.959, 0.967, and 0.938). Thus, the achievement of discriminant validity may be verified (Table 4).

Table 4. Discriminant Validating Analysis

	DIQ	DSQ	DEQ	DIU	DUS	AUI	DNB	AVE
DIQ	0.955							
DSQ	0.701	0.81						
DEQ	0.715	0.804	0.744					
DIU	0.957	0.785	0.772	0.868				
DUS	0.694	0.836	0.649	0.964	0.816			
AUI	0.993	0.976	0.686	0.794	0.639	0.655		
DNB	0.919	0.684	0.981	0.644	0.698	0.766	0.821	
AVE	0.891	0.908	0.912	0.825	0.909	0.914	0.731	0.874

5   Discussion

Empirical research indicates that the detailed information about technology and services offered of a high calibre has a bearing on the likelihood that a user would make a purchase. Therefore, system designers should be forthright and honest regarding the accuracy, understandability, completeness, and security of information to raise behaviour intention and user satisfaction. The suggested model and its components demonstrate how they can be utilised by enterprise and organisation decision-makers as a useful and efficient resource for evaluating information system implementation. Specifically, we have used the Information System Success Model developed by De Lone and Mc Lean to execute SCI's IoT strategy. We've used the Information System Success Model's building blocks to get here. On the other hand, we have added IoT-specific constructs to the Information System Success Model by intuition, such as the Deemed Intention to Use IoT (DIU), Deemed Users' Satisfaction Using IoT (DUS), Actual Usage of IoT (AUI), and Deemed Net Benefit of IoT (DNB). The statistical study indicates that these structures also contribute to users' adoption of IoT and are interconnected. Although we developed hypotheses about the relationship between DSQ and DUS using data mining and other means, it appears from the statistical analysis that neither H4 nor H6 is supported.

6 Concluding Remarks

This research set out to determine what criteria, if any, would be most important in determining whether or not an IoT-based information system would be successful in the context of the SCI.

The research shows that the Smart Citizens' perceptions of DIQ and DSQ have an impact on their adoption of IoT in the context of the proposed SCI. So, SCI leaders should prioritize the development of higher-quality information and systems to improve the performance of information systems, which in turn would increase users' motivation to employ IoT in SCI.

References

1. ArendeToth, J.B., Van dee Vijvr, F.J.R.: Acculturationattitudes: a comparisonof measurement methods. J. Appl. Soc. Psychol. **37**(7), 1462–1488 (2007)
2. Gupte, R.: Thepattern of urban land use changes, a case study of Indian cities. SAGE J. **5**(1), 83–104 (2014)
3. Gosgerov, V.: Smartcities: Introducing the IBM city operations and management solutions, IBM (2011)
4. Falconr, G., Mitchli.: SmartCity framework: a systematic process for enabling smart connected communities (2012). Retrieved February 12, 2017, http://www.cisco.com/c/dam/en_us/about/ac79/docs/ps/motm/Smart-City-Framework.pdf
5. Daves, F.D.: Perceivedeusefulness, perceived ease of use, and user acceptance ofinformation technology. MIS Q. **13**(3), 318–339 (1989)
6. Hullend, J.: Use of partialleastsquares (PLS) in strategic management research: a review of four recent studies. Strateg. Manag. J. **20**(2), 195–204 (1999)
7. Heir, J., Andeerson, R., Tathem, R., Black, W.: Multivariatedata analysis withreadings. MacMillan.Hair, J. F, New York (1998)
8. Venkatash, V., Morres, M.G., Daves, G.B., Daves, F.D.: User acceptance of information technology: toward a unified view. MIS Q. **27**(3), 425–478 (2003)
9. Dwivedi, Y.K., Rana, N.P., Jeyaraj, A., Clement, M., Williams, M.D.: Re-examining the unified theory of acceptance and use of technology (UTAUT): towards a revised theoretical model. Inf. Syst. Front. **21**(3), 719–734 (2017). https://doi.org/10.1007/s10796-017-9774-y
10. Grovar, P., Ker, A.K.: Bigdata analytics – a review on theoretical contributions and tools used in literature. Glob. J. Flex. Syst. Manag. **18**(3), 203–229 (2017)
11. Schlieck, J., Farber, S., Huppe, J.: IoT applications – Value creation for industry. River Publisher, Aalborg (2013)
12. Chatterji, S., Ker, A.K.: Smart cities in developing economies: a literature review and policy insights. In: IEEE International Conference on Advances in Computing, Communications and Informatics. Kochi, India, pp. 2335–2340 (2015)
13. Chatterji, S., Ker, A.K.: Successfu adoption of IT enabled services in proposedSmart City of India: a critical analysis for user experience perspective. J. Sci. Technol. Policy Manag. (2017). https://doi.org/10.1108/JSTPM-03-2017-0008
14. Dwivdi, Y.K., Sharif, M.A., Simintires, A.C., Lal, B., Werakody, V.: A generalisedadoption model for services: a cross-country comparison of mobile health(m-health). Gov. Inf. Q. **33**(1), 174–187 (2016)
15. Gubbe, J., Buyea, R., Mareusic, S., Palannswami, M.: Internet of Things (IoT): avision, architectural elements, and future directions. Future Gener. Comput. Syst. **29**(7), 1645–1660 (2013)

16. Kant, R., Kumar, S.: Future internet technologies. Int. J. Recent Adv. **34**(3), 33–42 (2012)
17. Verma, P., Awasti, S.P.: Future of Internet and Cities. Int. J. Adv. Trends **33**(2), 48–62 (2018)
18. Mohan, S.P., Abhishek, K.: Viability of IoT in smart cities. Int. J. Adv. Eng. Technol. **12**(6), 78–99 (2019)
19. Tau,L., Wang, N.: Future internet: the internet of things. In: Advanced Computer Theory and Engineering Proceedings of the International Conference, Chengdu, China, IEEE, Washington, DC, pp. 376–380 (2010)
20. Haller, S., Karnouskos, S., Schroth, C.: The internet of things in an enterprisecontext. In: Domingue, J., Fensel, D., Traverso, P. (eds.) Future Internet – FIS, pp. 14–28. Springer, Berlin (2009)
21. Peoples, C., Parr, G., Mcclean, S., Scotney, B., Morrow, P.: Performance evaluation of green data center management supporting sustainable growth of the internet of things. Simul. Model. Pract. Theory **34**, 221–242 (2013)
22. Yi, M.Y., Jackson, J.D., Park, J.S., Probst, J.C.: Understanding information technology acceptance by individual professionals: toward an integrative view. Inf. Manage. **43**(3), 350–363 (2006)
23. Mathieson, K.: Predicting user intentions: comparing the technology acceptance model with the theory of planned behaviour. Inf. Syst. Res. **2**(3), 173–179 (1991)
24. Luarn, P., Lin, H.H.: Toward an understanding of the behavioral intention to use mobile banking. Comput. Hum. Behav., **21**(6), 873–891 (2005)
25. Author, F.: Contribution title. In: 9th International Proceedings on Proceedings, pp. 1–2. Publisher, Location (2010)
26. LNCS Homepage. http://www.springer.com/lncs. Accessed 21 Nov 2016

Design of a Contextual IoT Framework
for the Improved User Experience and Services

Jaskaran Singh[1] (ID), Doman Sarkar[1] (ID), Mohammad Wazid[1] (ID), Ankit Taparia[2] (ID),
Dhaval Kishore Bisure[2] (ID), and Noor Mohd[1](✉) (ID)

[1] Department of Computer Science and Engineering, Graphic Era Deemed to Be University,
Dehradun 248002, India
jaskaran.jsk2001@gmail.com, domansarkar4@gmail.com,
wazidkec2005@gmail.com, noormohdcs@gmail.com
[2] Samsung R and D Institute, Bangalore 560037, India
{ank.taparia,d.bisure}@samsung.com

Abstract. Since the advent of IoT-enabled smart devices, researchers have been
engaged in research to extract contextual information about the user and manage
devices based on their environmental characteristics. However, very few practical
use cases to manage this growth of devices and control them based on features
like forecasted temperature and sleep patterns are being explored in this fairly
unexplored sub-domain. To resolve this issue, we propose this technique which is
a contextual engine which utilizes various APIs to gather data about the user and
uses this contextual awareness to assist the user in interacting with devices, creating
a contextually aware environment. In this paper, we propose novel algorithms to
deal with the influx of data, and we perform analyses based on its characteristics
and pattern. We evaluated our mobile application with a sample population and
retrieved an overall accuracy of 95.52% of working optimally.

Keywords: Internet of Things (IoT) · Application programming interface (API) ·
Android · Semantic search · Contextual awareness · Semantic communication

1 Introduction

Internet of Things (IoT) [1, 2] refers to the sensors, devices and the communication
network that connects the most common 'internet-enabled' devices with their capabilities
to process, sense, and act using inter-operability and communication over a local network
or the internet. This is the ecosystem created by these devices, as well as the software that
allows the end user to communicate better with these devices and derives results through
them optimally. By utilizing smart devices and the internet, IoT provides innovative
solutions for businesses, governments, and private individuals [24]. Our everyday lives
are becoming increasingly influenced by the Internet of Things, which is pervasive
everywhere. The main purpose of the Internet of Things is to make it possible for objects
to communicate with one another via any network, path or service at all times remotely.

Application Programming Interface (API) [9, 10] is a software interface that enables
two applications to communicate without the need for any user intervention. An API is

© The Author(s), under exclusive license to Springer Nature Switzerland AG 2023
R. K. Tiwari and G. Sahoo (Eds.): ICAII 2022, CCIS 1822, pp. 269–284, 2023.
https://doi.org/10.1007/978-3-031-37303-9_20

a collection of software procedures and protocols that allow applications to communicate with one another effectively [25]. API allows machines to exchange data, update themselves and be accessed without the need for human interaction. An API architecture can generally be categorized into two categories: client and server. The application sending the request is a client, and the application sending the response is the server. In this paper, we utilize several APIs, including the Open Weather Map API where our application serves as the client which asks for the current weather information, and the Open Weather Map is the server which provides the details as a response.

Android [7, 8] as described by its developers is an open-source operating system based on Linux, used in mobile devices and for building portable applications. In addition to its code and supporting data, Android comes with its own Software Development Kit (SDK). We also use Gradle, which is a build automation tool for the development of multi-language applications. It manages the entire development process including compilation, packaging, testing, deployment, and publication of Android code. For our application purpose, we utilize Android SDK 30.0.3, Gradle 7.2 and Kotlin Language for our code.

Contextual Awareness [3, 4] refers to the technology that analyses information about places, people, and objects to calculate subsequent steps and provide situation-specific functions and content. Combining context awareness with various streamlined applications benefits the end user by reducing their input and providing smart solutions that utilize various environmental, characteristic patterns [26]. Depending on the described entity, context information can be classified. The context of a user can be derived from a variety of factors, including the location of the user, the social context of the user, their interaction with the device, and their sentiments. Context-aware computing adapts to the circumstances around humans, their surroundings, and their use of software and hardware by utilizing intelligence-based decisions. Using IoT in context awareness we can better interact with smart devices and use this ambient knowledge to provide an enhanced user experience.

1.1 Motivation of This Work

With the inclusion of smart IoT devices in virtually every aspect of life, nowadays the number of devices with an individual has grown exponentially but controlling them in a centralized manner with the usage of automation remains an issue. So, there is a staunch need to utilize contextual clues from environmental and physical and logical conditions, for controlling smart devices and building a smart ecosystem. In lieu of this, we have envisioned a contextual engine that helps in managing multiple smart IoT devices through automation and providing context-based services.

1.2 Research Contributions

The research contributions of this paper are given below:

1. In this paper, we have proposed a contextual engine that provides multiple server space solutions to control and automate smart IoT devices

2. The practical effectiveness of the proposed algorithms has been conducted through a formal survey and its finding have been formulated.
3. The average computational time has been computed both without the contextual framework and using the contextual framework to compare the boost in performance.

2 Related Work

Context-Aware applications have been researched since the early 1990s [5]. Location-based contextual applications [6] have been talked about using location-aware services using GPS to locate people of interest or friends and relatives. Also, context-aware applications have been used to translate and bridge the barrier of languages [11] and textual data has been analyzed before to give smart context-aware responses [12].

Chen [19] proposes a contextual based search system that aims to create a hierarchical context model for the IoT devices in the ecosystem primarily for searches made by the user that takes into account the hidden context. Paper [20] also proposes a semantic reasoning model for making context-aware applications in a more realistic scenario taking into consideration resources constraints, scalability and mobility of the tools. They also verified the capabilities of these parameters of different approaches to reasoning in the paper in the paper [21], the author using a protocol bridge, develops a multi-agent protocol function that acts as an integration point for applications, providing access to relevant context, sharing it with other applications, and making relevant services available. Paper [22] discusses a domain-independent and semantic-based framework where the data and events are encapsulated in a separate context management layer that is dedicated solely to generating relevant context information. It also details upon novel rule structure for activity recognition.

The use-case discussed in the paper [13] discusses using contextual intrusion detection in a smart factory ecosystem and using sensors to solve decisions using contextual ambient intelligence. Paper [14] demonstrates a conventional context-aware technique to use ambient intelligence streaming in edge computing and reduces latency by a great margin. This area of study has been moderately researched with the advent of contextual awareness. An intriguing use-case that is described by [15] showcases to derive contextual information from industrial devices for the industrial Internet of Things domain. Paper [23] also discusses a conceptual framework for daily contextual-based activities, coupled with principles of Graph databases. They developed an inference engine for the device's services mapped with the data of context awareness.

3 Architecture of Proposed System

The architectural diagrammatic representation of our model is showcased in Figure 1. Out of the five layers bottom, three Layers are the core Android framework and, Drivers, Linux Kernel and all the applications. Rest two are specific to our framework and application:

1. **Linux Kernel** - It is the root layer of the architecture. It provides an abstraction layer between the device hardware and the remaining components of the architecture.

2. **Android Layer** - The second last layer comprises the core Android framework including platform libraries, Application Run-time and Application Framework.
3. **Applications** –Next is the application layer which has pre-installed applications like camera and other third-party application running on Android run-time.
4. **Contextual and APIs Layer** - This penultimate layer contains our main contextual application as well as the APIs that need to be called including Weather, Sleep and the motion device API. It also collects the sensor data using built-in Light and motion sensors.
5. **Smart Devices Layer** - The final layer of our architecture is the smart devices which are managed by our application and are registered and monitored through API calls to create a smart ecosystem.

4 Proposed Technique

This first version of our smart contextual application works on six major use cases and creates an ecosystem to manage these different IoT smart devices to create an IoT-enabled ecosystem:

– Smart Lights - Light and Bulbs
– Smart Cooling - Air Conditioner and Fans
– Smart Heaters - Centralised Heating and Heaters
– Smart Water geysers
– Smart Air Purifiers

We utilize the following API's and sensors to fulfil gather contextual and environmental information:

– Google's SLEEP API

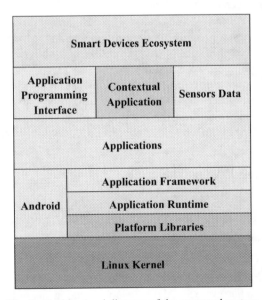

Fig. 1. Architectural diagram of the proposed system.

- OpenWeatherMap Current Weather API
- OpenWeatherMap 48 h Weather API
- OpenWeatherMap Air Pollution API
- Android Geo-Fencing API
- Ambient Brightness Light Sensor
- Accelerometer Motion Sensor

We have referenced these devices and APIs in Figure 2. Figure 2 illustrates IoT use cases being offered as a service to our users, and all the APIs that are being taken as input to the engine for the facilitation of the service. Now we'll discuss the five use cases and their generalised algorithmic intuition.

4.1   Usecase 1 - Geo-Fencing Triggered Device Management

Geo-Fencing is the capability to derive information from the user's current location and combines it with the proximity to some pre-targeted locations to influence the user's experience. A diagrammatic representation is showcased in Figure 3.

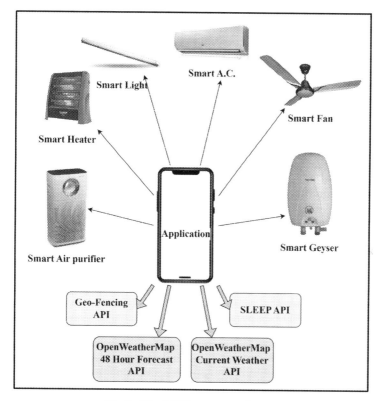

Fig. 2. The IoT Use-cases and APIs.

As demonstrated in Figure 3, we have illustrated the geo-fenced environment of the user. Once it is detected by the contextual engine that the user is in range, we move on to the phase of the environmental condition otherwise we check again after 10 seconds. As instructed by Algorithms 3, 4, 5 using the weather app if there is a need for any device we activate it, otherwise it is again checked for 10 seconds. Our application utilizes Android's Geo-Fencing API in conjunction with Weather API in order to contextually manage a wide range of smart devices such as ACs, Fans, heaters, and even small appliances such as smart microwaves based on our Algorithm 1 below.

Description of Algorithm 1

- The application takes the GPS permission and runs as a daemon process in the background.
- The user registers some smart devices whose location will be used to calculate the proximity.
- Once out, the user's location will be tracked every minute to update their live location and check if they are within range of the devices and fence that is created.
- If the proximity to the registered location is within a pre-computed range, then we move to step 5 otherwise steps 3–4 are carried out again with a buffer time of 1 min.

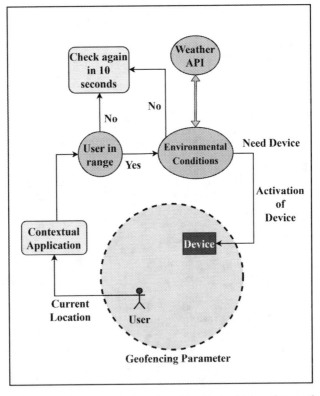

Fig. 3. Diagrammatic representation of the Geo-Fencing triggering mechanism.

- The application sends a triggered message that the user is within the range if it validates that the user is in range of the device for at least 1 min.
- Once the application 'triggers' we validate what should be the optimal device to be operated using Weather monitoring (Use-Case has been talked about in UseCase D) and then the application will interact and activate the pre-registered device.
- Once the user leaves the range again, the devices will be stopped and the user will get hereby notified.

4.2   Usecase 2 - Controlling Smart Lights and Geyser Based on Sleep Pattern

We utilise Sleep API provided by Google which analyses ambient light, motion sensor, and brightness information to determine when the user sleeps and wakes up and to update its status accordingly. A diagrammatic representation is showcased in Figure 4. Figure 4 demonstrates the Usecase for Sleep pattern identification. As shown, it takes an input of the Ambient Brightness, Motion sensing, and log-off time, to calculate sleeping patterns using Sleep API. This Service uses Activity Recognition to further give a sleep confidence value. This predicted sleep time is then used to turn off the Smart light at sleep time and activate the smart heater in winter before wake-up time. Our contextual application utilizes this information and uses it to control smart lights and heater based on sleep confidence value as detailed below.

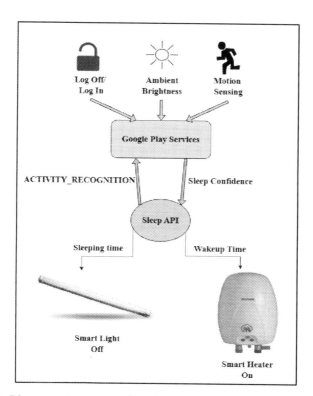

Fig. 4. Diagrammatic representation of Sleep API for Sleep Pattern Use-Case.

Description of Algorithm 2

- The user registers the application with Google Play Services and requests physical motion sensor's permission.
- The application uses Sleep API through Play Services to track the user's sleeping patterns and characteristics.
- The API takes into consideration the device Log In/ Log Off time, physical motion and ambient brightness to detect contextual information from the user.
- This data is collected by the API and it provides a sleep confidence value. If the value is above a threshold, it indicates the user is sleeping.
- The average Sleep and Wake-Up time over five days are taken into consideration and used in steps 6 and 7.
- The application uses the average Sleep time in order to dim and then turn off the smart lights currently on.
- The application uses the average Wake-Up in order to activate the smart geyser for bathroom applications as soon as the user wakes up.

4.3 Usecase 3 - Controlling Smart Air Purifier Based on Weather and Air Quality Pattern

We utilise OpenWeatherMap Air Pollution API to monitor the air quality forecast of the user's location and control smart air purifier based on the level of contamination in the area. The forecasted wind speed is also taken into account along with our initial AQI data, and modifying the prediction to activate more frequently as the wind speed increases, as high wind speeds can change the air quality more quickly.

Description of Algorithm 3

- The application takes the live location of the user using the underlying Android Global Positioning System (GPS).
- The location of the user is added and sent to the OpenWeatherMap Air pollution API which provides us with the current and forecasted Air quality of the current location.
- The received data is assessed by our application and a three-hour quality value is extracted for forecasted data.
- The OpenWeatherMap API is also assessed by the application to retrieve the wind speed of the area.
- Steps 2–4 will need to be repeated more frequently if the wind speed is more than 8km/hr due to the higher risk of pollution from the wind.
- We move to step 7 if the value of air quality drops below a threshold value. Otherwise, we repeat step 2 with a buffer time.
- As soon as the requirement is there, the smart air purifier will be activated or will be scheduled to activate at the appropriate time.

4.4   Usecase 4 - Weather Monitored Application for Controlling Smart Devices

In this Use-Case we use OpenWeatherMap Current weather API to retrieve the current location's weather, including the temperature, humidity, and pressure. A diagrammatic representation of the Use Case is showcased in Figure 5. We use this information in turn to monitor Smart AC, Heater and fans based on some underlying conditions as explained below.

Algorithm 1 Usecase 3 - Controlling Smart air purifier based on Weather and Air quality pattern

---

Input: User's current location coordinates
Output: Activation of Smart Purifier

1: **for** Every every 5 hours **do**
2:        **if** location of user is added **then**
3:location sent to OpenWeatherMap Air pollution API and get the current and
                forecasted Air quality
4:      **else**
5:           Ask for location permission
6:      **end if**
7:Received data is assessed by our application and three hour forecasted data is extracted.
8:Wind speed of the area is also extracted for response JSON.
9:**if** Wind speed is greater than 8Km/hr **or** Pollution Label is 'High'**then**
10:           Increase frequency of Inspection
11:**end if**
12:**if** Pollution Label is 'Low'**then**
13:**Goto**Step 3
14:      **else**
15:Activate air purifier one hour before the scheduled air quality drop
16:      **end if**
17: **end for**

The optimal temperature we take for our study is 26–30°C which may be altered depending on the user's location. We use the following papers [16–18] to utilise the optimal temperature and the effect of pressure and humidity on the relative temperature in our algorithm. The flowchart of the weather conditions that we use in weather monitoring and forecast is represented in Fig. 6.

Description of Algorithm 4

– The application takes the live location of the user using the underlying Android Global Positioning System (GPS).
– The location of the user is added and sent to the OpenWeatherMap Current weather API which details the quality of the current location.

- We use the conditions given in the flowchart to determine which device needs to be activated and at what output. Also, if the pressure is above 1000mm/hg we repeat step 2 more frequently (5 min).
- In addition to Smart A.C. and heater, we also switch on the nearest smart fan when the temperature moves out of the optimal range discussed in Algorithm2.
- As all conditions have passed, we switch off any available devices. – We repeat all these steps after 10 min.

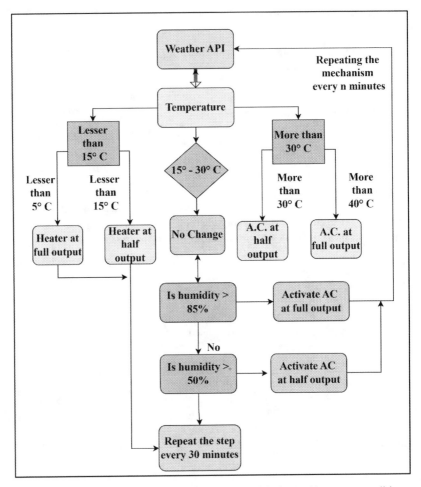

Fig. 5. Diagrammatic representation of activation of devices with current conditions.

Weather Forecast Application for Setting Smart Devices in Advance

We use OpenWeatherMap 48-h forecast to produce a schedule of the weather for the next 3 h, including the forecast temperature, humidity, and pressure. This Use-Case is built on top of our Weather Monitored Application and utilizes the same conditions that Usecase-4 utilizes as triggering points that help us schedule our smart devices for the future in the same notion that we use for current weather monitoring and is visualised in Fig. 6. All the underlying algorithmic conditions that are being used by the previous Use-Case will be considered and we will schedule the smart heater, A.C. and fans for half an hour before the forecast is scheduled.

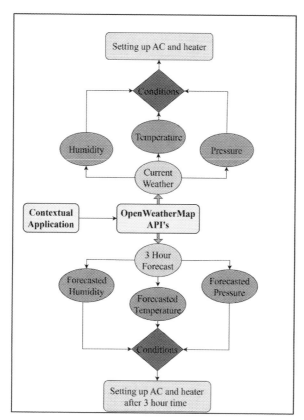

Fig. 6. Diagrammatic representation of activation of devices with current and forecast weather API calls.

Algorithm 2 Usecase 4 - Controlling Smart lights and geyser based on Sleep pattern

---

Input: User's current location coordinates
Output: Activation of Smart Heater and Air Conditioner

1: **for** Every every n minutes **do**
2:      **if** location of user is added **then**
3:          location sent to OpenWeatherMap Weather API and get the current and forecasted Weather condition
4:      **else**
5:          Ask for location permission
6:      **end if**
7:**if** Temperature is less than 5 degrees **then**
8:Activate heater at full output
9:**Goto**Step 20
10:**else if** Temperature is less than 15 degrees **then**
11:Activate heater at half output
12:      **Goto**Step 20
13:      **else if** Temperature is greater than 15 degrees **and** less than 30 degrees **then**
14:      No Change
15:**if** Humidity is greater than 85 **then**
16:          Activate AC at full output
17:**else if** Humidity is greater than 50 **and** less than equal to 85 **then**
18:          Activate AC at half output
19:      **else**
20:              **Goto**Step 2 after 30 minutes
21:      **end if**
22:      **else if** Temperature is more than 30 degrees **and** less than equal to 30 degrees **then**
23:          Activate AC at full output
24:      **else**
25:          Activate AC at half output
26:      **end if**
27: **end for**

4.5 Usecase 5 - Ambient Brightness Application to Monitor Smart Lights

The final Use-Case utilizes surrounding features in form of a built-in light sensor to derive context from the ambient brightness to activate smart lights with variable sensitivity.

Description of Algorithm 5

- Our application triggers this process in the background and retrieves the ambient brightness from the built-in environment light sensor using Sensor Manager.

- Our application refreshes these readings after an interval of 10 s in the background with the nearest smart light registered in our ecosystem.
- Based on the ambient brightness we categorize our actions from steps 4 -8
- If the light sensor returns a value of less than 5, we treat it as pitch black and activate the nearest smart light at 100% throughput
- If the light sensor returns a value greater than or equal to 5 and less than 15, the application treats it as very dark and activates the nearest smart light at 75% throughput
- If the light sensor returns a value greater than or equal to 15 and less than 30, the application treats it as moderately dark and activates the nearest smart light at 50% throughput
- If the light sensor returns a value greater than or equal to 30 and less than 50, the application treats it as slightly dark and activates the nearest smart light at 25% throughput.
- If the light sensor returns a value of greater than 50, the application treats it as normal lighting and deactivates the nearest smart light.

5 Practical Implementation

Our evaluation of the proposed scheme was conducted over a period of one month involving 250 users. Approximately 250 users had the engine installed in their machines, and after one month of use, they were asked whether the engine was functioning optimally.

The hardware and software requirements that were used for this implementation have been shared in Table 1. Details of this evaluation have been shared in Table 2.

Table 1. Parameters used in the practical demonstration

Parameter	Description
Android SDK	Version 30.0.3
Gradle	Version 7.2
Random-access memory (RAM) size 4 GB	
Programming Language	Kotlin
IoT Environment Samsung Smart Things	
Platform used for Implementation Android Studio Bumblebee	

Overall, the results were quite promising, with an average accuracy of across all five use cases of 95.52%.

Average overload and computational time were reduced by one-third by the algorithms. For all 250 users, the time taken to perform use cases conventionally was recorded, and the time taken to perform them with the framework was averaged Fig. 7 illustrates how the proposed framework increases the computational time for performing the usecases.

Table 2. Feedback Evaluation of all Use Cases Implementation

Usecase	Positive	Negative	Positive Percent
Usecase 1	241	9	96.4%
Usecase 2	234	16	93.6%
Usecase 3	244	6	97.6%
Usecase 4	230	20	92%
Usecase 5	245	5	98%

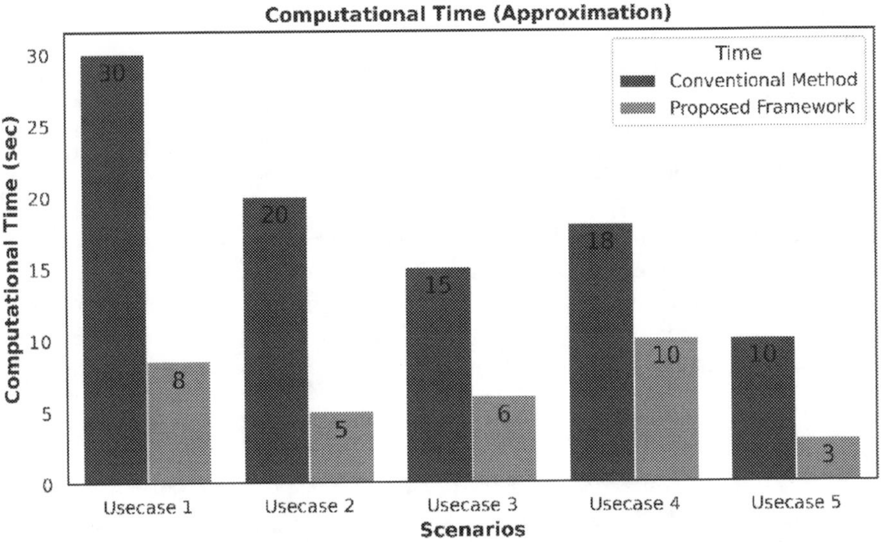

Fig. 7. Computational time with and without the frameworks.

6   Conclusion

In a conclusion, we explored the paradigm of contextual awareness and developed six practical methodologies to manage smart devices according to the different traits. We formulated six different Use-cases and manage to invoke and supervise different smart devices based on the trends in user behaviour and their environment.

There is a great deal of research potential in this field. There is a need to develop additional Use-Cases with more practical applications, such as psychological, environmental and physical context-based applications. Many more practical implications of context awareness have to be researched on the Internet of Medical Things, Industrial Internet of Things and personal users' Internet of Things ecosystem.

References

1. Li, S., Xu, L.D., Zhao, S.: The internet of things: a survey. Inf. Syst. Front. **17**(2), 243–259 (2014). https://doi.org/10.1007/s10796-014-9492-7
2. Madakam, S., Ramaswamy, R., Tripathi, S.: Internet of Things (IoT): a literature review. J. Comput. Commun. **3**, 164–173 (2015). https://doi.org/10.4236/jcc.2015.35021
3. Manaligod, H.J.T., Diño, M.J.S., Ghose, S., Han, J.: Context computing for internet of things. J. Ambient. Intell. Humaniz. Comput. **11**(4), 1361–1363 (2019). https://doi.org/10.1007/s12 652-019-01560-3
4. Schmidt, A.: Interactive context-aware systems interacting with ambient intelligence. Ambient Intelligence, 159–178 (2005)
5. Schilit, B., Theimer, M.: Disseminating active map information to mobile hosts. IEEE Network **8**(5), 22–32 (1994). https://doi.org/10.1109/65.313011
6. Pannevis, M.: I'm bored! Where is Everybody? Location Based Systems for Mobile Phones. MCs Thesis, University of Amsterdam (2007)
7. Jackson, W.: An introduction to android 7.0 nougat. In: Android Apps for Absolute Beginners. Apress, Berkeley, CA (2017). https://doi.org/10.1007/978-1-48422268-31
8. Developers, Android: What is android? Dosegljivo (2011). http://www.academia.edu/dow nload/30551848/andoid-tech.pdf
9. Joshua, B.: How to design a good API and why it matters. In: Companion to the 21st ACM SIG-PLAN Symposium on Object-Oriented Programming Systems, Languages, and Applications (OOPSLA '06). Association for Computing Machinery, New York, NY, USA, pp. 506–507 (2006). https://doi.org/10.1145/1176617.1176622
10. Ofoeda, J., Boateng, R., Effah, J.: Application programming interface (API) research: a review of the past to inform the future. Int. J. Enterp. Inf. Syst. (IJEIS) **15**(3), 76–95 (2019). https://doi.org/10.4018/IJEIS.2019070105
11. Schilit, B., Hilbert, D.M., Trevor, J.: Context-aware communication. IEEE Wirel. Commun. **9**(5), 46–54 (2002)
12. Nummiaho, A., Laakko, T.: A framework for mobile context-based messaging applications. In: Proceedings of the 4th International Conference on Mobile Technology, Applications, and Systems and the 1st International Symposium on Computer Human Interaction in Mobile Technology, MC'07 (Mobility'07). New York, NY, USA (2007)
13. Park, S.-T., Li, G., Hong, J.-C.: A study on smart factory-based ambient intelligence context-aware intrusion detection system using machine learning. J. Ambient. Intell. Humaniz. Comput. **11**(4), 1405–1412 (2018). https://doi.org/10.1007/s12652-018-0998-6
14. Kim, J., et al.: A context-aware adaptive algorithm for ambient intelligence DASH at mobile edge computing. J. Ambient. Intell. Humaniz. Comput. **11**(4), 1377–1385 (2018). https://doi.org/10.1007/s12652-018-1049-z
15. Lunardi, W.T., de Matos, E., Tiburski, R., Amaral, L.A., Marczak, S., Hessel, F.: Context-based search engine for industrial IoT: discovery, search, selection, and usage of devices. In: 2015 IEEE 20th Conference on Emerging Technologies & Factory Automation (ETFA), pp. 1–8 (2015). https://doi.org/10.1109/ETFA.2015.7301477
16. Patil, B.: Pulsating heat pipe for air conditioning system: an experimental study. Int. J. Sci. Res. Dev. **4**, 1312 (2016)
17. Diffey, B.: Time and place as modifiers of personal UV exposure. Int. J. Environ. Res. Public Health **15**, 1112 (2018). https://doi.org/10.3390/ijerph15061112
18. Zhu, M., Pan, Y., Wu, Z., Xie, J., Zhizhong, H., Kosonen, R.: An occupant centric air-conditioning system for occupant thermal preference recognition control in personal micro-environment. Build. Environ. **196**, 107749 (2021). https://doi.org/10.1016/j.buildenv.2021.107749

19. Chen, Y., Zhou, J., Guo, M.: A context-aware search system for Internet of Things based on hierarchical context model. Telecommun. Syst. **62**(1), 77–91 (2015). https://doi.org/10.1007/s11235-015-9984-x

20. Maarala, A.I., Su, X., Riekki, J.: Semantic reasoning for context-aware internet of things applications. IEEE Internet Things J. **3**, 1–13 (2016). https://doi.org/10.1109/JIOT.2016.2587060

21. Pradeep, P., Krishnamoorthy, S., Vasilakos, A.V.: A holistic approach to a context-aware IoT ecosystem with adaptive ubiquitous middleware. Pervasive Mobile Comput. **72**, 101342 (2021). https://doi.org/10.1016/j.pmcj.2021.101342

22. Elkady, M., ElKorany, A., Allam, A.: ACAIOT: a framework for adaptable context-aware IoT applications. Int. J. Intell. Eng. Syst. **13**(4), 271–282 (2020). https://doi.org/10.22266/ijies2020.0831.24

23. Li, M., Wu, Y.: Intelligent control system of smart home for context awareness. Int. J. Distrib. Sens. Netw. **18**(3), 155013292210820 (2022). https://doi.org/10.1177/15501329221082030

24. Pandey, N.K., Diwakar, M., Shankar, A., Singh, P., Khosravi, M.R., Kumar, V.: Energy efficiency strategy for big data in cloud environment using deep reinforcement learning. Mobile Inf. Syst. **2022**, 1–11 (2022). https://doi.org/10.1155/2022/8716132

25. Samant, S.S., Singh, V., Chauhan, A., Narasimaiah, J.D.: An optimized crossover framework for social media sentiment analysis. Cybern. Syst., 1–29 (2022). https://doi.org/10.1080/01969722.2022.2146849

26. Jain, P., et al.: Blockchain-enabled smart surveillance system with artificial intelligence. Wireless Communications and Mobile Computing **2022**, 2792639 (2022) https://doi.org/10.1155/2022/2792639

Internet of Things Enabled Framework for Sustainable Mobility and Clean Environment in Smart Cities

Surleen Kaur$^{(\boxtimes)}$ and Sandeep Sharma

Department of Computer Engineering and Technology, Guru Nanak Dev University,
Amritsar, India
{surleencse.rsh,sandeep.cse}@gndu.ac.in

Abstract. With people moving to cities for permanent settlements, there has been a rapid rise in urbanization worldwide. To accommodate such a vast number of citizens and provide them with quality life, the existing infrastructure of the cities requires transitioning into a more intelligent and safer environment. Hence, the aim of smart cities is to utilize the resources in order to offer a healthy and sustainable habitat to its citizens. Due to the increased urbanization; two significant issues which exist and are likely to persist as the cities grow are: the constant increase in transportation and the deterioration of environment as it's result. The ever-growing number of on-road vehicles eventually leads to increased emissions, which are detrimental to the environment and undermine the quality of life in the cities. This paper aims to explore Internet of Things-driven solutions to achieve sustainable mobility and to provide cleaner environment in smart cities. The implementation of intelligent services in smart cities is inextricably intertwined with the Internet of Things. IoT technologies such as sensors, communication gateways, cloud/edge computing, along with machine learning and artificial intelligence technologies, allow large-scale data collection, connectivity, storage, and processing; which facilitate availability of smart services through intelligent decision-making.

Keywords: Internet of Things · Smart Cities · Autonomous Vehicles · Electric Vehicles · Sustainability · Environment Monitoring

1 Introduction

With the growing population, the trend of urbanization is also growing at a fast pace; it is estimated that by the end of 2030 over 60% and by the end of 2050, almost 70% population will be living in cities [1, 2]. The resources are limited and continue to diminish due to continuously increasing consumption in urban areas. Such drastic expansion of smart cities requires measures such that the development can happen in a sustainable manner. Typically, smart cities aim to provide a live-able space which is sustainable and environment friendly [3]. However, the current scenario poses great threats to the environmental health as the increase in urbanization is often accompanied by increase in transportation; and among the total number of on-road vehicles, most of which are privately owned. Hence, mobility in cities becomes a major cause of concern as it is associated with various problems like congestion, collisions, larger energy consumption, and the most serious of them all, elevated carbon emission levels caused due to vehicle exhausts, which have severe impacts on the environment [4]. Thus, the cities need to be smart, equipped with intelligent systems that have the ability to combat such problems and promote sustainability.

With billions of devices connected with one another and the wide range of functionalities provided by these devices, Internet of Things can be regarded as the main driver of any smart city; where nearly everything, from people, buildings, roads, traffic lights, lamp posts, to vehicles is a 'thing' in this huge dynamic network of 'things' connected over the internet [5]. Thus, such huge infrastructure can be leveraged to achieve solutions to mobility and pollution related problems among other services provided by smart cities. Hence, the main objective of this paper is to explore Internet of Things based solutions in combating the above-mentioned issues in smart cities. The main objectives of this paper are:

a. To highlight the role of IoT in enabling intelligent services in smart cities with a special emphasis on environmental aspect of the cities.
b. To explore, how IoT technologies can be utilized in smart cities to achieve sustainable mobility and cleaner environment; discussing the case of connected and autonomous vehicles.
c. To analyze the intersection of IoT infrastructure and autonomous vehicles in order to facilitate better environmental conditions in future cities.
d. Finally, to propose a model for future implementation, by converging the aforementioned domains for efficient environmental monitoring and eventually taking control measures.

The rest of the paper has been organized into various sections. Section 2 discusses the relationship between a smart city and Internet of Things technology along with the importance of sustainable cities. Section 3 elaborates on the role of autonomous vehicles in achieving environment friendly and sustainable smart cities. Section 4, proposes a model which can be used in current scenario as well as future cities which can help achieve better environmental conditions. Finally, the paper has been concluded in Sect. 5 providing insights into the findings of the paper.

2   Role of IoT in Smart Cities

Smart city and Internet of Things are tightly coupled with each other; in other words, IoT can be regarded as a core enabler of smart cities. There has been a tremendous shift towards urbanization in the past few decades and it is estimated to grow further. With nearly 60% population located in the urban ecosystems, it becomes a basic requirement of the cities to incorporate intelligent systems in order to improve the quality of life and make them more livable, interactive and alert by providing smart services in all the aspects of day-to-day life [4, 6]. Some of the key services provided by a smart city include, smart transportation, healthy environment, smart economy, smart governance, smart industry, smart energy and various other facilities [7]. Hence, IoT with its vast range of technologies finds applicability in achieving almost every aspect of a smart city. As the name suggests Internet of Things is a huge dynamic network of heterogenous things where the 'things' are equipped with sensors, actuators, communication modules such that they are capable enough to generate and transmit data among themselves [8]. Internet of Things is a technology driven concept whereas smart city is user oriented; the intersection of the two thus has potential to provide all the aforementioned smart services [5]. Figure 1 below depicts various categories of IoT-based applications in a smart city.

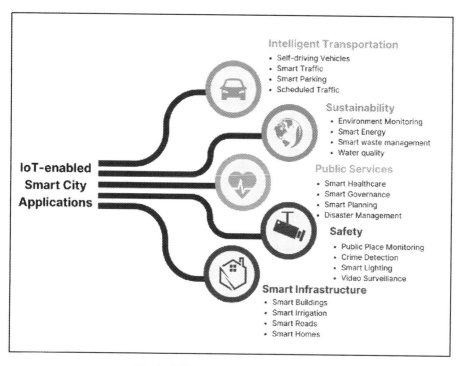

Fig. 1. IoT Applications in Smart Cities

2.1 Typical Smart City-IoT Infrastructure

A typical smart city offers numerous services to its citizens which can be achieved by deploying a multi-layered IoT infrastructure where each layer has a dedicated functionality [2]. To cover a city from end-to-end, a very huge number of IoT devices including sensors, actuators, RFID tags and readers, gateway, servers, need to be deployed to facilitate consistent data collection, constant connectivity among devices; such that there is an uninterrupted exchange of data and continuous service delivery [9]. These devices are often installed on street-side lights, buildings, parking lots, other public places and vehicles, such that a wide spatial coverage can be achieved. A smart city targets a wide variety of applications, as a result numerous types of devices are deployed which are typically heterogenous in nature; various distinct sensors generate all kinds of data, various wired and wireless communication standards are utilized to transmit data among these sensor nodes, gateways, clouds and end user devices, and finally this ginormous amount of data collected is processed on clouds or local servers to make cities more inhabitable, sustainable and safer for its people [1].

3   Environmental Aspect of Smart Cities

Providing environmentally sustainable space is regarded as the prime objective of any smart city. The increased urbanization and in turn increased transportation, industrialization and consumption have deteriorated the environmental health over the years. Utilizing the IoT infrastructure can facilitate in keeping track of the environment at all times, making the citizens aware of their surroundings and even taking counter measures [10]. Curbing carbon emissions is a fundamental requirement of any society to be able to control global heating and to improve the quality of air we breathe [11]; with IoT devices (static or moving) deployed all over a smart city, real-time environmental monitoring can be carried out. The biggest problem faced by today's urban habitats is the deteriorating air quality due to the increased levels of air pollution as a result of vehicle emissions, industries, construction, and buildings. With nearly 75% contribution towards air pollution, vehicle emissions remain the biggest culprit among all the contributors. Hence, alternative and optimal solutions to control vehicular emissions along with regular monitoring are being explored.

3.1   Sustainable Mobility

Realizing the harmful impacts of fossil-fuel-based vehicles on the environment, the automotive industry in the last few years has transitioned towards manufacture of electric vehicles (EVs) as they have nearly 58% lower lifecycle impact when compared with traditional internal combustion engine vehicles [12]. Various models of EVs are available which include battery electric vehicles, plug-in electric vehicles, hybrid electric vehicles, and fuel cell electric vehicles and their wide scale use will be beneficial for transportation sustainability in urban areas [13]. In the recent years, with the rise of IoT and with 5G technology underway, smart cities have developed more than ever. The industry is moving towards automation in every field, as a result autonomous transportation has also gained attention; connected and autonomous vehicles are being regarded as the future of mobility in smart cities [14]. Currently, the market of electric vehicles is slowly growing whereas the autonomous vehicle industry is still in its infancy; however, with the right amount of infrastructure, smart cities can go fully autonomous. Autonomous vehicles can benefit greatly from the smart city infrastructure and in turn smart cities can immensely benefit from the connected and autonomous vehicles for greener and more sustainable environment, efficient use of resources, safer roads, lesser traffic and much more [15].

3.2   Connected and Autonomous Vehicles

Connected and autonomous vehicles (CAVs) are regarded as the 'future of mobility', due the various benefits they offer including reduced congestion, reduced emissions, safety, better road designs and more [16]. Autonomous vehicles (also known as driverless cars) are the vehicles which can operate autonomously without any human intervention. Connected vehicles enable communication with other autonomous/non-autonomous vehicles, roadside infrastructure which aids in making better driving choices [17]. Thus, connected and autonomous vehicles offer combined benefits of both the technologies. These vehicles are equipped with a variety of sensors, LiDAR (Light Detection and Ranging), GPS (Global Positioning System) and computer vision technologies which allow them to obtain information about their surroundings and operate autonomously with very little or no assistance from the driver [18]. The developments in the fields of Internet of Things, cloud computing, machine learning and artificial intelligence have made it possible for the automotive industry to manufacture such vehicles. Moreover, with the widespread adoption of smart cities worldwide, the development of autonomous vehicles has further boosted. As per Society of Automotive Engineers (SAE), there are in total six levels of automation depending upon the level of assistance from the driver, with level zero being the no automation level and level 5 being the fully automotive where no driver involvement is needed [19]. Figure 2 here depicts the estimated and projected number of autonomous vehicles in the world from the years 2019 to 2024 [20]; and Fig. 3 shows the projected level of automation in the new cars sales for the year 2024 [21]. Out of the total 54.20 million units estimated, only 0.86 million units will have conditional to full automation.

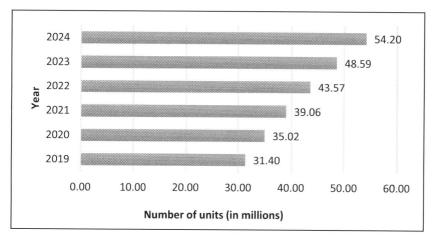

Fig. 2. Projected number of Autonomous Vehicles from 2019–2024

It can be derived that there still a long way to go before total automation of transportation industry as it requires complete transformation of infrastructure which is capable enough to support that level of automation. However, there is definitely an upward trend in the progression of autonomous vehicle industry; the global market size of automotive sensors stood at 30 billion US dollars in 2020 and as per reports it is expected to grow by at least 25 billion dollars till the year 2025 (refer Fig. 4) [22]. Furthermore, the share of various prominent sensor types in the global market size by the year 2030 is estimated as: 14 billion dollars for radar, 12 billion dollars for LiDAR, 8 for cameras and 9 for other automotive sensors like ultrasonic etc. (refer Fig. 5) [23]. These figures clearly support the fact that the automotive industry is gearing towards higher levels of automation in on-road vehicles for the coming years. (All of the abovementioned data represented through the following figures has been accessed from various reports published on https://www.statista.com/).

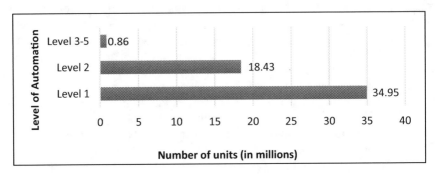

Fig. 3. Level of automation in cars in the year 2024

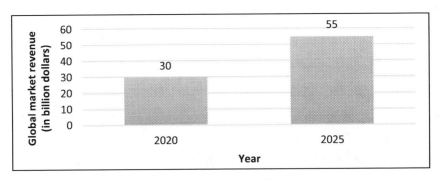

Fig. 4. Estimated global market size of Automotive Sensors

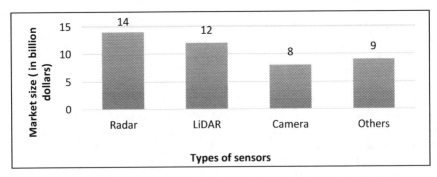

Fig. 5. Breakdown of Automotive Vehicles Market by Sensor Type in 2030

3.3 Intersection of Electric and Autonomous Vehicles

The magnitude of services offered by connected and autonomous vehicles have the capability to revolutionize the automotive industry and have direct impact on environmental health. With the ability to 1) sense the environment, 2) communicate with other devices of the smart city, 3) interact with other autonomous vehicles and 4) make onboard intelligent decisions, the autonomous vehicles act as mobile sensor platforms [24]. Autonomous vehicles come in different models based on the level of automation and the type of engine; these factors greatly influence the degree of impact an autonomous vehicle has on environment. To achieve the target of zero emissions from transportation, combination of fully electric and complete autonomous vehicle is inevitable. As of now, there is a negligible percentage of these vehicles; with internal combustion vehicles still constituting the largest chunk of total on-road vehicles, followed by hybrid and plug-in electric vehicles [25]. Hence, in a way, the pre-requisite of complete automation would be complete electrification of transportation supported by smart grids and energy efficient sources of electricity.

Along with reduced tailpipe carbon emissions, autonomous vehicles have the ability to regulate traffic flow, provide intelligent navigation, find more fuel-efficient routes resulting in lesser fuel consumption, decrease traffic congestion, reduce on-road collisions which are mainly caused due to human error and control noise pollution [26]. There are a lot of other potential benefits such as on-demand and shared mobility which are expected to further decrease greenhouse gas emissions, smart parking, changed driving behaviors, reduced travel time as a result of decreased congestion and more [19, 25]. Achieving this level of automation requires a robust infrastructure; which includes constant vehicle to vehicle (V2V) and vehicle to everything (V2X) communication, internet connectivity, efficient long-range and short-range communication standards (for reduced latency and optimized bandwidth), roadside sensors, smart streets, lane markings, parking facilities etc. for automated mobility in smart cities.

4 Proposed Framework

Vehicle emissions are the major reason behind deteriorating environmental health in urban areas and are the leading cause behind various health issues in people. In today's scenario, vehicle population mainly constitutes of gasoline and diesel engines, that emit various harmful pollutants into the air, deteriorating the air quality. The market of electric vehicles has gained pace in the recent years, but as of now the total percentage of on-road electric vehicles is still approximately 1% of total vehicle population; also, not all electric vehicles are fully electric [27]. Furthermore, the global market of autonomous vehicles is yet to gain pace; hence a large-scale adoption of autonomous vehicles is a thing of the future [28]. Moreover, the current testing of autonomous vehicles is mainly in combination with internal combustion engines or plug-in and hybrid electric vehicles; fully electric automated vehicles is still a far-fetched idea [25]. There are still decades to go before the world can completely phase out gasoline and diesel engine vehicles. Hence these calls for measures to monitor and control vehicular emissions in cities such that carbon emissions can be controlled and cleaner environments can be maintained.

The model proposed here (Fig. 6) suggests exploitation of IoT technologies available in today's time to improve environmental conditions of urban areas. A very diverse variety of pollution monitoring sensors are available which are capable enough to precisely and accurately sense pollution data [29]. These sensors can be deployed across the streets of smart cities; at intersections and pollution hotspots such that continuous pollution monitoring can be carried out and necessary actions can be taken. Moreover, RFID (Radio-Frequency Identification) technology allows identification of objects [30]; thus, the existing vehicles can be equipped with RFID tags such that vehicles emitting more than allowed pollution can be identified through RFID readers and their pollution data is sent to the environmental and governmental authorities. IoT along with edge-cloud and artificial intelligence technologies can make predictions based on environmental data, for instance pollution levels of an area can be predicted for a specific time interval and this information can be disseminated among citizens [31, 32]; which in turn can impact their driving choices.

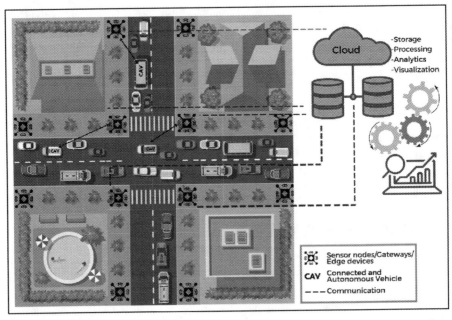

Fig. 6. A proposed model where the on-road vehicles and city's IoT infrastructure communicate with each other to share gathered environmental data and send it to cloud platforms for further actions

Furthermore, since the connected and autonomous vehicles are already equipped with sensors, artificial intelligence and GPS devices; pollution sensors can also be embedded in them such that whenever an autonomous vehicle moves around the city, it can sense the pollution levels of that area and can send location specific data to the cloud and that can be used to take control measures. Moreover, currently not all the on-road vehicles are fully electric, hence they are responsible for carbon emissions to a great extent; in such cases, even a single vehicle equipped with the pollution sensors can help monitor pollution levels around it and assist the driver to make driving decisions accordingly. Thus, along with vehicle's own emissions, the sensors can also obtain pollution data of nearby vehicles. In a way, the autonomous vehicles can act as mobile wireless sensor nodes that can communicate with each other and with the smart city's infrastructure [33]. Hence, the proposed IoT-enabled framework can help control carbon emissions caused due to transportation in smart cities. With proper infrastructure and connectivity, the number of connected and autonomous vehicles are estimated to increase in the future; in which case the proposed system can prove even more efficient. The aim is to explore the intersection of 1) IoT and automation; 2) IoT and environment monitoring; and manner in which these domains merged together can facilitate the implementation of the proposed system.

4.1 IoT: The Core Enabler

Role of IoT in Facilitating Automation. Internet of things plays a very crucial role in facilitating smooth functioning of an automated driving ecosystem. By definition, the Internet of Things is a paradigm that allows connectivity among multiple devices over the internet. Any autonomous vehicle continuously collects and acts upon a very huge amount of data at any given time [34]. The sensors equipped on the vehicle collect an insurmountable quantity of data from the surroundings and this data needs to be sent to edge/cloud for analysis such that the vehicle can take further action. The data collected by the vehicle is highly heterogeneous in nature; which includes data obtained by on-vehicle radar system that is used to measure distance from other objects; data from the camera which includes traffic signals, nearby pedestrians, lane markers, etc.; and data regarding road conditions, weather conditions, location data, and so on. All this gathered data needs to be instantly shared such that the vehicle can operate smoothly. In other words, constant connectivity between the vehicle and the environment is fundamental in the working of connected and autonomous vehicles. Internet of Things has the capability to connect all sorts of devices via its wide range of communication technologies. It has already transformed the traditional vehicular ad hoc networks into a new domain i.e., Internet of Vehicles (IoV) which is now further progressing towards a more advanced domain, Internet of Autonomous Vehicles (IoAV) [35].

It can be said that the Internet of Things technologies are indispensable for deployment of autonomous vehicles owing to the intelligent connectivity provided by these. As per the AUTOPILOT project an autonomous vehicle communicates with various entities that include the on-vehicle units, roadside objects, people, etc.; and hence the connectivity domain of an autonomous vehicle is quite wide which requires secure, reliable communication between the vehicle and all the other entities (basically vehicle to everything/ environment communication) [36]. Internet of Things offers numerous sensing and communication facilities that makes this possible. Table 1 below enlists the several categories of vehicle to environment connections along with the communication protocols utilised by each.

Further, apart from sensing and communication technologies, autonomous ecosystem also heavily relies on cloud/fog/edge for processing and analysis of data [37]. It is where all the high-level intelligent decisions are made based on which the vehicle plans

Table 1. Connectivity domain of autonomous vehicles

Type of Connectivity	Communication Protocols*	Communicating Entities and Purpose
V2V (Vehicle to Vehicle)	ITS-G5, LTE-V2X, 5G NR -V2X	Wireless mode of communication between a vehicle and its surrounding vehicles for their speed and position information
V2C (Vehicle to Cloud-Edge)	LTE-V2X Long range, 5G NR -V2X	Wireless communication between vehicle and cloud datacenters for tracking information etc
V2I (Vehicle to Infrastructure)	ITS-G5, LTE-V2X, 5G NR -V2X	Vehicle communicating with roadside infrastructure, such as traffic lights, road, weather condition alerts etc
V2N (Vehicle to Network)	LTE-V2X Long range, 5G NR -V2X, GPS	Wireless communication between a vehicle and cellular networks for routing information, or charging station locations
V2P (Vehicle to Pedestrian)	5G, 4G, Wi-Fi, LTE-V2X Long range, 5G NR -V2X	Communication between the vehicles and the road users to ensure their safety
V2H (Vehicle to Home)	5G, 4G, GPS	Wireless communication between a vehicle and its permanent /temporary home
V2U (Vehicle to Users)	5G, 4G, Wi-Fi, BLE, NFC, NB-IoT, GPS	Wired/ wireless communication taking place between the vehicle and the person using it regarding the current state of affairs
V2O (Vehicle to Owner)	5G, 4G, GPS	Wireless communication between a vehicle and its owner regarding location the vehicle, rental management, etc
V2D (Vehicle to Device)	BLE, Zigbee, NFC, CAN, RFID, LoRA, 6LoWPAN, NB-IoT	Wired/wireless communication between the vehicle and the IoT devices equipped on-board or on roadside
V2G (Vehicle to Grid)	5G, 4G, Wi-Fi, BLE, Zigbee NFC, PLC	Wired/wireless communication between a vehicle and the charging grid about information regarding an electric vehicle's battery status, charging information, etc

(*continued*)

Table 1. (*continued*)

Type of Connectivity	Communication Protocols*	Communicating Entities and Purpose
V2M (Vehicle to Maintenance)	5G, 4G, GPS	Wireless communication between the vehicle and the party responsible for maintenance of vehicle's health and repair (could be the owner or the manufacturer)

* ITS: Intelligent Transportation System; LTE: Long-Term Evolution; NR: New Radio; BLE: Bluetooth Low Energy; NFC: Near Field Communication; NB-IoT: Narrowband Internet of Things; CAN: Controller Area Network; LoRA: Long Range; 6LoWPAN: IPv6 over Low-power Wireless Personal Area Networks

its path. Thus, for real-time and logical movement of an autonomous vehicle, Internet of Things is absolutely necessary [38].

IoT- Enabled Environmental Monitoring. Air pollution has been regarded as the biggest cause of concern for the deteriorating environmental health [39]. One of the major reasons behind the alarming levels of air pollution is rapid urbanization which has skyrocketed the manufacturing of personal as well as public vehicles; which in turn are the biggest contributors of ambient air pollution. Over the last decade, numerous IoT-based studies have been undertaken by researchers who have integrated a wide range of technologies, to develop environmental monitoring frameworks which are capable of monitoring various harmful pollutants emitted by vehicles [40]. Among these studies, wireless sensor networks (WSNs) -based systems (Mobile Sensor Network, Vehicular Sensor Network) have been mainly suggested when aiming at vehicular pollution monitoring on large scale. Wireless Sensor Networks offer benefits of a distributed system where the overall system comprises of multiple entities which are capable obtaining data, processing it and sharing it among themselves [41, 42]. Moreover, WSNs are easily scalable and offer wider spatial coverage as there are multiple sensor nodes moving at different locations [43]. However, it has also been observed in the existing literature that deployment of sensors and implementing standardized communication protocols remain a concern [44]. Thus, drawing motivation from these concerns this paper has proposed a system where various domains can co-benefit; the CAVs which are already quite equipped with a system of sensors of their own can act as sensor nodes for environment monitoring as well. Further, the IoT infrastructure set-up for smart cities can be utilized by CAVs for smooth operation.

5   Conclusion

Internet of things has allowed anything and everything to be connected to the network via various sensor and communication technologies. Advancements in fields of cloud computing, machine learning and artificial intelligence have further allowed collection and processing of huge amounts of data to make intelligent decisions. Hence, IoT has always been tightly coupled with smart cities owing to its distinct characteristics like connectivity, reliability, scalability and flexibility. Smart cities are those urban habitats which aim at providing better living experience, enhanced quality of life, clean and safe environments; and IoT provides the required set of technologies to achieve the same. This paper focuses on the sustainability aspect (with special emphasis on sustainable mobility and clean environments) of smart cities and explores ways in which IoT infrastructure of any smart city can be utilized to develop sustainable and eco-friendly cities. As a result, role of IoT-based solutions to handle increased transportation, the associated emissions and their potential implementation is discussed to provide insights into the current scenario. It has been found that regulating mobility in smart cities is one of the most sought-after goals of future cities and that can be greatly improved by deployment of connected and autonomous vehicles. In addition to enhanced mobility services, electric- autonomous vehicles promote healthy environments too. However, there are still some major challenges that need to be addressed before cities can go fully electric and completely autonomous. The sensor technologies need to be highly efficient in terms of speed, accuracy and processing; energy consumption of these sensing devices is another major challenge. Much more advanced and intelligent software solutions are required such that path can be planned accurately with precision. Robust and fault-tolerant intelligent systems and technologies need to be developed for the smart cities to go fully autonomous. It can be further emphasized that automation is not the only solution to transportation challenges faced by growing cities, the environmental impacts of vehicular emissions also need to be tackled; which requires more deployment of electric vehicles and continuous monitoring of existing fossil fuel-based vehicles. Hence, leveraging Internet of Things technologies to work out these issues can prove beneficial for smart cities.

References

1. Jin, J., Gubbi, J., Marusic, S., Palaniswami, M.: An information framework for creating a smart city through internet of things. IEEE Internet Things J **1**, (2014). https://doi.org/10.1109/JIOT.2013.2296516
2. Gaur, A., Scotney, B., Parr, G., McClean, S.: Smart city architecture and its applications based on IoT. In: Procedia Computer Science (2015)
3. Silva, B.N., Khan, M., Han, K.: Towards sustainable smart cities: a review of trends, architectures, components, and open challenges in smart cities. Sustain Cities Soc 38 (2018)
4. Kirimtat, A., Krejcar, O., Kertesz, A., Tasgetiren, M.F.: Future trends and current state of smart city concepts: a survey. IEEE Access 8 (2020)
5. Alavi, A.H., Jiao, P., Buttlar, W.G., Lajnef, N.: Internet of Things-enabled smart cities: State-of-the-art and future trends. Measurement (Lond) **129**, (2018). https://doi.org/10.1016/j.measurement.2018.07.067
6. Das, S.K.: Smart design and its applications: challenges and techniques (2021)
7. Dameri, R.P., Ricciardi, F.: Leveraging smart city projects for benefitting citizens: The role of ICTs. In: Springer Optimization and Its Applications (2017)
8. Kim, T., Ramos, C., Mohammed, S.: Smart City and IoT. Future Gener. Comput. Syst. 76 (2017)
9. Theodoridis, E., Mylonas, G., Chatzigiannakis, I.: Developing an IoT Smart City framework. In: IISA 2013 - 4th International Conference on Information, Intelligence, Systems and Applications (2013)

10. Almalki, F.A., Alsamhi, S.H., Sahal, R., et al.: Green IoT for Eco-friendly and sustainable smart cities: future directions and opportunities. Mobile Netw. Appl. (2021). https://doi.org/10.1007/s11036-021-01790-w

11. Ahvenniemi, H., Huovila, A., Pinto-Seppä, I., Airaksinen, M.: What are the differences between sustainable and smart cities? Cities **60**, (2017). https://doi.org/10.1016/j.cities.2016.09.009

12. Virta: Electric cars & pollution: facts and figures (2022). https://www.virta.global/blog/electric-cars-pollution-facts. Accessed 30 May 2022

13. Sanguesa, J.A., Torres-Sanz, V., Garrido, P., et al.: A review on electric vehicles: Technologies and challenges. Smart Cities 4 (2021)

14. Vaidya, B.T., Mouftah, H.: Connected autonomous electric vehicles as enablers for low-carbon future. In: Research Trends and Challenges in Smart Grids (2020)

15. Coumans, F.: Smart cities benefit from infrastructure for autonomous vehicles (2021). https://www.gim-international.com/content/article/smart-cities-benefit-from-infrastructure-for-autonomous-vehicles. Accessed 30 May 2022

16. Elliott, D., Keen, W., Miao, L.: Recent advances in connected and automated vehicles. J. Traffic Transp. Eng. (English Ed.) 6 (2019)

17. Rana, M.M., Hossain, K.: Connected and autonomous vehicles and infrastructures: a literature review. Int. J. Pavement Res. Technol. (2021)

18. Gerla, M., Lee, E.K., Pau, G., Lee, U.: Internet of vehicles: from intelligent grid to autonomous cars and vehicular clouds. In: 2014 IEEE World Forum on Internet of Things, WF-IoT 2014 (2014)

19. Kopelias, P., Demiridi, E., Vogiatzis, K., et al.: Connected & autonomous vehicles – environmental impacts – a review. Sci. Total Environ. **712**, (2020). https://doi.org/10.1016/j.scitotenv.2019.135237

20. Statista: Projected number of autonomous cars globally from 2019 to 2024 (2021). https://www.statista.com/statistics/1230664/projected-number-autonomous-cars-worldwide/. Accessed 28 Jul 2022

21. Statista: New car sales worldwide in 2024, by autonomous vehicle level (2022). https://www.statista.com/statistics/1071071/new-car-sales-by-autonomous-level/. Accessed 28 Jul 2022

22. Statista: Size of the global market for automotive sensors in 2020, with a forecast for 2025 (2021). https://www.statista.com/statistics/1011203/projected-global-automotive-sensor-market/. Accessed 28 Jul 2022

23. Statista: Breakdown of the market for sensor types in ADAS/AD systems in 2030, by type (2022). https://www.statista.com/statistics/1076066/adas-autonomous-drive-system-sensor-market-by-type/. Accessed 28 Jul 2022

24. Guevara, L., Cheein, F.A.: The role of 5G technologies: challenges in smart cities and intelligent transportation systems. Sustainability (Switzer-land) 12 (2020). https://doi.org/10.3390/su12166469

25. Rojas-Rueda, D., Nieuwenhuijsen, M.J., Khreis, H., Frumkin, H.: Autonomous vehicles and public health. Ann. Rev. Public Health 41 (2019)

26. Seuwou, P., Banissi, E., Ubakanma, G.: The future of mobility with connected and autonomous vehicles in smart cities. In: Internet of Things (2020)

27. IEA: Electric Vehicles (2021). https://www.iea.org/reports/electric-vehicles. Accessed 30 May 2022

28. Businesswire global autonomous vehicles market trajectory & analytics report (2022). https://www.businesswire.com/news/home/20220114005334/en/Global-Autonomous-Vehicles-Market-Trajectory-Analytics-Report-2022. Accessed 30 May 2022

29. Idrees, Z., Zheng, L.: Low cost air pollution monitoring systems: a review of protocols and enabling technologies. J. Ind. Inf. Integr. **17**, (2020). https://doi.org/10.1016/j.jii.2019.100123

30. Jia, X., Feng, Q., Fan, T., Lei, Q.: RFID technology and its applications in Internet of Things (IoT). In: 2012 2nd International Conference on Consumer Electronics, Communications and Networks, CECNet 2012 – Proceedings (2012)

31. Shetty, C., Sowmya, B.J., Seema, S., Srinivasa, K.G.: Air pollution control model using machine learning and IoT techniques. Adv. Comput. (2020)

32. Kaur, S., Sharma, S.: Edge-Assisted IoT architecture: a case of air pollution monitoring frameworks. In: Luhach, A.K., Jat, D.S., Hawari, K.B.G., et al. (eds.) Advanced Informatics for Computing Research, pp. 244–256. Springer International Publishing, Cham (2022). https://doi.org/10.1007/978-3-031-09469-9_21

33. Zakaria, N.A., Zainal, Z., Harum, N., Chen, L., Saleh, N., Azni, F.: Wireless internet of things-based air quality device for smart pollution monitoring. Int. J. Adv. Comput. Sci. Appl 9(11), (2018). https://doi.org/10.14569/IJACSA.2018.091110

34. Lonari, Y., Zhou, X., Kumar, S.: IoT-enabled AI technologies for self-driving connected cars (2020). https://www.hitachi.com/rd/sc/aiblog/023/index. Accessed 29 Jul 2022

35. Nanda, A., Puthal, D., Rodrigues, J.J.P.C., Kozlov, S.A.: Internet of autonomous vehicles communications security: overview, issues, and directions. IEEE Wireless Commun. 26, (2019). https://doi.org/10.1109/MWC.2019.1800503

36. Vermesan, O., Bahr, R., Falcitelli, M., et al.: IoT technologies for connected and automated driving applications. In: Internet of Things - The Call of the Edge: Everything Intelligent Everywhere (2020)

37. Lee, J., Lee, K., Yoo, A., Moon, C.: Design and implementation of edge-fog-cloud system through HD map generation from lidar data of autonomous vehicles. Electronics (Switzerland) 9, 1–15 (2020). https://doi.org/10.3390/electronics9122084

38. Bathla, G., Bhadane, K., Singh, R.K., et al.: Autonomous vehicles and intelligent automation: applications, challenges, and opportunities. Mobile Inf. Syst. 2022, 1–36 (2022). https://doi.org/10.1155/2022/7632892

39. Balakrishnan, K., Dey, S., Gupta, T., et al.: The impact of air pollution on deaths, disease burden, and life expectancy across the states of India: the Global Burden of Disease Study 2017. Lancet Planet Health 3, (2019). https://doi.org/10.1016/S2542-5196(18)30261-4

40. Kalajdjieski, J., Stojkoska, B.R., Trivodaliev, K.: IoT based framework for air pollution monitoring in smart cities. In: 2020 28th Telecommunications Forum, TELFOR 2020 - Proceedings. Institute of Electrical and Electronics Engineers Inc. (2020)

41. Ma, Y., Richards, M., Ghanem, M., et al.: Air pollution monitoring and mining based on sensor Grid in London. Sensors 8, (2008). https://doi.org/10.3390/s8063601

42. De, D., Mukherjee, A., Das, S.K., Dey, N.: Wireless sensor network: applications, challenges, and algorithms. In: De, D., Mukherjee, A., Das, S.K., Dey, N. (eds.) Nature Inspired Computing for Wireless Sensor Networks, pp. 1–18. Springer, Singapore (2020). https://doi.org/10.1007/978-981-15-2125-6_1

43. lo Re, G., Peri, D., Vassallo, S.D.: Urban air quality monitoring using vehicular sensor networks. Adv. Intell. Syst. Comput. 260, (2014). https://doi.org/10.1007/978-3-319-03992-3_22

44. Cordova-Lopez, L.E., Mason, A., Cullen, J.D., et al.: Online vehicle and atmospheric pollution monitoring using GIS and wireless sensor networks. J. Phys. Conf. Ser. 76, (2007). https://doi.org/10.1088/1742-6596/76/1/012019

Human Motion Detection Using Ultra-Wide Band Radar

Hanish Saini[1], Siddhartha Sarkar[2,3(✉)], Ashish Gaurav[2,3], Vaibhav Kumar[2], Lini Mathew[1], and Satish Kumar[2,3(✉)]

[1] National Institute of Technical Teachers Training & Research, Chandigarh 160019, India
[2] CSIR – Central Scientific Instruments Organisation, Chandigarh 160030, India
{ssarkar,satish}@csio.res.in
[3] Academy of Scientific and Innovative Research (AcSIR), Ghaziabad 201002, India

Abstract. The detection of presence of human is a scientific challenge in the area of automatic target recognition. Researchers have presented different sensing modalities for human detection such as seismic, acoustic and imaging. All the sensing modalities impose different environmental challenges. To overcome these challenges, Ultra-Wide Band (UWB) radar is used as sensing modality for static and moving human detection. UWB PulsON 440 radar detects human targets in indoor and outdoor scenarios using monostatic mode. This study describes the experimental results in which a monostatic UWB radar detects human presence. Different techniques such as Short-Term Average to Long Term Average ratio (STA/LTA), wavelet transformation, mean averaging, background removal, and CFAR-based approaches are developed and presented here. The performance of the presented methods is evaluated on the collected radar return signals in different scenarios where STA/LTA, mean averaging, wavelet and CFAR provided average accuracy of 87.1%, 84.1%, 78.3%, and 73.6% respectively. These approaches could be useful in coal mines for human safety, real-time target detection, industrial applications, human posture classification, military surveillance, and pedestrian safety.

1 Introduction

Ultra-Wide Band radar has been immensely popular over the last decade due to its broad bandwidth, inherent high resolution and immunity from external interference. Automatic target detection has been performed by using different sensing approaches such as thermal cameras, video imaging, radar systems, etc. A UWB radar system for target detection is mainly used to identify partially or fully covered targets [1–3]. UWB has several applications and uses in the military, industries, medical care, and emergency response due to its ability to penetrate diverse walls or buildings and dense foliage. Ultra-Wide-Band radar technology is a complementing technology for detecting and tracking persons since it works effectively in situations where other sensing modalities operate weakly (such as in the dark or in dusty, foggy, rainy environments). In UWB sensing, human motion are detected by processing the received pulse waveforms. The frequency, phase, amplitude, and arrival time of the reflected signal may be used to examine signal variation due to human presence and gestures. The clutter reflected by non-human targets is an extra energy signal that suppresses the needed signal from the targets. As a result, to decrease clutter, proper preprocessing of UWB signals is necessary [4, 5].

Nguyen and Pyun developed a unique combined technique that employs a Kalman filter in the clutter-reduction phase and CLEAN algorithm improvements in the target identification stage [6]. Clutter is reduced using weighted Range Profile Subtraction on each recorded scan of human motion. Nezirovic introduced this method in which a weighted array is used to multiply each range profile for background subtraction without changing the signal's strength [7]. Wavelet transform is also a useful tool for suppressing the ground clutter and noise from air turbulence echo at time series. Wavelet decomposition splits a signal into a set of basic functions high-frequency and low-frequency coefficients known as detailed coefficients and approximation coefficients [8]. Human target detection via Empirical Mode Decomposition (EMD) is developed and tested by Narayanan et al. on detecting changes in signal patterns for stationary human detection behind the wall [9]. The person is located using simple moving averages of radar signal by computing the square of the difference between two successive scans eliminates stationary clutter from the signal, and feature extraction indicates the presence of a human [10]. Maali et al. proposed the Cell Averaging Constant False Alarm Rate (CA-CFAR) to detect the target's motion [11]. Katwijk and Verton used a method that filtered the noise in the received signals using an FIR motion filter [12]. Singh et al. suggested a unique method for detecting humans behind walls using a combination of Singular Value Decomposition (SVD) and Short Time Fourier Transform (STFT), where based on the material of the wall different results are obtained [13]. The short-time-average to long-time-average (STA/LTA) approach is most commonly used to detect any abrupt change in signal amplitude [14]. In this paper, the comparative analysis of different signal processing techniques has been presented for human detection under different environmental conditions. The paper is structured as follows: Data collection from UWB radar and preprocessing are covered in Sect. 2. The experiment setup is discussed in Sect. 3. Methodology in part Sect. 4. Results and discussion are presented in Sect. 5, followed by the Conclusion.

2   Data Generation and Preprocessing

UWB radar has several significant benefits over continuous wave radars, as the pulses having a broad frequency range and may readily travel through obstacles. The PulsON 440 is monostatic UWB Radar i.e both the transmitter and receiver antennas are placed close to each other. It is a single-board ultra-wideband radio component with an operating frequency range of 3.1 to 4.8 GHz. The PulsON 440 uses a modified gaussian pulse, and its range resolution is calculated by the product of the travelling speed of Radio wave and time required for one pulse width of 61.023 picoseconds. The P440 module, as shown in Fig. 1, is the new Fully Integrated Front End (FIFE) custom chip, which is provided with two antennae that offers multiple interface choices (USB, Ethernet, serial, SPI, and CAN) and consume less power of the previous generation P410 and P412 platforms [15].

Fig. 1. PulsON 440 Module

The range of the radar, scan start, scan stop time, pulse integration index, and transmit gain are all configured using PulsON 440 Monostatic Radar Module software during data generation and these parameters are stored for offline processing.

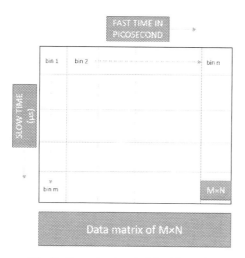

Fig. 2. Recorder data in M × N matrix

The recorded scan is placed parallel as a rake receiver as depicted in Fig. 2. The received amplitude is recorded and kept in each bin. The amplitude of the received signal with respect to distance is recorded horizontally in each bin, corresponding to the fast time axis and scans with respect to time are gathered vertically. The time interval between repeated scans can be specified in milliseconds. It is the difference in time between two scans. The Radar can record several scans, and acquired scans can be shown as reflected signals from human targets [16]. The vertical axis represents the amplitude or strength of recorded scans and it also shows the mutual coupling of the antenna, commonly known as antenna crosstalk in the initial segment of the fast time axis which is also shown in Fig. 3.

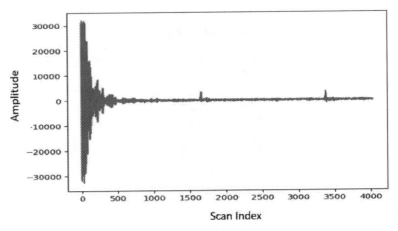

Fig. 3. Recorded Scan by UWB Radar

3   Detail of Experiment Setup

Two independent scenarios are considered for data generations i.e., outdoor and indoor environment with the walking and standing of a human target in a clear line of sight as shown in Figs. 4 and 5. P440 Radar module on a tripod stand and Table 1 lists critical parameters used for carrying out the experiment. The UWB radar installation and configuration parameters are managed via Ethernet and Wi-Fi to prevent any other possible target in the radar's range.

Table 1. Selected Parameters for Experimental Setup

Parameters	Values
Detection Range	Indoor 5 m and Outdoor 30 m
Successive Scan Interval	125 ms
Transmit Gain	0–63
Pulse Integration Index	6–12

A human target may walk towards the radar and then return to its original place. The first set of data is acquired in an outside situation with a direct line of sight for detection

Fig. 4. Outdoor experimental setup

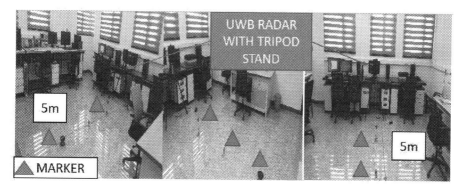

Fig. 5. Indoor experimental setup under laboratory condition

of walking persons up to 30 m away, and the second set of data is obtained indoors for the identification of static humans at a distance of 5 m.

Table 2 shows the details about recorded scans at different ranges with human targets in outdoor an indoor scenarios.

Table 2. Details about Recorded Scans Using UWB Module

Experimental Setup (Distance of Human Target from Radar)	Number of Scans with No Human Target (Background)	Number of Scans with One Human Target	Number of Scans with Two Human Targets
Outdoor (1.5 m–30 m)	2500 Scans	100800 Scans	20160 Scans
Indoor (1 m–5 m)	1000 Scans	4500 Scans	2250 Scans

4 Methodology

The input signal is varied along the fast time axis throughout time t, due to leg, arm, and other micro motion of the human body. These scans are monitored at each time instant (in picoseconds range). An IIR bandpass filter eliminates unwanted band frequencies that are outside the range of 3.1–4.8 GHz at each scan. Clutters and out-of-band signals are minimized by including a specific number of previous scans values passed over to determine the output k which is shown in (1)

$$k = s[i] - \left(\frac{s[i+1]}{2}\right) - \left(\frac{s[i+2]}{4}\right) - \left(\frac{3 * s[i+3]}{20}\right) - \left(\frac{s[i+4]}{40}\right) \ldots \quad (1)$$

Where s is the input signal, and i is the recent scan iterator, which passes values accumulatively through the equation. Every scan reflects a change in human micro-motion, non-stationary clutter, and noise in the system. These changes occur over time in each scan. Figure 6 depicts the block diagram of detection procedures and methodology employed. The study was conducted at the CSIR-CSIO Laboratory in Chandigarh.

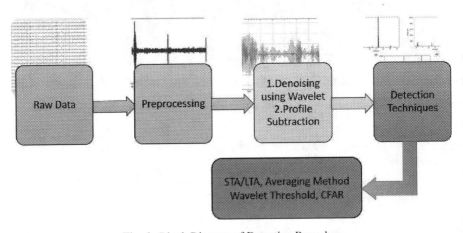

Fig. 6. Block Diagram of Detection Procedure

The de-noising of the signal is achieved using wavelet decomposition which is a combination of low-pass and high-pass filtering processes as shown in Fig. 7, up to the five level of signal decomposition. Wavelets are small waves that are localized in both the time and frequency domains. Wavelet decomposition divides a signal into a set of basis functions, high- and low- frequency coefficients known as detailed coefficients and approximation coefficients.

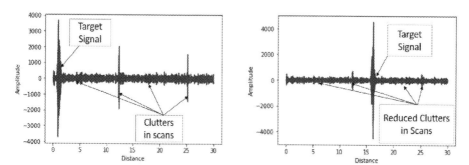

Fig. 7. Clutters with moving Target Signal and Removal of Clutters using profile subtraction method

The signal denoted by the sequence s [.], where n is an integer, is processed by a [.] series of high-pass and low-pass filters. The Daubechies wavelet is the finest wavelet for extracting meaningful movement data [17, 18]. The high-pass filter provides detailed coefficients at level one, whereas the low-pass filter produces approximation coefficients. The output of the highpass and lowpass filter can be expressed in (2) and (3)

$$ylowpass[s] = \sum_{n} a[n] \, w[2s - n] \tag{2}$$

$$yhighpass = \sum_{n} d[n] w[2s - n] \tag{3}$$

Figure 8 depicts the recorded background signal in indoor environment without the presence of any human target within the configured range of the radar i.e., 5 m. Here, the blue signal indicates the recorded raw signal and the signal plotted in red color indicates the de-noised signal after applying pre-processing i.e., transformations using db4 wavelet. The received signal comprises of the target information along with the background noise because of unwanted movements in the range of the radar. These signals are non-stationary and correspond to various wave-like structures in the shape. Therefore, selection of wavelet based on the energy of the signal is important factor for signal characterization and de-noising [19].

4.1 STA/LTA Technique

The STA/LTA approach uses an envelope of preprocessed signals, as seen in Fig. 9(a). Detections are achievable for defined window length. This method divides scans into two adjacent windows of differing lengths and determines the ratio of their summation divided by the number of points in each scan. If the STA/LTA ratio (10:50) exceeds a predetermined threshold, the detection is performed [20, 21]. It is observed that, the

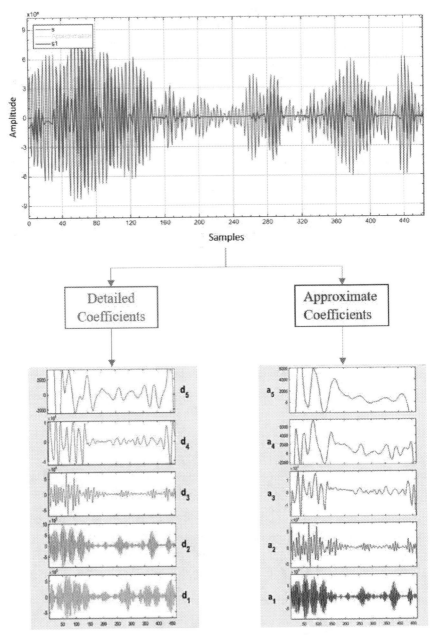

Fig. 8. (a) Raw Data Signal using Wavelet, (b) Wavelet Detailed Coefficients with Original Input signal d5 to d1 (c) Wavelet Approximate Coefficients with Original Signal a5 to a1

slight changes in the defined ratio due to walking human target is not detected at larger distances as the amplitude of the envelope falls below the defined threshold value.

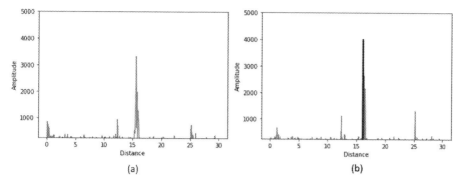

Fig. 9. (a) Envelope of Moving Target Signal (b) Detection of Moving Target Using STA/LTA

Figure 9 indicate the event detection utilizing short-term and long-term averaging when the threshold value is exceeded, the movement of individual is detected as shown in red color. The disadvantage of this approach is that it can produces false and missed detections on fluctuation of short-term and long-term averages. As larger LTA window duration suppresses the background noise, which improves the triggering sensitivity to the target signal. The accuracy of STA/LTA technique has shown an accuracy of 87.1% as it is affected by a false detections as shown in Fig. 10.

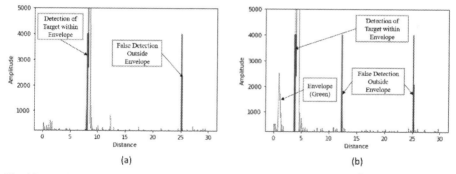

Fig. 10. (a) One true and one False Detection Observed by STA/LTA (b) One True and Three False Detections Observed by STA/LTA

The experiment is carried out in lab environment where a single individual was standing 5m away from the Radar in static position. The peak of the detection is not sharp in indoors because the collected samples is less than outdoor scenarios which is depend upon the distance parameter and also on the preprocessed values stored in envelope but for small range single individual detection like, if the individual moves from 3.5 m to 5 m, an appropriate change is detected, as shown in Fig. 11.

4.2 Detection using CFAR

Constant False Alarm Rate (CFAR) technique is applied under lab indoor scenario and outdoor environment. In this, a sliding window is moved over the scans and the samples

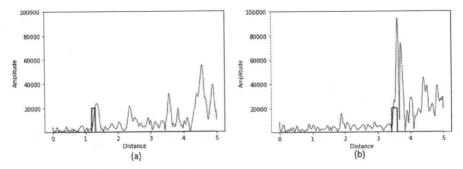

Fig. 11. (a) STA/LTA Detection Indoor Environment (b) Moving Target Detection Indoor Environment using STA/LTA

present in the guard cells is compared with adjacent cells [4, 22]. This technique is applied for both static and moving target i.e., human within range of 30 m. The results are shown in Fig. 12 (a), red peaks are appearing of targets on a single event, and the rate of false positives appears to be higher than the rate of true positives. It is observed that false detections due to moving objects other than standing human are generated by this technique, as shown in Fig. 12 (b). To overcome this problem, wavelet with threshold techniques is suggested.

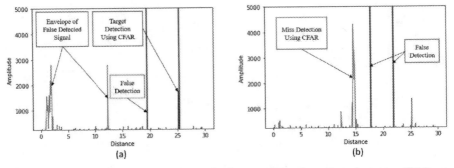

Fig. 12. (a) Target Detection by CFAR (b) Constant False alarm Detection using CFAR

4.3 Mean Window Comparison

This technique is applicable to both adaptive and static background and hence developed for detection of moving human target [23–25]. The mean of the first 100 scans is computed for the static background, which is then compared for detection against the remaining motion scans. The target is detected, if the computed mean value of the scans under consideration deviates beyond a predefined threshold. These 100-scan box windows are scrolled over the whole set of data for the adaptive backdrop to compute the mean at each event based on its previous 99 scans. After denoising, the scan envelopes are computed by applying the Hilbert transform to one scan at a moment. Each measurement in the scan is compared with the corresponding data from the 99 previous scans. This technique worked well both in adaptive and static situations (Fig. 13). However, missing detection was observed after 30 m. Furthermore, the algorithms were not adequate for the task when there is feeble motion.

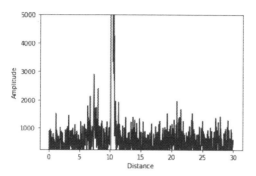

Fig. 13. Detection using Mean Averaging

4.4   Wavelet Transform

The detailed and approximation coefficients of the scans are computed utilizing db4 wavelet transform [26–28]. The thresholding for detection is computed using the Py-Wavelet Library; with soft and hard thresholding. As the detection peaks of the target are missing after 15 m, resulting in miss detection, which has been avoided by using hard thresholding.

The detection peak is caused by values that exceed the specified threshold values which is decided by receiving de-noising coefficients, the detection peak with the envelope is moved with the reference of moving human target but sometimes target detection peak is outside the envelope this is mostly due to the difference between detailed and approximation coefficients. The envelope (green curve) as shown in Fig. 14 (a) & (b) used for signature collection does not always overlap with the detection points (blue curve). The red line in Fig. 14 (a) & (b) represents the detection of a person, in indoor scenario and Fig. 14 (c) & (d) shows the detection of human target in outside environment. The envelope (green curve) as shown in Fig. 14 (a) & (b) used for signature collection does not always overlap with the detection points (blue curve). This is mostly due to the difference between detailed and approximation coefficients.

The technique is also applied for detection of more than one human targets, as shown in Fig. 14 (e). The original signal information is retrieved using the inverse discrete wavelet transform.

5   Discussions

Monostatic Ultra-wideband processed radar scans and appropriate values of threshold are required to test human detection. The presented approaches perform well in both indoor and outdoor environments, although there is a difference in detection rates in the outside

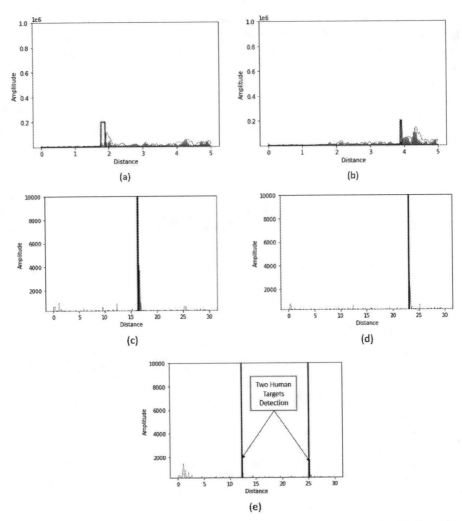

Fig. 14. (a) Detection of Person in Indoor Environment at 2 m (b) Detection Indoor Environment at 4 m by Wavelet (c) Outdoor Target Detection by Wavelet (d) Detection of Target at 25 m using Wavelet (e) Detection of Two Targets Present by Wavelet

environment, which has a greater false detection rate than the interior environment due to additional clutters that raise false alarms. The identification of false and missing detection is based on a threshold comparison, which is the difference between the target value and the values surpassing the target values. The performance of detecting algorithms is represented in ROC curves as well as numerically. The ROC curve compares the True Positive rate to the number of false positive rates based on the threshold used in the proposed algorithms [29–31]. The detection matrix, which includes detection points and an envelope that retains the values of real scans, with the help of a classifier the results are obtained.

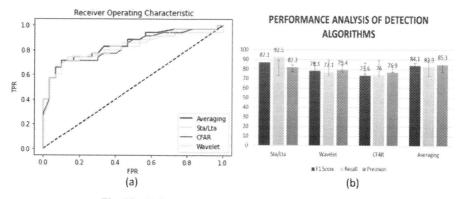

Fig. 15. (a) Roc curve and (b) Performance of detection

Receiver operating characteristic (ROC) curves for the developed detection techniques is shown in Fig. 15 (a). All the techniques performed similarly and lie closer to the top left corner, which indicates that their performances are acceptable for the moving target detection. From the result it is indicated that, more than 90% recall performance of STA/LTA detection technique, as shown in Fig. 15 (b), is achieved. It further indicates that it is statistically most sensitive, as compared to other techniques. Although, the performance of CFAR based detection technique is not evident to be performing poorer in ROC plot, its average detection Recall is below 75%. The comparison is helpful while applying the technique for real world scenario of moving target detection. STA/LTA-based human detection technique performs well with F1-score 87.1%, whereas, Mean Averaging has a F1-score of 84.1%, Wavelet has an F1-score of 78.3%, and CFAR has an F1-score of 73.6%.

6 Conclusion

This research work demonstrated a non-contact method for detecting indoor and outdoor human movements using UWB radar. For the detection of human motion, STA/LTA, wavelet, mean averaging, and CFAR techniques are developed, implemented and compared. Wavelet is suited for clutter removal and denoising whereas the profile subtraction approach does not adequately reduce the amount of noise. The performance of these techniques has been compared which concluded that STA/LTA detection technique shown good performance i.e. F1-score of 87.1 as compared to other techniques. The wavelet is effectively implemented for clutter removal, and the same approach is utilized for detection using the threshold. In future, the approaches must be tested and validated for different scenarios in which multiple targets are situated within the same range of the radar. The same techniques will be used to detect and localize targets in an outside area with extended limits of detections.

References

1. Rovňáková, J., Kocur, D.: UWB radar signal processing for positioning of persons changing their motion activity. Acta Polytechnica Hungarica **10**(03) (2013)

2. Nanzer, J.A.: A review of microwave wireless techniques for human presence detection and classification. IEEE Trans. Microw. Theory Tech. **65**(5), 1780–1794 (2017). https://doi.org/10.1109/TMTT.2017.2650909

3. Novák, D., Švecová, M., Kocur, D.: Multiple person localization based on their vital sign detection using UWB sensor. In: Goudos, S.K. (ed.) Microwave Systems and Applications. InTech (2017). https://doi.org/10.5772/66361

4. Quan, X., Choi, J.W., Cho, S.H.: A miss-detection probability based thresholding algorithm for an IR-UWB radar sensor. In: Proceedings International Radar Symposium, 2018-June (2018). https://doi.org/10.23919/IRS.2018.8448111

5. Jang, M.K., Cho, C.S.: Target detection for UWB radars using the standard deviation. In: Asia-Pacific Microwave Conference Proceedings, APMC, pp. 663–665 (2013). https://doi.org/10.1109/APMC.2013.6694898

6. Nguyen, V.H., Pyun, J.Y.: Location detection and tracking of moving targets by a 2D IR-UWB radar system. Sensors **15**(3), 6740–6762 (2015). https://doi.org/10.3390/s150306740

7. Nezirovic, A.: Stationary clutter- and linear-trend suppression in impulse-radar-based respiratory motion detection. In: Proceedings - IEEE International Conference on Ultra-Wideband, pp. 331–335 (2011). https://doi.org/10.1109/ICUWB.2011.6058857

8. Allabakash, S., Yasodha, P., Reddy, S.V., Srinivasulu, P.: Wavelet transform-based methods for removal of ground clutter and denoising the radar wind profiler data. IET Signal Process. **9**(5), 440–448 (2015). https://doi.org/10.1049/iet-spr.2014.0312

9. Narayanan, R.M., Shastry, M.C., Chen, P.-H., Levi, M.: Through-the-wall detection of stationary human targets using Doppler radar. Prog. Electromag. Res. B **20**, 147–166 (2010). https://doi.org/10.2528/PIERB10022206

10. Ma, Y., et al.: Multiscale residual attention network for distinguishing stationary humans and common animals under through-wall condition using ultra-wideband radar. IEEE Access **8**, 121572–121583 (2020). https://doi.org/10.1109/ACCESS.2020.3006834

11. Maali, A., Mesloub, A., Djeddou, M., Baudoin, G., Mimoun, H., Ouldali, A.: CA-CFAR threshold selection for IR-UWB TOA estimation. In: 7th International Workshop on Systems, Signal Processing and their Applications, WoSSPA 2011, pp. 279–282 (2011). https://doi.org/10.1109/WOSSPA.2011.5931473

12. Šabanović, A., van Katwijk, A., Verton, P.: Person detection using ultra-wideband radars UWB indoor person tracking (2017). https://repository.tudelft.nl/islandora/object/uuid%3A6d621ed9-970a-47cf-8d2d-bce2e13d063a

13. Singh, S., Liang, Q., Chen, D., Sheng, L.: Sense through wall human detection using UWB radar. EURASIP J. Wireless Commun. Netw. **2011**(1), 1–11 (2011). https://doi.org/10.1186/1687-1499-2011-20/FIGURES/21

14. Rane, S.A., Sarkar, S., Gaurav, A.: Moving target localization using Ultra WideBand sensing. In: Proceedings of 2016 Online International Conference on Green Engineering and Technologies, IC-GET 2016 (2017). https://doi.org/10.1109/GET.2016.7916628

15. Focsa, A., Toma, S.-A., Gorgoteanu, D.: On the interferometric capabilities of the Pulson P440 UWB radar. In: 2021 IEEE International Geoscience and Remote Sensing Symposium IGARSS, pp. 8201–8204. IEEE (2021). https://doi.org/10.1109/IGARSS47720.2021.9553329

16. Duan, Z., Zhang, Y., Zhang, J., Liang, J.: Non-contact detection of vital signs via a UWB radar sensor. In: Liang, Q., Liu, X., Na, Z., Wang, W., Mu, J., Zhang, B. (eds.) CSPS 2018. LNEE, vol. 516, pp. 708–716. Springer, Singapore (2020). https://doi.org/10.1007/978-981-13-6504-1_86

17. Liu, Y., Liu, Y.: Adapting seismic processing techniques for data preconditioning in radar imaging of highly dissipative and dispersive media (2017). https://doi.org/10.11575/PRISM/24699. https://prism.ucalgary.ca/handle/11023/4163

18. Guo, T., Zhang, T., Lim, E., Lopez-Benitez, M., Ma, F., Yu, L.: A review of wavelet analysis and its applications: challenges and opportunities. IEEE Access **10**, 58869–58903 (2022). https://doi.org/10.1109/ACCESS.2022.3179517

19. Crozier, J., Karlstrom, L.: Wavelet-based characterization of very-long-period seismicity reveals temporal evolution of shallow magma system over the 2008–2018 eruption of kīlauea volcano. J. Geophys. Res. Solid Earth **126** (2021). https://doi.org/10.1029/2020JB020837

20. Sun, Y., Fei, T., Li, X., Warnecke, A., Warsitz, E., Pohl, N.: Real-time radar-based gesture detection and recognition built in an edge-computing platform. IEEE Sensors J. **20**, 10706–10716 (2020). https://doi.org/10.1109/JSEN.2020.2994292

21. Gan, L., Liu, Y., Li, Y., Zhang, R., Huang, L., Shi, C.: Gesture recognition system using 24 GHZ fmcw radar sensor realized on real-time edge computing platform. IEEE Sensors J. **22**, 8904–8914 (2022). https://doi.org/10.1109/JSEN.2022.3163449

22. Jang, M.K., Cho, C.S.: Target detection of marine radars using Matrix Bank filters. In: Asia-Pacific Microwave Conference Proceedings, APMC, pp. 1046–1048. IEEE (2012). https://doi.org/10.1109/APMC.2012.6421820

23. Baird, Z., Rajan, S., Bolic, M.: Classification of human posture from radar returns using ultra-wideband radar. In: Proceedings of the Annual International Conference of the IEEE Engineering in Medicine and Biology Society, EMBS, 2018-July, pp. 3268–3271 (2018). https://doi.org/10.1109/EMBC.2018.8513094

24. Li, Q., Liu, J., Gravina, R., Li, Y., Fortino, G.: A UWB radar-based approach of detecting vital signals. In: 2021 IEEE 17th International Conference on Wearable and Implantable Body Sensor Networks, BSN 2021. 2021–2024 (2021). https://doi.org/10.1109/BSN51625.2021.9507032

25. Qi, R., Li, X., Zhang, Y., Li, Y.: Multi-classification algorithm for human motion recognition based on IR-UWB radar. IEEE Sensors J. **20**, 12848–12858 (2020). https://doi.org/10.1109/JSEN.2020.3000498

26. An, Q., Li, Z., Liang, F., Lv, H., Chen, F., Qi, F., Jianqi: Wavelet based human target detection in complex ruins using a low center frequency UWB radar. In: 2016 Progress in Electromagnetics Research Symposium, PIERS 2016 - Proceedings, pp. 744–1747 (2016). https://doi.org/10.1109/PIERS.2016.7734777

27. Song, Y., Chen, Z., Fan, W.: A novel scheme based on variational mode decomposition and multiple denoising technologies for heartbeat rate estimation. In: 2016 Progress In Electromagnetic Research Symposium. IEEE, Shanghai (2022)

28. Liu, S., Qi, Q., Xian, W., Chai, J., Wu, B., Ma, T.: UWB vital sign signal recognition method based on SVM. In: 2022 7th International Conference on Signal and Image Processing, ICSIP 2022, pp. 126–130 (2022). https://doi.org/10.1109/ICSIP55141.2022.9886084

29. Ntanis, A., Kostikis, N., Tsimperis, I., Tsiouris, K., Rigas, G., Fotiadis, D.: Evaluating parameters of the tug test based on data from IMU and UWB sensors. In: International Conference on Wireless and Mobile Computing, Networking and Communications. 2022-October, pp. 142–147 (2022). https://doi.org/10.1109/WiMob55322.2022.9941700

30. Bhole, D., Liang, Q.: Machine learning enabled sense-through-foliage target detection using UWB radar sensor network. In: Liang, Q., Wang, W., Liu, X., Na, Z., Zhang, B. (eds.) CSPS 2021. LNEE, vol. 878, pp. 1239–1246. Springer, Singapore (2022). https://doi.org/10.1007/978-981-19-0390-8_156

31. Moro, G., Di Luca, F., Dardari, D., Frisoni, G.: Human being detection from UWB NLOS signals: accuracy and generality of advanced machine learning models. Sensors **22**, 1–22 (2022). https://doi.org/10.3390/s22041656

Realization of MUX, DEMUX and ADD – DROP of Wavelength Using Bragg Grating and Optical Circulator

Ajay Yadav[✉], Amit Prakash, Rakesh Choudhary, Sushanta Mahanty,
Raj Ranjan Singh, Shiva Nand Singh, and Ajay Kumar

Fiber Optics Laboratory, Department of Electronics and Communication Engineering,
National Institute of Technology, Jamshedpur 831014, India
`ajayyadavnitjsr@gmail.com`, {`amitprakash.ece`,`snsingh.ece`,
`ajay.ece`}`@nitjsr.ac.in`

Abstract. Optical fiber communication is a fundamental component in optical communication systems that greatly influences the possible data transfer rate. Due to recent improvements in manufacturing and processing techniques, switching, multiplexing, and de-multiplexing of optical wavelengths are getting more attention. Optical fiber technologies have a wide range of technical contributions to the development and implementation of a worldwide, high-performance, and highly reliable Internet of Things (IoT). An experimental kit of CWDM (Coarse Wavelength Division Multiplexing) is used to add and drop optical signal of wavelength 1550 nm using Bragg grating and circulator. Four wavelength sources of 1510 nm, 1530 nm, 1550 nm, and 1570 nm are available for wavelength multiplexing and de-multiplexing. The Bragg grating used in the CWDM kit is designed to reflect a wavelength of 1550 nm. Therefore, out of four wavelength sources, optical wavelength of 1550 nm is added and dropped in the experiment. The work presents an experimental demonstration of the add and drop of optical wavelength (1550 nm). A detailed mathematical description of the coupled mode theory of fiber Bragg gratings is presented along with MATLAB simulation results. The discussed approach ensures low optical cost in the performance of all experiments.

Keywords: Fiber Bragg grating · Multiplexer · De-multiplexer · Optical circulator · Couple mode theory · Optical fiber communication using IoT

1 Introduction

The development of optical fiber technology has completely changed the telecom industry by enabling high-speed, high security, high data carrying capacity and long-distance telephone communications. Fiber Bragg grating (FBG) is a viable alternative for optical fiber sensors for strain or temperature measurements due to its easy manufacturing process, low cost, less maintenance, and very potent reflected signal. FBG are produced in a variety of ways, including periodic modulation along the core refractive index of single mode optical fiber in the longitudinal direction. FBG is one of several technologies being

R. K. Tiwari and G. Sahoo (Eds.): ICAII 2022, CCIS 1822, pp. 314–327, 2023.
https://doi.org/10.1007/978-3-031-37303-9_23

employed in optical communication systems to improve the optical communication system. The design of uniform FBG exhibiting constant modulation of index is shown in Fig. 1. According to the Bragg's law, the Bragg wavelength can be represented as:

$$\lambda_B = 2n_0\Lambda \tag{1}$$

where, λ_B is the Bragg wavelength, n_0 and Λ represents core refractive index and grating period refractive index perturbation respectively. That the first paragraph of a section or subsection is not indented.

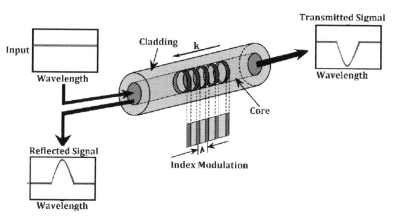

Fig. 1. Design of uniform FBG exhibiting constant index modulation.

A multi-port device exhibiting properties of non-reciprocal transmission of an optical signal is known as an optical circulator. A three-port optical circulator is used in the experimental procedure of add- drop of optical wavelengths. The optical signal enters the circulator through port 1 and leaves through port 2. If an optical signal enters through port 2 of the circulator, it now emerges from port 3 instead of port 1. This kind of device can be used in a number of ways, such as using FBGs to change the way the signal is spread out, add/drop multiplexers, and de-multiplexer, etc. [1–6]. There are several other more devices available for building all-optical logic gates, such as the Mach-Zehnder Interferometer (MZI), Micro-ring Resonator (MRR), Surface Plasmon Resonance (SPR), etc. [8–10]. Other essential properties of a circulator besides these are its polarization dependency, which is measured in terms of polarization dependent loss (PDL) and polarization mode dispersion (PMD), the wavelength of operation, and the power handling capability. If you add the right equipment to the experimental kit, you can also use it to measure these parameters. The detailed mathematical expression for the coupled mode theory [7] of the FBG is discussed along with the MATLAB simulation results. This paper is intended to optimize the reflectivity of the FBG to achieve maximum efficiency, and the experiment is performed to show the reflectivity of the FBG. Optical fiber communications have developed as a more cost-effective means of enhancing the capabilities of IoT networks. When IoT is added to optical fiber communication [11], it could have a big impact, however it is important for every industry to choose the best network to get the best communication and connections between networks.

2   Coupled Mode Theory of Fiber Bragg Grating (FBG)

Fiber Bragg grating is made up of grating structure inside the core of optical fiber. Figure 2. Represents the periodic variation of refractive index inside fiber core.

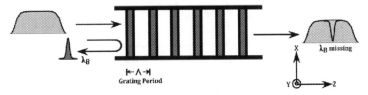

Fig. 2. Schematic representation of FBG.

The variation in refractive index is given below in Eq. (2)

$$n(x, z) = n_1(x) + \delta n(z) \tag{2}$$

The value of $\delta n(z)$ can be represented as $\delta n(z) = \Delta n sin(Kz)$, where $K = \frac{2\pi}{\Lambda}$. Λ is the grating period and K is the grating wave-vector. After above modification Eq. (2) can be represented as,

$$n^2 = n_1^2 + \sigma sin\left(\frac{2\pi}{\Lambda}z\right) \tag{3}$$

The total field in the device as is defined as the combination of forward propagation and backward propagation of wave. Amplitude associated with forward propagating wave is represented as A(z) as a function of z and B(z) for the backward propagating. Using the coupled mode theory, our purpose is to find out the dA/dz and dB/dz. The wave equation in the slab waveguide is given as follows:

$$\frac{d^2\psi_1}{dx^2} + \left(k_0^2 n_1^2 - \beta_1^2\right)\psi_1(x) = 0 \tag{4}$$

where, ψ_1 and β_1 represents the guided field and propagation constant of the guided wave respectively. FBG are produced in a variety of ways, including periodic modulation along the core refractive index of single mode optical fiber in the longitudinal direction; therefore, the wave equation for the FBG can be given as:

$$\nabla^2\psi = \frac{n^2}{c^2}\frac{\partial^2\psi}{\partial t^2} \tag{5}$$

In this case, $n = n(x, z)$ and the operator $\nabla^2 = \partial_x^2 + \partial_y^2$. The forward traveling wave (ψ_f) and the backward moving wave (ψ_b) may now be viewed separately from ψ. Consequently, it may be stated as,

$$\psi = \left(\psi_f + \psi_b\right) \tag{6}$$

The mathematical expression for forward propagation of wave (ψ_f) and backward propagating wave (ψ_b) is as follows:

$$\psi_f(x, z) = A(z)e^{i(\beta_1 z - \omega t)}\psi_1(x) \tag{7}$$

$$\psi_b = B(z)e^{i(-\beta_1 z - \omega t)}\psi_1(x) \tag{8}$$

where, A(z) and B(z) represents the amplitude for ψ_f and ψ_b. And $\psi_1(x)$ represents the transverse distribution of the field. Hence, the combined form of Eq. (7) and (8) can be written as,

$$\psi(x, z) = \left[A(z)e^{i(\beta_1 z)} + B(z)e^{i(-\beta_1 z)}\right]e^{-i\omega t}\psi_1(x) \tag{9}$$

After putting these values in the Maxwell's wave equation, which is shown below,

$$\nabla^2\psi = \frac{n^2}{c^2}\frac{\partial^2\psi}{\partial t^2} \tag{10}$$

The L.H.S can be represented as $.\nabla^2\psi = \left(\partial_x^2 + \partial_z^2\right)\psi$
Now, we can write the first part as:

$$\frac{\partial^2\psi}{\partial x^2} = \frac{\psi}{\psi_1(x)}\frac{\partial^2\psi_1(x)}{\partial x^2} \tag{11}$$

As we know, the Eq. (4) will be fulfilled in the absence of any perturbation. It may be expressed as follows in FBG:

$$\frac{\partial^2\psi}{\partial x^2} = \frac{\psi}{\psi_1(x)}\left(\beta_1^2 - k_0^2 n_1^2\right)\psi_1(x) \tag{12}$$

As a result,

$$\frac{\partial^2\psi}{\partial x^2} = \left(\beta_1^2 - k_0^2 n_1^2\right)\psi \tag{13}$$

Again, the computation for $\partial_z^2(\psi)$ is as follows:

$$\partial_z^2(\psi) = \left[\frac{\partial^2 A}{\partial z^2}e^{i(\beta_1 z)} + 2(i\beta_1)\frac{\partial A}{\partial z}e^{i(\beta_1 z)} - \beta_1^2 A e^{i(\beta_1 z)} + \frac{\partial^2 B}{\partial z^2}e^{-i(\beta_1 z)}\right.$$
$$\left. -2(i\beta_1)\frac{\partial B}{\partial z}e^{-i(\beta_1 z)} - \beta_1^2 B e^{-i(\beta_1 z)}\right]e^{-i\omega t}\psi_1(x) \tag{14}$$

As a result, we may rewrite the Eq. (14), as follows, using a slowly changing approximation.

$$\partial_z^2(\psi) = 2(i\beta_1)\left[\frac{\partial A}{\partial z}e^{i(\beta_1 z)} - \frac{\partial B}{\partial z}e^{-i(\beta_1 z)}\right]e^{-i\omega t}\psi_1(x) - \beta_1^2\psi \tag{15}$$

Now, computing the R.H.S part,

$$\frac{n^2}{c^2}\frac{\partial^2\psi}{\partial t^2} = -\omega^2\frac{n^2}{c^2}\psi = -k_0^2 n^2\psi \tag{16}$$

As we know that,

$$n^2 = n_1^2 + \sigma \sin(Kz) \tag{17}$$

$$\frac{n^2}{c^2} \frac{\partial^2 \psi}{\partial t^2} = -k_0^2 \left(n_1^2 + \sigma \sin(Kz)\right)\psi \tag{18}$$

According to the wave equation,

$$\frac{\partial A}{\partial z} - \frac{\partial B}{\partial z}e^{-2i(\beta_1 z)} + \frac{k_0^2 \sigma \sin(Kz)}{2(i\beta_1)}\left[A(z) + B(z)e^{-2i(\beta_1 z)}\right] = 0 \tag{19}$$

Now, the term $\sin(Kz) = \frac{e^{iKz} - e^{-iKz}}{2i}$, using in the Eq. (19),

$$\frac{\partial A}{\partial z} - \frac{\partial B}{\partial z}e^{-2i(\beta_1 z)} - \frac{k_0^2 \sigma}{4\beta_1}\left[A(z)\left(e^{iKz} - e^{-iKz}\right) + B(z)\left(e^{i(K-2\beta_1)z}\right) - B(z)\left(e^{-i(K+2\beta_1)z}\right)\right] = 0 \tag{20}$$

There are five exponential terms in Eq. (20)

$$\begin{cases} e^{-2i\beta_1 z} \\ e^{iKz} \\ e^{-iKz} \quad 5\,exponential\,term \\ e^{i(K-2\beta_1)z} \\ e^{-i(K+2\beta_1)z} \end{cases}$$

Neglecting these rapidly varying terms, the simplified form of the equation can be expressed as

$$\frac{\partial A}{\partial z} \approx \frac{k_0^2 \sigma}{4\beta_1}B(z)e^{i(K-2\beta_1)z} \tag{21}$$

We have simple expression, which tells us that how A(z) is varying.
Let us assume, $\kappa = \frac{k_0^2 \sigma}{4\beta_1}$ and $\Gamma = K - 2\beta_1$.
Hence, finally we can write,

$$\frac{\partial A}{\partial z} \approx \kappa B(z)e^{i\Gamma z} \tag{22}$$

Similarly,

$$\frac{\partial B}{\partial z} \approx \kappa A(z)e^{i\Gamma z} \tag{23}$$

The coupling co-efficient is an essential parameter since it connects A(z) and B(z).
Now, we have defined $\kappa = \frac{k_0^2 \sigma}{4\beta_1}$, where $k_0^2 = \frac{4\pi^2}{\lambda_0^2}$, $\beta_1 = k_0 n_1 = \frac{2\pi}{\lambda_0}n_1$ and $\sigma = 2n_1 \Delta n$.
Thus,

$$\kappa = \frac{\Delta n\pi}{\lambda_0} \tag{24}$$

Equation (24) reveals that the coupling co-efficient depends upon Δn and λ_0. In the Bragg condition: $\Gamma = 0$, (phase matching condition). As a result, $K = 2\beta_1$. It can be observed as $K = \beta_1 - (-\beta_1)$. Where K represents grating wave-vector, $K = \frac{2\pi}{\Lambda}$.

$$\beta_1 = \frac{\pi}{\Lambda} = n_{eff} k_0 = \frac{2\pi}{\lambda_B} n_{eff}$$

From above analysis, Bragg condition λ_B can be reparented as $\lambda_B = 2n_{eff} \Lambda$. Bragg wavelengths that meet the standard phase matching criteria. As a result, under the pure phase matching condition ($\Gamma = 0$).

$$\frac{dA}{dz} = \kappa B \ and \ \frac{dB}{dz} = \kappa A \tag{25}$$

Hence, if we make derivative of first equation,

$$\frac{d^2 A(z)}{dz^2} = \kappa \frac{dB}{dz} = \kappa^2 A \tag{26}$$

Similarly,

$$\frac{d^2 B(z)}{dz^2} = \kappa \frac{dB}{dz} = \kappa^2 B \tag{27}$$

In order to solve the differential equation, the boundary condition is applied for FBG (Fig. 3).

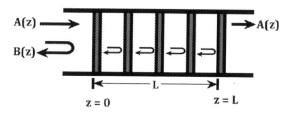

Fig. 3. Boundary Condition in FBG.

When the light will reflect, then at $z = L$, there should not be any kind of B. As a result, one boundary condition may be noticed as,

$$B(z = L) = 0 \tag{28}$$

General form of Eq. (27) can be written as,

$$B(z) = C_1 e^{\kappa z} + C_2 e^{-\kappa z} \tag{29}$$

Now applying boundary condition in the Eq. (29),

$$C_2 = -C_1 e^{2\kappa L} \tag{30}$$

As a result,

$$B(z) = C_1 e^{\kappa z} - C_1 e^{2\kappa L} e^{-\kappa z} \tag{31}$$

$$B(z) = C_1 e^{\kappa L}\left(e^{\kappa(z-L)} - e^{-\kappa(z-L)}\right) \tag{32}$$

$$B(z) = F \sinh[\kappa(z-L)] \quad \text{where } F = 2C \text{ and } C = C_1 e^{\kappa L} \tag{33}$$

Computing A(z), Hence

$$A(z) = \frac{1}{\kappa}\frac{dB}{dz}$$

$$A(z) = \frac{1}{\kappa}(\kappa F)\cosh[\kappa(z-L)] = F\cosh[\kappa(z-L)] \tag{34}$$

Now, A $(z=0) = A_0, A_0 = 1$, without loss of generality, Then, $A_0 = 1 = F\cosh[\kappa L]$

$$F = \frac{1}{\cosh(\kappa L)} \tag{35}$$

Putting the value of F from Eq. (35) in the Eqs. (33) and (34),

$$\left.\begin{array}{l} A(z) = \frac{1}{\cosh(\kappa L)}\cosh[\kappa(z-L)] \\ B(z) = \frac{1}{\cosh(\kappa L)}\sinh[\kappa(z-L)] \end{array}\right\} \tag{36}$$

The Eq. (3), represents the phase matching condition, where $\Gamma = 0$. Now, the reflectivity is defined as,

$$R = \frac{|B(z=0)|^2}{|A(z=0)|^2} = \tanh^2(\kappa L) \tag{37}$$

We further note,

$$|A(z)|^2 - |B(z)|^2 = \frac{1}{\cosh^2(\kappa L)} = constant \tag{38}$$

That means difference between $|A(z)|^2$ and $|B(z)|^2$ is constant. Essentially, the given equation reflects energy conservation. Because the two waves are traveling in different directions, the negative sign appears.

$$\left.\begin{array}{l} R = \tanh^2(\kappa L) \\ \kappa = \frac{\Delta n \pi}{\lambda_B} \\ R = \tanh^2\left(\frac{\Delta n \pi}{\lambda_B}L\right) \end{array}\right\} \tag{39}$$

Another generalized case, $K \neq 2\beta_1$, where $K = \frac{2\pi}{\Lambda}$. Hence, the Bragg condition is not satisfied under that condition, we have two general conditions,

$$\left.\begin{array}{l} \frac{dA}{dz} = \kappa B e^{i\Gamma z} \\ \frac{dB}{dz} = \kappa A e^{-i\Gamma z} \end{array}\right\} \tag{40}$$

Now, further simplifying,

$$\frac{d^2B}{dz^2} + i\Gamma \frac{dB}{dz} - \kappa^2 B = 0 \qquad when \; \Gamma \neq 0 \qquad (41)$$

The differential equation should be in the form of

$$m^2 + i\Gamma m - \kappa^2 = 0$$

where, we can write $m_{1,2} = -i\frac{\Gamma}{2} \pm \sqrt{\kappa^2 - \frac{\Gamma^2}{4}}$,

Now, if $\kappa^2 > \frac{\Gamma^2}{4}$, then suppose, $\sqrt{\kappa^2 - \frac{\Gamma^2}{4}} = \alpha$, when α is real and real and positive $(\alpha > 0)$ and $\kappa = \frac{\Delta n\pi}{\lambda_B}$ and $\Gamma = (K - 2\beta_1)$. Then solution of the above equation can be represented as follow,

$$B(z) = e^{-\frac{\Gamma}{2}z}\left[c_1 e^{\alpha z} + c_2 e^{-\alpha z}\right] \text{general solution of B}$$

Applying the boundary condition we get,

$$\frac{dB}{dz} = Fe^{-\frac{\Gamma}{2}z}\alpha \, cosh\,[\alpha(z - L)] + Fe^{-\frac{\Gamma}{2}z}\left(-\frac{\Gamma}{2}z\right) sinh\,[\alpha(z - L)] \qquad (42)$$

Now, the generalized equation of A(z) can be written as follow,

$$A(z) = \frac{F}{\kappa}e^{i\Gamma z}\left[\alpha cosh[\alpha(z - L)] + Fe^{-\frac{\Gamma}{2}z}\left(-\frac{\Gamma}{2}z\right)sinh[\alpha(z - L)]\right] \qquad (43)$$

We can apply the boundary condition, at $z = 0$, $A = 1$

$$F = \frac{\kappa}{[\alpha cosh(\alpha L) + sinh(\alpha L)]} \qquad (44)$$

Hence,

$$|F|^2 = \frac{\kappa^2}{\left[\alpha^2 cosh^2(\alpha L) + \frac{\Gamma^2}{4}sinh^2(\alpha L)\right]} \qquad (45)$$

The reflection co-efficient can be represented as follow,

$$R = \frac{|B(z = 0)|^2}{|A(z = 0)|^2} = |B(z = 0)|^2$$

$$B(z) = \frac{\kappa}{[\alpha cosh(\alpha L) + sinh(\alpha L)]}e^{-\frac{\Gamma}{2}z}sinh[\alpha(z - L)] \qquad (46)$$

Hence, reflectivity can be represented as,

$$R = \frac{\kappa^2 sinh^2(\alpha L)}{\left[\alpha^2 cosh^2(\alpha L) + \frac{\Gamma^2}{4}sinh^2(\alpha L)\right]}$$

Reflectivity $\Gamma \neq 0$ .where, $\alpha = \sqrt{\kappa^2 - \frac{\Gamma^2}{4}}$, $\alpha > 0$(Real)

When, $\Gamma = 0, \alpha = \kappa$

$R = \tanh^2(\kappa L)$, which is already computed.

Now, when $\Gamma \neq 0$ i.e. hence, $\Gamma = K - 2\beta_1$, hence $K - 2\beta_1 \neq 0$

$$K = \frac{2\pi}{\Lambda}, \beta_1 = \frac{2\pi}{\lambda_0}n_{eff}$$

We know that, $\lambda_B = 2n_{eff}\Lambda$, hence, $\frac{1}{\Lambda} = \frac{2n_{eff}}{\lambda_B}$

$$\Gamma = 4\pi n_{eff}\left[\frac{1}{\lambda_B} - \frac{1}{\lambda_{op}}\right] \qquad \lambda_{op} \text{ is the operating wavelength}$$

When $\Gamma = 0$, $\lambda_{op} = \lambda_B$, If we change the value of Γ, then the reflectivity will change, Variation of R with λ_{op} can be represented as,

$$R = \frac{\kappa^2 \sinh^2(\alpha L)}{\alpha^2 \cosh^2(\alpha L) + \frac{\Gamma^2}{4}\sinh^2(\alpha L)} \qquad (47)$$

$$\alpha = \sqrt{\kappa^2 - \frac{\Gamma^2}{4}} \qquad \alpha > 0 \qquad \kappa > \left|\frac{\Gamma}{2}\right|$$

Now,

$$\frac{\Gamma}{2} = 2\pi n_{eff}\left[\frac{1}{\lambda_B} - \frac{1}{\lambda_{op}}\right]$$

$$\kappa > 2\pi n_{eff}\left|\frac{1}{\lambda_B} - \frac{1}{\lambda_{op}}\right|$$

$$\left|\frac{1}{\lambda_B} - \frac{1}{\lambda_{op}}\right| < \frac{\kappa}{2\pi n_{eff}} \qquad (48)$$

Now, we can have the possibility, that with change in λ_{op}, $\left|\frac{1}{\lambda_B} - \frac{1}{\lambda_{OP}}\right|$ may be greater than $\frac{\kappa}{2\pi n_{eff}}$. In that condition also, the reflectivity expression will change as,

$$R = \frac{\kappa^2 \sinh^2(\alpha L)}{\alpha^2 \cosh^2(\alpha L) + \frac{\Gamma^2}{4}\sinh^2(\alpha L)} \qquad (49)$$

We can write the reflectivity in another convenient form,

$$R = \frac{\kappa^2 \sinh^2(\alpha L)}{(\kappa^2)\cosh^2(\alpha L) + \frac{\Gamma^2}{4}} \qquad (50)$$

where,

$$\kappa = \frac{k_0^2 \sigma}{4\beta_1}, \beta_1 = \kappa_0 n_{eff}, and \sigma = 2n_1 \Delta n$$

$$\kappa = \frac{k_0^2 2 n_1 \Delta n_1}{4 k_0^2 n_{eff}} = \frac{n_1 \Delta n \pi}{\lambda_{op} n_{eff}}$$

When, $\lambda_{op} = \lambda_B = 2 n_{eff} \Lambda$

$$\kappa = \frac{n_1 \Delta n \pi}{2 n_{eff}^2 \Lambda} \qquad \text{for the Bragg Wavelength} \tag{51}$$

As, we know that, we have the differential equation,

$$\frac{d^2 B}{dz^2} + i\Gamma \frac{dB}{dz} - \kappa^2 B = 0$$

We are expecting the solution in the form of $B \sim e^{mz}$, hence if $\kappa^2 < \frac{\Gamma^2}{4}$, then we must have a solution,

$$m_{1,2} = -i \left[\frac{\Gamma}{2} \pm \sqrt{\kappa^2 - \frac{\Gamma^2}{4}} \right]$$

$$m_{1,2} = -i \frac{\Gamma}{2} \pm i\gamma \quad where, \ \gamma = \sqrt{\frac{\Gamma^2}{4} - k^2}$$

Hence, the general solution can be represented as,

$$B(z) = M_1 e^{-im_1 z} + M_2 e^{im_2 z}, \ where \ m_1 = \frac{\Gamma}{2} + \gamma \ and \ m_2 = \frac{\Gamma}{2} - \gamma \tag{52}$$

Now, according to the boundary condition

$$B(z = L) = 0$$

$$B(L) = M_1 e^{-im_1 L} + M_2 e^{im_2 L} = 0$$

$$M_2 = M_1 \frac{e^{-im_1 L}}{e^{im_2 L}} \tag{53}$$

Putting above value of M_2 from Eq. (53) in the Eq. (52),

$$B(z) = M e^{-i\frac{\Gamma}{2}z} sin \left[(z - L)\gamma \right] \tag{54}$$

In the similar way, we can write the solution of $A(z)$

$$A(z) = \frac{M}{\kappa} e^{-i\frac{\Gamma z}{2}} \left[\gamma cos\{(z - L)\gamma\} - i\frac{\Gamma}{2} sin\{(z - L)\gamma\} \right] \tag{55}$$

Hence, at $A(z = 0) = 1$

$$M = \frac{\kappa}{\left[\gamma cos\{(L)\gamma\} + i\frac{\Gamma}{2} sin\{(L)\gamma\} \right]} \tag{56}$$

Now, the reflectivity can be represented as:

$$R = \frac{\kappa^2 sin^2(\gamma L)}{\left[\frac{\Gamma^2}{4} - \gamma^2 cos^2(\gamma L)\right]}$$

(57)

Final equation of reflectivity can be represented as:

$$R = \frac{\kappa^2 sinh^2(\alpha L)}{\left[\alpha^2 cosh^2(\alpha L) + \frac{\Gamma^2}{4} sinh^2(\alpha L)\right]}, \quad where \left|\frac{1}{\lambda_0} - \frac{1}{\lambda_B}\right| < \frac{\kappa}{2\pi n_{eff}}$$

$$R = \frac{\kappa^2 sin^2(\gamma L)}{\left[\frac{\Gamma^2}{4} - \gamma^2 cos^2(\gamma L)\right]}, \quad where \left|\frac{1}{\lambda_0} - \frac{1}{\lambda_B}\right| > \frac{\kappa}{2\pi n_{eff}}$$

$$R = tanh^2(\kappa L), \qquad where \; \lambda_0 = \lambda_B$$

(58)

Figure 4. Shows the MATLAB simulation of the reflectivity curve of uniform FBG, which shows that the wavelength of 1550 nm is reflected with a reflectivity value of 0.999.

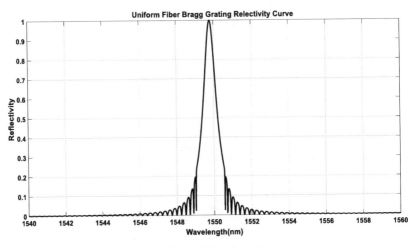

Fig. 4. Uniform FBG reflectivity curve.

Using the Eq. (58), the reflectivity curve for uniform FBG is obtained for grating length L = 4.00 mm, $n_1 = 1.50$, $\Delta n = 1.4 \times 10^{-3}$, grating period 535.90 nm and the effective refractive index is $n_{eff} = 1.447$. Now, computing the value of k_B at the Bragg wavelength can be written as,

$$k_B = \frac{\pi \Delta n}{\lambda_B}$$

(59)

The strength of grating reflectivity is determined by the value of $k_B L$. The $k_B L = 8$ is illustrated in Fig. 4, indicating a high reflectivity strength, with a reflectivity value of 0.9999 at the Bragg wavelength. Figure 5. Illustrates the less reflectivity of 0.94 for the $k_B L = 2$.

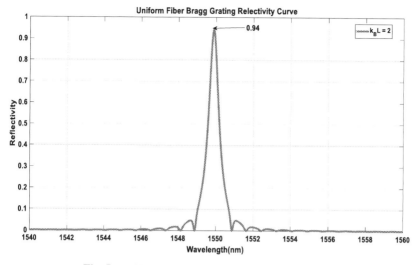

Fig. 5. Uniform FBG reflectivity curve for $K_B L = 2$.

3 Experimental

To perform the experimental realization of a Bragg grating and optical circulator for multiplexing, de-multiplexing, and Add – Drop of optical wavelengths, a CWDM kit is required with a power cord, USB A to B cord, SC/PC to SC/PC fiber patch cord connector, and an optical power meter to perform the experiment. Figure 6. Depicts an experimental CWDM kit with a port number of source, multiplexer, FBG 1550 nm, optical circulator, demultiplexer, and detector.

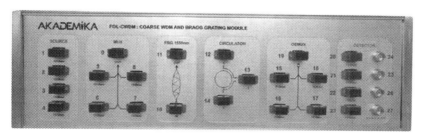

Fig. 6. An experimental kit of coarse wavelength division multiplexing.

Four wavelength sources of 1510 nm, 1530 nm, 1550 nm, and 1570 nm are available for wavelength multiplexing. The source wavelengths link the source port to the MUX ports: 1 to 5, 2 to 8, 3 to 6, and 4 to 7. The output of port 9 is the output multiplexer.

The Bragg grating of the CWDM kit is optimized to reflect a 1550 nm wavelength. FBG and an optical circulator are utilized to add-drop wavelengths of 1550 nm. In order to drop wavelength of 1550 nm, output port 9 of MUX is connected to the input port 12 of the circulator. Output port 11 of FBG is connected to the input port 19 of the

DE-MUX. The optical circulator functions in the forward direction; therefore, energy input to port 12 appears at port 13 but not at port 14. Similarly, energy input to port 13 appears up at port 14 but not at port 12. Here, four wavelengths are fed into circulator port 12 and routed to a Bragg grating linked to circulator port 13. As a result, the 1550 nm wavelength is reflected by the Bragg grating, while the rest of the wavelengths are sent through to the DE-MUX input. The reflected 1550 nm wavelength enters the circulator via port 13 and exits through port 14. A wavelength of 1550 nm is detected at port 14 by connecting the output of port 14 to the optical power meter.

In order to add wavelength of 1550 nm, only the wavelengths of 1510 nm, 1530 nm, and 1570 nm is being multiplexed. The SC/PC – SC/PC fiber patch cords is connected to the source ports to the MUX ports: 1 to 5, 2 to 8 and 4 to 7 and the multiplexed output of three wavelengths is output is shown at the MUX port 9. The wavelength of source 1550 nm coming out from the port 3 is connected to the input port of circulator in port 12. The output of MUX (port 9) is connected to the input port 10 of the Bragg grating. The wavelengths coming out from the output port 11 Bragg grating is connected to the input port 13 of the circulator. In this instance, 1550 nm wavelength input to circulator port 12 is transmitted to the Bragg grating and reflected back to port 13. This 1550 nm wavelength is the input to the circulator at port 13 and the output at port 14. Also, the three multiplexed wavelengths that are input to the Bragg grating are sent straight to circulator port 13, where wavelength 1550 nm is already reflected. Now, all four wavelengths from port 13 of the circulator are emitted from port 14. Thus, at port 14 of the circulator, both multiplexed and reflected wavelengths are added. As a consequence, port 14 of the circulator is linked to the input port 19 of the DE-MUX which shows the demultiplexed output of wavelengths at ports 15, 16, 17, and 18.

4   Result and Discussion

This paper describes the fundamental concept of multiplexing, de-multiplexing, and ADD - DROP of optical wavelength (1550 nm) using Bragg grating and an optical circulator for its applications in optical fiber communication networks. The experiment is carried out using CWDM and Bragg grating as the base technologies. The optical sources (1510 nm, 1530 nm, 1550 nm, and 1570 nm), multiplexer, Bragg grating, optical circulator, de-multiplexer, and detectors are part of the experimental setup. The Bragg grating is optimized to reflect a 1550 nm wavelength. Therefore, out of four wavelength sources, optical wavelength of 1550 nm is added and dropped in the experiment. As a result, the experiment for add- drop of wavelength 1550 nm is successfully performed. The detailed mathematical expression for the coupled mode theory of the FBG is discussed along with the MATLAB simulation results. The reflectivity of the FBG is optimized to achieve maximum efficiency, and the experiment is performed to show the reflectivity of the FBG. IoT can be used to improve optical communication technology to meet the technological needs of the present era.

References

1. Okayama, H., Ozeki, Y., Kamijoh, T., Xu, C.Q., Asabayashi, I.: Dynamic wavelength selective add/drop node comprising fibre gratings and optical switches. Electron. Lett. **33**(5), 403–404 (1997)
2. Dejun, F., Guiyun, K., Weigang, Z., Yonglin, H., Zhiguo, L., Xiaoyi, D.: Experiment on channel-switching add/drop multiplexer in a multi-channel WDM system. Chinese J. Lasers B. **11**(1), 57 (2002)
3. Okamoto, K., Takiguchi, K., Ohmori, Y.: 16-channel optical add/drop multiplexer using silica-based arrayed-waveguide gratings. Electron. Lett. **31**(9), 723–724 (1995)
4. Bilodeau, F., Johnson, D.C., Theriault, S., Malo, B., Albert, J., Hill, K.O.: An all-fiber dense-wavelength-division multiplexer/demultiplexer using photoimprinted Bragg gratings. IEEE Photon. Technol. Lett. **7**(4), 388–390 (1995)
5. Ortega, B., Dong, L., Reekie, L.: All-fiber optical add-drop multiplexer based on a selective fused coupler and a single fiber Bragg grating. Appl. Opt. **37**(33), 7712–7717 (1998)
6. Moores, J.D., et al.: Optical switching using fiber ring reflectors. JOSA B **8**(3), 594–601 (1991)
7. Mahanty, S., Kumar, A.: Implementation of all-optical 4 bit binary to gray code converter based on cross-phase modulation effect in a phase shifted fiber Bragg grating. Opt. Quant. Electron. **54**, 601 (2022)
8. Yadav, A., Kumar, A., Prakash, A.: Design and analysis of optical switches using electro-optic effect-based Mach-Zehnder interferometer structures. Mater. Today Proc. **56**(1), 462–467 (2022)
9. Kumar, A., Kumar, S., Raghuwanshi, S.K.: Implementation of XOR/XNOR and AND logic gates by using Mach-Zehnder interferometers. Optik **125**(19), 5764–5767 (2014)
10. Choudhary, R., Kumar, A.: Design and analysis of all-optical nibble multiplexer with tri-stated outputs using micro-ring resonator structure. Eur. Phys. J. D **76**, 42 (2022)
11. Aleksic, S.: A survey on optical technologies for iot, smart industry, and smart infrastructures. J. Sens. Actuator Netw. **8**, 47 (2019)

Author Index

R. K. Tiwari and G. Sahoo (Eds.): ICAII 2022, CCIS 1822, pp. 329–330, 2023.
https://doi.org/10.1007/978-3-031-37303-9